perspectives

Aging

Academic Editor
Kathleen Doyle
Eastern Illinois University

coursewise
publishing
inc.

St. Paul • Bellevue • Boulder • Dubuque • Madison

Our mission at **coursewise** is to help students make connections—linking theory to practice and the classroom to the outside world. Learners are motivated to synthesize ideas when course materials are placed in a context they recognize. By providing gateways to contemporary and enduring issues, **coursewise** publications will expand students' awareness of and context for the course subject.

For more information on **coursewise,** visit us at our web site: http://www.coursewise.com

To order an examination copy, contact Houghton Mifflin Sixth Floor Media: 800-565-6247 (voice); 800-565-6236 (fax).

coursewise publishing editorial staff

Thomas Doran, ceo/publisher: Journalism/Marketing/Speech
Edgar Laube, publisher: Political Science/Psychology/Sociology
Linda Meehan Avenarius, publisher: **courselinks**™
Sue Pulvermacher-Alt, publisher: Education/Health/Gender Studies
Victoria Putman, publisher: Anthropology/Environmental Science/Geography
Tom Romaniak, publisher: Business/Criminal Justice/Economics
Kathleen Schmitt, publishing assistant

coursewise production staff

Lori A. Blosch, permissions coordinator
Mary Monner, production coordinator
Victoria Putman, production manager

Note: Readings in this book appear exactly as they were published. Thus, inconsistencies in style and usage among the different readings are likely.

Library of Congress Catalog Card Number: 98-87649

ISBN 0-395-95464-9

Printed in the United States of America by **coursewise publishing,** Inc.
1559 Randolph Avenue, St. Paul, MN 55105

10 9 8 7 6 5 4 3 2 1

from the
Publisher

Sue Pulvermacher-Alt
coursewise publishing

Pilot to Pilot

Golda Meir, the Prime Minister of Israel from 1969–1974, once said:

> Old age is like a plane flying through a storm. Once you're aboard, there's nothing you can do.

She's right, of course; aging is inevitable. If you're the pilot, however, you can make decisions that affect the quality of the flight. Maintain the equipment, know the flight plan, make adjustments through the storm, stay in touch with air traffic control, etc. You get the picture. YOU are the pilot of your own aging process. Aging will happen no matter what you do. How you age, however, is up to you.

We've tried to put together readings in this volume that help you to sort out the important issues so you can better understand the process of aging. We want to help you—and others you will work with—age well. In the first section, we include readings that focus on characteristics of our aging population. In the second and third sections are readings that examine changes associated with aging—both normal, expected changes and changes that are common but not necessarily a normal part of the aging process. The next several sections explore healthy aging and the impact of aging on society (and the impact of society on aging). The final section offers readings that explore dying and death, the final stage of living.

In addition to the readings in this volume, you'll find web sites that we hope will expand your understanding of the issues. The R.E.A.L. sites you'll find throughout this *Perspectives: Aging* volume and at the **courselinks**™ site have been chosen because they are particularly useful sites. You, however, still need to be the pilot of this flight of aging. You need to build your own flight plan. Read our annotations and decide if the site is worth visiting. Do the activities so you can get to know the site better. Search our **courselinks**™ site by key topic and find the information you need to be better informed.

As publisher for this volume, I had the good fortune to work with Kathleen Doyle as the Academic Editor. I've worked with Kathy on several projects, and I continue to be amazed at her easygoing style, which is coupled with a laserlike efficiency. She knows her stuff. Kathy Doyle is also the **courselinks** editor for the **courselinks** site on Aging. You can rest assured that the readings in this volume speak to the variety of resources you'll find at the **courselinks** site.

We were helped by a top-notch Editorial Board. At **coursewise** we're working hard to publish "connected learning" tools—connecting theory to practice and the college classroom to the outside world. Readings and web sites are selected with this goal in mind. Members of the Editorial Board offer critical feedback and pose interesting challenges. They know their content and are a web-savvy bunch. My thanks to Kathy and the entire Editorial Board.

As you use our print and online resources and build your understanding of aging, I invite you to share your reactions to our materials. How'd we do in representing the subject of aging? What worked and what didn't work in this *Perspectives: Aging* volume and the accompanying **courselinks** site? Does the plane need repair? Do we need to modify our flight plan to build better course materials for you? I'd love to hear from you—as one pilot on this stormy journey to another.

Sue Pulvermacher-Alt, Publisher
suepa@coursewise.com

from the
Academic Editor

Kathleen Doyle
Eastern Illinois University

Gerontology, the scientific approach to the study of the aging phenomenon, is a relatively new field. Interest in gerontology expanded around World War II. However, the significant increase in interest concerning the topic was made evident when the National Institutes of Health created the Institute on Aging in 1974. Today, gerontology is a discipline that is recognized by most of society.

Aging implies process. We begin "aging" at birth and continue to "age" daily throughout life. So it only makes sense to study and understand this process just as we study other biological, psychological, and sociological processes. In the past, aging often was addressed as a component or unit within other courses at the college level. Today, many courses are devoted entirely to aging. Because of their interdisciplinary nature, aging courses are found within psychology, sociology, physiology, and health education departments. Departments such as business, education, recreation, the arts, and humanities also recognize how aging is connected to their disciplines and offer courses related to the topic.

Perspectives: Aging approaches the topic from this multidisciplinary aspect, as evidenced by the titles of the six sections: Profile of Aging, the Aging Process, Chronic and Acute Conditions, Healthy Aging, Aging and Society, and Dying and Death. The main purpose of *Perspectives: Aging* is to promote a positive aspect of aging by providing a wide variety of practical information concerning individual aging and the aging of those around us.

Section 1, Profile of Aging, introduces the characteristics of the aging population to promote an awareness of the diversity within this group. Several of the selections address the changes in life expectancy since the turn of the century and the impact of people living longer. General demographic trends are highlighted, including mortality trends among the oldest old. And one thought-provoking article presents the public health challenges associated with an aging population from a global perspective.

Sections 2 and 3 approach aging from different perspectives. The normal changes that we associate with aging are highlighted in Section 2. These articles provide practical suggestions for coping with or compensating for these changes and thereby attaining a healthier quality of life as you age. Section 3 addresses diseases or conditions that are common among the elderly but that are not part of the normal aging process. Typical conditions such as osteoporosis and vision problems are discussed. In addition, some not-so-typical conditions associated with aging, such as sexually transmitted diseases and risks for HIV/AIDS, are covered. One article provides a comprehensive overview of the special health considerations among African-American elders.

Kathleen Doyle attended Slippery Rock University as an undergraduate, and received a Master's degree from Western Illinois University. Kathleen earned her Ph.D. at Southern Illinois University, and has been teaching at Eastern Illinois in health studies for 20 years. In that time, she's been honored with a Faculty Excellence Award four times. Kathleen is also the Academic Editor for *Perspectives: Drugs and Society*.

Section 4 focuses on healthy aging by emphasizing wellness and prevention. Nutrition and exercise are the most common factors identified as improving the lives of older adults. Proper use of medications can also add to the quality of later life. Lastly, myths and misconceptions about aging and sexuality are addressed, and the role of normal sexual activity among the elderly is explored.

Section 5 addresses the impact of aging on society and the impact of society on aging. Several selections discuss problems in the health-care delivery system and the care of the elderly. These discussions include possible solutions. Information about specific concerns, such as elder abuse and long-term care, is also provided. And a discussion of the factors that influence how African-Americans view the health-care system brings the diversity issue to the forefront.

The final section, Dying and Death, explores this final stage of living and the unique perspectives of the elderly concerning these issues. Living wills, the right to die issue, the funeral industry, and death and grief in the later years are some of the topics explored. Section 6 presents not only the older individual's thoughts on dying and death, but also insights into the medical-care provider's role in dealing with the dying individual.

◆ ◆ ◆

About 15 years ago, I was given the challenge of developing a course about aging that would be appropriate for the health education majors in our department. I wanted a course that focused mainly on understanding the differences between normal aging changes and changes associated with disease, while also devoting time to health-related issues facing the aging individual. Every year since that first semester the course was offered, I have been looking for an appropriate book to complement these specific course objectives. After working with **coursewise** on another resource (*Perspectives: Drugs and Society*), I knew I had found the solution to my problem. The **coursewise** approach to material development incorporates current, readable, interesting, user-friendly, and affordable resources for the college classroom. I found the opportunity to put together a true "health and aging" book that not only allows for the multidisciplinary aspect of aging but remains focused on practical, health-related information. In working with the **coursewise** staff, I have found individuals genuinely interested in the usefulness and applicability of the final product. In the end, both instructors and students benefit from this combination.

Editorial Board

Judith McLaughlin

Georgia Southern University

Judith McLaughlin is an associate professor and Director of the M.P.H. program in the Department of Health and Kinesiology at Georgia Southern University. She previously taught health promotion and behavior courses at the University of Georgia, where she was a Gerontology Fellow at UGA's Gerontology Center during 1991–1992 and a member of the Gerontology and Women's Studies Faculties. She earned her doctorate in health education from Southern Illinois University, Carbondale; an M.S. in pathology from the Ohio State University; an M.T. in medical technology from Duke University; and a B.A. in biology from Berea College.

Manoj Sharma

University of Nebraska at Omaha

Manoj Sharma, MBBS, Ph.D., is an assistant professor of Community Health Education at the University of Nebraska at Omaha. He earned his Ph.D. in Preventative Medicine/Health Behavior & Health Promotion from The Ohio State University, his M.S. from Mankato State University, and his Bachelor of Medicine and Bachelor of Surgery (equivalent to MD) from the University of Delhi, Delhi, India. He has coauthored two books, published fifteen articles in peer reviewed journals, and presented seventeen papers at National and International Conferences. In 1997 he received the Best Dissertation Award from both the Society of Public Health Education (SOPHE) and the American School Health Association (ASHA).

S. Maggie Reitz

Towson State University

S. Maggie Reitz, Ph.D., OTR/L, is an associate professor of Occupational Therapy at Towson State University. She received her Ph.D. in health education from the University of Maryland at College Park, and both an M.S. in Gerontic Occupational Therapy and a B.S. in Occupational Therapy from Towson State University. She has also served as Associate Chief and Director of Field Work Program for the Department of Occupational Therapy of the Greater Southeast Community Hospital in Washington, D.C.

Mike Jackson

Western Illinois University

Mike Jackson, CHHS, Ph.D. is an Associate Professor in the Department of Health Education and Promotion at Western Illinois University. He received his Ph.D. from Southern Illinois University; his professional interests include community health, program planning and evaluation, and health ethics.

Beverly Ovrebo

San Francisco State University

Beverly Ovrebo is a Professor in the Health Education Department at San Francisco State University. She earned her Dr.P.H. and M.P.H. in Community Health Education from the University of California at Berkeley, and a B.A. in Philosophy from Kalamazoo College. She was the Principal Investigator/ Founding Director of the Bay Area Homelessness Program from 1989 to 1994. She currently serves as Principal Investigator for the Robert F. Kennedy AmeriCORPS Fellows Program.

WiseGuide Introduction

Critical Thinking and Bumper Stickers

Question Authority

The bumper sticker said: Question Authority. This is a simple directive that goes straight to the heart of critical thinking. The issue is not whether the authority is right or wrong; it's the questioning process that's important. Questioning helps you develop awareness and a clearer sense of what you think. That's critical thinking.

Critical thinking is a new label for an old approach to learning—that of challenging all ideas, hypotheses, and assumptions. In the physical and life sciences, systematic questioning and testing methods (known as the scientific method) help verify information, and objectivity is the benchmark on which all knowledge is pursued. In the social sciences, however, where the goal is to study people and their behavior, things get fuzzy. It's one thing for the chemistry experiment to work out as predicted, or for the petri dish to yield a certain result. It's quite another matter, however, in the social sciences, where the subject is ourselves. Objectivity is harder to achieve.

Although you'll hear critical thinking defined in many different ways, it really boils down to analyzing the ideas and messages that you receive. What are you being asked to think or believe? Does it make sense, objectively? Using the same facts and considerations, could you reasonably come up with a different conclusion? And, why does this matter in the first place? As the bumper sticker urged, question authority. Authority can be a textbook, a politician, a boss, a big sister, or an ad on television. Whatever the message, learning to question it appropriately is a habit that will serve you well for a lifetime. And in the meantime, thinking critically will certainly help you be course wise.

Getting Connected

This reader is a tool for connected learning. This means that the readings and other learning aids explained here will help you to link classroom theory to real-world issues. They will help you to think critically and to make long-lasting learning connections. Feedback from both instructors and students has helped us to develop some suggestions on how you can wisely use this connected learning tool.

WiseGuide Pedagogy

A wise reader is better able to be a critical reader. Therefore, we want to help you get wise about the articles in this reader. Each section of *Perspectives* has three tools to help you: the WiseGuide Intro, the WiseGuide Wrap-Up, and the Putting It in *Perspectives* review form.

WiseGuide Intro

WiseGuide Intro

In the WiseGuide Intro, the Academic Editor introduces the section, gives you an overview of the topics covered, and explains why particular articles were selected and what's important about them.

Also in the WiseGuide Intro, you'll find several key points or learning objectives that highlight the most important things to remember from this section. These will help you to focus your study of section topics.

At the end of the WiseGuide Intro, you'll find questions designed to stimulate critical thinking. Wise students will keep these questions in mind as they read an article (we repeat the questions at the start of the articles as a reminder). When you finish each article, check your understanding. Can you answer the questions? If not, go back and reread the article. The Academic Editor has written sample responses for many of the questions, and you'll find these online at the **courselinks**™ site for this course. More about **courselinks** in a minute. . . .

WiseGuide Wrap-Up

Be course wise and develop a thorough understanding of the topics covered in this course. The WiseGuide Wrap-Up at the end of each section will help you do just that with concluding comments or summary points that repeat what's most important to understand from the section you just read.

In addition, we try to get you wired up by providing a list of select Internet resources—what we call R.E.A.L. web sites because they're **R**elevant, **E**xciting, **A**pproved, and **L**inked. The information at these web sites will enhance your understanding of a topic. (Remember to use your Passport and start at http://www.courselinks.com so that if any of these sites have changed, you'll have the latest link.)

Putting It in *Perspectives* Review Form

At the end of the book is the Putting It in *Perspectives* review form. Your instructor may ask you to complete this form as an assignment or for extra credit. If nothing else, consider doing it on your own to help you critically think about the reading.

Prompts at the end of each article encourage you to complete this review form. Feel free to copy the form and use it as needed.

The courselinks™ Site

The **courselinks**™ Passport is your ticket to a wonderful world of integrated web resources designed to help you with your course work. These resources are found at the **courselinks** site for your course area. This is where the readings in this book and the key topics of your course are linked to an exciting array of online learning tools. Here you will find carefully selected readings, web links, quizzes, worksheets, and more, tailored to your course and approved as connected learning tools. The ever-changing, always interesting **courselinks** site features a number of carefully integrated resources designed to help you be course wise. These include:

- **R.E.A.L. Sites** At the core of a **courselinks** site is the list of R.E.A.L. sites. This is a select group of web sites for studying, not surfing. Like the readings in this book, these sites have been selected, reviewed, and approved by the Academic Editor and the Editorial Board. The R.E.A.L. sites are arranged by topic and are annotated with short descriptions and key words to make them easier for you to use for reference or research. With R.E.A.L. sites, you're studying approved resources within seconds—and not wasting precious time surfing unproven sites.

- **Editor's Choice** Here you'll find updates on news related to your course, with links to the actual online sources. This is also where we'll tell you about changes to the site and about online events.

- **Course Overview** This is a general description of the typical course in this area of study. While your instructor will provide specific course objectives, this overview helps you place the course in a generic context and offers you an additional reference point.

- **www.orksheet** Focus your trip to a R.E.A.L. site with the www.orksheet. Each of the 10 to 15 questions will prompt you to take in the best that site has to offer. Use this tool for self-study, or if required, email it to your instructor.

- **Course Quiz** The questions on this self-scoring quiz are related to articles in the reader, information at R.E.A.L. sites, and other course topics, and will help you pinpoint areas you need to study. Only you will know your score—it's an easy, risk-free way to keep pace!

- **Topic Key** The Topic Key is a listing of the main topics in your course, and it correlates with the Topic Key that appears in this reader. This handy reference tool also links directly to those R.E.A.L. sites that are especially appropriate to each topic, bringing you integrated online resources within seconds!

- **Web Savvy Student Site** If you're new to the Internet or want to brush up, stop by the Web Savvy Student site. This unique supplement is a complete **courselinks** site unto itself. Here, you'll find basic information on using the Internet, creating a web page, communicating on the web, and more. Quizzes and Web Savvy Worksheets test your web knowledge, and the R.E.A.L. sites listed here will further enhance your understanding of the web.

- **Student Lounge** Drop by the Student Lounge to chat with other students taking the same course or to learn more about careers in your major. You'll find links to resources for scholarships, financial aid, internships, professional associations, and jobs. Take a look around the Student Lounge and give us your feedback. We're open to remodeling the Lounge per your suggestions.

Building Better Perspectives!

Please tell us what you think of this *Perspectives* volume so we can improve the next one. Here's how you can help:

1. Visit our **coursewise** site at: http://www.coursewise.com

2. Click on *Perspectives*. Then select the Building Better *Perspectives* Form for your book.

3. Forms and instructions for submission are available online.

Tell us what you think—did the readings and online materials help you make some learning connections? Were some materials more helpful than others? Thanks in advance for helping us build better *Perspectives*.

Student Internships

If you enjoy evaluating these articles or would like to help us evaluate the **courselinks** site for this course, check out the **coursewise** Student Internship Program. For more information, visit:

http://www.coursewise.com/intern.html

Contents

section 1

Profile of Aging

section 2

The Aging Process

section 3

Chronic and Acute Conditions

section 4

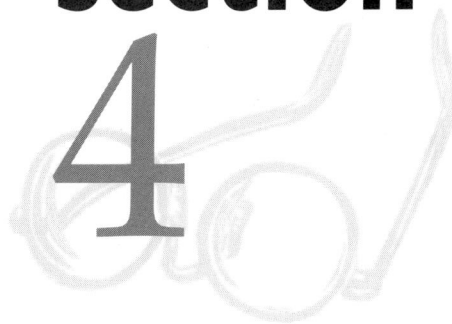

Healthy Aging

section 5

Aging and Society

section

6

Dying and Death

Topic Key

This Topic Key is an important tool for learning. It will help you integrate this reader into your course studies. Listed below, in alphabetical order, are important topics covered in this volume. Below each topic, you'll find the reading numbers and titles, and also the R.E.A.L. web site addresses, relating to that topic. Note that the Topic Key might not include every topic your instructor chooses to emphasize. If you don't find the topic you're looking for in the Topic Key, check the index or the online Topic Key at the **courselinks**™ site.

Aging Minorities

6 Demography and Gerontology: Mortality Trend Among the Oldest Old
12 Special Health Considerations in African-American Elders
21 The Healthiest Women in the World
27 Under the Shadow of Tuskegee: African Americans and Health Care

National Aging Information Center Website
http://www.aoa.dhhs.gov/naic

Health Status of Racial/Ethnic Older Women
http://www.bphc.hrsa.dhhs.gov/omwh/omwh_9.htm

Native American Elder Population
http://www.aoa.dhhs.gov/ain/naepop90.html

Aging Stereotypes

2 Myths of Ageing: Ageing Today and Tomorrow

Healthy Aging
http://www.healthy.net/wellness/aging/index.html

Alcohol

18 Alcohol Consumption among the Elderly in a General Population, Erie County, New York

National Institute on Aging (NIA)
http://www.nih.gov/nia/

Administration on Aging Fact Sheets
http://www.aoa.dhhs.gov/factsheets/

Healthfinder
http://www.healthfinder.gov

Alzheimer's Disease

26 Medicare Managed Care Partnership: Kaiser Permanente and the Alzheimer's Association

Ask NOAH about Aging and Alzheimer's Disease
http://www.noah.cuny.edu:8080/aging/aging.html

Alzheimer's Disease Education and Referral Center (ADEAR)
http://www.alzheimers.org/

Family Care Resources
http://www.ncoa.org/

Assisted Suicide

30 Deciding Life and Death in the Courtroom: From Quinlan to Cruzan, Glucksberg, and Vacco—A Brief History and Analysis of Constitutional Protection of the 'Right to Die'
32 Decisions and Care at the End of Life

Association for Death Education and Counseling (ADEC)
http://www.adec.org/

GriefNet
http://www.omhrc.gov/frames.htm

Baby Boomers

3 What If . . . ?

Health and Retirement Study (HRS) and Asset and Health Dynamics Among the Oldest Old (AHEAD)
http://www.umich.edu/~hrswww/

Cardiorespiratory System

9 Assessing the Older Patient
10 What Is Normal Aging?
17 New Success Against Stroke

American Heart Association
http://www.americanheart.org/catalog/Health_catpage9.html

American Lung Association
http://www.lungusa.org/index2.html

National Heart, Lung, and Blood Institute (NHLBI)
http://www.nhlbi.nih.gov/nhlbi/nhlbi.htm

Cognitive Aging

7 Aging and Decision Making: Driving-Related Problem Solving
8 Fear of Forgetting

34 Caring for the Older Patient, Part III: Ethical Issues in Gerontology

The National Center on Elder Abuse (NCEA)
http://www.gwjapan.com/NCEA/

Area Agencies on Aging - Description
http://208.209.106.2/aaa_desc.html

Dementia

2 Myths of Ageing: Ageing Today and Tomorrow
12 Special Health Considerations in African-American Elders
14 Recognizing and Treating Depression in the Elderly
26 Medicare Managed Care Partnership: Kaiser Permanente and the Alzheimer's Association

Alzheimer's Disease Education and Referral Center (ADEAR)
http://www.alzheimers.org/

Demographics

1 Telomeres, Cancer, and Aging: Altering the Human Life Span
3 What If . . . ?
4 Population Ageing: A Public Health Challenge
5 Record High U.S. Life Expectancy
6 Demography and Gerontology: Mortality Trends among the Oldest Old

Profile of Older Americans: 1997
http://www.aoa.dhhs.gov/aoa/stats/profile/

National Institute on Aging (NIA)
http://www.nih.gov/nia/

We the American Elderly
http://www.census.gov/apsd/wepeople/we-9.pdf

Administration on Aging Statistical Information on Older Persons
http://www.aoa.dhhs.gov/aoa/stats/statpage.html

section

1

Key Points

- The aging process is complex and not well understood.

- The demographics of the elderly population are diverse and unique.

- Life expectancy has increased, but life span has remained basically the same.

- Many implications are associated with increases in both life expectancy and life span.

- Misconceptions and myths associated with the aged affect the way they are treated in society.

Profile of Aging

WiseGuide Intro

Aging is an inevitable process. It happens no matter what we do. Stopping or reversing human aging has been the pursuit of many throughout history. What is aging? Why do we age at different rates? Do we really want to live longer? These are some of the questions that the readings in this section address.

The aging process is complex. Many theories have been developed and suggested to help define it, but none can completely explain the mystery. Some of the currently accepted theories of aging are mentioned and explored in a few of the readings in this section. Several other readings provide excellent overviews and discussions concerning life expectancy and maximum life span. While life expectancy has consistently increased since the early 1990s, maximum life span has remained pretty much the same. The changes in expectancy have shaped the demographics of many countries, both developing and developed. Some good summaries of the demographics of an aging society, and the implications of the demographics, are found in this section.

As with other subgroups in society, the elderly are not exempt from myths, misconceptions, and prejudices. Unfortunately, *ageism* is a term that has emerged within the last few decades. One of the readings identifies some of the myths associated with aging and explores ways to help change some of the stereotypical views of the elderly.

Questions

Reading 1. How is cancer used in the study of aging? What are some of the social implications of altering human aging?

Reading 2. What is a common myth about old age? How can myths about aging affect the way people view the elderly?

Reading 3. What are some negative or "doomsday" predictions associated with changing demographics? How does migration impact the demographics of an aging society?

Reading 4. How does mortality and fertility impact aging demographics? What are some of the health challenges that an aging population will bring to developing countries?

Reading 5. What is the average number of years a person in the United States can expect to live? Do women or men live longer?

Reading 6. Who are the "old-old"? How do African-American elderly compare to White American elderly concerning life expectancy?

How is cancer used in the study of aging? What are some of the social implications of altering human aging?

Telomeres, Cancer, and Aging

Altering the human life span

Dwayne A. Banks

Richard and Rhoda Goldman School of Public Policy and Center for the Economics and Demography of Aging, University of California, Berkeley

Michael Fossel

Michigan State University College of Human Medicine, East Lansing

Any cost projections for treating elderly people in the future need to consider the fact that scientists may be able to change the aging process. While the average lifespan has increased in the past 200 years, the maximum age remains at about 120 years. However, animal research has shown that maximum lifespan can be extended by restricting dietary calories. Cellular aging is believed to result from genetic changes that prevent the cell from neutralizing damaging free radicals. Many cancer cells are immortal and can continue dividing indefinitely without aging.

Population projections of the aging global society and its fiscal and social impact have depended on assumptions regarding the human life span. Until now, the assumption that the maximum human life span is fixed has been justified. Recent advances in cell biology, genetics, and our understanding of the cellular processes that underlie aging, however, have shown that this assumption is invalid in a number of animal models and suggest that this assumption may become invalid for humans as well. In vitro alteration of telomeres affects cellular senescence, and in vivo manipulation of genes and diet can increase maximum life span in animal models if these discoveries are extended to humans. We may soon be able to extend the maximum human life span and postpone or prevent the onset of diseases associated with aging. Such a possibility requires that we recognize a growing uncertainty in any attempt to project international health care costs into the next few decades. The costs may be significantly lower than projections, if life span increases and age-related disabilities are postponed or less severe,

or perhaps higher, if life span increases without altering the onset and severity of disability. An appropriate uncertainty regarding the human life span undermines any attempt to accurately predict health costs in the next century.

The same forces which operate in the birth and temporal existence of the human being operate also in his destruction and death.

Maimonides, the Guide for the Perplexed

Historically, there has been an—as yet well-founded—assumption that although we may alter the course of age-related diseases, such as emphysema by smoking cessation and atherosclerosis by lowering cholesterol and blood pressure, the underlying process of aging cannot itself be altered.[1] The actual life span of any single individual is determined by a multitude of factors including lifestyle, socioeconomic status, diet, environmental conditions, and genetic endowments.[2,3] Some of these factors can be altered with consequent alteration of the individual (or the mean) life span, but not with any known increase in the maximum human life span. Currently, the longest anyone has ever lived is 122 years.[4] The biological origin of this maximum life span has been controversial. Is there a "clock" regulating the aging process? Or is there a biological limit that cannot be surpassed—irrespective of our genes? These are questions that gerontologists, geneticists, and molecular and cell biologists have been pondering for decades.

Recently, there has been a conceptual shift in our understanding of aging. The possibility of extending the maximum human life span has gone from legend to laboratory.[5] This change has been prompted by a growing academic literature that suggests that the aging process itself, as well as the consequent and fundamental cellular changes that occur in age-related diseases, is modifiable. This revision in views, if borne out, has profound clinical implications for the incidence of age-related diseases. Furthermore, the fiscal impact on government expenditures in the areas of health and social security will be perplexing even if only a modicum of these views hold true.

Aging is often seen from two vantage points: damage theories and programmed theories. Damage theories view aging as the result of accumulated errors, from free radicals for example. Programmed theories view aging as the result of genetic regulation. These paradigms are not contradictory, but complementary. Changes in gene expression that occur with cellular aging permit damage that does not occur (or accumulate) in immortal cell lines such as germ cells. The issue is not whether free radical damage underlies much of aging—it clearly does—but the more complex question of whether we may learn to control the onset and timing of such damage, which ultimately determines our health and our maximum life span.

Clones, Cancer, and Aging Cells

The mean human life span has been extended remarkably over the past two centuries; the maximum life span has not.[6] This has resulted in a "rectangularization" of life span, in which mortality is increasingly becoming compressed against an apparently fixed end point, the maximum human life span of approximately 120 years.[7] Over the past decade, however, several laboratories have successfully extended the maximum life spans of at least two multicellular species genetically (*Drosophila*[3] and *Caenorhabditis elegans*[8–10]) and several more by dietary restriction.[11–13] That this increase in maximum life span can occur at all invalidates the dogma that maximum life span is fixed, and it thus invalidates the inevitability of the rectangularization model described above. That it occurs with such minimal genetic manipulation and that the effect is so substantial two gene mutations increase the maximum life span of *C elegans* six-fold) raise the provocative question of what might lie in store for clinical medicine. To a first approximation, the increased life span occurs predominantly through the genetic control of free radical metabolism. This is not unexpected: cellular aging (and modifications of maximum life span) operates predominantly through the damaging effects of free radicals.[14,15] Not only does free radical production increase substantially as cells age, but the free radicals produced are less well contained and less efficiently mopped up by free radical scavengers, and their consequent damage is less efficiently repaired. This simplification leaves unanswered the questions of how cancer cells and the germ cell lines avoid aging damage, though they have comparable genomes, mitochondria, and free radicals. Telomere shortening (and its consequent effects on gene expression and cell cycle mechanisms) is implicated in allowing cancer and other cell lines to avoid cell senescence.[16,17] Free radical damage appears to be the major cause of the damage that occurs in aging cells,[18,19] but the more complex issue lies in the control of the timing and release of such damage.[20]

What is the age of a cell? Unless we measure age from every new division (as we do in Saccharomyces, for example, in which the asexual form shows aging in that "maternal" cells have a limited number of divisions, but the number is "reset" in each new "daughter" cell), newly divided cells each inherit the same age as the single cell from which they derived. All cells—as unbroken cell lines—have, reductio ad absurdum, the same age. Life on this planet is 3.5 billion years old, and all life and every cell are equally old in a peculiar sense. But then how is the onset of free radical damage timed, if not simply by years of a cell's life? Aging does not occur for 3.5 billion years in the germ cell line, yet it clearly does so beginning sometime after fertilization. Free radical aging is not timed by the profoundly archaic age of the entire cell lineage, but rather by a clock that begins running only after fertilization (in multicellular organisms; in the asexual phase of unicellular organisms such as yeasts, aging is considered to commence at the asymmetric division of a daughter cell as she buds off the larger mother cell). Humans and other multicellular organisms derive from cells that do not show the loss of replicative ability and the morphologic and gene expression changes that are characteristic of senescent cells[1,21,22] until after the organism achieves multicellularity. Age per se does not determine aging; it is altered genetic expression that somehow permits the onset of aging to occur.

The onset and progression of aging is strongly affected by chromosomal structure[23] and gene expression.[24] Evidence from work on early aging syndromes (progerias) supports this observation. Patients with Werner syndrome have an average life span of 47 years and a known defect in helicase metabolism that results in abnormal chromosomal "unwinding" and replication.[25] Patients with Hutchinson-Gilford syndrome have an average life span of 12.7 years, and their skin fibroblasts have telomere lengths characteristic of cells from far older patients.[26,27]

The cloning of mature ovine mammary cells likewise raises the question of whether age can be reset. Wilmut et al.[28] have shown that gene expression can be reset: in this case at least, the 6-year-old adult mammary cells from the donor have not yet been irreversibly aged by time per se or by the aging of the donor organism. To the contrary, successful cloning demonstrates that these cells still have sufficient intact genetic information available to allow reconstitution of an apparently healthy multicellular organism. But was Dolly—the cloned organism—6 years old at birth, or

had her cells been reset to age 0? The most tempting and certainly viable hypothesis is that genes can be reset to reflect the cellular age consistent with a developing organism,[29] a hypothesis that is now (in Dolly's case) finally being tested. A considerable body of evidence suggests that cell aging does not occur because of accumulated DNA damage or poor transcription fidelity;[30] rather, the DNA is intact and transcription is intact, but transcription occurs at lower rates and in significantly altered patterns as cells age.[21,23] If Dolly's cells show normal ovine aging for her "new" age rather than being 6 years old at birth, then this will provide further support for the hypothesis that age can be reset even after it has been in progress. The nature of this putative resetting mechanism will be a prime target for further research.

Cancer research has also prompted revision of our views of cell aging.[22] The problem in oncology is not that cells age and die, but that they do not. Normal somatic cells have well-defined limits to replication. Young skin fibroblasts typically have 50 divisions before they show cellular senescence. Within the past 7 years, there has been increasing support for the model that cellular senescence in normal (noncancerous) human cells is the result of an altered (and, for the cell, dysfunctional) pattern of gene expression, and that the onset and progression of this pattern of senescent gene expression is regulated (through insufficiently understood mechanisms likely to involve heterochromatin changes) regulated by the telomeres.[31-33] Most cancer cells, however, are biologically immortal and will continue dividing indefinitely under appropriate condi-

tions. This potential is linked to their expression of telomerase.[34,37] Additionally, it appears that most, perhaps all, cancer cells are fundamentally different with regard to their aberrant cell cycle braking systems. Typically, 60% of combined human cancers (70% of colon cancers, 40% of breast cancers) have an aberrant p53. If we include p21, D cycling, cyclin-dependent kinases, and other parts of the cell cycle "machinery," the percentage of cell cycle abnormalities might approach 100% of cancers.[38,39] More recently, evidence is accumulating that at least 90% of cancer cells from human malignancies are also capable of resetting their telomere lengths and evading cell senescence.[40] This model has proven a powerful predictor not only of cell aging, but also of cancer cell survival.[41]

This realization—that the aging process is mutable at the cellular level and the implications of this for age-related diseases—has itself spawned more than a dozen targeted biotechnology companies over the past 4 years.[42] Not only does this realization have implications for cellular aging, but it has also prompted rethinking of the historically warranted pessimism about curing cancer. As a *Science* editorial put it at the end of 1996, predicting whether we might cure cancer, "the standard answer—'No'—may be up for revision."[43] Such optimism is not novel, but a comprehensive conceptual base, good supporting data, and promising clinical trials are new and very welcome.

The recent cloning of the protein component of human telomerase[36] will only accelerate this already rapid progress in understanding cancer and cell senescence. More importantly, to the extent that we can affect cell senescence therapeutically, we may stand to alter age-related diseases and thereby their economic, social, and human outcomes.

An Evolving Model

Previously, aging was seen as an immutable, passive accumulation of entropic damage in the cell. The evolving paradigm, in which cell aging results from and is coordinate on altered gene expression,[29,32,33] is growing in acceptance. Although still nascent, the Senescent Gene Expression (SGE) model is a model that encompasses both the programmed and damage schools of thought on aging. It suggests that aging is a complex cascade of processes that include repeated cell division, telomere effects at the chromosome ends (due to both their lengths and their associated heterochromatin), a significantly altered pattern of senescent gene expression in "old" cells, and consequent alternations in cell metabolism in general and free radical metabolism (production, sequestration, trapping, and damage repair) in particular. In addition, even cells that do not directly demonstrate aging changes (e.g., myocardial cells) depend on those that do (e.g., vascular endothelial cells). Together this cascade of processes play a coordinated but complex role in aging and—far more importantly—identification of each step could provide a basis for developing therapeutic interventions to affect a single step or the whole. This model—that the process of aging in the cell can be altered or reset (as may be true in the cloning of adult sheep cells and as is demonstrably true in senescent fibroblast hybridomas[44]—undermines the historical certainty that aging and age-related diseases are immutable at the cellular level. Coordinate and similar shifts are occurring in our understanding of cancer. Differences at the heart of cancer cells, such as cell cycle errors and telomerase expression, may provide leverage to draw far clearer therapeutic lines than we now can between cancers and normal cells. While none of our currently altering views of cancer or aging promise a cure, enormous clinical potentials may be opening for us where none existed previously.[43,45,46]

These changes in our theoretical understanding of cell aging and the availability of data to support the mutability of cell aging together call into question our ability to provide accurate extrapolations of the social and economic consequences of projected aging in developed countries. In 1950, 4 years before the Salk vaccine, if we were to have predicted the medical costs (e.g., iron lungs) that would accrue from polio over the next decade, we would have risked similar inaccuracies. Predictions of the costs of aging will be hollow unless they factor in the ongoing, nascent, and fundamental changes in our understanding of aging and age-related diseases.

Policy Implications of Extending Life

We are currently incapable of altering the aging process in any meaningful way, and any assertion to the contrary is misleading and not supported by fact. It is, however, equally misleading and disingenuous as well to ignore the ongoing shift in our knowledge of cell biology as we attempt to predict the future of health care and social policy in the United States and other developed countries. The assumptions on which we base our predictions need to be clearly understood, and there exists a reasonable degree of uncertainty in assuming that aging and age-related diseases will remain immutable in the coming decades.

The fiscal and social implications of this possibility cannot be underestimated. Any increase in the life span will be accompanied by concomitant shifts in social spending on the aged, but we cannot reasonably estimate the timing, magnitude, or fiscal outcome of altering the maximum human life span and age-related diseases. Even if one denies the possibility of such alteration, the upward trend in median age of the world's population is substantial but of uncertain magnitude. Even assuming that the lifespan is fixed, the consequent rectangularization of the survival curve, described by Fries,[7] will exert fiscal and social pressures on our ability to care for the elderly.[43,47] The magnitude of these pressures, their global distribution, and their effect on well-being will depend on several factors.

First, while there exists some variation internationally in the health status of elderly cohorts,[49,50] the social costs of increasing the maximum human life span will largely depend on the level of functional impairments and chronic disabilities among the aged.[51,52] Recent research suggests that, at least in the United States, increases in the mean life span have been accompanied by a concomitant decline in the prevalence of morbidity and disability among the aged.[53,54] The magnitude of any such decline and its overall impact on health care costs, relative to prior elderly cohorts, will vary internationally as a function of a nation's health care system, preventive health measures, rate of technological diffusion, advances in the treatment of acute and chronic diseases, social and political structures, and economic systems—to mention a few. The possibility that we might delay or prevent aging and associated disabilities only increases the already considerable variance in estimating such costs. However, the impact of such innovations would be determined by the political, social, regulatory, and economic structures of each country.

Second, innovations in medical technology (therapeutic, diagnostic, or organizational) for age-related conditions need not coincide with the health care needs or necessarily promote the well-being of those in developing countries. The immediate and future medical and public health concerns of sub-Saharan Africa are not in the research, development, and diffusion of age-related technologies, but in the development of effective mechanisms for controlling the spread of infectious diseases (such as the acquired immunodeficiency syndrome,[55] malaria, and tuberculosis), and the fatal consequences of drought, famine, and civil wars, which lead to mean life spans in these countries of approximately 48 years.[56] Therefore, when considering the international fiscal effects of increasing the maximum healthy human life span and the impact of these innovations on functional impairment among the aged, it is important to acknowledge that these advances are likely to benefit developed nations preferentially.

Third, the continued decline in the level of functional impairment among the elderly populations in developed countries, along with increases in active life expectancy,[57,58] has profound implications for work and retirement years. Even though the effect of longevity on work and retirement choice remains unclear,[59] developed nations can expect years of productive life among elderly age-specific cohorts to increase. How altering the maximum human life span—by whatever magnitude—would alter this effect cannot be reliably projected, but contrary to what one might expect, increased life expectancy in the United States has been associated with an accelerated decline in the labor force participation rates of older persons for the past 50 years.[60] To sustain current levels of well-being, however, longer life spans will have to be accompanied by either correspondingly longer work years, or higher premiums to enhance private contributions to retirement accounts, or higher taxes to enhance contributions into social insurance accounts. The magnitude of the latter will be determined by the willingness of current generations to subsidize future generations, as well as the ratio of workers to retirees. Further, the structure of public and private pension funds can in themselves affect the labor force participation rates of individuals. The retirement income provided by the funds allows older workers to leave the labor force at younger ages and still support themselves in retirement years.[60] Hence, it is the interplay among mortality, health status, work, and retirement and the structure of retirement accounts that will determine the overall impact of the burgeoning aging population

and any increase in the maximum human life span on the fiscal health of nations.

Finally, with increasing relative numbers of the aged, along with the growth in the proportion of the oldest old by the year 2040,[61] the international demand for long-term care could impose unexpected pressures on governments and individuals. This will be exacerbated if the proportion of offspring willing to live with their elderly parents continues to decline internationally,[62] therefore placing greater pressures on the public and private sectors for the establishment of innovative alternatives to long-term care—such as home or community-based care. The magnitude and direction of these pressures depend critically on the extent to which the maximum life span may be altered and the degree to which the prevalence of disabilities will be modified. Neither of these effects can be reliably estimated, yet current research suggests there is a reasonable possibility that both might alter within the time frame of current attempts to project future trends in international health and social welfare expenditures.

Conclusion

We should exercise extreme caution in projecting the future social and economic impact of an aging global society. This is particularly so because our understanding of the biology of aging is changing. The unquestioned conviction that we cannot alter aging and the cellular underpinnings of the diseases that accompany the aging process is no longer strictly tenable. The possibility that aging and its consequent clinical outcomes may be alterable at the cellular and chromosomal levels remains merely speculative and needs to be considered cautiously. However, such speculation becomes increasingly appropriate if we are to make any attempt to predict the future costs of an aging global society. It is important that we qualify and carefully define our assumptions to include the possibility that the morbidity and the mortality rates of age-related diseases, along with the maximum human life span itself, may be altered in the near future.

References

1. Hayflick, L. *How and Why We Age.* New York: Ballantine Books; 1994:313.
2. Finch CE. *Longevity, Senescence and the Genome.* Chicago: University of Chicago Press; 1990.
3. Jazwinski SM. Longevity, genes, and aging. *Science.* 1996;273:54–59.
4. Jeanne Calment, born 21 February 1875 in Arles, died 4 August 1997 in Paris, France: world's oldest woman dies at 122. *Baltimore Sun.* August 5, 1997:B5.
5. National Institute on Aging, National Institutes of Health; 1997.
6. Smith DWE. *Human Longevity.* New York: Oxford University Press; 1993.
7. Fries JF, Crapo LF. *Vitality and Aging: Implications of the Rectangular Curve.* San Francisco: WH Freeman; 1981.
8. Lakowski B, Hekimi S. Determination of life-span in Caenorhabditis elegans by four clock genes. *Science.* 1996;272:1010–1013
9. Ewbank JJ, Barnes TM, Lakowski B, Lussier M, Bussey H, Hekimi S. Structural and functional conservation of the Caenorhabditis elegans timing gene elk-1. *Science.* 1997;275:980–983.
10. Larsen PL, Albert PS, Riddle DL. Genes that regulate both development and longevity in Caenorhabditis elegans. *Genetics.* 1995, 139:1567–1683.
11. Weindruch R, Walford RL. *The Retardation of Aging and Disease by Dietary Restriction.* Springfield, IL: Charles C Thomas Publisher Inc; 1988.
12. Sohal RS, Weindruch R. Oxidative stress, calorie restriction, and aging. *Science.* 1996;273:59–63.
13. Lane MA, Ingram DK, Roth GS. Beyond the rodent model: calorie restriction in rhesus monkeys. *Age.* 1997; 20:45–56.
14. Harman D. The biologic clock: the mitochondria? *J Am Geriatr Soc.* 1972; 20:145–147.
15. Orr WC, Sojal RJ. Extension of life-span by overexpression of super oxide dismutase and catalase in Drosophila melanogastsr. *Science.* 1994;263:1128–1138.
16. Lundblad V, Wright WE. Telomeres and telomerase: a simple picture becomes complex. *Cell.* 1996;87:369–375.
17. Holt SE, Wright WE, Shay JW. Regulation of telomerase activity in immortal cell lines. *Mol Cell Biol.* 1996; 16:2932–2939.
18. Harman D. Aging: a theory based on free radical and radiation biology. *J. Gerontol.* 1956;11:298–300.
19. Sohal RS, Weindruch R. Oxidative stress, calorie restriction, and aging. *Science.* 1996;273:59–63.
20. Fossel M. *Reversing Human Aging.* New York: William Morrow & Co; 1996.
21. Dimri GP, Lee X, Basile G, et al. A biomarker that identifies senescent human cells in culture and in aging skin in vivo. *Proc Natl Acad Sci USA.* 1995;92:9363–9367.
22. Smith JR, Pereira-Smith OM. Replicative senescence: implications for in vivo aging and tumor suppression. *Science.* 1996;273:63–67.
23. Guarente L. Do changes in chromosomes cause aging? *Cell.* 1996;86:9–12.
24. Campisi J. Replicative senescence: an old live's tale. *Cell.* 1996;84:497–500.
25. Yu CE, Oshima J, Fu YH, et al. Positional cloning of the Werner's syndrome gene. *Science.* 1996; 272:258–262.
26. Allsopp RC, Vaziri H Patterson C, et al. Telomere length predicts replicative capacity of human fibroblasts. *Proc Natl Acad Sci USA.* 1992;89:10114–10118.
27. Oshima J, Brown WT, Martin GM. No detectable mutations at Werner helicase locus in progeria. *Lancet.* 1996;348:1106.
28. Wilmut I, Schnieke AK, McWhir J, Kind AJ Campbell KHS. Viable offspring derived from fetal and adult mammalian cells. *Nature.* 1997;385:810–813.
29. Stewart C. An udder way of making lambs. *Nature.* 1997;385:769–771.
30. Harley CB, Pollard JW, Chamberlain JW, Stanner CP, Goldstein S. Protein synthetic errors do not increase during aging of cultured human fibroblasts. *Proc Natl Acad Sci USA.* 1980;77:1885–1889.
31. Harley CB, Futcher AB, Greider CW. Telomeres shorten during aging of human fibroblasts. *Nature.* 1990;345:458–460.
32. Guarante L. Do changes in chromosomes cause aging? *Cell.* 1996;86:9–12.
33. Marcand S, Gasser SM, Gilson E. Chromatin: a sticky silence. *Curr Biol.* 1996;6:1222–1225.
34. Kim NW, Piatyszek MA, Prowse KR, Harley CB, West MD, Ho PLC. Specific association of human telomerase activity with immortal cells and cancer. *Science.* 1994;266:2011–2015
*35. Shay JW, Bacchetti S. A survey of telomerase activity in human cancer. *Eur J. Cancer.* 1997;33:787–791.
36. Nakamura TM, Morin GB, Chapman KB, et al. Telomerase catalytic subunit homologs from fission yeast and human. *Science.* 1997;277:955–959.
37. Meyerson M, Counter C, Eaton EN, et al. hEST2, the putative human telomerase catalytic subunit gene, is up-regulated in tumor cells and during immortalization. *Cell.* 1997;90:785–795.
38. Rao RN. Targets for cancer therapy in the dell cycle pathway. *Curr Opin Oncol.* 1996;8:516–524.
39. Sherr CJ. Cancer cell cycles. *Science.* 1996;274:1672–1677.
40. Shay JW, Gazdar AF. Telomerase in the early detection of cancer. *J Clin Pathol.* 1997;50:106–109.
41. Feng J, Funk WD, Wang SS, et al. The RNA component of human telomerase. *Science.* 1995;269:1236–1241.

This research was partially supported by the National Institute on Aging-funded Center on the Economics and Demography of Aging (P20-AG-12839)

The authors gratefully acknowledge the advice of Donald Ingram, David Smith, Robert Arking, David Kirp, Ron Lee, and Jane Mauldon.

*These references do not appear in this reading.

*42. Jazwinski SM, Martin GM, Schellenberg GD, et al. *Molecular and genetic strategies for treatment of age-related diseases.* Presented at the National Managed Health Care Congress: Bio/technology Conferences; July 14–15, 1997; Seattle, Wash.

43. Scanning the research horizon. *Science.* 1996;274:1989. Editorial box.

44. Wright WE, Brasiskyte D, Piatyszek MA, Shay JE. Experimental elongation of telomeres extends the life span of immortal x normal cell hybrids. *EMBOJ* 1996;15:1734–1741.

45. Hartwell LH, Kastan MB. Cell cycle control and cancer. *Science.* 1994;266:1821–1828.

46. Jacks T, Weinberg RA. Cell-cycle control and its watchman. *Nature.* 1996;381:643–644.

47. Winker MA, Glass RM. Aging global population: a call for papers. *JAMA.* 1996;276:1758.

*48. Marwick C. Longevity requires policy revolution. *JAMA.* 1995;273:1319–1321.

49. Manton KG, James VW. Survival after the age of 80 in the United States, Sweden, France, England, and Japan. *N Engl J. Med.* 1995;333:1232–1235.

50. Sallar AM, Hogg RS, Schechter MT. Survival after age 80. *N Engl J Med.* 1996;334:537–538.

51. Lubitz J, Beebe J, Baker C. Longevity and Medicare expenditures. *N Engl J Med.* 1995;332:999–1003.

52. Schneider EL, Guralnik JM. The aging of America: impact on health care costs. *JAMA.* 1990; 263:2335–2340.

53. Manton KG, Corder L, Stallard E. Chronic disability trends in the elderly United States populations: 1982–1994. *Porch Natl. Cad SCI USA.* 1997;94:2593–2598.

54. Alliance for Aging Research. *Seven Deadly Myths: Uncovering the Facts About the High Cost of the Last Year of Life.* Washington, DC: Alliance for Aging Research; May 1997.

55. Van De Walle E. The social impact of AIDS in sub-Saharan Africa. *Milbank Q.* 1990;68(1):10–32.

56. US Bureau of the Census. *Statistical Abstract of the United States*, 115th Edition. Washington, DC: US Bureau of the Census; 1995.

57. Manton KG, Stallard E, Liu K. Forecasts of active life expectancy: policy and fiscal implications. *J Gerontol.* 1993;48:11–26.

58. Sullivan DF. A single index of mortality and morbidity. *HSMHA Health Rep.* 1971;86:347–354.

59. Lee R, Tuljapurkar S. Death and taxes: longer life, consumption, and social security. *Demography.* 1997;34(1):67–81.

60. Wise DA. Retirement against the demographic trend: more older people living longer, working less, and saving less. *Demography.* 1997;34(1):83–95.

61. US Bureau of the Census. *Statistical Abstract of the United States*, 1995. Washington, DC: US Bureau of the Census, 1996.

62. Okamoto Y. Health care for the elderly in Japan: medicine and welfare in an aging society facing a crisis in long term care. *BMJ* 1992;305:403–405.

Reprints: Michael Fossel, MD, PhD, St. Mary's Hospital, 200 Jefferson SE, Grand Rapids, MI 49503 (e-mail: *Mfossel@aol.com*).

Article Review Form at end of book.

*These references do not appear in this reading.

What is a common myth about old age? How can myths about aging affect the way people view the elderly?

Myths of Ageing

Ageing today and tomorrow

Graham P. Mulley

Abstract

Accepting myths about old age may affect the way the elderly are treated. The belief that getting very old inevitably means being physically decrepit, diseased, and disabled can lead to negative attitudes and behaviors concerning the elderly. The concept that older people may not benefit from medical interventions as much as younger ones has led to their exclusion from investigational research and less than optimum therapeutic treatment in many instances. In order to improve the quality of life of the aged, we must eradicate these damaging prejudices.

"Old age" is synonymous with frailty, decrepitude, and senility. As people age, they inevitably develop degenerative disease for which little can be done. Very old people can no longer cope at home, and now that families no longer care for their elders most go into institutional care.

The medical profession is to blame for the burgeoning numbers of aged people. These are some of the myths of ageing which are reflected in apocalyptic terminology (rising tides, demographic time-bombs, grey hordes), negative stereotypes, and suboptimal care. Myths (from the Greek muthos, a fable or legend) are invented stories, imaginary ideas, fictions. How have the myths of ageing affected the way we think and talk about older people and our attitudes and behaviour towards them?

In the Graeco-Roman era average life expectancy in Europe was 20 years. By the year 1000 it had risen to about 30. By the mid-19th century, an American could expect to live for 39 years; by 1911 the figure was 46 and in 1930 it was 55.[1] Over the past 100 years, the proportion of Britons over 65 has risen from 5% to 16%.[2] Population prediction is not a precise science but, assuming unchanged fertility patterns and barring environmental catastrophe, the projected increase in the over-65 population of England and Wales is only 8% for the period 1991–2031.[3] This modest increase is at odds with the myth of an inexorable rise in the older population but it warrants closer scrutiny. Over the same period there will be a 48% increase in those aged 75–84 and a 138% increase in the over-85s. Few now consider 65–74 as old; we generally reserve that term for the over-75s, those over 85 being of advanced age.

The myth of medicated survival is at best a half-truth. The profound changes in population structure have more to do with public-health measures (improved hygiene, housing, and nutrition) and improved perinatal care than with artificially prolonging life by drugs, surgery, and medical technology. In 1919, 12% of deaths in Britain were in the first year of life (the current figure is less than 1%); 65% of people died before they were 65 (today 19%).[4] The "greying of nations" is therefore largely the result of the great reduction in premature deaths. Lately, however, prolongation of life does seem to be related to medical intervention: in the USA, much of the improvement in life expectancy has been attributed to access to the Medicare and Medicaid services.[5]

In Britain, only 3% of men and 64% of women over 65 are in residential or nursing homes. The proportion of people in care rises steeply with age (but varies greatly between countries); even so, four-fifths of those over 85 live in their own homes. The older you are, the more likely it is that you will live alone. Two-thirds of people aged 65–74 are married compared with one in six of those over 85.[2] Being alone does not mean being lonely; although 90% of the general population believe that loneliness is a problem in old age only one in ten older people feels lonely very often.[6]

The myth of selfish relatives who fail to meet their responsibilities to older people is as unfortunate as it is mistaken. Most support is still given by families.

Many caregivers are spouses; one-third of us can expect to become caregivers in retirement.[7] The belief that relatives of ethnic elders can support almost any chronic disease in old age is questionable.[8]

Forbidden phrases in geriatric medicine include "It's just your age" and "What do you expect at your age?" If a condition were solely due to ageing, it would become progressively common with advanced age and be universal in very late life. It would be equally common in older people of different races and at different times.

Some disorders do increase exponentially with age (e.g. fracture of the proximal femur) but cataract may be one of the few conditions which everyone will develop if they live long enough. Age-related macular degeneration clinically affects only a minority of older people, and is uncommon in blacks. Edentulousness is becoming less common: we do not lose our teeth because of age but because of caries and periodontal disease. The reduced muscle strength and bulk of older people is related to lack of exercise. Though self-rated

perception of smell declines with age, this is not uniform and varies with different odorants.[9] People in their 70s and 80s can still smell the roses.

Cognitive decline in healthy old people has been confirmed by metaanalysis[10] but cannot be attributed to age alone.[11] It's consequences for everyday living are usually trivial. Though the prevalence of dementia doubles every 5 years above 65,[2] the prevalence in people over 80 does not show an exponential pattern: there is a flattened S-curve, with a levelling off in the very old.[12]

The prevalence of disability rises with age but differs in social groups and in different parts of the country. In recent years there has been a decline in chronic disability in older Americans. Over a seven-year period, the probability of someone aged 85 or over remaining free from disabilities increased by nearly 30%.[13]

Our use of words reflects our attitudes and beliefs. "Geriatric" is an adjective; we should no more call an older person "a geriatric" than a child "a pediatric". The word "senile" is pejorative, with a resonance of therapeutic futility. "Decrepit" (literally, noiseless, from the Latin crepare, to crackle) evokes a feeble, tottery person worn out by age, whereas much of what has been attributed to age is caused by lifestyle or environmental factors. The concept of "frailty" is developing: it is now considered as a multisystem reduction in capacity, leading to an inability to withstand environmental stresses.[14] "She's a social problem" is another forbidden phrase, which often overlooks multiple medical, psychological, and functional problems. Geriatricians see few older people whose difficulties are exclusively social.

The unquestioning acceptance of the myth that old age is associated with a poor prognosis is one factor in the exclusion of elderly patients from investigations and new therapies.[3] Purely on grounds of age, people were excluded from the earlier trials of antihypertensive drugs and thrombolytic agents (later it was found that older patients benefited more from these treatments than middle-aged ones did). In the UK old people are excluded from screening programmes for cervical cancer. Those with established cancers are less likely to be referred for specialist treatment, to be properly investigated, or to receive optimum therapy. Older patients are less likely to have coronary artery bypass surgery or aortic-value replacement. Negative views of ageing are reflected in the false beliefs that rehabilitation is ineffective[15] or that geriatric medicine as a career is unrewarding, frustrating, and dull.

References

1. Agate J. *The practice of geriatrics.* London: Heinemann, 1970.
2. Mann A. Epidemiology. In: Jacoby R, Oppenheimer C, eds. *Psychiatry in the elderly.* Oxford: Oxford University Press, 1996: 89–112.
3. Medical Research Council. *The health of the UK's elderly people: MRC topic review.* London: Medical Research Council, 1994.
4. Markowe H. Health trends in the last 75 years. *Health Trends* 1994, 26: 98–105.
5. Manton KG, Vaupel JW. Survival after the age of 80 in the United States, Sweden, France, England

I hope that this collection of Lancet essays will challenge negative views about ageing, old people, their careers and what can be done to improve the wellbeing and independence of elderly people—and also that it will introduce young doctors to the absorbing range of opportunities that constitute the art, philosophy, and science of geriatric medicine.

and Japan. *N Engl J Med* 1995; 333: 1232–35.

6. Forbes A. Loneliness. *BMJ* 1996; 313: 352–54.
7. Travers AF. Carers. *BMJ* 1996; 313: 482–86.
8. Ebrahim S. Ethnic elders. *BMJ* 1996; 313: 610–13.
9. Wysocki CJ, Gilbert AN. National Geographic smell survey: effects of age are heterogenous. *Ann NY Acad Sci* 1989; 561: 12–28.
10. Verhaegen P, Marcoen A, Goossens L. Facts and function about memory aging: a quantitative integration of research findings. *J Gerontol* 1993; 48: 157–71.
11. Starr JM, Deary IJ, Inch S, Cross S, MacLennan WJ. Age-associated cognitive decline in healthy old people. *Age Ageing* 1976; 26: 295–300.
12. Ritchie K, Kildea D. Is senile dementia "age-related?": evidence from metaanalysis of dementia prevalence in the oldest old. *Lancet* 1995; 346: 931–34.
13. Manton KG, Stalland E, Corder I. Changes in morbidity and chronic disability in the US elderly population: evidence from the 1982, 1984, and 1989 national long-term care survey. *J. Gerontol* 1995; 50: 5104–204.
14. Campbell AJ, Buchner DM. Unstable disability and the fluctuations of frailty. *Age Ageing* 1997; 26: 317–18.
15. Young J. Rehabilitation. *BMJ* 1996; 313: 677–81.

Article Review Form at end of book.

What are some negative or "doomsday" predictions associated with changing demographics? How does migration impact the demographics of an aging society?

What If . . .?

What if some of the trends touted in the media came true during the next few decades? Here's American Demographics' contribution to millennial type.

Diane Crispell, Shannon Dortch, Brad Edmondson, Nancy Ten Kate, Matthew Klein, Matthew Cravatta

Abstract

More mothers are opting to stay at home rather than work, but if all mothers quit the workforce, family income would decrease a median of 32%. More men are leaving college before graduation, and at the current dropout rate, the last man will graduate in 2144. If boomers continue to spend rather than save for retirement, many could find themselves working way into their retirement years. Americans are aging as a group, but this will stabilize at 38 years of age after 2020.

When the first issue of this magazine appeared, manuscripts were laboriously typed on canary-yellow paper on real typewriters (remember those?), then sent to a typesetter. Charts were hand-drawn using rulers, and everything was assembled with Exacto-knives and lots of hot wax. It was a dangerous time for the production staff. Who would

have thought that 20 years later, we would nimbly cut and paste using our fingertips on a keyboard, and that the biggest health risk we would take is to destroy our backs and eyes being chained to chairs and computer monitors?

We have no idea how we'll be producing magazines in 20 years. But human beings can't resist speculating. This tendency is especially pronounced as we approach the year 2000. Forecasters and fortunetellers abound, expounding their visions of the good and bad in store for us. Some prognosticators are frivolous, but most are earnest. Some are optimistic; many are doomsayers.

Here are ten of our favorite futuristic scenarios, accompanied by our efforts to sort the reality from the hype. As befits any self-respecting grandiose millennial story, they also include our thoughts about why these things might or might not happen, and why it matters—or not.

Women Didn't Work?

"In just the past two years, a quiet counterrevolution has begun the exodus of women from the labor

force."—Maggie Mahar (*Forbes*, March 21, 1992).

"Heard enough about women in the work force? Well, so (arguably) have younger women."—Peter Brimelow (*Forbes*, January 13, 1997).

This persistent myth appears to revolve around the wishful thinking of both men and women, that mothers should stay home while their children are young, at least those who are married to men who can supposedly support them. In 1996, the U.S. had 7.3 million workers who were married women with children under age 6. What would happen if they all went home?

For starters, they would see their family income fall a median of 32 percent, according to the Bureau of Labor Statistics. Furthermore, "the wages of women who have taken a leave from the labor market never catch up to the wages of women who never left," according to research published in *Family Economics and Nutrition Review*.

At the same time, families with at-home mothers have lower expenses, notably for child care and commuting. An analysis of

1980–83 Consumer Expenditure Survey data shows that two-earner couples spent as much as 68 percent of their second-income advantage on work-related expenses they wouldn't have otherwise incurred. Even after taking into account these "opportunity costs," however, families suffer a net income loss by reverting to single-earner status. Furthermore, the share of wives in two-income families who earn more than their husbands was 22 percent in 1995, according to the Bureau of Labor Statistics. In these families, the husband's job is more dispensable.

If married mothers of preschoolers didn't work, Americans would spend less on women's clothes, eating out, housecleaning services, and transportation. They would probably also reduce discretionary spending on clothing and entertainment. They would spend more on food at home. They might also spend more on health insurance and put more aside to make up for lost employer-provided retirement benefits.

If married moms of young kids stopped working, U.S. employers would lose 1 in 20 workers. They wouldn't need to replace them all because of reduced consumer demand. They would find some replacements among the hundreds of thousands of displaced workers from the largely wiped-out child-care industry, but many wouldn't be suitable substitutes.

If mothers stopped working, some would get a little crazy. We're talking about a generation of women for whom a job is much more than a paycheck. Yes, some are willing to give up the economic and ego rewards, at least for a while. And yes, the ones who keep working often feel guilty. But 63 percent of married women with children under age 6 work because it pays, one way or another. There's nothing to suggest they won't keep doing so.

Men Didn't Go To College?

"What is wrong with the guys? When the labor market offers such rich rewards for the college-educated, why have only women responded, while men pass on the opportunity?"—Thomas G. Mortenson (*Postsecondary Education Opportunity*, September 1995)

The U.S. economy loves a college graduate. And it shows it by insuring greater lifetime earnings for college-educated men and women than for their less-educated counterparts. In the 30 years between the end of World War II and the end of the Vietnam War, men, in particular, made astounding progress in their rates of earning college diplomas.

But things have changed. Men are falling behind women in crossing the three main hurdles to a college degree: graduating from high school, continuing directly to college, and staying there until completing a degree, according to analysis by the newsletter *Postsecondary Education Opportunity*.

Men have slightly lower high school graduation rates than women, but the difference is small. The problem for men is in going to college and staying there. Until the early 1970s, men were much more likely than women to go to college within a year of completing high school. (College completion rates are greatest for those who proceed directly to college.) Since then, their continuation rates have fluctuated wildly. By the late 1980s, women surpassed men in the rate

at which they pursued higher education right after high school; men have never caught up.

Since 1990, smaller shares of both men and women aged 25 to 29 have stuck with college long enough to earn a bachelor's degree. Some of this decline may be due to changes in the way the Census Bureau measures educational attainment. Even so, there's no disputing that women continue to earn the lion's share of bachelor's degrees. The last year men earned the majority of sheepskins was 1981.

If the share of bachelor's degrees earned by men continues to shrink at the same rate as it has since 1870, the last American man will graduate from college in 2144. This could happen more quickly if the share of men who are incarcerated continues to grow rapidly.

If women were the only college-educated workers around, the jobs they do might become devalued, in which case employers could realize substantial payroll savings. Even so, the number of college-educated wives out-earning less-educated husbands would undoubtedly skyrocket. Other developed countries are further along in realizing this scenario; women earned 63 percent of the bachelor's degrees awarded in Norway in 1991.

Boomers Couldn't Retire?

"The savings crisis is far worse than previously imagined. Unless baby boomers become significantly more frugal, many will be forced to accept dramatically lowered standards of living during retirement, or else postpone retirement indefinitely." —Dr. B. Douglas Bernheim (*The Merrill Lynch Baby Boom Retirement Index: Update '97*)

Blaring sirens, warning bells, crunch time—these phrases pepper reports on the retirement prospects of America's roughly 76 million baby boomers. The idea is that profligate boomers have frittered their wages on high living and face economic risk when their working years end.

What if boomers get old without enough savings to sustain them? They may work until they die. Life expectancy for the oldest boomers is 78.5 years, so they could lose out on almost 15 years of golf and bingo. This would put a damper on some of the anticipated recreational boom. Ever-toiling boomers couldn't spend four weeks in Greece or travel America in an RV.

If boomers didn't retire, many would die on the job. Between 1991 and 1995, 4,612 people died of heart attacks while on the job. The majority of workplace deaths today are due to accidents, but that would change if legions of 75-year-old workers succumbed to old-age diseases on the spot. As it is, workers aged 65 and older are four times as likely as younger ones to die from job-related causes.

Before they kicked the bucket, never-quitting boomers would wreak havoc on younger workers. Employee attrition would slow, and competition between older and younger workers would intensify. In 1996, less than 4 million Americans aged 65 and older were in the paid labor force, accounting for 3 percent of workers. If men and women currently aged 45 to 54 kept up the same work rates they have now (82 percent), we would have 26 million workers aged 65 to 74 in 2020.

This is unlikely, however. Economists disagree on whether

boomers are heading toward a financial emergency. The widely publicized *Merrill Lynch Baby Boom Retirement Index* reports that in 1997, boomers are saving 39 percent of the funds they will need for retirement. "Don't believe it," says financial writer Jane Bryant Quinn in a December 1996 *Newsweek* article. "For middle-class workers, the news ain't all bad."

Evidence suggests that Americans with modest savings will live OK in retirement, albeit at a reduced level. If they want to maintain their current standard of living, however, they'll have to be a little more creative. Only 14 percent of boomers surveyed by Merrill Lynch in 1996 plan to use the equity in their homes, but they have plenty of time to change their minds. Elderly boomers could also just keep spending until they're broke, then cast themselves on the mercy of others. Provisions of adequate food, housing, and medical care for these nouveau indigent would fall to taxpayers.

Here's another novel idea. Young and middle-aged adults could reduce their living standards now and put more away for retirement. This might mean fewer big-screen TVs and sport-utility vehicles now, but more motor-coach tours and golf clubs later.

America Were Really Aging?

"By the year 2020, the old will control America and youth will be at their mercy."—Ken Dychtwald, popular speaker on aging and business.

Holy Metamucil, Batman! Is America doomed to a future of menopause and mall-walking? We don't think so. While "the

aging of America" is real, it won't be as scary or dramatic as Dychtwald suggests. In 1980, the median age of the United States was 30. Today, it is 35. Shortly after 2020, according to Census Bureau projections, it will stabilize at 38.

The U.S. has been gradually aging for more than a hundred years because of advances in life expectancy. The process is in the midst of a temporary acceleration, thanks to the baby boom. This will culminate around 2030, when the youngest boomers will be in their late 60s.

But America is more than just baby boomers. And older adults may have more power in 2020 than they do today, but they already have the bulk of it. Take property ownership: in 1996, 34 percent of homeowners were aged 55 and older, and another 18 percent were aged 45 to 54. Or government support: Medicare and Social Security claimed 33 percent of all federal outlays in 1996. How about political leadership? Most members of the House of Representatives are over age 50; in the U.S. Senate, 41 are aged 50 to 59 and 44 are aged 60 and older. In universities, 44 percent of instructional faculty and staff are aged 50 and older. Aging baby boomers will add a few percentage points to these figures, but they won't dramatically shift the balance of power.

If the old control America, will youth be at their mercy? As the kids would say: "You wish." The number of 18-to 24-year-olds is projected to increase from 25 million today to 30 million in 2020. At the same time, the annual number of births is projected to increase from about 3.9 million to 4.6 million, as a steady stream of immigrants comes to the U.S. and start families.

One-third of current population growth comes from immigration. If we shut off the immigration tap, as some recommend, America would age much more rapidly. Demographically speaking, the U.S. is beginning to resemble West Germany, Japan, and other highly developed countries. Our native-born population is aging rapidly because of low fertility, and we are relying more on immigrants to do the tasks of youth. It's not really an age wave. It's more like ebb tide for Anglos.

Whites Become a Minority?

"A half century from now, when your own grandchildren are in college, there will be no majority race in America."—President Clinton (1997 commencement speech at the University of California at San Diego)

Close, but no cigar. Although technically wrong, the President was on the right track. In 2050, three in four Americans will belong to the white race, but many will be Hispanics, who are currently viewed as minorities. Non-Hispanic whites will still be a majority of the population, but barely, at 53 percent, according to the Census Bureau's middle-series projections.

Shortly after 2050, non-Hispanic whites may become a true minority. Hispanics are poised to overtake blacks as the largest minority group. Asians and Pacific Islanders could almost double their numbers by 2020. And interracial marriages will add children to the population who cannot be easily labeled using current categories.

Non-Hispanic whites are already a minority in central cities of large metropolitan areas. Hawaii has always had a minor-ity majority, and New Mexico attained the distinction in 1990. Large numbers of immigrants will add California and Texas to the list by 2000 and 2010, respectively. The under-18 population will attain a minority majority long before the general population.

These changes will take place at this pace only if immigration continues at its present rate and in its present form (from Asia and Latin America), and if total fertility rates of nonwhites remain higher than for whites. Neither trend is certain, but it would take substantial changes in both to push back the timeline on a "minority majority."

The question isn't really whether non-Hispanic whites become a minority; it's a question of when. The even bigger question is: "So what?" For one thing, the 21st century may find young minorities working to support an older and whiter population. This could spur increased racial/ethnic tension across generational lines. Eventually, however, so-called Anglos will no longer dominate older age groups or control the government and economy. At that point, it's possible that divisions between haves and have-nots will be drawn less along white/nonwhite lines. (This doesn't mean they won't be drawn along other ones.) Transitions in the balance of power will occur gradually, however, and are already well underway. When we actually reach the day of a minority majority, nothing much will change.

Only a few decades ago, many non-Hispanic whites were considered minorities because they were recent non-English speaking immigrants who received less-than-equal social and economic treatment—Jews, Italians, Irish, and Poles. The "majority minority" of the future will not suffer from such new-comer disadvantages, but they may be put in their place to some extent. In the international scheme of things, non-Hispanic whites are a pretty small minority. The U.S. of the 21st century will merely be closer to reflecting this global reality.

Juvenile Crime Explodes?

"Unless we act today, we're going to have a bloodbath when these kids grow up."—James Alan Fox (news conference at American Association for Advancement of Sciences, February 1995)

Experts thought crime would drop when the teenage population hit a slump in the 1980s. It didn't. Now that the teen population's on the rise, media reports of "super predators" are fueling fears that the next decade will be even worse.

Some Americans in gang-war-torn neighborhoods already live with criminologist Fox's grim bloodbath scenario. Between 1985 and 1995, the rate at which teens aged 14 to 17 murdered people rose 165 percent. If this trend continues, "the number will double by the year 2010," according to *The New York Times*. This is not media hype; it is a straight-forward projection from the Department of Justice.

Drugs get most of the blame for rising crime and arrest rates among America's youth. Drugs, gangs, and guns go together. Ninety percent of juvenile homicides are committed with hand-guns. Childhood abuse and neglect also play a big role. Ninety percent of girls with a criminal record in Connecticut have a history of physical or sexual abuse, according to the state's justice department.

There is much debate about how to treat youth offenders. Is incarceration the answer? One study estimates that society more than benefits in dollar terms from incarcerating violent criminals who commit murder, assault, and robbery. It's less clear that we see a net gain from locking up cat burglars, though, and the analysis doesn't estimate the cost benefit of locking up drug offenders.

Even criminologist Fox isn't convinced that the Justice Department's dire prediction will come true, however. "It would be hard to keep on going straight up," he told *The New York Times*. Let's hope he's right. The number of federal and state prisoners (of all ages) grew 107 percent between 1986 and 1995, while the total population grew 9 percent. If the prison population continues to grow at the same average annual pace, one in four Americans will be living behind bars by 2050. And that doesn't count those living behind bars in their own homes for fear of the "super predators."—Diane Crispell

Everyone Was Wired?

"As the Internet becomes our new town square, a computer in every home—a teacher of all subjects, a connection to all cultures—will no longer be a dream, but a necessity. And over the next decade, that must be our goal."—President Clinton (1997 State of the Union address.

In his dream of an information nation, President Clinton hopes the Internet will change the American public. It will. But the public may change the Internet more.

Clinton's statement implies a vast electronic library and communications network hooked to a computer, which is how the Internet looks today. But to become a universal fixture in American homes, it needs to be both more and less. A fair share (41 percent) of the vast number of Americans without an Internet connection don't see a need for one, according to FIND/SVP's 1997 American Internet User Survey. That translates into 66 million Mohammeds who don't want to go to the mountain.

One chunk of the mountain, in the form of Bill Gates, is heading toward reluctant Mohammeds in two ways. Both take advantage of relationships Americans already have with home electronics. On the high end, full-strength PCs are designed to be the heart of the home-entertainment system, controlling televisions and stereos, and adding e-mail and browsing capabilities to the mix. For those without the means or desire to own a PC, Gates suggests a TV-set-top box connected to the Internet.

Although WebTV and similar ventures imply that the Net will be colonizing television, the opposite may be true in the future, as the spirit of TV becomes the approach that makes the Internet universally accepted. In 1997, the Internet is a super research mechanism that doubles as an instant letter-delivery system. But these functions have their limits. Look at all the encyclopedias collecting dust in countless homes. Americans aren't big on letter writing, either. They sent an average of 2.3 personal letters per month in 1995, according to Roper Reports.

The real key to universal adoption of the Internet is the same as it has been for virtually every successful mass medium the world has ever known, from print to radio and television—entertainment, not education. In the end, a nation bound by electronic connections may look pretty much like the nation currently united by networks of telephone lines, mail delivery, and mass media. In other words, it will still have a healthy supply of couch potatoes whose interactive pursuits are limited to channel changing.

There Was One Car For Every Adult?

"Look at some of the main thoroughfares in London, and you can see the future. And it isn't moving."—Neil Kinnock, transport commissioner for the European Union (*Newsweek*, August 25, 1997)

The future London faces is reality in parts of the U.S. We will have one vehicle for every American adult aged 18 and older by 2005, according to the Bureau of Transportation Statistics. Nearly every eligible American has a driver's license (175 million in 1994), and the number of vehicles (198 million in 1994) exceeds the number of drivers.

Other parts of the world might eventually face this situation, too. The world has 2.6 billion people and 50 million vehicles in 1950. Today, it has 5.5 billion people and 500 million vehicles. We add about 50 million cars and trucks to the global inventory each year. In the next 30 years, the auto industry will produce as many cars as it did in its first century.

The U.S. has reached a seeming saturation point for several reasons. For one thing, we're a prosperous nation in which most people can afford cars. Second, we're a spread-out nation of commuters. Most work traffic is now from suburb to suburb, making it difficult to travel with others or use public transport.

Perhaps most significant, American women have become a major car-owning force. Their jobs and other activities warrant the need for second cars in many households. "Women buy 52 percent of new and 48 percent of used cars," according to Courtney Calwell, editor and publisher of *American Woman Motorscene* magazine. "In the next three to five years, women will account for 60 percent of all new-car sales."

So what do London and other places have to look forward to in an era of universal car ownership? During its lifetime, an average car travels 100,000 miles, consumes more than 3,000 gallons of fuel and 50 gallons of oil, and discharges more than 35 tons of carbon in the form of various gases and particles. The physical and social costs of driving in the U.S. average an estimated $2,000 a year per vehicle, which covers building and repairing roads, loss of economic activity from congestion, cost of illnesses caused by air pollution, and medical care for the victims of accidents. One radical proposal by the mayor of Sao Paulo, Brazil, is to charge drivers an annual tax to cover the real costs of their actions.

The number of vehicles in the U.S. is beginning to stabilize. But what if we decide at some point that we "need" more than one car per person? We will doubtless face more pollution, bad roads, and longer commutes. One problem that might ease is the risk of injury or death. It's hard to be badly injured in a car accident when the traffic's not moving.

The Oceans Rose Three Feet?

"As the heating of the atmosphere intensifies, it will increase sea levels by as much as three feet in the next century, causing disastrous floods." (projections from the U.N. Intergovernmental Panel on Climate Change)

If the oceans rose three feet, coastal cities like New York, Miami, and New Orleans would be faced with two costly choices: build dikes or move. Pricey real estate in Rhode Island, Cape Cod, and the Outer Banks would turn back into submerged sandbars. Land that is miles from the ocean in 1997 would turn into shoreline and salt marsh. And land that is now safe from ocean storm surges would become vulnerable flood zones. About four in ten Americans live within 50 miles of a coastline, according to the Census Bureau.

Rising sea levels could lead to famine in low-lying countries such as Bangladesh that depend on small farms for food. Flooded salt marshes could decrease seafood harvests. Controlling the ocean would be a serious financial burden for affluent overseas markets like Tokyo and Singapore. Worldwide, 14 of the fastest-growing urban centers are located on coasts.

Most climate change models indicate that the potential effects of global warming go far beyond rising ocean levels. Winters are likely to become warmer and more stormy in temperate and arctic latitudes. Summers could be hotter with less rain, and summer rains more likely to come in the form of thunderstorms instead of gentle showers.

How likely is a 3-foot rise? The earth's atmosphere has warmed about 1 degree Fahrenheit in the last century, and global sea levels have risen about 10 inches, according to the United Nations Intergovernmental Panel on Climate Change (IPCC). The leading explanation for these events is the "greenhouse effect," caused by increased levels of carbon dioxide in the atmosphere, which in turn is caused by burning fossil fuels. Rising temperatures cause polar ice to thaw and oceans to rise. According to the IPCC's 1995 report, written and reviewed by 1,000 leading climate experts, global warming is most likely to contribute a 6-inch increase in sea levels by 2050 and an increase of about 14 inches by 2100. They give a 3-foot rise a 1 percent probability.

An international agreement to stabilize carbon-dioxide emissions could reduce the long-term effects of global warming if it is ratified at a U.N. conference in Kyoto this month. But even if the agreement is made and upheld, says the IPCC, we'll keep heating up for at least a few decades. And some of the ice will melt.

Everyone Stopped Smoking?

"The forces that lead people to light up their first cigarette are largely external. Therefore, it should be no surprise that external forces also will be necessary to reach the goal that many Africans now hope we can achieve—a smoke-free, healthier society."—Richard A. Levinson (Richard A. Levinson heads the District of Columbia Public Health Commission's Preventative Health Care Administration)

What if the nation's cigarette smokers woke up gasping one morning and discovered there wasn't a cigarette to be found, nor a single tobacco plant growing in the rich soils of the Tobacco Belt? What if cigarette prohibition became the law of the land in the blink of an eye?

No smoke-choked taverns; no yellowed fingers, teeth, or lungs; no hazy chats in school bathrooms; no coffee-and-cigarette breakfasts; no "Got a light?" chance encounters. It may or may not happen, but if the current decline in cigarette-smoking rates continues, there's a slim chance that by the year 2060 or so, finding a lit cigarette will be as difficult as finding a parking space.

The U.S. has roughly 61 million cigarette smokers, or about 29 percent of the population aged 12 and older.

Social repercussions aside, the change in the national landscape would be astronomical. For starters, the roughly 76,000 tobacco manufacturing employees and 600,000 tobacco farm families would have a tough time in the New Clean Age. Tobacco farmers would see a big change in per acre gross income, as tobacco (the nation's fifth-largest cash crop) pulls in 12 to 15 times more than an acre of corn or soybeans.

State and federal governments would surely scramble to replace the missing $20 billion in tax revenue that cigarettes generate (I'm sure they'd find something to tax). On the other hand, we'd spend less on health care related to smoking (conservative estimates are around $60 billion a year, not including lost productivity time).

It would probably take at least a couple of generations of smokeless Americans to see any substantial changes in mortality rates (an estimated 400,000 deaths per year are attributed to cigarette consumption). It takes years for former smokers to eliminate the damage to their bodies; and, as most of us know, cigarettes not only negatively affect the smoker, but also nearby nonsmokers via secondhand smoke. Ultimately, however, a smokefree society would be an older one. People would live longer and die of illnesses other than smoking-related diseases.

Some of the health-care savings related to cigarette abstinence might be balanced out by the negative effects of nicotine withdrawal: mass depression and irritability, higher incidence of overweight (men gain an average of 10 pounds after quitting, women gain 11), chronic nail-biting and knuckle-gnawing, not to mention pencil-tip desecration, teeth-grinding, and sarcastic remarks.

On a positive note, people owning stock in chewing gum, lollipop, and other candy industries are bound to strike it rich; sales of anything that people like to put in their mouths, from popsicles to chicken legs, would likely go through the roof. Retail clothing sales should also see a boom, as ex-smokers' waistlines gradually expand. These substitutes might replace at least some of the jobs and dollars lost in the tobacco industry. Dentists might make out OK, too.

Taking It Further

Mothers stopped working: statistics on number and income of married working mothers from the Bureau of Labor Statistics; "Effects of Intermittent Labor Force Attachment on Women's Earnings," Family Economics and Nutrition Review, U.S. Department of Agriculture, Vol. 9, No. 2, 1996; "The Economic Costs and Rewards of Two-Earner, Two-Parent Families," by Sandra L. Hanson and Theodora Ooms, Journal of Marriage and the Family, August 1991.

Men didn't go to college: For more information on college continuation and completion, see the September 1995 and February 1996 Postsecondary Education Opportunity, P.O. Box 127, Iowa City, IA 52244; telephone (319) 351-4913. The National Center for Education Statistics annually publishes projections of college enrollment, degrees awarded, and other measures. Its most recent data are published in Projections of Education Statistics to 2007, available from the Government Printing Office, Washington, DC 20402-9328; telephone (212) 512-1800. For more on the declining number of men on college campuses, see "Hey Guys: Hit the Books" in the September 1997 American Demographics.

Boomers couldn't retire: The Merrill Lynch Baby Boom Retirement Index is conducted annually by Merrill Lynch & Company, Inc.; telephone (212) 449-7293. Data on workplace fatalities are available from the Bureau of Labor Statistics' Census of Fatal Occupational Injuries. For information, call (202) 606-6175, e-mail CFOOSTAFF@bls.gov, or see Internet site http://www.stats.bls.gov/oshfat1.htm.

America were really aging: Ken Dychtwald in "21st Century Online Magazine," Internet address http://www.21net.com/online/agewave.htm; "Population Projections of the United States . . . " Current Population Reports No. P25–1130; Housing Vacancy Survey, second quarter 1997, Census Bureau; Office of Management and Budget, Historical Tables; Congressional Quarterly, Washington, DC; The New Americans: Economic, Demographic, and Fiscal Effects of Immigration, National Research Council (National Academy Press, Washington, DC, 1997).

Whites became a minority: U.S. Census Bureau middle-series projections; Demographic Statistics Branch, Immigration and Naturalization Service, Department of Justice; Roper Starch Worldwide, New York, NY; National Science Foundation, Washington, DC; National Review, June 16, 1997.

Juvenile crime explodes: "Murder by Teens Has Soared," Newsday, February 17, 1995; "Grim Forecast Is Offered on Rising Juvenile Crime," The New York Times, September 8, 1995; "Search for Answers to Juvenile Crime," The Christian Science Monitor, June 17, 1996;

"Wayward Youth, Super Predator," *Corrections Today*, June 1997; "The Effect of Prison Population Size on Crime Rates: Evidence from Prison Overcrowding Litigation," *The Quarterly Journal of Economics*, May 1996; Bureau of Justice Statistics, U.S. Department of Justice, Washington, DC.

Everyone was wired: 1997 American Internet User Survey, FIND/SVP, New York, NY; "The Future of the Internet: The Internet PC," by Bill Gates, Microsoft Web site: http://www.microsoft.com; Roper Starch Worldwide, New York, NY.

One car per adult: *Statistical Abstract of the United States 1996; Commuting in America II*, by Alan Pisarski, August 1997, Eno Foundation for Transportation, Inc., Westport, CT;

Surface Transportation Policy Project, Environmental Working Group, *USA Today*, September 16, 1997; "Taming the Beast: a survey on living with the car," *The Economist*, June 22, 1996; "The Car Trap," *World Press Review*, December 1996; "2020 Vision," *Chemistry & Industry* magazine.

Oceans rose three feet: "Experts on Climate Change Ponder: How Urgent Is It?" *The New York Times*, September 9, 1997; journalist Ross Gelbspan in The American Prospect, March 1997; "The Rising Risk of Rising Tides," Forum for Applied Research and Public Policy, Summer 1996; "The Probability of Sea Level Rise," by James Titus et al., U.S. Environmental Protection Agency, and Second Assessment Report of the IPCC, both available at Internet address http://www.epa.gov/globalwarming, or via fax request to EPA Publication Office, (513) 489-8695.

Everyone stopped smoking: Centers for Disease Control's Office on Smoking and Health; Reuters Health Information Services, *New England Journal of Medicine; Statistical Abstract of the United States, 1996; The Psychology of Everyday Living* by Ernest Dichter; Forum for Applied Research and Public Policy, Fall 1995; Berkeley Economic Research Associates; *The Politics of Our National Addiction* by Gwenda Blair.

Article Review Form at end of book.

How does mortality and fertility impact aging demographics? What are some of the health challenges that an aging population will bring to developing countries?

Population Ageing

A public health challenge

By 2020 more than 1,000 million people aged 60 years and older will be living in the world, 710 million of them in developing countries.

One of the main achievements in the 20th century has been a considerable increase in the numbers and proportions of older people in both developed and developing countries. This phenomenon is referred to as "population ageing."

- Today, there is an estimated 540 million elderly people (60 years and more) living in the world with around 330 million of them in developing countries.

From a demographic point of view population ageing is characterized by a shift towards lower mortality and lower fertility. In other words, more people reach old age while fewer children are born.

- Over the last fifty years mortality rates in developing countries have declined dramatically raising the average life expectancy at birth from around 46 years in the early 1950s to almost 64 years in 1990. By 2020, it is projected to reach 72 years.

- More recently equally sharp falls have occurred in birth rates in nearly all developing countries except for most of Sub-Saharan Africa. Total fertility rates in China, for example, declined from 5.4 in 1970 to the current 2.0 level, respective figures for Brazil being 5.0 and 2.8.

Population ageing has become an important development issue that requires urgent action. If left unattended now, it may have far-reaching consequences for public health services throughout the world. Projections for the first quarter of the 21st century, prepared independently by a number of organizations and scientists, merit the closest attention.

- By 2020 the number of elderly people worldwide will reach more than 1,000 million with some 710 million of them in developing countries.

- Within the next quarter-century Europe is projected to retain its title of the "oldest" region of the world (elderly people represent around 19% of the total population now and will represent 24% by 2020).

- The "oldest" country by 2020 will be Japan (31%), followed by Italy, Greece and Germany (all above 28%) and Switzerland (27.4%). Today, the country with the highest proportion of elderly people is Greece (22%).

- By 2020 the proportion of population aged 60 and over is projected to reach 23% in North America, 17% in East Asia, 12% in Latin America and 10% in South Asia.

- By 2020 seven developing countries will be among the ten countries with the largest elderly populations in the world: China (231 million), India (145), Brazil (30), Indonesia (29), Pakistan (18), Mexico (15) and Bangladesh (14 million).

"Population Ageing: A Public Health Challenge" Fact Sheet N135 from www.who.ch/inf/fs/fact135.html. Reprinted by permission of the World Health Organization.

In developed countries, population ageing has evolved gradually as a result of improving living standards of the majority of the population over a relatively long period of time after the industrial revolution. Technological breakthroughs in the field of medicine, including the development of new and effective drugs and vaccines, contributed to this process much later.

In developing countries, population ageing has a more rapid character. It is being accompanied by persistent poverty and misery and is mostly accounted for by medical interventions based on the use of advanced technology and drugs. These have provided effective means to treat and prevent many diseases that kill people prematurely.

- In France, it has taken 115 years (1865–1980) for the proportion of the elderly population to double from 7 to 17%. It is projected that the same doubling in China will take 27 years (2000–2027), or will occur four times as rapidly.

- From 1985 to 2025 the rate of increase of elderly populations in developing countries is expected to be up to 10 times higher in countries such as Colombia, the Philippines, Kenya, and Thailand, as compared, for example, with the United Kingdom and Sweden. These developing countries are expected to experience a 300% increase in their elderly populations over a period of only 40 years.

The rapidly growing numbers and proportions of older people in both developed and developing countries mean that more and more people will be entering the age when the risk of developing certain chronic and debilitating diseases is significantly higher. As such, population ageing presents new and serious challenges for national and international public health.

By 2020 three-quarters of all deaths in developing countries will be ageing-related and caused by non-communicable diseases (NCDs) such as diseases of the circulatory system (CSDs), cancers, hypertension and diabetes.

- In Latin America, NCDs are on a steady increase. In Argentina, Cuba and Uruguay, for example, CSDs together with cancers are already responsible for around two-thirds of all deaths. In Cuba, hypertension prevalence in men and women had reached 34.5% and 27.1%, while diabetes affects 5.7% of women and 2.9% of men.

- Population surveys in a number of African countries indicate that hypertension rates are on the rise, as is the prevalence of diabetes. In Seychelles, hypertension affects 22% of the population; in South Africa—16%; in Mauritius—14%. Diabetes affect from 4 to 15% of the population in the three countries.

- In South East Asia, with an average life expectancy of about 60 years, CSDs and cancers are now the two leading causes of mortality. Hypertension has been found in India, Indonesia and Thailand to affect up to 15% of the adult population. Diabetes reaches industrialized-country proportions in urban populations.

- NCDs have a major impact on health economics. According to the American Heart Association in 1996, cardiovascular diseases in the U.S.A. will cost $151.3 billion, including medical treatment and lost productivity from disability.

- Diabetes mellitus alone, which affects some 100 million people worldwide, claims on the average around 8% of total health budgets in industrialized countries.

Population ageing has also been projected to aggravate the magnitude of mental health problems within the next quarter-century. This will happen because of the increasing life expectancy of those with mental disorders and an ever-growing number of people reaching the age at which the risk of such disorders is high.

- Estimated at 22 million today, the number of people affected by senile dementia in Africa, Asia and Latin America may exceed 80 million in 2025.

Visual impairment and vision loss increase dramatically with age. One disease that is especially notorious in this respect is cataract. Cataracts may have different origins, but they are mostly related to the ageing process.

- Today, there about 38 million blind people in the world and a further 110 million have low vision. Cataract is responsible for 16 million cases of blindness worldwide. In most countries of Asia and Africa, it accounts for more than 50% of all blindness and more than 40% of all low vision cases.

- Usually, ageing-related cataract can be treated with a relatively simple operation to remove the opaque lens. Increasingly, cataract surgery includes the use of intraocular lens implantation, which, however, requires sophisticated technology and adequately trained personnel. In the U.S. alone there are some 1.35 million cataract operations performed each year at a cost of $3.4 billion.

These are but a few examples that can demonstrate the magnitude of the public health aspects of population ageing. They certainly do not cover the whole range of the ageing-related public health aspects. Furthermore, many developing countries are already facing a double affliction: the newly-emerging health problems of an aging population, and continuing high rates of communicable disease.

The emerging social and public health consequences of ageing, especially in developing countries, need to be taken very seriously. In the majority of these countries, poverty, lack of social security schemes, continuing urbanization and the growing participation of women in the workforce—all contribute to the erosion of traditional forms of care for elderly people.

In order to respond to public health challenges of population ageing, the World Health Organization (WHO) launched in April 1995 a new programme on ageing and health which stems from and builds upon the achievements of its predecessor—the programme of health of the elderly.

The emphasis of the new programme is on healthy ageing rather than on "the elderly." Its key components include policy development, data base development, advocacy, community-based programmes, training and research.

Living longer offers unprecedented opportunities for creative personal and social lives, but it also presents individual and societal challenges related to quality of life in old age, including independence, social interaction, health care and community involvement. In order to answer these challenges countries have to develop sound and affordable policies that perceive ageing as a natural process which continues throughout one's lifetime. Effective community-based programmes need to be part and parcel of such healthy ageing policies.

The creation and strengthening of a reliable data base is a prerequisite for the development of national policies on healthy ageing. It is also crucial for awareness-raising among policy-makers and decision-makers about the magnitude of population ageing and its public health consequences. This awareness is still low, particularly in developing countries.

National policies on ageing should rely on the results of research aimed at cost-effective public health interventions to improve the quality of life in old age. Such results need to be widely shared among countries.

Improved knowledge and skills of primary health workers to deal with ageing-related problems could be achieved through training activities.

Living longer is both an achievement and a perpetual challenge. Investing in health and promoting it throughout their lifetime is the only way to ensure that more people will reach old age in good health and capable of contributing to society intellectually, spiritually and physically.

For more information, please contact Health Communication and Public Relations, WHO, Geneva, Tel (41 22) 791-2532, Fax (41 22) 791-4858. All WHO Press Releases, Fact Sheets and Features can be obtained on Internet on the WHO home page http://www.who.ch/

Article Review Form at end of book.

What is the average number of years a person in the United States can expect to live? Do women or men live longer?

Record High U.S. Life Expectancy

Stanley Kranczer

Medical Statistician and Demographer

In 1996 expectation of life at birth for all newborns and for infant boys reached new highs. According to preliminary life tables prepared by MetLife statisticians, average future lifetime for all babies reached 75.9 years or 0.1 year higher than the previous peak established in 1992 and matched in 1995 (Table 1*). For infant boys, average future lifetime rose to 72.8 years in 1996, 0.3 years more than the 1995 high of 72.5 years. Among newborn females, life expectancy at birth rose from 78.9 years in 1995 to 79.0 years in 1996. However, this expectancy is still below the peak of 79.1 years reached in 1992.

The life expectancy sex differential has narrowed considerably due to changes in the longevity patterns of newborn boys and girls (Figure). During 1996 baby girls could expect to live, on the average, 6.2 years more than baby boys; in 1992 their longevity advantage was 6.8 years and in 1990 and 1986 it was 7.0 years. These changes occurred because life expectancy reflects underlying death rates. More specifically, at ages 65 and over—the age group where most deaths occur—mortality rates among men have rapidly declined since 1990, while those for women have hardly budged.

Gains in life expectancy at each age can be attributed to the small decline in overall mortality between 1995 and 1996. According to provisional data there were 2,311,000 deaths last year compared with a final total of 2,312,132 in 1995 and 2,278,994 in 1994. The corresponding death rates were 8.7 per 1,000 in 1996 and 8.8 per 1,000 during the two previous years.[1,2] In 1996 preliminary data indicate that there were meaningful mortality declines from the major cardiovascular diseases, pneumonia and influenza, chronic liver diseases and cirrhosis and human immunodeficiency virus infection (HIV).[1]

Infant Mortality Progress

Along with the encouraging increase in longevity, the downward trend in infant mortality rates continues to be extremely positive. During 1996 the estimated death rate in the first year of life fell substantially to 7.2 per 1,000 live births. This is another record low and represents the 34th consecutive annual decline. In 1995 the infant death rate was 7.6 per 1,000 and in 1994 it was 8.0 per 1,000.

Age Analysis

Past childhood, 1996 estimated male longevity values also increased to new record highs (Table 1*). For example, at age 25, average remaining lifetime for men was 49.5 years compared with 49.2 years in 1995 and 49.1 years in 1994 and 1992. Male average future lifetime at ages 45 and 65 in 1996 was 31.5 years and 15.7 years, respectively For women, the average number of remaining years increased slightly at ages 15–45. Nonetheless, their 1996 life expectancies still are below their longevity peaks recorded in 1992.

*Not included in this publication.

Reprinted courtesy of Metropolitan Life Insurance Company, STATISTICAL BULLETIN, "Record High U.S. Life Expectancy," Vol. 78, No. 4, pp. 2–8, 1997.

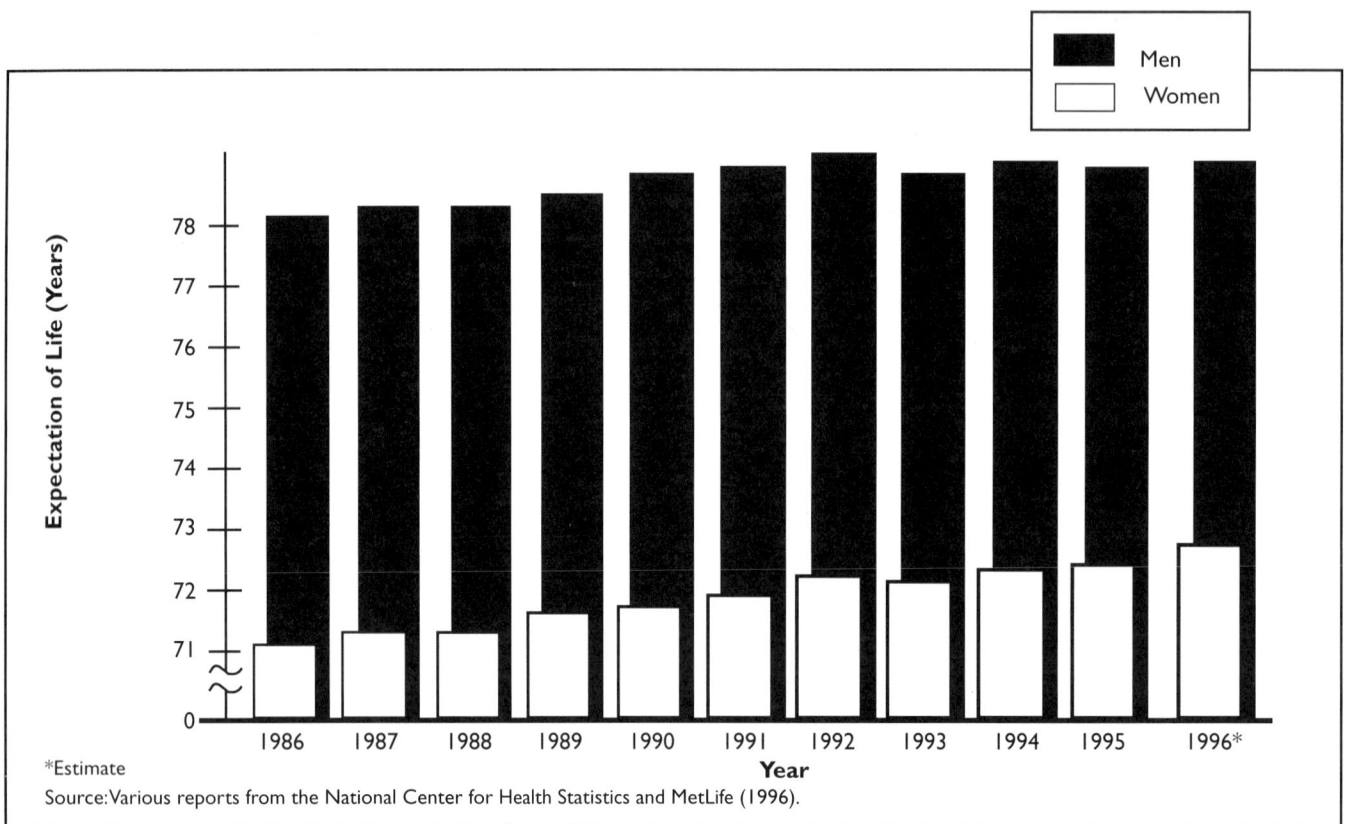

Figure—Trend in expectation of life at birth by sex, United States, 1986–1996.

Recap: Expectation of Life Increases

In 1996 life expectancy in the United States rose to a record high of 75.9 years for all persons combined. A new peak was also recorded among newborn boys—72.8 years—while average future lifetime for infant girls increased to 79.0 years—0.1 year shy of the 1992 record of 79.1 years. In recent years longevity gains among males have outpaced those for females, with the result that the sex differential in longevity at birth in favor of females has narrowed considerably. In 1996 newborn girls could anticipate living 6.2 years longer than boys—the gap was 6.8 years in 1992 and 7.0 years in 1990. Projections indicate that the trend in longevity improvements in favor of males will continue. As a consequence, the sex differential gap in average future lifetime is anticipated to diminish to 4.6 years by 2050.

Changes Over Time

The trend in life expectancy by race and sex since the turn of the century is presented in Table 2*. Significant improvement in expectation of life has been recorded for each racial group. However, since 1989–91, the longevity advances have been markedly larger for men than for women. Between 1989–91 and 1995, expectation of life for infant white boys increased by 0.7 years, while the comparable gain among girls was 0.1 year.

For newborns of all other races, the rise among boys was 0.9 years and for girls 0.3 years. African-American infant boys gained 0.7 years of additional life in the period,

> In 1996 life expectancy at birth values for all newborns and for infant boys recorded new highs.

while the increase among girls was 0.2 years. Thus, the advantage in longevity at birth among women has declined to 6.2 years among whites and 7.8 years among nonwhites. The longevity gap between the sexes was somewhat higher for blacks, namely, 8.7 years.

Differentials by Race and Sex

Older men in each of the three racial groups fared better than the women (Table 2*). Between 1994 and 1995 male longevity either increased slightly or remained unchanged in virtually each age category, while that for females declined, for the most

*Not included in this publication.

part. For example, past childhood expectation of life for white men rose by at least 0.1 year (except at age 85) to new record highs; on the other hand, among white women average remaining lifetime declined in half of the eight ages shown. Life expectancy among men of all other races combined and for African Americans fell only at the extreme ages but was diminished among females in all but one instance.

Notwithstanding the larger recent improvements in nonwhite men's longevity, their average future lifetime still is less than that for whites. For example, in 1995 newborn white boys could expect to outlive black babies by 8.2 years. At age 25 the differential was 7.0 years and at age 45 white men could expect 5.0 more years of additional lifetime. The racial difference diminished with advance in age and by age 85 it was only 0.1 year. Among women the longevity differentials were much smaller but have not materially narrowed.

> Since 1989–91, the longevity advances have been markedly larger for men than for women.

> The likelihood of reaching an 85th birthday is much smaller for men than for women.

Chances of Survival

Racial differences in longevity are also evident in comparing chances of survival. Thus, among 1,000 white girls born in 1995, 987 could expect to survive to age 25, 969 to age 45, and 714 to age 75; the comparable age survival for black girls was 974, 927 and 566, respectively. Among men the like-

lihood of surviving to celebrate a 75th birthday was 556 per 1,000 for whites but only 359 per 1,000 for blacks. The likelihood of reaching an 85th birthday was also much smaller for men than for women.

Single Years of Age Details

Table 3* shows expectation of life values and mortality rates by single years of age from the final 1995 National Center for Health Statistics "life tables."[3] The longevity advantage at birth in favor of women has been discussed previously. Additionally, in 1995 at age 25 white women could expect to outlive white men by 5.6 years and at age 45 by 4.6 years. By age 65 the longevity differential narrowed to 3.4 years but was still 1.1 years at age 85. Among persons of all other races, women's longevity advantage over men was 7.1 years at age 25, 5.4 years at age 45, 3.4 years at age 65 and 1.1 years at age 85.

In 1995 death rates were less than one per 1,000 at ages 1–35 among white women and at ages 1–25 among nonwhite women. This low level of mortality was only recorded for white males aged 1–16 and nonwhite males at ages 2–14. Mortality rates of less than five per 1,000 were experienced among white men through age 48 and among white women

through age 54. Among persons of all other races, rates of this magnitude prevailed through age 37 for men and age 49 for women.

Projections

Continued slow improvements in life expectancy are likely. The latest projected life tables for the year 2050, prepared by the Bureau of the Census, indicate that expectation of life at birth could rise to 82.0 years for all persons combined and reach 79.7 years for men and 84.3 years for women.[4] These figures represent an increase for men and a decrease for women from the previous published projections.[5]

References

1. Anderson, R.N., Kochanek, K. D., Murphy, S. L. "Report of final mortality statistics, 1995." *Monthly Vital Statistics Report*, 45(11, Suppl. 2). Hyattsville, MD: National Center for Health Statistics, 1997.
2. National Center for Health Statistics. "Births, marriages, divorces, and deaths for 1996." *Monthly Vital Statistics Report*, 45(12). Hyattsville, MD: National Center for Health Statistics. 1997.
3. National Center for Health Statistics, "Life tables." *Vital Statistics of the United States.* 11(6): Hyattsville, MD, 1997.
4. Day, J. C. "Population projections of the United States, by age, sex, race, and Hispanic origin: 1995 to 2050." *Current Population Reports.* P25–1130. Washington, DC: U.S. Gov. Print. Office, 1996.
5. Day, J. C. "Population projections of the United States, by age, sex, race, and Hispanic origin: 1992 to 2050." *Current Population Reports.* P25–1092. Washington, DC: U.S. Gov. Print. Office. 1992.

Article Review Form at end of book.

*Not included in this publication.

Who are the "old-old"? How do African-American elderly compare to White American elderly concerning life expectancy?

Demography and Gerontology

Mortality trends among the oldest old

Emily Grundy

*Age Concern Institute of Gerontology,
King's College, Cornwall House,
Waterloo Road, London SE1 8WA, UK*

Abstract

This paper provides a brief introduction to demography and population science and the newly emerged subfield of the demography of ageing. Links with gerontology are explored. Recent work on mortality at very high ages and on the black-white mortality 'cross-over' reported from the United States is then reviewed. These topics are important substantively and theoretically and also serve to illustrate demographic approaches to data and data analysis. Analytic approaches to the topics reviewed have had to be imaginative as there are major problems with data on very old people. Recent work indicates that the mortality of very old people, including centenarians, has fallen considerably, at least in those countries where good data exist. The mortality 'cross-over', however, appears to be artefactual, at least at ages under 95 years.

Introduction

This paper provides a short introduction to the fields of demography, population science and the demography of ageing before focusing in more detail on trends in the mortality of the oldest-old and on the apparent black-white mortality 'cross-over' in the United States. This research is likely to be of substantive and theoretical interest to gerontologists, because it provides insights into what levels of life expectancy may be attainable in the short and medium terms and how the health status of the older population may be influenced by 'selection' effects. This research also illustrates well demographic approaches to data and their analyses.

Demography

Demography is essentially concerned with the 'numbering of the people' and with understanding population dynamics—how populations change in response to the interplay between fertility, mortality and migration. 'Formal'

or pure demography is focused on answering questions about *how* populations change in size and age structure. Early theoretical work demonstrated the central role of fertility in influencing age structure (Coale 1957; Lotka 1907), more recently, demographers have shown that in low fertility, low mortality populations with mature age structures, changes in mortality play a major part in determining the extent of further population ageing (Preston *et al.* 1989).

The broader field of population science also embraces the question of *why* demographic parameters change and with what consequences. Recent very low levels of fertility in much of Europe, for example, have been analysed in relation to economic changes, including the increased participation of women in paid work, in relation to changes in contraceptive technology and its availability and in relation to attitudinal shifts. All are probably important and all may have interactive effects (Becker 1981; Murphy 1993). This debate is relevant to gerontology not just because of the effects of very low fertility on age structure, but also because if there has been a 'second demographic transition' involving a 'cultural shift' from family to individual values, then this has far reaching implications for intergenerational relationships and support exchanges (Grundy 1996; Inglehart 1990; van de Kaa 1987).

Demographic Methods and Materials

Much of the raw material for demographic and related analyses comes from censuses and surveys. The growing availability of micro-data from record-linkage studies and surveys, including longitudinal surveys, has provided new opportunities for the analysis of demographic change at the levels of the individual and family as well as the population. However, as data are generally collected from individuals or households, information on non-coresidents is sparse. As a result there is a substantial literature (reviewed in: Glaser 1997; Grundy 1992) on the living arrangements of elderly people and on intra-household intergenerational resource exchanges, but much less is known about exchanges with non co-resident kin. A prior topic, important in itself, is the estimation of potential kin resources and how these may have changed. As empirical sources of data on kin availability are far from adequate, demographers are turning to macro- and micro-simulation to estimate kin availability in populations with different demographic parameters (Bongaarts *et al.* 1986; Keilman *et al.* 1988).

Demographic analysis involves the use of various specialist techniques, such as life table methods and the indirect estimation of demographic events, together with more general statistical techniques. While predominantly a quantitative discipline, demographers have also embraced other methods to study particular problems. Knodel *et al.* (1992), for example, have used focus-group discussions to investigate links between declining fertility and familial support for older people in Thailand; and Cain (1991) used non-participant observation to study the relationship between age and hours-of-work in rural Bangladesh. Historical demographers have used a range of methods, including family reconstruction—a form of record-linkage, which allows reconstruction of individual families—and back-projection (population projection from the present to the past) to reveal a wealth of information about population in the past. This work means that we now have quite detailed information about both population structure and dynamics, and also about families, households and the position of older people in a number of historical populations, including that of England and Wales (Kertzer and Laslett 1995; Laslett 1977; Pelling and Smith 1991; Wrigley and Schofield 1981).

Demography, like gerontology, has close links with many other disciplines and fields of study, including human biology; epidemiology; sociology and social history; economics and economic history; geography and planning; and mathematics and statistics. A further strong link with gerontology comes from the demographic approach to analysing time dependent change. The demographic behaviour of any individual at any one time is conditioned by age, period (current circumstances) and the accumulated experience of the individual. Since this latter may be shared by others born at the same time (birth cohort), it is often termed a cohort effect (Hobcraft *et al* 1982; Pressat and Wilson 1989). Any one of these is a function of the other two in combination, and the long demographic tradition of using cohorts, which may be defined through the common timing of some event other than birth, such as marriage (Ryder 1964), as well as periods as units of analysis is in accord with much gerontological work which stresses the importance of past events and experiences on later-life characteristics.

The use of age as a classificatory variable is contentious in some quarters and demographers are sometimes accused of overusing age-based measures, such as 'dependency' ratios. It is of course the case that the use of ratios of the population aged 65 years and over to the population aged 20–64 years as an indicator of the economic costs of age-structure change is simplistic and involves several assumptions which are often not valid. In the United Kingdom, for example, only half of 60–64 year old men in 1994 were still in the labour force, although the state pension age of 65 years is still often treated as the age of withdrawal from the labour market (Central Statistical Office 1996). Moreover, of those in the labour force, a substantial minority, particularly in young age groups, are not actually in work: in Britain, 20 per cent of teenage males who have left education are unemployed. However, demographers have been among those who have challenged the use of such ratios without qualification (Falkingham 1989; Grundy 1983). Moreover, while age may be a poor predictor of performance at the individual level (Brouwer 1992), studies show that it remains in general useful as an indicator at the population level (Siegel 1992). It is hard to see how we can usefully study ageing and its effects without some reference to such a basic parameter. Demographers have, however, often used in their analyses *duration*, or length of exposure (*e.g.* duration of marriage) or life cycle stage rather than or as well as age as a way of organising elapsed time. This approach is followed in some gerontological work.

The Demography of Ageing

Until relatively recently research on the topic of the 'demography of ageing' largely comprised studies of the mechanisms of age-structure change and descriptive accounts of the extent of population ageing in various parts of the world, with consideration of some of the consequences of population ageing particularly the economic consequences (Clark and Spengler 1980; Grundy 1983; Livi-Bacci 1982; Myers 1985; Siegel 1980). Both the volume and purview of work in this area has however expanded enormously, particularly in the United States, during the 1980s and 1990s, to the extent that the demography of ageing has been described as a sub-discipline of demography (Suchindran and Koo 1997). There is a considerable overlap between some areas of this recent work; particularly those focused on intergenerational relationships, retirement behaviour, caring and the support of frail older people; and the concerns of social gerontologists. Much demographic work of this kind will be familiar to readers of this journal (Crimmins and Ingegneri 1990; Ettner 1995; Quinn and Burkhauser 1994; Weinick 1995). Recent research in other, more specialised, areas may be less well known to social gerontologists. This review focuses on one such topic, the ascertainment and analysis of late-age mortality and the controversy surrounding the 'cross-over' in mortality rates of Blacks and Whites in the United States population. This debate, far from being an arcane example of demographers' notorious obsession with data quality, has important implications for the planning of services for the oldest-old, for our understanding of ageing processes, and for projections fof health status in the older populations of the future.

Mortality at Very Old Ages

Changes in age structure and in the risks of death in younger age groups mean that late-age mortality is now a much more important component of overall mortality than in the past. Consequently, trends in late-age mortality, including mortality at very old ages, have a much greater demographic impact. In Japan, half of the increase in female life expectancy at birth achieved between 1985 and 1990 was due to reductions in the death rates among those aged 85 years and over (Kono 1994). Projections of the size of the very old population depend crucially on the assumptions made about mortality which have often proved wrong (Murphy 1995). There is no consensus about the future. Bennett and Olshansky (1996) have recently drawn attention to the large discrepancy between projections of the size of the United States elderly (and very old) populations made by the US Social Security Administration (SSA) and the US Bureau of the Census. Whereas the SSA projects that the population aged 85 years and over will increase from 3.3 million in 1990 to 14.5 million in 2050, the Census Bureau projects a population of 18.9 million by 2050: the difference between the two projections exceeds the current total population in the age groups considered. A further very important reason for investigation of trends and differentials in the mortality of the oldest old is that the results may aid understanding of senescence itself.

Unfortunately, addressing these important issues is not a straightforward as it might seem as there is a prior problem of assessing the validity of data on death rates among the very old. In all but the largest national populations, the number of survivors and of deaths at very old ages (95 years and over) is small and the extent of random fluctuation correspondingly great. Apart from this random error, the two major non-random errors that bedevil analysis of mortality at very old ages are age mis-statement and numerator-denominator bias. Age mis-statement has long been recognised as a problem and various strategies have been devised for coping with common errors such as the 'heaping' of reported ages on numbers ending in 0 or 5. At older ages the main problem is age exaggeration, especially among men. As a general rule, 'when the quality of demographic data improves, the number of alleged very old declines' (Daugherty and Kammeyer 1995: 138). Accounts of 'super-longevity' invariably turn out to reflect weak authentication procedures rather than the effects of eating yoghurt or living in the shadow of the 'air-recycling' huilco tree (Garson 1991). If ages are exaggerated, calculated death rates at old ages will be too low, even if the extent of exaggeration is the same on death certificates and in the census (Coale and Kisker 1986; Thatcher 1992). If, as is common, exaggeration is greater in the census than at time of registration of death, then further under-estimation of the true level of mortality results (Coale and Kisker 1990).

Several approaches to this problem have been tried. If the problem appears largely to rest with the denominator data and consequent numerator-denominator bias, then information on deaths can be used to provide both numerator and denominator using the 'extinct generation' method developed by Vincent (1951) and used on British data by Humphrey (1970) and Thatcher (1992). The logic of this method is simply that someone who dies aged 99 years in year x must have been alive and aged 98 in year x—1; 97 in year x—2, and so on. The total population of, for example, 95-year-olds in 1985 comprises 96-year-olds dying in 1986, 97-year-olds dying in 1987, 98-year-olds dying in 1988 and so on. Once the members of a cohort have died, information on their dates of birth and death can thus be used to reconstruct the cohort. As Thatcher (1992) showed, it is not necessary to wait until all the members of a cohort have died before using this approach. By the time the members of a cohort have reached an advanced age, only a small proportion will still be alive and the ratio of survivors to the number who have died during the recent past can be estimated from the experience of previous cohorts. Thatcher also used other methods in his investigation of centenarians and of mortality at very high ages, including 'reverse' survival techniques (backward projection of the population) and comparisons with other sources.

Comparison with other sources has been one of the main approaches used in the United States where the quality of data on the oldest old is worse than in much of Europe. *Medicare* data, for example, have been used in preference to census data to give estimates of the size of the elderly and very old population both by researchers and government (Kestenbaum 1992; Rosenwaike 1985). The other main method involves using models, including model life-tables, in themselves derived from populations with good data to estimate patterns of late-age mortality. Coale and Kisker (1990), for example, estimated mortality rates in the United States population aged 65 years and over by assuming that the rate of increase followed a Gompertz (exponentially increasing) function, and estimating the rate at which mortality increased with age from data from countries with reliable data. As it is known that the Gompertz model does not provide a good fit at the oldest ages (when rates of increase in death rates tend to slow down), Coale and Kisker made further assumptions about the rate of change in risk of death with age in the oldest age groups. These assumptions were tested against empirical data for Sweden and Japan by Wilmoth (1995) and found to fit well. Himes *et al* (1994) followed a broadly similar approach, although choosing a different type of model, to estimate generalisable patterns of mortality change at older ages using data when passed various checks on validity.

Given this and other methodological work, together with advances in verifying death data and bringing together data sets on the mortality of the oldest-old, have the problems involved in resolving questions about mortality trends in this age group now been resolved? The answer to this is yes and no. Painstaking work by Thatcher (1992; 1997) and by Kannisto (1994) and others (Vaupel and Lundström 1994) has now definitively established that in a number of countries with good data, mortality rates at very old ages, including ages over 100 years, have fallen substantially since 1950. Kannisto and colleagues assembled a data base of mortality rates for those aged 80 and over for 31 countries. The data were subjected to a range of checks for validity and a time-series of mortality among the oldest-old was constructed. This was based only on data assessed as valid. The results of this show a clear downward movement of death rates among very old people, including centenarians, since the mid-1950s in some cases, more recently in others. However, the range of countries included in these data was necessarily limited, and major questions remain about between-country differences in mortality at older ages. The United States, for example, appears to have low mortality at older ages compared with other developed countries, even though at younger ages death rates are similar to, or worse, than those of many European countries. As United States mortality data at older ages are known to be defective, at least part of this difference may be artefactual (Himes, Preston and Condran 1994). Some analysts (using adjusted data) have also argued that there is a real difference, perhaps reflecting current income and health care advantages of the oldest Americans when compared with those in other populations (Himes, Preston and Condran 1994), or advantages earlier in life (Manton and Vaupel 1995). However, the issue remains a matter of debate (Bennett and Olshansky 1996) Apart from the question of differences between the very old American population and populations elsewhere, the investigation of differentials in mortality within the United States, particularly differentials by race has also provoked considerable controversy.

Ageing, Race and Health in the United States

Numerous studies of health differentials, however measured, show that African-Americans are seriously disadvantaged compared with whites (Markides and Keith 1995). Although the extent of the difference in life expectancy at birth has diminished from nearly 15 years at the beginning of the century, in 1990 life expectancy at birth was still 7 years longer for whites than for African-Americans (Rogers 1992). In the 1970s some analysts hypothesised that the disadvantages of African-Americans might be even worse in old age as the difficulties of facing discrimination were compounded by the difficulties of growing old (Dowd and Bengston 1978). However, empirical analyses suggested that black-white differentials in mortality and other health indicators in fact declined with age to the extent

that at age 75 years or so, mortality rates 'crossed over' and were subsequently lower in the black than in the white population (Manton and Stallard 1984; Markides 1983; Nam et al. 1978). Data for the late 1980s suggested that the 'cross-over' age had shifted upwards a decade to 85 years (U.S. Bureau of the Census 1992).

This mortality crossover has been attributed to a selective survival effect; because African-Americans are exposed to far greater health challenges at younger ages, only those with particularly favourable health characteristics survive to old age (Manton and Stallard 1981; Markides and Machalek 1984). However, as indicated in the title of an influential paper by Ansley Coale and Ellen Kisker (1986), 'Mortality cross-overs: reality or bad data?' not everyone was convinced that the phenomenon existed and the debate has continued (Nam 1995). Recently, Preston et al. (1996) investigated the 'cross-over' further by linking a sample of death certificates for elderly African-Americans to individual records from early 20th century censuses and records held by the Social Security Administration. This showed that the ages recorded on death certificates were too young; paradoxically too many deaths were reported at ages 95+ years and late-age mortality was underestimated. This is because the steeply declining age pattern of deaths gives a much larger base for upward transfers into an age category than for downward transfers out of it. Using corrected mortality data for African-Americans, the 'cross-over' disappeared, although the data were not good enough (among either African-Americans or whites) to

allow differentials after age 95 years to be examined. This latest contribution to the debate is of interest not only for ethnic and racial differences in later life, but also because of its relevance to the wider 'selective survival' argument. Do groups disadvantaged in early life paradoxically appear more advantaged in later life due to a survival-of-the-fittest effect, or are early disadvantages carried throughout life and perhaps compounded in old age? If the former, then the increasing proportions surviving to very old ages might be expected to be less healthy as a group than their more 'selected' predecessors; if the latter, then health in very old age groups might improve as those who survive include higher proportions with favourable health legacies. This is a question of major importance; even more fundamental are questions about the levels of life expectancy that might be achieved by advantaged populations in the long-term, and what the consequences of upward gains might be. Demographers, particularly in the United States, are now addressing these questions Manton et al. 1991, 1993; Olshansky et al. 1990; Vaupel and Lundström 1994).

Life expectancy—average further years lived after a specified age, often birth, under existing mortality conditions—is not equivalent to life span, or maximal life span, which means the maximum number of years a member of a species might live under optimum conditions. Currently there are major debates about both the levels of life expectancy and the maximal life span that might be achieved and how these may be related. Approaches to the former question include extrapolation from current mortality rates and the application of models based on the elimination or reduction of particular causes of death (Bourgeois-Pichat 1978; Manton and Stallard 1994; Manton, Stallard and Tolley 1991; Siegel 1992). Early estimates of maximum life expectancy, which yielded values in the 70s, have already been surpassed in low mortality populations. Currently some research groups suggest an achievable life expectancy of around 85 years (Olshansky, Carnes and Cassel 1990), while others have produced estimates close to 100 years and raise the possibility of even higher life expectancies in the distant future (Manton *et al* 1994). The former estimate is lower because Olshansky and colleagues argue that eliminating risk factors in the entire population is not feasible and also that there is a biological 'law of mortality'. This group also raises the interesting possibility that interventions could allow human life expectancies that exceed the biological life span as 'extra' time 'manufactured' through pharmaceuticals or other technologies may be added to biologically allotted time (Olshansky, Carnes and Cassel 1990). These differences in ideas about achievable levels of life expectancy rest partly on different assumptions about biological limits. Few demographers accept the idea of a fixed limit to the life span in the sense of a particular duration of existence after which further life is impossible (as opposed to highly improbable), and many have pointed out that the empirical evidence for such a hypothesis is far from convincing (Gavrilov and Gavrilova 1991; Grundy 1983; Schneider 1983). Recent declines in death rates at very extreme ages (Thatcher 1997), and a widening in the distribution of ages at death (Wilmoth and Lundstrom 1996), both run counter to some arguments raised in favour of a 'fixed' limit (Fries 1980).

The fact that many demographers question the evidence for a predetermined moment at which a person's life will end, does not of course mean that they believe in eternal life on earth or refuse to incorporate biological evidence into their calculations. On the contrary, there have always been very strong links between biology and some areas of demography (particularly the study of fertility) and these are now being strengthened in order to develop new approaches to the study of late-age mortality and longevity (Carey 1997; Olshansky and Carnes 1997; Yashin and Iachine 1997). Similar strong links need to be maintained and developed with social gerontologists—both academics and practitioners—to further our knowledge of some of the consequences of recent demographic transformations, on, for example, family relationships, economic indicators and the support of disabled older people.

References

Becker, G. S. 1981. *A Treatise on the Family*. Cambridge, Massachusetts: Harvard University Press.

Bennett, N. G. and Olshansky, S. J. 1996. Forecasting US age structure and the future of social security: the impact of adjustments to official mortality schedules. *Population and Development Review*, 22 (4), 703–727.

Bongaarts, J., Burch, T. K. and Wachter, K. W. (eds) 1986. *Family Demography: Methods and Their Application*. Oxford: Oxford University Press.

Bourgeois-Pichat, J. 1978. Future outlook for mortality decline in the world. *Population Bulletin of the United Nations*, **11**, 12–41.

Brouwer, A. 1992. The nature of ageing. In Horan, M. A. and Brouwer, A. (eds), *Gerontology: Approaches to Biomedical and Clinical Research*. London: Edward Arnold.

Cain, M. T. 1991. The activities of the elderly in rural Bangladesh. *Population Studies*, **45**, 189–202.

Carey, J. R. 1997. What demographers can learn from fruit fly actuarial models and biology. *Demography*, **34** (1), 17–30.

Clark, R. L. and Spengler, J. J. 1980. *The Economics of Individual and Population Ageing*. Cambridge: Cambridge University Press.

Coale, A. 1957. The effects of changes in mortality and fertility on age composition. *Millbank Memorial Fund Quarterly*, **34**, 79–114.

Coale, A. and Kisker, E. 1986. Mortality crossovers: reality or bad data? *Population Studies*, **40**, 389–401.

Coale, A. J. and Kisker, E. E. 1990. Defects in data on old age mortality in the United States: new procedures for calculating mortality schedules and life tables at the highest ages. *Asian and Pacific Population Forum*, **4** (1), 1–31.

Crimmins, E. M. and Ingegneri, D. G. 1990. Interaction and living arrangements of older parents and their children. *Research on Aging*, **12** (1), 3–35.

Daugherty, H. G. and Kammeyer, K. C. W. 1995. *An Introduction to Population*. New York: The Guildford Press.

Dowd, J. J. and Bengston, V. L. 1978. Aging in minority populations: an examination of the double-jeopardy hypothesis. *Journal of Gerontology*, **33**, 427–436.

Ettner, S. L. 1995. The impact of 'parent care' on female labour-supply decisions. *Demography*, **32** (1), 63–80.

Falkingham, J. 1989. Dependency and ageing in Britain: a re-examination of the evidence. *Journal of Social Policy*, **18** (2), 211–233.

Fries, J. F. 1980. Aging, natural death and the compression of morbidity. *New England Journal of Medicine*, **303** (3), 130–135.

Garson, L. K. 1991. The centenarian question: old-age mortality in the Soviet Union, 1897 to 1970. *Population Studies*, **45**, 265–278.

Gavrilov, L. A. and Gavrilova, N. S. 1991. *The Biology of Life Span: A Quantitative Approach*. London: Harwood Academic Publishers.

Glaser, K. 1997. The living arrangements of elderly people. *Reviews in Clinical Gerontology*, **7**, 63–72.

Grundy, E. 1983. Demography and old age. *Journal of the American Geriatrics Society*, **31** (6), p. 325–332.

Grundy, E. 1984. Mortality and morbidity among the old. *British Medical Journal*, **288**, 663–664.

Grundy, E. 1992. The living arrangements of elderly people. *Reviews in Clinical Gerontology*, **2**, 353–361.

Grundy, E. 1996. Population ageing in Europe. In Coleman, D. (ed.) *Europe's Population in the 1990's*. Oxford: Oxford University Press.

Himes, C. L., Preston, S. H. and Condran, G. A. 1994. A relational model of mortality at older ages in low mortality countries. *Population Studies*, **48**, 269–291.

Hobcraft, J., Menken, J. and Preston, S. 1982. Age, period and cohort effects in demography: a review. *Population Index*, **48**, 4–43.

Humphrey, G. T. 1970. Mortality at the oldest ages. *Journal of the Institute of Actuaries*, **96**, 105–119.

Inglehart, R. 1990. *Culture Shift in Advanced Industrial Society*. Princeton: Princeton University Press.

Kannisto, V. 1994. *Development of the Oldest-Old Mortality, 1950–1990: Evidence from 28 Developed Countries*. Odense: Odense University Press.

Keilman, N., Kuijsten, A. and Vossen, A. (eds) 1988. *Modelling Household Formation and Dissolution*. London: Clarendon Press.

Kertzer, D. L. and Laslett, P. (eds) 1995. *Aging in the Past: Demography, Society and Old Age*. Berkeley: University of California Press.

Kestenbaum, B. 1992. A description of the extreme aged population based on improved Medicare enrolment data. *Demography*, **29**, 411–426.

Knodel, J., Chayovan, N. and Siriboon, S. 1992. The impact of fertility decline on familial support for the elderly: an illustration from Thailand. *Population and Development Review*, **18** (1), 79–103.

Kono, S. 1994. Demography and population ageing in Japan. *Ageing in Japan*, Tokyo: Japan Ageing Research Centre.

Laslett, P. 1977. *Family Life and Illicit Love in Early Generations*. Cambridge: Cambridge University Press.

Livi-Bacci, M. 1982. Social and biological aging: contradictions of development. *Population and Development Review*, **8** (4), 771–781.

Lotka, A. 1907. Relation between birth rates and death rates. *Science*, **26**, 21–22.

Manton, K. and Stallard, E. 1994. Medical demography: interaction of disability dynamics and mortality. In Martin, L. G. and Preston, S. H. (eds), *Demography of Aging*. Washington D.C.: National Academy Press.

Manton, K. G., Singer, B. H. and Suzman, R. M. (eds) 1993. *Forecasting the Health of Elderly Populations*. New York: Springer-Verlag.

Manton, K. G. and Stallard, E. 1981. Methods for evaluating the heterogeneity of aging processes in human populations using vital statistics data: explaining the black/white mortality crossover by a model of mortality selection. *Human Biology*, **53**, 47–67.

Manton, K. G. and Stallard, E. 1984. *Recent Trends in Mortality Analysis*. New York: Academic Press.

Manton, K. G., Stallard, E. and Singer, B. H. 1994. Methods for projecting the future size and health status of the U.S. elderly population. In Wise, D. A. (ed.), *Studies in the Economics of Aging*. Chicago, Illinois: University of Chicago Press.

Manton, K. G., Stallard, E. and Tolley, H. D. 1991. Limits to human life expectancy: evidence, prospects, and implications. *Population and Development Review*, **17** (4), 603–637.

Manton, K. G. and Vaupel, J. W. 1995. Survival after the age of 80 in the United States, Sweden, France, England and Japan. *New England Journal of Medicine*, **333**, 1232–1235.

Markides, K. S. 1983. Minority aging. In Riley, M. W., Hess, B. B. and Bond, K. (eds), *Aging in Society: Reviews of Recent Literature*. Hillsdale, New Jersey: Erlbaum.

Markides, K. S. and Keith, V. M. 1995. Race, ageing and health in the USA. *Reviews in Clinical Gerontology*, **5**, 332–345.

Markides, K. S. and Machalek, R. 1984. Selective survival, aging and society. *Archives of Gerontology and Geriatrics*, **3**, 207–229.

Murphy, M. 1993. The contraceptive pill and women's employment as factors in fertility change in Britain 1963–1980: a challenge to the conventional view. *Population Studies*, **47**, 221–244.

Murphy, M. J. 1995. Methods for forecasting mortality and their performance. *Reviews in Clinical Gerontology*, **5** (2), 217–227.

Myers, G. C. 1985. Aging and worldwide population change. In Binstock, R. H. and Shanas, E. (eds), *Handbook of Aging and the Social Sciences*. New York: Van Nostrand Reinhold.

Nam, C., Weatherby, N. and Ockay, K. 1978. Causes of death which contribute to the mortality crossover effect. *Social Biology*, **25**, 306–314.

Nam, C. B. 1995. Another look at mortality crossovers. *Social Biology*, **42** (1–2), 133–142.

Central Statistical Office 1996. *Social Trends*. London: HMSO.

Olshansky, S. J. and Carnes, B. A. 1997. Ever since Gompertz. *Demography*, **34** (1), 1–15.

Olshansky, S. J., Carnes, B. A. and Cassel, C. 1990. In search of Methuselah: estimating the upper limits of human longevity. *Science*, **250**, 634–640.

Pelling, M. and Smith, R. M. (eds) 1991. *Life, Death and the Elderly: Historical Perspectives*. London: Routledge.

Pressat, R. and Wilson, C. 1989. *The Dictionary of Demography*. Oxford: Basil Blackwell.

Preston, D. B., Himes, C. and Eggers, M. 1989. Demographic conditions responsible for population aging. *Demography*, **26**, 691–704.

Preston, S. H., Elo, I. T., Rosenwaike, I. and Hill, M. 1996. African-American mortality at older ages: results from a matching study. *Demography*, **33** (2), 193–209.

Quinn, J. F. and Burkhauser, R. V. 1994. Retirement and labour force behavior of the elderly. In Martin, L. G. and Preston, S. H. (eds), *Demography of Aging*, Washington, D.C.: National Academy Press.

Rogers, A. 1992. Living and dying in the USA: Socio-demographic determinants of death among blacks and whites. *Demography*, **29**, 287–303.

Rosenwaike, I. 1985. *The Extreme Aged in America: A Portrait of an Expanding Population*. Westport, Connecticut: Greenwood.

Ryder, N. B. 1964. Notes on the concept of a population. *American Journal of Sociology*, **61**, 447–463.

Schneider, E. 1983. Aging, natural death, and compression of morbidity: another view. *New England Journal of Medicine*, **309**, 854–856.

Siegel, J. S. 1980. On the demography of aging. *Demography*, **17**, 345–364.

Siegel, J. S. 1992. *A Generation of Change: A Profile of America's Older Population*. New York: Russell Sage Foundation.

Suchindran, C. M. and Koo, H. P. 1997. Demography and public health. In Detels, R., Holland, W. H., McEwen, J. and Omenn, G. S. (eds), *Oxford Textbook of Public Health*, Third edition, vol. 2. Oxford: Oxford University Press.

Thatcher, A. R. 1992. Trends in numbers and mortality at high ages in England and Wales. *Population Studies*, **46**, 411–426.

Thatcher, A. R. 1997. Trends and prospects in mortality at very high ages. In Charlton, J. C. and Murphy, M. (eds), *The Health of Adult Britain 1841–1991*, London: HMSO.

U.S. Bureau of the Census 1992. *International Populations Reports: An Aging World II*. Washington DC, U S Government Printing Office.

van de Kaa, D. J. 1987. *Europe's Second Demographic Transition* (Population Bulletin 42). Washington, D.C.: Population Reference Bureau.

Vaupel, J. W. and Lundström, H. 1994. Longer life expectancy? Evidence from Sweden of reductions in mortality rates at advanced ages. In Wise, D. A. (ed.), *Studies in the Economics of Aging*. Chicago: University of Chicago Press.

Vincent, P. 1951. La mortalité des vieillards. *Population*, **6**, 181–204.

Weinick, R. M. 1995. Sharing a home: The experiences of American women and their parents over the twentieth century. *Demography*, **32** (2), 281–297.

Wilmoth, J. 1995. Are mortality rates falling at extremely high ages? An investigation based on a model proposed by Coale and Kisker. *Population Studies*, **49** (2), 281–295.

Wilmoth, J. R. and Lundstrom, H. 1996. Extreme longevity in five countries: presentation of trends with special attention to issues of data quality. *European Journal of Population/Revue Européenne de Demographie*, **12** (1), 63–93.

Wrigley, E. A. and Schofield, R. S. 1981. *The Population History of England: A Reconstruction*. London: Edward Arnold.

Yashin, A. I. and Iachine, I. A. 1997. How frailty models can be used in evaluating longevity limits. *Demography*, **43** (1), 31–48.

Article Review Form at end of book.

WiseGuide Wrap-Up

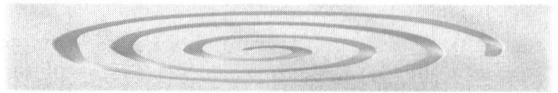

- Science is getting closer to understanding the aging process but the ability to control or affect it is still in the future.

- The demographics of aging can help experts plan for the future needs of the elderly population.

- Society will need to change to better adapt to increases in both life expectancy and life span.

- Dispelling aging myths and misconceptions will improve attitudes of both society and the elderly themselves.

R.E.A.L. Sites

This list provides a print preview of typical **coursewise** R.E.A.L. sites. There are over 100 such sites at the **courselinks**™ site. The danger in printing URLs is that web sites can change overnight. As we went to press, these sites were functional using the URLs provided. If you come across one that isn't, please let us know via email to: webmaster@coursewise.com. Use your Passport to access the most current list of R.E.A.L. sites at the **courselinks**™ site.

Site name: Profile of Older Americans: 1997

URL: http://www.aoa.dhhs.gov/aoa/stats/profile/

Why is it R.E.A.L.? Need statistics on the elderly? This site provides quick and easy access to population data about the elderly, such as education levels, income, housing and living arrangements, marital status, employment, ethnic distributions, and health care.

Key topics: aging minorities, demographics, life expectancy

Activity: What is the current sex ratio among people over 65 in the United States?

Site name: National Institute on Aging (NIA)

URL: http://www.nih.gov/nia/

Why is it R.E.A.L.? This is a premier site for the latest research in the area of aging as well as useful information on health information about aging.

Key topics: demographics, psychological aging

Activity: What's the focus of the latest news release by this agency?

Site name: Theories on the Cause of Aging

URL: http://www3.hmc.edu/~clewis/aging/theories.html

Why is it R.E.A.L.? This site is part of an aging course webpage. Eight current theories of aging are discussed. The theories are divided into two categories: DNA Damage theories and Built-in Breakdown theories. Each theory is neatly summarized in a single paragraph.

Key topics: theories of aging

Activity: List the two current theories discussed at this site.

Site name: Native American Elder Population, 1990

URL: http://www.aoa.dhhs.gov/ain/naepop90.html

Why is it R.E.A.L.? This link provides a quick and easy-to-read summary of demographic information about Native American elders.

Key topics: aging minorities, demographics, life expectancy

Activity: Identify the state where most of the Native American elders live.

section

2

Key Points

- General decline should be expected as we age.

- Many serious conditions associated with aging are symptoms of disease.

- Recognizing and preparing for the general changes enables individuals to maintain a quality life as they age.

The Aging Process

WiseGuide Intro

Many people associate aging with decline. But many of the detrimental events associated with growing older are not normal changes but rather symptoms of disease. Granted, there are some inevitable changes and slowing down of the systems. However, most of the changes can be compensated for or at least slowed. This section investigates some of the common changes associated with normal aging.

Psychological changes, or changes in the cognitive process, are examined in several of the readings. Myths and misconceptions regarding senile dementia, changes in intelligence, loss of memory, and the decision-making process are addressed. Information is provided to help individuals compensate and adjust to the changes.

The physiological changes are highlighted in several other readings. Both normal aging changes and changes associated with common conditions in the elderly are discussed. Several of the readings take the approach that we must understand the differences in these changes to effectively deal with the elderly as well as our own aging.

Questions

Reading 7. How can performance be improved or maintained with the elderly and the decision-making process? What are the age-related effects on the decision-making process of the elderly?

Reading 8. What role does nutrition, specifically choline, have in memory? When should we worry about memory loss?

Reading 9. What are some common aging changes associated with the cardiovascular system? What are some of the most noticeable changes in the aging body?

Reading 10. What are the components of cellular production that decline most noticeably and contribute to the most noticeable changes associated with aging? How do the senses change with age?

Reading 11. Why, as we get older, does novelty become less appealing? Does it really matter whether people are open to novelty in their cultural and social choices? Why or why not?

How can performance be improved or maintained with the elderly and the decision-making process? What are the age-related effects on the decision-making process of the elderly?

Aging and Decision Making

Driving-related problem solving

Neff Walker

Neff Walker received his Ph.D. in psychology from Columbia University in 1983. He is currently an assistant professor in engineering psychology at the Georgia Institute of Technology.

W. Bradley Fain

W. Bradley Fain received an M.S. in psychology (1994) from the Georgia Institute of Technology. Currently, he is pursuing a Ph.D. while working in the Human Factors branch of the Georgia Tech Research Institute.

Arthur D. Fisk

Arthur D. Fisk is currently a professor in both the general-experimental and the engineering psychology programs at the Georgia Institute of Technology in the School of Psychology. He is coordinator of the engineering psychology program. He received a Ph.D. in psychology from the University of Illinois in 1982.

Christy L. McGuire

Christy L. McGuire received a B.S. in psychology from Mississippi State University in 1994 and is currently pursuing a Ph.D. in experimental psychology at the Georgia Institute of Technology.

Abstract

We examined age-related effects on decision making in a task environment familiar to most younger and older adults. Participants made route-selection decisions in real time. Participants received information about traffic density and expected speed limits of main and alternative routes, from which they determined the optimality of their present route versus alternative routes. The experiment evaluated the effects of information type, amount of congestion, alternative route speed limit, and age on speed and quality of decision making. Measures of optimal route selection revealed main effects of alternative route speed limit, congestion level, and message type, but there was not a main effect of age, and age did not interact with any variable. In terms of decision speed (but not quality of decision making), older participants were slower, and age interacted with alternative route speed and with message type. The data are interpreted in relation to previous data examining everyday problem solving and aging.

Introduction

Decision making is a critical aspect of daily life. There is an assumption that older adults will make decisions differently than younger adults and that they will perform worse because of the high cognitive demands of many decision tasks. Most of the studies documenting age-related differences in decision making have relied on tightly controlled laboratory tasks, with limited real-world familiarity or applicability. However, other studies that have investigated decision making in more natural settings have found a different pattern of results (see Marsiske & Willis, 1995, for a review). In these studies, performance levels among older adults are more similar to those of their younger counterparts. Previous research has also found that age-related differences in decision making, when present, are often related to the nature of the task and to the level of experience that older adults have with the task. In the study reported here, we in-

vestigated age-related differences in decision making in a real-world task domain.

Three specific characteristics of many real-world decision making tasks are the focus of the study: (a) lack of precise feedback after decisions have been made about the relative correctness of the chosen option relative to the alternatives that were not chosen; (b) presence of a random component in the situation, preventing absolute certainty about the correctness of the decision; and (c) the availability of multiple sources and types of information that may inform the decision.

Examples of real-world tasks with these characteristics include investing in retirement funds, purchasing a residence, deciding where to go on a vacation, and responding to traffic information. A fuller understanding of how older adults respond to situations with these characteristics can serve as the basis for interventions designed to maintain and enhance their life skills.

In this experiment, we used a route selection task characterized by the three aforementioned features. In this task, participants were told that they were driving a car and were asked to minimize the time needed to drive from Point A to Point B. For each trial, they received information about each route's distance, level of traffic congestion, and speed limit, in addition to a real-time traffic message providing information about the level of congestion on the main route and, in some trials, advice about which route to take. They were then asked to decide whether they would remain on the main route or divert to an alternate route to reach their destination. This task was designed to limit the precise feedback offered about whether

or not a route would have reduced overall driving time. There was a random component preventing an algorithmic selection of the optimal route, and multiple types of information were provided in each experimental trial. The outcome measures used to describe performance included percentage of trials in which participants diverted to the alternate route, percentage of trials in which the optimal route was chosen, decision making time, and a measure of the participants' confidence in their route choice. Previous research with this simulated task (Fain, 1994) had shown that drivers made route selection decisions in the same manner as they reported during driving and that they used all of the available sources of information in making their decisions.

Based on previous literature, three hypotheses were posited about the pattern of possible results. First, some studies have demonstrated that older adults perform less effectively in decision tasks because of cognitive overload (e.g., Salthouse, Legg, Palmon, & Mitchell, 1990). Given the amount and complexity of information in the route decision task used in this experiment, if the cognitive efficiency hypothesis translates from simple tasks to everyday decision making situations, then older adults' decision making quality should suffer relative to that of younger adults.

Second, other research (Johnson, 1990) has suggested that older adults can maintain performance levels by using strategies that effectively reduce the complexity of the decision task. In the current experiment, this explanation led to the possibility that older adults might perform as well as their younger counterparts but that their deci-

sions would be made in a different manner. This hypothesis is based on the assumption that older adults use a heuristic that allows them to use a reduced set of information variables relative to those used by younger adults. This heuristic-switching hypothesis can be investigated by examining the interactions between age and the use of the various types of information available.

Third, earlier studies have found that when older adults have previous experience with a specific task type, they can often maintain their level of performance (e.g., Morrow, Leirer, Altieri, & Fitzsimmons, 1994). Such data provide support for a "skill maintenance" hypothesis, which posits that older, experienced drivers will perform as well as younger drivers on the experimental task and will take the full range of types of information into account in the same way as younger adults.

Method

Participants

Thirty-three young adults (mean age 19.7 years; range 18–24 years; SD 1.53) and 30 older adults (mean age 71.6 years; range 64–80 years, SD 4.62) from the Atlanta metropolitan area participated in this study. All were paid for their participation, had at least the equivalent of 20/40 correct vision, continued to be active drivers on both surface streets and highways, and were taking no more than one drug that was rated to have more than minimal effects on attention (Giambra & Quilter, 1988). The participants completed five general ability tests, which revealed age-related patterns consistent with the general population. (These data are available from the first author at

School of Psychology, Georgia Institute of Technology, Atlanta, GA, 30332–0170.)

Apparatus and Materials

The experimental software consisted of a simulated route selection interface with graphical map and instruction screens. Data were collected using IBM PS/2 computers equipped with standard 101-button keyboards and 14-inch color VGA monitors.

There were five message types: (a) information currently available to drivers without access to real-time traffic information systems (i.e., only information that could be obtained from maps or posted speed limit signs for the purpose of making route choice decisions; (b) descriptive information describing the source of congestion, if any, for the routes; (c) advisory information that recommended a route based on current traffic conditions; (d) two redundant descriptive messages, each describing the same traffic event using different words (the redundant message type was included to control for message length rather than content); (e) combined descriptive and advisory messages that described the source of congestion and made a recommendation for the main or alternative route based on current traffic conditions.

Design

The independent variables were message type, degree of main route congestion, speed limit on alternate route, and age. Age was a quasi-experimental variable, and all others were manipulated within subjects. The first variable, message type, was described in the previous paragraph. The second variable consisted of four levels of main route congestion (zero to three lanes closed). The levels of main route congestion were directly related to the type of incidents reported by the descriptive component of the real-time information system. The third variable manipulated the alternative route speed as either 40 to 50 miles/h (approximately 64 or 80 km/h). There were four trials with each of the 40 traffic conditions (Message Type × Congestion Level × Alternate Route Speed). The experimental session was divided into four blocks of 40 route selection decisions each. Within each block, a travel scenario was selected from the route selection database at random, with the restrictions that no two route selections could be selected more than once during any given block and that each trial must differ by more than one independent variable. Dependent variables were route selection decision (percentage diversion and optimal route decisions), static information evaluation time (measured as the time viewing the navigation screen), route selection time (measured as time from receiving traffic message to decision), and confidence for each route selection.

Procedure

Participants were scheduled for two sessions occurring on consecutive days. On the first day, they completed the consent, demographic, health, and medication forms and the abilities tests. During the second day, the computer simulation was explained and the participants practiced the task. Data collection began after this practice. The participants were told that they were taking part in an experiment to evaluate the relative merits of real-time traffic information systems. It was explained that they would be placed in a number of hypothetical situations in which they would be required to navigate from one section of the city to another during morning rush-hour traffic. Their task was to evaluate the situation and information provided and to make the best possible decision in a timely fashion concerning the optimal route. The participants were fully informed that, as in real-world driving, random events could occur that would slow or speed expected travel time (expected based on the information displays) on the main and alternative routes. The participants entered their responses by pressing keys labeled as the main or alternative route and then entered their level of confidence concerning the decision. For the confidence rating, they viewed a Likert-type scale and entered a response on a scale from 1 (no confidence) to 7 (completely confident). Participants were provided with computer-generated travel-time feedback after every fourth route selection.

Results

The analyses are outlined in four sections. First, we analyzed the percentage of diversions from the main route. The purpose of this analysis was to determine whether factors shown to affect decisions about diverting to an alternate route in actual driving would affect decision making in the simulation (for those data see Fain, 1994). Next, we analyzed the proportion of optimal route decisions. Then we analyzed the time taken to make the route diversion decision. Finally, we analyzed the measure of confidence in route diversion decision. A summary of the data is provided in Table 1*. For all analyses, we utilized an Age (young, old) × Congestion Level (0, 1, 2, 3 lanes closed) × Alternate Route Speed Limit (40, 50 miles/h) × Message Type (advisory, descriptive, combination, redundant, no information) analysis of variance (ANOVA). For main effects we used Bonferroni pairwise comparisons. Simple effects tests were used to follow up significant interactions.

Percentage Route Diversion

This analysis indicates that the data from the present simulation study replicate earlier work in that they show that the factors people report as affecting their route selection decision (alternate route speed limit, congestion level on the main route) also affect route decision in this task. The four-factor ANOVA yielded eight significant effects. As expected, there were main effects of alternate route speed limit, $F(1, 62) = 110.75$, MSE = 0.06614, $p. < 001$, and congestion level, $F(3, 186) = 424.64$, MSE = 0.1178, $p. < 001$. People chose the alternate route more when the alternate route speed limit was 50 miles/h (mean = 52%) than when the alternate route speed limit was 40 miles/h (mean = 41%). Follow-up analyses revealed that percentage route diversion went up with congestion level (means = 11%, 37%, 64%, and 73% for 0, 1, 2, and 3 lanes closed, respectively). These two analyses strongly suggest that the participants were attending to the information presented about traffic patterns and used this information in making decisions about route selection. There was also a main effect for message type

*Not included in this publication.

$F(4,248) = 231.84$, MSE = 0.1268, $p. < .001$. Follow-up analyses revealed that all pairwise comparisons were significantly different except for that between descriptive and combination message types.

The interaction of alternate route speed and age, $F(1, 62) = 9.10$, MSE = 0.06614, $p. < .01$, was significant. Follow-up analyses revealed that older adults were significantly more affected by alternate route speed in their decision to take the alternate route (means = 40% and 54% for 40 and 50 miles/h, respectively) than were younger adults (means = 42% and 49% for 40 and 50 miles/h, respectively). There was a significant interaction of alternate route speed and congestion level, $F(3,186) = 92.49$, MSE = 0.0320, $p.< .001$. Follow-up analyses revealed that the source of this interaction lay in the difference in choice of the alternate route when one lane of traffic was closed. Here there was a significant difference attributable to alternate route speed limit on diversion (means = 21% and 52% for 40 and 50 miles/h, respectively). For the other levels of traffic congestion, alternate route speed limit had a nonsignificant effect. None of the other significant effects involved age, and they will not be presented here in consideration of space constraints.

Optimal Decision Making

The analyses evaluating percentage of time an optimal decision was made clearly show that there were no age-related differences in optimal route decision. Older adults made the same decisions as did younger adults, and they used the same information to make their decisions. The four-

factor ANOVA revealed six significant effects but none involving age. There were significant main effects of alternate route speed, $F(1, 62) = 20.68$, MSE = 0.0866, $p. < .001$, congestion level, $F(3, 186) = 60.91$, MSE = 0.1402, $p. .001$, and message type, $F(4, 248) = 18.46$, MSE = 0.1029, $p. < .001$. Optimal route selection was higher when the alternate speed limit was 40 miles/h (mean = 75%) than when the speed limit was 50 miles/h (mean = 70%). Optimal route selection was significantly higher when no lanes were closed (mean = 89%) than for the other three levels of congestion. Selection of the optimal route for three lanes closed (mean = 72%) was significantly higher than for one lane closed (mean = 65%) and two lanes closed (mean = 64%). The percentage of optimal route selection when there was no real-time information (mean = 39%) was significantly lower than for the other four message types. The combination message yielded a significantly higher optimal route selection rate. In addition to the significant main effects, there were significant interactions of alternate route speed and congestion level, $F(3, 186) = 28.82$, MSE = 0.1142, $p. < .001$, of congestion level and message type, $F(12, 744) = 151.46$, MSE = 0.0442, $p. < .001$, and of alternate route speed, congestion level, and message type, $F(12, 744) = 34.67$, MSE = 0.0320, $p. < .001$.

Route Decision Time

When decision time is assessed, an effect of age emerges; however, even with this dependent variable, age does not interact with other variables. The four-factor ANOVA on decision time revealed four significant main effects and three significant interactions. The main effect of age, F $(1, 62)$ = 22.76, MSE = 41.0971, $p. < .001$, revealed that older adults took longer to make their route decision (mean = 3.240 s) than did younger adults (mean = 2.029 s). The main effect of alternate route speed, $F(1, 62)$ = 5.41, MSE = 1.2298, $p. < .05$, revealed that decision time was longer when the alternate route speed limit was 40 miles/h (mean = 2.286 s) than when it was 50 miles/h (mean = 2.583 s). Follow-up analyses revealed that decision time was less for no lanes closed (mean = 2.408 s) and three lanes closed (mean = 2.485 s) than for one lane (mean = 2.858 s) and two lanes closed (mean = 2.714 s). Follow-up analyses for main effect of congestion level, $F(3, 186)$ = 11.49, MSE = 1.8934, $p. < .001$, revealed that decision time was faster when no lanes or three lanes of traffic were closed (means = 2.280 s and 2.486 s, respectively) than when one or two lanes of traffic were closed (means = 2.858 s and 2.714 s, respectively). Follow-up tests for the main effect of message type, $F(4, 248)$ = 9.71, MSE = 0.6940, $p. < .001$, revealed that decision time was significantly faster when there was no real-time message (mean = 2.322 s) and an advisory message (mean = 2.209 s) than for descriptive, combination, and redundant message types (means = 2.761, 2.884, and 2.996 s, respectively).

Confidence in Decisions

Overall, decision confidence varied little as a function of age. However, older adults were more confident than young adults that they had made the correct decision when the main route was not at the extreme level of congestion. Also, older and younger adults'

confidence level varied differentially as a function of alternative route speed. The main contribution of the confidence data suggests that the age-related difference in speed of decision making was not attributable to hesitation resulting from uncertainty about the decision. The four-factor ANOVA yielded eight significant effects. There were significant effects of congestion level, $F(3, 186)$ = 13.71, MSE = 0.9095, $p. < 0.001$, and message type, $F(4, 248)$ = 12.20, MSE = 1.6128, $p. < 0.001$. Follow-up analyses revealed that confidence was higher when no lanes of traffic (mean = 6.17) or three lanes of traffic (mean = 6.17) were closed than when one lane (mean = 6.01) or two lanes of traffic were closed (mean = 5.85). Follow-up analyses revealed that confidence was higher when there was no real-time message (mean = 6.39) than for the other four message types (means = 6.01, 5.93, 6.03, and 5.91 for advisory, descriptive, combination, and redundant message types, respectively).

There were also significant interactions of age and congestion level, $F(3, 186)$ = 6.20, MSE = 0.9095, $p. < .001$, and age and alternate route speed limit, $F(1, 62)$ = 8.29, MSE = 0.2035, $p. < .01$. The locus of the interaction of age and congestion level was that older adults had higher confidence levels than young adults when zero, one, or two lanes of traffic were closed. When three lanes of traffic were closed, there was no age difference in confidence rating. The interaction of age and alternate route speed limit was attributable to a slight crossover effect. Older adults had slightly higher mean confidence in their decision when the alternate route speed was 50 miles/h than when it was 40 miles/h (means = 6.20 and 6.15,

respectively). For younger adults, confidence was slightly higher when the alternate speed limit was 40 miles/h than when it was 50 miles/h (means = 5.97 and 5.90, respectively). There were also significant two-way interactions of alternate route speed and congestion level, $F(3, 186)$ = 13.98, MSE = 0.1610, $p. < .001$, and congestion level and message type, $F(12, 744)$ = 21.08, MSE = 0,2594, $p. < .001$. There were significant three-way interactions of alternate route speed, congestion level, and message type, $F(12, 744)$ = 6.74, MSE = 0.1540, $p. < .001$, and of congestion level, message type, and age, $F(12, 744)$ = 21.08, MSE = 0.2594, $p. < .001$.

Conclusions

The present study evaluated possible age-related effects on variables known to contribute to mute-selection decision making. Previous research evaluating real-time traffic information systems revealed effects of type of advisory message, alternative route speed, and route congestion on decision speed, decision quality, and decision confidence (see Fain, 1994, for a review). The present study also found that these effects were quite strong. However, from an age-related perspective, there was only one main effect of age (time to make decision) and two significant interactions with age (older adults varied their route selection more according to alternative route speed, and they were differentially confident about their decision as a function of alternative route speed). From a decision-making perspective, there was no evidence that reduced cognitive efficiency reduced decision-making quality; older and younger adults made the same route decisions with the same level of selection optimality. There was also no evidence of qualitatively different decision heuristics: Older and younger adults used the same set of information for their decisions.

The present data support other studies that suggest that task familiarity helps to maintain quality of decision making across age groups (e.g., Morrow et al., 1994). Older adults made the same decisions as younger adults, and these decisions were affected by the same types of information. The difference was quantitative in terms of time required to make the decision. These data suggest that as long as the task remains familiar and allows sufficient time for the decision process, older adults will simply require more time than younger adults but will make the same decision. (Obviously, if sufficient time is not provided, then older adults may not reach the optimal decision outcome.) Indeed, the familiarity hypothesis does help explain the present data. Also, the present data together with other data in the literature suggest that task familiarity will lessen or overcome cognitive age-related performance differences to the extent that familiarity is broadened to include content, context, and presentation of information (see Fisk & Kirlik, 1996). With this multifaceted view of familiarity, a unifying principle can emerge. If the task is truly familiar within a familiar context (e.g., playing bridge; Charness, 1985), full compensation can be expected. When the task context is modified, then partial compensation can be expected (Morrow et al., 1994). Finally, if only the familiar, but

primitive, information processing components are maintained outside of a familiar environment, then little compensation can be expected (e.g., the Salthouse, Babcock, Mitchell, Skovronek, & Palmon, 1990, study examining architects' visualization capabilities on primitive information processing tasks).

The focus and contribution of the study was twofold. First, we were able to assess the effects of age on decision making when the decisionmaking component was embedded within a familiar task domain. This assessment was important because domain familiarity has been shown to influence age-related effects in other areas of learning and performance (Fisk & Kirlik, 1996). Second, the study was directly relevant to design decisions for traffic advisory message construction. The data suggest that when designing familiar environments, cognitive decline (for healthy older adults) may be of less concern than overall speed of performance factors; the designer need not consider two qualitatively different design approaches for older and younger adults. One must be cautious, however, because careful analysis is still required to ensure that design changes do not turn the familiar into the unfamiliar.

References

Charness, N. (1985). Aging and problem-solving performance. In N. Charness (Ed.), *Aging and human performance* (pp. 225–259). Chichester: Wiley.

Fain, W. B. (1994) *Analysis of route selection behavior in the presence of real time traffic information.* Unpublished master's thesis, Georgia Institute of Technology, Atlanta, GA.

Fisk, A. D., & Kirlik, A. (1996). Practical relevance and age-related research: Can theory advance without practice? In W. A. Rogers, A. D. Fisk, & N. Walker (Eds.), *Aging and skilled performance: Advances in theory and application* (pp. 1–15). Mahwah, NJ: Erlbaum.

Giambra, L. M., & Quilter, R. E. (1988). Sustained attention in adulthood: A unique, large-sample, longitudinal, and multicohort analysis using the Mackworth clock test. *Psychology and Aging, 3,* 75–83.

Johnson, M. M. S. (1990). Age differences in decision making: A process methodology for examining strategic information processing. *Journal of Gerontology: Psychological Sciences, 45,* P75–P78.

Marsiske, M., & Willis, S. L. (1995). Everyday problem solving in older adults. *Psychology and Aging, 10,* 269–283.

Morrow, D., Leirer, V., Altieri, P., & Fitzsimmons, C. (1994). When expertise reduces age differences in performance. *Psychology and Aging, 9,* 134–148.

Salthouse, T. A. Babcock, R. L., Mitchell, D. R., Skovronek, E., & Palmon, R. (1990). Age and experience effects in spatial visualization. *Developmental Psychology, 26,* 128–136.

Salthouse, T. A., Legg, S., Palmon, R., & Mitchell, D. (1990). Memory factors in age-related differences in simple reasoning. *Psychology and Aging, 5,* 9–15.

Acknowledgments: This research was supported in part by NIH Grant No. P50 AG 11715 under the auspices of the Center for Applied Cognitive Aging Research on Aging (one of the Edward R. Roybal Centers for Research on Applied Gerontology). Portions of this research were presented at the Cognitive Aging Conference (Atlanta, Georgia, 1996).

Article Review Form at end of book.

What role does nutrition, specifically choline, have in memory? When should we worry about memory loss?

Fear of Forgetting

"Honey. Have you seen my keys? I've got to go to the store to get some . . . uh . . . now what was it we needed?"

David Schardt and Stephen Schmidt

"Memory does begin to slip in some people as early as their 40s," says memory expert Thomas Crook. "It's a normal part of growing older and doesn't necessarily mean you're going to develop Alzheimer's disease."

Normal? Maybe for other people. But when *you* can't connect that face with its name, or don't have a clue where you parked your car, it's unnerving.

Relax.

"As we age, we don't normally lose a substantial number of cells in the part of the brain essential for complex thought," says Marilyn Albert, director of gerontology research at Massachusetts General Hospital in Boston.

"Our vocabularies usually improve, and our ability to reason and solve problems is retained," points out Paul Costa, Jr., of the Baltimore Longitudinal Study of Aging. "But it's true that many of us need more time to make and execute decisions, and our memories aren't as sharp."

There's that memory thing again. Its loss seems to irk us no end. Which might explain why we spend millions each year on memory supplements. Anything to stave off that shift into the slow lane.

"It makes perfect sense to want to find something that will help restore our mental quickness and memory to what it once was," says Barry Lebowitz, chief of the Mental Disorders of the Aging Research Branch at the National Institute of Mental Health in Rockville, Maryland.

Does that something exist? Supplement makers would like you to think so. Here's a peek behind the hype that's propping up the most popular ingredients in memory pills.

No-Brainers

Some are easy. Pregnenolone, DHEA, DHA, DMAE. If you see any of them in a memory tonic, don't waste your money. Most are still in the early stages of animal testing, and the results, though occasionally promising, say nothing about their ability to help you find your keys.

Other ingredients have a far longer research trail.

Choline and Lecithin

Choline is found in a wide variety of foods, especially egg yolks, liver, soybeans, and peanuts. It's also found in popular memory supplements like lecithin, Brain Fuel, BrainStorm, and Food for Thought.

What's the memory connection?

"Choline is an essential part of the neurotransmitter acetylcholine, which relays messages from nerve cell to nerve cell in the areas of the brain responsible for memory and learning," explains neuropsychologist Paul Spiers of the Massachusetts Institute of Technology.

In fact, by using drugs to lower the brain's supply of choline in animals and human volunteers, scientists can mimic the memory disturbances that are typical of aging.

But that's a far cry from proving that taking choline can help shore up fading memories. In the only two long-term studies that tested choline or lecithin in humans, "the results haven't been promising in people with either normal or impaired memories," says Spiers.

In one, 16 healthy older people did no better on word and picture memory tests five weeks after they started taking three grams of choline a day.[1]

In the other, after taking eight grams of choline a day for three weeks, ten elderly adults with mild memory impairment were no better at remembering a list of 15 or 20 words.[2]

"Eat enough choline and you'll smell like a fish," concludes Spiers. "But that's its only effect." (Bacteria in the intestines convert excess choline into trimethylamine, a fishy-smelling compound.)

Of course it's always possible that choline keeps flunking memory tests because it never gets to where it's needed.

"We've found that, beginning in middle-age, people seem to lose their ability to transport choline from the blood into the brain," says Bruce Cohen, director of the Brain Imaging Center at McLean Hospital in Belmont, Massachusetts.[3]

"Maybe by taking enormous amounts it's possible to force choline in, but we didn't see it with even three grams or more." Cohen is exploring ways to coax aging brains into absorbing more choline, but he doesn't expect a solution soon.

The bottom line: *There's no good evidence that taking choline or lecithin will help prevent or treat memory loss.*

Ginkgo Biloba

"The thinking person's supplement," says a television ad for the Ginkoba brand of ginkgo. "Taken as directed, Ginkoba will help you remember where you put things," says the company's site on the World Wide Web (www.ginsana.com).

Ginkgo biloba is an herbal supplement that's extracted from the leaves of the ginkgo tree. Is there good evidence that it can help the memories of healthy people like those pictured in Ginkoba's ads?

"No," says Jerry M. Cott, director of the Psychotherapeutic Medication Development Program at the National Institute of Mental Health.

No studies have looked at what happens to the memories of healthy people who take ginkgo regularly. And only two studies have even tested short-term effects. Both gave their volunteers a single dose of ginkgo and tested their memories just an hour later.

In one, ginkgo did nothing for the memories of eight young women who took 120 mg—the usual recommended dose.[4] Only at a huge dose—600 mg—were the women better able to memo-rize a series of numbers. But a second study of 12 different women who also took a single dose of 600 mg of ginkgo came up empty.[5]

If that's all the evidence, how can Pharmaton, the Ridgefield, Connecticut, company that manufactures Ginkoba, claim that its product improves memory?

"We're basing this claim on what Schwabe of Germany, our source of ginkgo, says and we believe they substantiate those claims," said Pharmaton's general manager, Tom Peterson.

But when we contacted Schwabe, the company couldn't produce any evidence that the regular use of ginkgo improves the memories of healthy people.

"Schwabe is naturally not responsible for statements made by any independent company and we are unable to speak to those," said Werner Busse, Schwabe's head of regulatory and scientific affairs.

And what about research on people who already have mild memory problems? Only one good study has been done.

After three months of taking 120 mg of ginkgo a day, 27 men and women aged 62 to 85 performed better on just one of 13 tests of memory and thinking ability than 27 people who were given a (look-alike but inactive) placebo.[6]

"It is nonsense to conclude from one small study—where findings on 12 of 13 tests were negative—that ginkgo improves memory," says Thomas Crook, who is a former chief of the Geriatric Psychopharmacology Program at the National Institute of Mental Health. "Further research is clearly needed before ginkgo can be regarded as even a possible treatment for memory loss."

There's memory loss . . . and there's *memory* loss.

While most lapses aren't signs of Alzheimer's disease or other forms of dementia, the symptoms listed below could be early warning signs. They're from a checklist that the Department of Health and Human Services gives health professionals to help evaluate patients. A "yes" answer to any category "generally indicates the need for further assessment for the presence of dementia."

Does the person have increased difficulty with any of these activities:

- **Learning and retaining new information.** Is more repetitive; has trouble remembering recent conversations, events, appointments; frequently misplaces objects.

- **Handling complex tasks.** Has trouble following a complex train of thought or performing tasks that require many steps, such as balancing a checkbook or cooking a meal.

- **Reasoning ability.** Is unable to respond with a reasonable plan to problems at work or home, such as knowing what to do if the bathroom is flooded. Shows uncharacteristic disregard for rules of social conduct.

- **Spatial ability and orientation.** Has trouble driving, organizing objects around the house, finding his or her way around familiar places.

- **Language.** Has increasing difficulty with finding the words to express what he or she wants to say and with following conversations.

- **Behavior** Appears more passive and less responsive; is more irritable than usual; is more suspicious than usual. Misinterprets [what he or she sees or hears].

The clinician can also look for failure to arrive at the right time for appointments, difficulty discussing current events in an area of interest, and changes in behavior or dress.

Source: *Recognition and Initial Assessment of Alzheimer's Disease and Related Dementias*, AHCPR Publication No. 97-0702, November 1996, U.S. Dept. of Health and Human Services.

The bottom line: *There's no evidence that ginkgo helps memory in healthy people. The evidence that it helps people with mild memory loss is very preliminary. More studies are needed.*

Phosphatidylserine (PS)

"I've tested close to a hundred compounds for their effects on human memory, and phosphatidylserine (PS) is the most impressive one I've found so far," says Crook.

Phosphatidylserine [foss-fuh-TID-ill-SEER-een] is a substance that occurs naturally in the membranes of all nerve cells.

In 1991, Crook and researches at Stanford and Vanderbilt Universities recruited 149 volunteers aged 50 to 75 who had the "normal" memory loss of people 50 and older. Half were given 300 milligrams of PS each day for 12 weeks, and half got a placebo.[7]

"The group given PS, especially those who were most impaired, improved in their ability to learn and recall names, faces, and numbers," reports Crook. "The most memory-impaired among them reversed, in three months, an estimated 12 years of decline in being able to match a name with a face."

A much larger study in Italy found that elderly people with moderate to severe memory loss could improve their ability to store and recall verbal information after taking 300 mg a day of PS for three months.[8]

But these and other studies used PS that had been extracted from cows' brains, not exactly a hot commodity in the wake of "mad cow disease," a fatal neurological disorder that scientists think can be transmitted to humans.

PS made from soybeans is now available, "but there's no proof that it's equivalent to cow PS until a good human study is done," says biochemist Lloyd A. Horrocks of Ohio State University. The only study to use soy PS in people was inconclusive.

The bottom line: *Phosphatidylserine (PS) may help shore up declining or impaired memories, but the only kind currently on the market hasn't been adequately tested.*

The Wisdom of Age

Not convinced that there's a magic bullet that will restore your memory? You don't need one, says memory expert Paul Costa.

"Conscientious, organized older people will beat out unorganized young people all the time," he says. Costa should know. The Baltimore Longitudinal Study of Aging tracks memory changes in 500 volunteers every two years.

"Given enough time," Costa explains, "older people can usually perform at the same levels and learn to the same levels as before."

A key "memory prosthesis," says Costa, is to write things down. "You need to set up multiple redundancies," he explains. "That means lists, reminders, tickler files that tell you to do things at certain times."

Exercising the Mind

"Use it or lose it" doesn't just apply to your muscles. K. Warner Schaie is a psychologist at Pennsylvania State University and an expert on how people can help keep their minds sharp as they age. He spoke to *Nutrition Action's* David Schardt by phone.

Q: How important is it to exercise our brains?

A: If you don't exercise your muscles, they get flabby. If your brain isn't stimulated, you don't keep growing the new connections that are necessary to maintain optimal mental functioning.

The worst thing people do to themselves, particularly when they retire, is they say: "Oh, I've worked all my life, now I deserve to do nothing." If you don't do anything, pretty soon you *can't* do anything.

Q: What happens to our minds as we get older?

A: In our Seattle Longitudinal Study, we've been examining changes in mental abilities. In most people, we haven't found a significant cognitive decline prior to their 60s. By their 80s, virtually everybody has some partial decline in mental function. It's very unusual to find an 80-year-old who is functioning the same as he or she did 20 years earlier.

But from your 60s to your 80s, how much you slip really depends on a lot of things, some of which are under your control and others of which are not.

Q: What can we control?

A: Education. It's very clear that life gets more complex as you go along. People who are well-educated have developed ways of solving problems and figuring things out that less-well-educated people haven't.

Q: What if you've finished your formal education?

A: To maintain cognitive function at a high level, you need continuing mental stimulation.

People with good support systems have more opportunities for stimulating activities. People who live by themselves, who have no friends, lack these kinds of supports. The smaller your support system, the less likely you are to go to the theatre or to a movie because you have nobody to go with.

Q: What else can we control?

A: People who maintain their mental abilities tend to seek out activities that require thinking and decision-making. For example, playing bridge is probably a lot better for you than playing bingo, unless you're playing 25 bingo cards and have to remember them all. If you feel that you are beginning to have trouble thinking of the right word, crossword puzzles are a great exercise.

As they get older, people—especially women—have increasing problems with orienting themselves in space and doing things that involve spatial abilities. Things like translating from a map which way you should turn, or buying a piece of furniture from a mail-order catalog and trying to assemble it, figuring out which piece goes where.

Q: How can people work on that?

A: We find that people who do jigsaw puzzles are better at spatial orientation than people who don't do them. Of, people who do square dancing, because it means you both have to orient yourself in space and you have to know what the sequence of steps is. That's a very important skill, because, even

though people aren't always aware of it, in most of our problem solving activities we have to figure out what's step number one, what's step number two, and how to work ourselves through a complex problem.

Q: Are there programs that can help?

A: Yes. We trained 229 men and women aged 64 to 95.[1] The inductive reasoning program helped them to recognize patterns in order to predict what should come next. The spatial orientation training helped them to mentally rotate two-dimensional figures in order to match them with other figures.

Q: Why these two skills?

A: These are the two that start declining beginning in the mid-60s. Among the participants, about half had declined in one or both of these skills over the preceding 14 years.

With training, about 40 percent of both the men and women reversed their 14-year slide. And the women, who had always lagged behind the men in spatial skills, not only made up what they had lost—they actually caught up to the men.

Q: Does it help to marry a stimulating mate?

A: Yes. Over time, the cognitive abilities of spouses become more similar. Surprisingly, the lower-functioning spouse moves in the direction of the higher-functioning spouse. Which makes some sense because positive change requires cognitive stimulation. If you're married to someone brighter than you are, you're going to have to deal with that.

---

[1] *Psychology and Aging* 1: 239, 1986.

It's also important to keep in mind, says Costa, that age has no effect on the ability to think.

"Unless you've had a stroke or have Alzheimer's disease or some other condition that shouldn't be confused with aging itself, age doesn't influence the ability to reason at all. The higher mental processes aren't affected."

1. *Neurology* 32: 944, 1982.
2. *Neurobiology of Aging* 1: 21, 1980.
3. *J. Amer. Med. Assoc.* 74: 902, 1995.
4. *Presse Médicale* 15: 1592, 1986
5. *Thérapie* 46: 33, 1991.
6. *Human Psychopharmacology* 2: 159, 1987.
7. *Neurology* 41: 644, 1991.
8. *Aging Clin. Exp. Res.* 5: 123, 1993.

Article Review Form at end of book.

What are some common aging changes associated with the cardiovascular system? What are some of the most noticeable changes in the aging body?

Assessing the Older Patient

Gayle P. Andresen, RN, C, MS, ANP/GNP

Gayle Andresen, formerly a senior instructor in family medicine at the University of Colorado School of Medicine in Denver, is a geriatric nursing consultant in private practice.

Staff Editor: *Paul L. Cerrato*

Nowhere in clinical nursing does the adage "If it ain't broke, don't fix it" hold truer than in geriatric care. While aging causes a steady decline in organ system reserves, it would be a grave mistake to assume that these physiologic changes need to be "cured" or aggressively treated.

Trying to eliminate all audible crackles from the lungs of an elderly patient who has severe kyphosis but is otherwise doing well, for example, may actually do more harm than good. Such "fixes" may needlessly expose older patients to the adverse effects of medication, burden them with added medical bills, and diminish their quality of life.

By the same token, ignoring complaints or dismissing them with comments like, "Oh, it's just old age" isn't good either. Signs and symptoms of disease and in-jury are often vague or atypical in these patients. A 75 year old who comes to the ED short of breath with undefined pain, mild confusion, and decreased appetite shouldn't be shrugged off. Evaluation may reveal ECG changes indicative of recent MI; a medication history may uncover a drug reactin.

This review will help you better understand the physiologic changes that accompany aging and how they should guide clinical interventions.

Heart and Lungs Work Less Efficiently

Older patients are prone to fatigue, dizziness, and falls in part because the older heart can't respond quickly to sudden movements, exertion, or changes in position, particularly during physical or emotional stress. The myocardium loses elasticity with age as some muscle fibers are replaced by fibrotic collagen and others become hypertrophied. These changes, along with thicker and stiffer valves, may reduce cardiac output.[1] On auscultation, you may hear an S4 heart sound even in the absence of disease. The presence of an S3 heart sound, however, is abnormal.[2]

Within coronary and peripheral blood vessels, elastin fibers straighten, fray, and fragment and atherosclerotic plaque builds up. Together, these changes may decrease the vessels' elasticity by as much as 70%. Peripheral resistance increases, and systolic BP rises in response. To maintain perfusion in the face of reduced cardiac output, the diastolic pressure also rises.

Despite age-related hemodynamic changes, don't assume that hypertension is a normal consequence of aging. While diastolic pressure rises with age, it should stabilize after age 60.[3] Systolic pressure, on the other hand, continues to rise after age 55. But if it reaches 160 mm Hg or greater, take heed. Readings this high, with a diastolic reading below 90 mm Hg, point to isolated systolic hypertension. An elevated systolic pressure accompanied by a diastolic reading of 95 mm Hg or higher is considered full-blown hypertension.

Older patients are also prone to orthostatic hypotension. That's because baroreceptors in the aortic arch and carotid sinus become less sensitive, so blood vessels are less able to constrict in response to rapid changes in position.[1]

The elderly are predisposed to cardiac conduction disorders, too. They're caused by the buildup of connective tissue in the SA and AV nodes and a decline in the number of pacemaker cells. Although resting heart rate is not significantly affected by age, heart rate under stress takes longer to speed up and return to normal.

Valves in the peripheral venous circulation also work less effectively. Vessels become tortuous and engorged, sometimes leading to varicose veins, edema, peripheral vascular disease, or, indirectly, stroke.

Pulmonary function begins to decline relatively early—after about age 40. The lungs lose elasticity, reducing vital capacity. The alveolar ducts and bronchioles enlarge and the number of alveoli decreases—especially at the bases of the lungs.[1] When that happens, the lungs don't inflate well during inhalation, and patients have a harder time expelling secretions. Residual volume—the amount of air left in the lungs after maximum expiration—also increases.

When you assess the patient, expect to see a decrease in oxygen saturation to around 93%–95%. You'll probably observe an overall slowing of respiratory rate, too, and shortness of breath during episodes of increased oxygen demand, the exact opposite of what occurs in younger adults.[3] That's partly because, in the elderly, arterial chemoreceptors don't respond as well to changes in pulmonary gases.

You may also note an increase in the anteroposterior diameter of the chest and some kyphosis. Loss of water from the intervertebral discs and bone demineralization help account for these changes. In addition, calcification of costal cartilage and partial contraction of the inspiratory muscles limit the older person's ability to fully expand the chest. Cough and gag reflexes and ciliary action in the bronchial lining are also less efficient, making it even more difficult to clear secretions. These changes help explain why respiratory infection is always a threat to the elderly patient.[2,4]

Digestive and Urinary Functions Slow Down

Nutritional problems are common among the elderly, and poor appetite is a frequent complaint. There are a number of reasons: Saliva secretion decreases by as much as 66%, and salivary ptyalin is reduced, inhibiting the digestion of complex carbohydrates. Taste buds also atrophy and gastric secretion drops considerably, reducing the absorption of iron, calcium, and vitamin B12.

Peristalsis in the esophagus is no longer triggered with each swallow. The lower esophageal sphincter often fails to relax, delaying the entry of food into the stomach and causing a premature feeling of fullness. Weakening of sphincter tone and the diaphragm muscle around the hiatus can cause heartburn, or reflux. These factors, along with a weakened gag reflex, heighten the risk of aspiration.[4]

Even if your patient has no problem eating or digesting food, elimination difficulties may inhibit the adequate intake of solids and liquids. Elders are prone to constipation, largely because the intestinal tract loses neurons over time; inadequate fluid and fiber intake only add to the problem.

Diminished anal sphincter control, on the other hand, can lead to fecal incontinence.

Nocturia, frequency, and urgency are common complaints as bladder capacity decreases. The response to vasopressin—a hormone with an antidiuretic effect—diminishes, causing urine to become more dilute and output to increase.

Bladder and pelvic muscles and sphincter tone can weaken as well. Problems with urinary control may arise in older women with perineal muscle weakness and in men with enlarged prostates. Incontinence, however, is not a normal part of aging, and your patients deserve to have this problem thoroughly evaluated. Because a patient may be reluctant to discuss incontinence, always include the subject in your assessment interview.

The kidneys are also affected by aging. Tissue growth and renal blood flow decrease, and there is a loss of nephron units. By age 90, the glomerular filtration rate declines by as much as 50%.

Physical Changes Are Obvious

One of the most easily noticed signs of aging is the wrinkling and loss of resiliency of the skin. As subcutaneous fat diminishes, elastin fibers are replaced with collagen fibers, and sebaceous and sweat gland activity decrease, the skin becomes thinner, drier, less elastic, and more fragile.[5]

Capillary blood flow decreases too, slowing wound healing as fewer macrophages are available to respond to injury. Natural aging of cells and exposure to the environment cause lesions and pigmentation changes. Fingernails can thicken, become ridged and brittle, and grow more slowly.

An older patient may mention that she is not as tall as she once was. Height decreases as the intervertebral discs and vertebrae thin. Bone loses mineral as it ages—rapidly in women just past menopause—increasing the risk of fractures. Immobilization or excessive calcium loss via the bowel or kidney can accelerate the process, while regular, graded exercise and proper diet appear to slow it. Cartilage around the joints deteriorates and there is a gradual reduction in bone mass. This occurs in men as well, though at a more gradual rate than in women.

An older person's strength and endurance decline, too. Muscle fibers become smaller and fewer and motor neurons decline in number, affecting reaction time and coordination. Encouraging patients to include weight lifting in their exercise regimen can improve bone density and help maintain muscle strength[6]

Senses Are Less Acute, Reaction Time Slows

Decreased sensitivity to outside stimuli also slows response time. That's one reason the elderly are more prone to injury.

A person may not realize, say, that air temperature is too cold or too hot. Physiologic reactions to temperature extremes—shivering, peripheral vasoconstriction or dilation, or muscle contraction—may be inadequate.

All senses, in fact, become less acute. Your patient may complain of a loss of appetite as the sensitivity of taste buds and olfactory receptors declines. Sweet and salt tastes, especially, are dulled. The ability to distinguish items exclusively by touch diminishes, too.[7]

Vision is particularly affected by aging. The lens of the eye begins to stiffen and lose water, compromising its ability to change shape for focus. The lens yellows and becomes cloudy, which may cause problems with color vision. Blues and greens may be hard to distinguish, for instance.

Pupils change, too. They get smaller, decreasing the amount of light reaching the retina, so an older person may find it hard to see in a dimly lit setting. The eyes take longer to adjust to darkness and to glare. Diminished peripheral vision can lead to auto accidents and physical injury when objects go unnoticed.[7,8] Decreased tear production may lead to corneal irritation and a predisposition to conjunctivitis.

Hearing difficulties, often caricatured in an older person, may be mechanical or the result of normal aging. Inability to hear high-frequency sounds often results from degeneration in the cochlea. Sometimes, wax may simply be clogging the ear. Although less copious in an older person, ear wax—or cerumen—is harder because it contains a greater amount of keratin.

Another physiologic change of aging affects not only sensory perception, but many other functions. Beginning at birth, the brain loses neurons. By age 80, brain weight may be as much as 10% less than at birth. Blood flow to the brain also decreases, and brain metabolism slows. Intellectual function can remain intact despite these changes, however.[8,9]

Neurotransmitter levels also change. Monoamine oxidase and norepinephrine production often increase with age while serotonin production may go up or down. Depression may be the result.

The sensory deficits and neurotransmitter changes that accompany aging may make it difficult for older people to process information at a normal rate. Keep this in mind as you perform your assessment and take the nursing history. Speak slowly and distinctly with your mouth visible to the patient. Keep questions simple and allow sufficient time for him to respond. If the question must be repeated, use the same words you used the first time; otherwise, the patient will have two questions to process.[5]

Glandular Activity— Its Complex Effects

One reason the elderly have lowered resistance to disease and infection can be traced to the thymus gland. Between sexual maturity and middle age, this essential component of the immune system—which regulates the development of T-lymphocytes—normally shrinks by approximately 90%. By about age 60, thymic hormones are completely absent. In addition, naturally-occurring antibodies decline, affecting antibody-antigen responses.

Much research remains to be done on the effect of aging on the endocrine glands. Results of many studies are inconclusive or controversial, so only generally agreed on changes are reviewed here:

Pituitary function drops slightly and endorphin levels rise with age. The latter may explain why elderly patients have decreased awareness of painful events like an MI.

The thyroid gland seems to function normally despite alterations in hormone secretions, but changes in other glands—the pituitary and adrenals—may hamper its activity. Thyroxine (T_4) levels remain normal but triiodothyronine (T_3) levels tend to decrease after age 75. Thyroid-stimulating hormone (TSH) is the best measure of the gland's function in the elderly.

The adrenal glands' secretion of glucocorticoids, which are involved in reactions to stress, decrease by 25% in those over 70. Circulating levels of the hormone aldosterone which helps regulate the excretion and retention of sodium, chloride, and potassium, are also lower.

Delayed insulin release by the pancreas, reduced tissue sensitivity to insulin, or both, cause decreasing glucose tolerance with advancing age. At age 75, the average two-hour serum glucose level is 30 mg/100 dL higher than during young adulthood. A fasting blood glucose of 126 mg/dL or greater is the newest standard for determining the presence of diabetes mellitus.[10]

Body temperature regulation, which is under the control of several glands, is somewhat impaired in the elderly. That's partly because of a drop in metabolic rate. The result is a lower normal range, which averages between 96° and 98.8° F.[4]

Despite these changes, organ systems generally continue to function adequately even in the very old unless injury, illness, or intense stress—whether physical, emotional, or social—taxes them beyond their limits. Trouble in one system can have a domino effect. A patient immobilized by a fractured hip, for example, can quickly develop problems with circulation, skin breakdown, pulmonary function, voiding, and constipation.

All patients—regardless of age—dread losing control of normal functioning and fear illness and disability. One of the best ways to help your older patients regain their health and maintain or even strengthen their reserves is by continuing to nurture the vigorous spirit within while caring for the aging body.

For more on the physiologic changes that accompany aging and how they should guide clinical interventions, see the box that begins on page 50.

References

1. Goldman, R. (1986). Aging changes in structure and function. In D. Carnevali & M. Patrick (Eds.), *Nursing Management for the Elderly* (2nd ed.). Philadelphia: J. B. Lippincott.
2. Kane, R., Ouslander, J., & Abrass, I. (1994). *Essentials of Clinical Geriatrics* (3rd ed.) New York: McGraw-Hill.
3. Abrams, W. B., Beers, M. H., et al. (1995). *Merck Manual of Geriatrics* (2nd ed.). Whitehouse Station, NJ: Merck & Co.
4. Blair, K. (1990). Aging: Physiological aspects and clinical implications. *Nurse Pract., 15*(2), 14.
5. Hanson, C. (1996). *Delmar's Instant Nursing Assessment: Gerontologic.* Albany: Delmar Publishers.
6. Nelson, M. (1997). *Strong Women Stay Young.* New York: Bantam Books.
7. Gallman, L. (1995). The sensory system and its problems in the elderly. In M. Stanley & P. Beare (Eds.), *Gerontological Nursing.* Philadelphia: F. A. Davis.
8. Roussel, L. (1995). The neurological system and its problems in the elderly. In M. Stanley & P. Beare (Eds.), *Gerontological Nursing.* Philadelphia: F. A. Davis.
9. Cooper, J., Bloom, F., & Roth, R. (1991). *The Biochemical Basis of Neuropharmacology* (6th ed.) New York: Oxford University Press.
10. American Diabetes Association. (1997). *Revised Clinical Guidelines.* Alexandria, VA: Author.

Clinical Assessment: Findings and Interventions

Assessment Findings	Physiologic Cause	Nursing Implications
Cardiovascular		
Early systolic murmur (S4) Fatigue	Valves more rigid and thicker	Take apical pulse for one minute. Auscultate heart sounds. Observe for syncopal episodes, falls, dizziness. Encourage slow rising when changing positions. Provide a safe environment.
Premature beats and arrhythmias	Conduction deficiencies	Take pulse apically for full minute so that you don't miss premature beats. Bradycardia is defined when heart rate is below 55; tachycardia above 110. Encourage slow rising when changing positions. Provide a safe environment.
Under conditions of stress, the pulse is slow to respond and slow to return to normal	Diminished baroreceptor response Myocardium loses elasticity	Check postural blood pressure. Ask about syncopal episodes, falls, dizziness. Encourage daily graded exercise. Teach stress reduction techniques.
Increased systolic and diastolic blood pressures	Blood vessels lose elasticity	Check blood pressure in both arms.
Widened pulse pressure	Peripheral resistance increases	Monitor peripheral circulation: Check pulses, color, temperature, edema.
Vascular tortuosity and prominence in the forehead, neck, and extremities Varicose veins Edema	Blood vessels lose elasticity Peripheral valves weaken Blood vessels kink Decreased activity resulting in decreased venous return	Teach leg exercises, leg elevation while sitting. Monitor closely for signs of peripheral vascular disease and stroke. Tell patient not to wear garters, tight knee-highs, or rolled stockings.
Respiratory		
Decreased breath sounds at bases Fatigue and breathlessness with sustained activity	Lung tissue loses elasticity Respiration compromised Slow cardiac response to increased oxygen demand	Auscultate lung sounds. Encourage influenza and pneumonia immunization. Encourage regular paced activities. Teach deep-breathing exercises.
Decreased effectiveness of cough Difficulty coughing up secretions	Reflexes diminished Decreased ciliary action	Have patient sit upright for meals. Humidify room air and promote adequate fluid intake to keep secretions liquefied. Tell patients to avoid people with upper respiratory infections.
Increase in the anteroposterior diameter of the chest Kyphosis (rounding of the shoulders) Decreased chest expansion Decreased depth of respiration	Intervertebral disc collapse Demineralization of bone Costal cartilage calcification Respiratory muscle weakness	Teach upper extremity and trunk strengthening exercises. Monitor for mechanical and respiratory complications of surgery and prolonged bed rest. Respirations are often hard to see because of decreased chest expansion.

Assessment Findings	Physiologic Cause	Nursing Implications
Gastrointestinal		
Atrophy of gums with loss of teeth or decay Dry mouth	Poor dental care Bone loss Decreased saliva production	Monitor closely for adequate nutrition. Provide semi-solid foods if needed. Encourage and provide fresh fluids.
Decreased appetite and thirst Early satiety Cough or choking Dysphagia Heartburn, or reflux	Diminished esophageal peristalsis Delayed emptying Gag reflex diminished Hiatal hernia	Monitor for signs of dehydration—assessing mucous membranes rather than skin turgor—and assess electrolyte imbalance. Monitor for choking. Encourage semi-solid foods and small meals. Give medicines with 4–6 ounces of fluid. Have patient remain upright for one hour after meals. Encourage low-fat, low-caffeine diet.
Constipation/fecal impaction Fecal incontinence	Decreased intestinal motility Decreased anal sphincter tone	Encourage adequate fiber and liquids. Encourage mobility. Teach bowel training. Discourage chronic laxative use.
Genitourinary		
Increased nocturia, frequency, and urgency	Diminished sensation, hormone response Decreased bladder capacity	Ensure ready access to commode or bathroom. Assess for urinary tract infection even when patient is afebrile.
Dehydration	Decreased thirst Increased body water storage	Maintain 1,500–2,000 cc of fluids daily. Monitor for dependent edema. Assess weight, intake and output, urine specific gravity, color and condition of mouth, tongue, and mucous membranes.
Increased toxic effects from certain medications, dyes	Decreased renal clearance	Evaluate creatinine clearance before administering nephrotoxic drugs. (Note: Serum creatinine alone is not an adequate measure of renal status because its value doesn't rise with age in proportion to the fall in renal function.)
Decreased glycosuria in diabetics	Increased renal threshold	Monitor blood glucose, not urine tests.
Incontinence: Urge Overflow Stress	 Decreased bladder capacity Decreased bladder innervation Weakened musculature and sphincter tone	Suggest medical evaluation of incontinence. Teach bladder training: toileting program, Kegel exercises, patient to Crede bladder after voiding.
Males: Difficulty initiating urine stream	Enlarged prostate	Suggest medical evaluation. Provide privacy while voiding. Have patient stand and tip forward.
Females: Painful intercourse Delayed orgasm	Vaginal changes	Encourage use of water-soluble lubricant with intercourse.
Males: Delayed erection and achievement of orgasm	Diminished hormonal and sensory cues	Check for possible medication effect. Explain that orgasm and satisfaction may require longer stimulation and foreplay.

Clinical Assessment (continued)

Assessment Findings	Physiologic Cause	Nursing Implications
Musculoskeletal		
Decrease in height Kyphosis	Weakened spinal structures Shrinking of intervertebral discs Bone demineralization	Protect the patient from injury—good lighting, clean, dry floor, side rails. Encourage high calcium, low phosphorus diet, supplemented with 400 I.U. of vitamin D. Encourage moderate exercise: walking or swimming.
Decrease in muscle mass, tone, and strength Diminished mobility, flexibility, and range of motion Diminished balance and reaction time	Decreased muscle fibers Decreased physical activity Decreased capillary circulation Decreased innervation Decreased physical activity	Maintain range of motion and physical activity (especially weight-bearing). Provide assistive devices (cane, walker, nurse's arm) if needed to encourage ambulation.
Joint pain	Joint and cartilage erosion Bony overgrowths	Provide diversional activities to encourage full range of motion.
Integumentary		
Skin: thin, dry, fragile, decreased turgor, increased wrinkles	Thinning of skin layers Decease in gland activity Loss of subcutaneous fat	Suggest fewer baths and the use of unscented soaps. Encourage and provide fresh fluids.
Injuries slow to heal	Diminished capillary flow	Monitor for tearing, bruising, and pressure ulcers. Protect from trauma. Inspect the skin frequently. Remind patient of his decreased cold tolerance. Caution patient to avoid chemical (detergents, harsh household cleansers) and thermal (sun, cold exposure, hot dishes) irritants. Encourage use of sunscreens, hat, skin lubricants.
Decreased perspiration Lesions: Seborrheic keratoses, senile, angioma, pigmentation deposits, senile keratosis, basal cell carcinoma	Decreased sweat gland activity Cellular changes Environmental injury	Monitor for signs of heat intolerance. Differentiate cancerous from precancerous lesions.
Nails: thickened, yellowed, and ridged	Cellular changes	Teach nail-care cleansing and trimming. Suggest podiatry consult.
Taste/Smell		
Poor nutrition Decreased appetite Foods taste bland	Reduced taste buds and olfactory receptors	Encourage use of herb seasoning, lemon, and spices (non-salty) to enhance flavor. Encourage social dining. Encourage nutritional supplements.
Touch		
Diminished sensitivity to pain, heat, pressure Diminished ability to distinguish items by touch (stereognosis)	Conduction deficiencies	Remind the patient he faces a greater chance of accident or injury. Encourage use of other senses. Suggest avoiding temperature extremes without sufficient protection. Suggest frequent position changes. Teach daily skin inspection. Encourage use of a bath thermometer.

Assessment Findings	Physiologic Cause	Nursing Implications
Vision		
Dry eyes	Decreased tear production	Assess for corneal irritation.
		Encourage liberal use of artificial tears (not astringent OTC products).
Problem reading at close range	Lens hardens	Encourage eye exams and use of eyeglasses or magnifying glass.
Pupils slow to react to light	Possibly diminished muscle response	Realize that pupil check on a neuro assessment may be misleading.
Pupils react unequally to light Clouding of lens	Corneal changes	Document unequal pupil size as part of baseline assessment.
Requires more light to see Slow adaptation to dark, poor night vision	Decreased light perception threshold	Provide adequate, indirect, non-glare lighting. Provide night light.
Diabetics: Inability to accurately read blood glucose strips	Yellowed keratin deposits Alteration in blue-green discrimination	Use glucometer or audible meter for blood glucose monitoring. Check patient's ability to distinguish among colors.
Hearing		
Speech discrimination difficulty Decreased ability to hear high-pitched sounds	Ear wax impaction Degenerative changes	Recommend formal hearing test. Check ears for impacted cerumen and infection. Instruct in the proper use of a hearing aid. Do not shout or raise pitch of voice. Face patient directly, with adequate lighting. Reduce background noises.
Neurological		
Sleep disturbances: More wakeful periods, need for naps, insomnia	Stages of sleep altered Chronic or acute disorders Medication effect Decreased physical activity	Evaluate for physical discomforts. Evaluate for sedative or hypnotic abuse. Encourage decreased caffeine intake. Suggest patient avoid evening naps. Encourage increase in daily activities.
Slowed reaction time Learning takes longer	Conduction deficiencies	Allow time for the patient to process questions. Decrease the number of simultaneous stimuli. Divide tasks into short segments.
Mild, recent memory losses or confusion	Conduction deficiencies Reduced cerebral blood flow	Keep teaching sessions short. Minimize environmental stress. Display pictures of familiar faces, suggest family bring in familiar objects. Encourage visitors. Avoid room changes. Offer orienting objects: calendars, clock, TV, newspaper. Write instructions simply.
Depression	Alteration in naturally occurring chemicals and hormones	Suggest diversionary activities. Encourage social interaction. Consider antidepressant drugs.

Article Review Form at end of book.

What are the components of cellular production that decline most noticeably and contribute to the most noticeable changes associated with aging? How do the senses change with age?

What Is Normal Aging?

The passage of time, which can enrich the spirit, usually has the opposite effect on the flesh. Age alone is a principal risk factor for myriad ills, including arthritis, heart disease, cancer, adult-onset diabetes, and osteoporosis. Yet many women make it into their eighth, ninth, and even tenth decades seemingly untouched by degenerative disease. In a sense, one of the goals of modern medicine is to bring all of us into that enviable category.

Of course, slowing the aging process requires understanding it. Although no one has unlocked the secret of senescence, scientists have proposed several theories. One of the most popular and plausible is that aging involves several processes that are interrelated. Each process moves at a slightly different rate within the body and among individuals.

In this scheme of things, cell loss is the major determinant of aging. Cells have finite lives. In most instances, those that have expired are replaced through cell division, but at a slowly declining rate. Neurons (brain cells) and myocytes (heart cells) do not divide at all after reaching maturity; so when those cells are lost, they are gone forever.

As cell populations decline, so do cellular products. Among the most noticeable losses are those of collagen and elastin, which shore up and provide resilience for bone, muscle, and skin. Hormones—which influence tissue growth and proliferation—and enzymes—which officiate in chemical reactions—also diminish.

While heredity may set the cellular stopwatch, environmental factors can influence how fast it runs. Some of the most important and best documented influences are those like tobacco smoke and ultraviolet radiation, which stimulate the production of oxygen-free radicals. These oxygen compounds are unstable and eager to pair with the next available molecule. The resulting union results in oxidation of the target molecule, which often sets off an unfortunate chain of events. For example, through oxidation LDL-cholesterol is readied for deposit into arterial plaque.

Over time, these processes take a toll on the body. The evidence of their effects is quantified in standard screening tests—blood pressure creeps upward, cholesterol levels rise, serum glucose increases.

In determining normal aging, researches tend to rely on averages. They take the range of values in a given age group for a physiologic test, such as serum cholesterol, and compute the mean. It is generally assumed that being within the normal range for one's age group is a sign of good health.

However, normal is not necessarily optimal. Observational investigations, such as the Nurses' Health Study, have determined that low-fat diets, regular exercise, and low body weight in relation to height favor longevity, while the National Health and Nutrition Examination Survey indicates that the average woman eats more fat, gets less exercise, and has a higher body mass index than those who live the longest. Thus, when scientists compare a statistically normal 60-year-old to a 40-year-old or a 20-year-old, they are probably observing not only the effects of aging, but also the effects of 20–40 years of excessive dietary fat, inactivity, and extra poundage.

The following system-by-system account of what to expect of the aging process is based on this imperfect situation. It is accompanied by estimates of what we could do to slow the aging process by being closer to perfection.

The Skin

We tend to think of the skin as the fabric of our presentation to the world, but it also acts as a barrier against foreign substances, a temperature regulator, and a transmitter of sensations. With age, it becomes less capable of carrying out these functions.

The epidermis, or top layer of the skin, experiences a substantial loss of cells. As keratinocytes, which constitute 90% of this layer, decline in numbers, the epidermis not only becomes thinner, it is less firmly attached to the dermis, or underlying layer. The shrinking keratinocyte population also accounts for a decline in provitamin D_3—a substance that is necessary for the manufacture of vitamin D, and consequently a reduction in the body's supply of vitamin D, which plays a vital role in building bone.

The loss of melanocytes—pigment-producing cells—renders us more susceptible to the effects of ultraviolet radiation. The depletion of Langerhans cells, which remove foreign substances, lowers our susceptibility to skin infections, but also makes allergic reactions less common.

The dermis also loses volume. Most of the shrinkage is due to a reduction in fibroblasts, the cells that secrete collagen and elastin—the two proteins that are responsible for the skin's elasticity. The number of microscopic vessels that nourish the dermis also decreases substantially. As a result of these changes, the skin is thinner, less resilient, and less capable of responding to changes in temperature and to sensation.

The Brain

Thanks to advances in brain imaging, scientists have come to realize that brain loss with aging is not as severe as once thought. However, the brain is one organ in which it is particularly difficult to tease apart the effects of aging and experience. There is increasing evidence that environmental stimulation has a great deal of influence on the state of our brains later in life. Knowledge is still incomplete, though rapidly evolving.

While some researchers are puzzling over the structure and chemistry of the aging brain, others are collecting information about brain function from cognitive studies. The results of tests administered to large numbers of people of different ages indicate that short-term memory begins to decline in one's 50s; general intelligence, in one's 60s, and capacity for abstract thought, in one's 70s. However, the variation among individuals is great.

The Cardiovascular System

Like the skin, the arteries become less elastic, probably due to changes in collagen and elastin in the arterial walls. This reduces the vessels' ability to relax to accommodate changes in blood volume as the heart beats, and blood pressure increases slightly. Although most people in industrialized nations develop some degree of atherosclerosis with age, the degree of plaque that is due to age, rather than genetics or diet, remains to be seen.

The wall of the heart's left ventricle, or pumping chamber, becomes somewhat thicker with age, due to an increase in the size of the myocytes, or heart muscle cells, and a build-up of collagen. The heart is a highly adaptive organ that can modify the way it works to accommodate changes in the vessels that feed it. Heart rate during exercise doesn't rise as much as it once did, but the heart dilates more to admit the same volume of blood and expels it as forcefully as it ever did. However, when the heart has to counter the effects of high blood pressure, or if the heart muscle is deconditioned from inactivity, it loses much of its contractile force.

The Respiratory System

Most of us attain our maximal lung function (measured by the amount of air that can be forced out in 1 second) when we're in our early 20s. From then on, it declines steadily, falling to about 70% of peak by age 75.

The decline in function is thought to be due to several factors, primarily the loss of elastic fibers that keep the bronchioles—the tiny airways in the lungs—open. The lungs not only retain a larger amount of the air from breath to breath, oxygen doesn't diffuse as readily from the lungs into the blood, reducing the volume of oxygen that gets into circulation. Even so, the effects of age aren't nearly as important as those of smoking in limiting the ability to exercise.

The Musculoskeletal System

The bone density of the skeleton reaches its peak during one's 20s and remains stable for about two decades. Around the time of menopause, resorption—the process by which bone is broken down and calcium is released from the bone for use by the body—increases, but formation—the bone-rebuilding process—fails to keep pace. This imbalance, which is triggered by declining estrogen levels, leads to rapid bone loss during the first decade following menopause, with moderate bone loss thereafter. In women with low peak bone mass, it can result in osteoporosis.

Muscle mass also declines, due to a loss of some fibers and of nerves that stimulate others. However, muscle strength can be maintained through exercise well into one's 70s.

The Digestive System

The gastrointestinal tract ages well. The alimentary organs—esophagus, stomach, small intestine, and colon—like all muscular structures, lose some tone with age. Still, they manage to perform almost as well in age as in youth.

The production of gastric acid and some digestive enzymes declines during middle age, but usually not enough to have much of an effect. Some nutrients, particularly calcium, are not as well absorbed as they once were.

The gallbladder releases less bile into the liver, allowing more time for gallstones to develop. The liver shrinks somewhat, requiring more time to process drugs and alcohol. The pancreas, which regulates glucose levels and secretes enzymes that break

down fats and proteins, has such a large reserve capacity that 90% of its function would have to be lost before we begin to suffer ill effects.

The Reproductive System

By middle age, the ovaries, which once held about two million eggs, have resorbed or shed nearly all of them. At menopause, these glands produce only a small fraction of the estrogen and progesterone they once did. This decline has effects throughout the body, often resulting in hot flashes, vaginal dryness and other symptoms associated with menopause. These effects are highly variable from woman to woman.

The endometrium—uterine lining—and the vaginal lining begin to atrophy. Glandular tissue in the breast shrinks. Although natural pregnancy is no longer possible, recent events have indicated that women in their 60s who have undergone hormonal therapy and donor-egg implantation can still bear children.

The Excretory System

The gradual reduction of blood flow to the kidneys is coupled with a reduction in nephrons—the units that extract wastes from the blood and concentrate them in the urine. As a result, the volume of urine increases somewhat. A reduction in bladder capacity increases the number of times one urinates in a day. Moreover, the urinary timetable changes as well. While the kidneys produce most of the urine during the day in young people, they segue to the night shift over time, making one or two nocturnal trips to the bathroom commonplace.

The Immune System

The gradual degeneration of the thymus, a small gland in the neck that is responsible for training T-lymphocytes to coordinate the body's immune system, produces most of the effects of age on the immune system. T-cells decline in number and those that remain don't function as well. B-lymphocytes, the cells that send out antibodies, also lose their edge. Both the capacity to respond to a new microscopic invader and the ability to release antibodies are impaired somewhat with age. The overall effect is an increased susceptibility to infection with advancing years.

However, the antibody decline has certain benefits. As the cells responsible for allergic reactions wear down, conditions like hayfever may diminish.

The Endocrine System

Although estrogen and progesterone decline more dramatically, other hormones fall off as well. A dampening of the function of the adrenal glands results in lower levels of dehydroepiandrosterone (DHEA), the hormone from which most androgens, including testosterone, are derived in women. Growth hormone, which helps to build muscle mass, also drops as pituitary function declines. Luteinizing hormone (LH) and follicle-stimulating hormone (FSH) increase during perimenopause, in an effort to stimulate waning ovarian function. These levels remain elevated during the early years after menopause, but decline thereafter.

Levels of some hormones actually increase with age. Parathyroid hormone (PTH), which stimulates the release of calcium from the bones, rises in response to reduced intestinal absorption of that mineral. The increase in PTH contributes to a reduction in bone-mineral density. Endorphin levels rise with age, reducing sensitivity to pain.

Production of thyroid hormone, which regulates metabolism, and insulin, which helps to move glucose out of the blood and into the cells, doesn't change much. However, slightly higher glucose levels are necessary to prompt insulin secretion.

The Senses

Our sensory organs are among the hardest hit by passing time. The attrition of hair cells, which are actually nerve cells in the ear that conduct sound signals to the brain, is the principal cause of presbycusis, or age-related hearing decline. This results in a gradual decline in the ability to hear high-pitched sounds. As hair-cell loss continues, lower pitches go unheard.

Presbyopia, age-related vision loss, is what sends many of us to the drugstore for reading glasses in middle age. It is a result of the lens's loss of elasticity, which diminishes our capacity to change focus as we redirect our glance from distant to near objects. The lens becomes more opaque, reducing the amount of light that reaches the retina. However, as is the case with the skin, many of the changes to the lens are the result of sun exposure.

The number of taste buds declines, reducing the range of flavors we can savor. Although there is little scientific evidence to that effect, our ability to appreciate subtle scents is thought to diminish as well.

Slowing the Process

As the biggest bolus of our population passes beyond their 50th birthdays, the commercial development of anti-aging products is booming. The greatest emphasis is on estrogen, progesterone, DHEA, human growth hormone, testosterone, and agents that mimic their activities. The role of these hormones, for the most part, is to rev up desirable functions—such as the production of collagen and elastin, muscle development, the immune response, and tissue repair—and to dampen undesirable ones—such as bone resorption and atherosclerotic plaque formation. As the experience with postmenopausal estrogen has taught us, the trick is to avoid stimulating or suppressing the wrong activities.

Even if these hormonal remedies fulfill their promise, they can't fully compensate for damage previously incurred. As gerontologists point out, most of the vestiges of age are not the work of time, but of our own hands. The secrets of slower aging are simple ones:

- *Sun shields:* The skin is one organ in which it is relatively easy to isolate the changes due to age from those caused by sun exposure, by comparing skin from the buttocks or other habitually covered regions to skin on the hands and face. These comparisons indicate that sun damage is responsible for as much as 90% of the unwanted cosmetic changes, such as wrinkling, mottled pigmentation, spider veins, and easy bruising, that we mistakenly attribute to age. Apply sunscreen with SPF 15 or more whenever the sun is high in the sky. From the skin's point of view, there is no such thing as a healthy tan. Sunglasses with maximum protection against ultraviolet light slow the development of cataracts.

- *Micronutrients:* Antioxidants soak up oxygen-free radicals to minimize damage to tissues. Although study after study continues to suggest the benefits of vitamins E, C, and beta-carotene for protection against cancer and heart disease, recent research indicates that these antioxidants are best acquired through a diet abundant in fruits, vegetables, and grains rather than through supplements. Adequate B-vitamins, especially B12 and folate, appear to reduce the risk of atherosclerosis. In this case, a multivitamin supplement may be necessary.

- *Exercise:* In reports analyzing the effects of aging on the respiratory, musculoskeletal, and cardiovascular systems, researchers state time and again that it is virtually impossible to separate the effects of age from those of inactivity. Exercise increases lung capacity, builds muscle and bone, and conditions the heart and blood vessels. It also promotes a favorable shift in the ratio of lean tissue to fat. Give all your muscles a workout; include a session of Kegels for the pelvic floor.

- *Peace and quiet:* Keeping the volume down—even if it necessitates wearing earplugs on occasion—reduces damage to hair cells and slows hearing loss. It may also reduce stress, an issue we'll explore in a future article.

Article Review Form at end of book.

Why, as we get older, does novelty become less appealing? Does it really matter whether people are open to novelty in their cultural and social choices? Why or why not?

Open Season

When do we lose our taste for the new?

Robert M. Sapolsky

Despite my best efforts to ignore him, Paul, my fresh-out-of-college administrative assistant, was getting on my nerves. The problem wasn't his work, which was superb. It was his taste in music. Shortly after his arrival at my neurobiology lab, his CD player started blasting something horrendous by whatever group twenty-year-olds were listening to. But that wasn't what bothered me. What bothered me was the way he kept switching what he listened to. One day it would be Sonic Youth for hours, and the next day later Beethoven. Irish folk music would give way to Gregorian chants, and then to Shostakovich, John Coltrane, big-band hits, Yma Sumac, Puccini arias, Philip Glass, and klezmer classics. He was spending the paychecks from his first real job on a methodical exploration of different types of music, giving them a careful listening, and forming opinions—hating some of the stuff, loving the process. What was irritating was how open-minded he was, how amenable to novelty.

He was like that in every respect. He had a beard and longish hair until, one day, he came into the lab with a bald pate. "I thought it would be interesting to try out this appearance for a while—see if it changes the way people interact with me," he explained. In his time off, he would spend a weekend at a film festival of Indian musicals, just for the experience. He'd pore over Melville, then Chaucer, then contemporary Hungarian realists.

All this was more than irritating. It was depressing, because it made me reflect on my own narrowing. At the age of forty, I listen to music constantly, but I can't remember the last time I listened to a new composer. And while I love all Mahler's music, I now seem to listen only to the same two symphonies of his. The same goes for reggae: it's always the same trusted tape of Bob Marley's greatest hits. And if I'm going out to dinner I'm more and more likely to order my usual favorites.

How did this happen? When did it become so important to have familiar ground underfoot? For many people, that question would lead to some heavy soul-searching. Being a scientist, I decided to avoid this by Studying the Subject. A quick survey revealed that this all too familiar tendency had been ignored in the scientific literature. Though there is research into why highly creative people tend to become less creative over time, no one knows why, as we age, we start buying those "Best of" anthologies advertised on late-night television. I figured I could at least get a better fix on the phenomenon, but I needed some data.

I wanted to test whether there were any clear-cut maturational time windows during which we form our cultural tastes, are open to new experience, even gravitate to it for its own sake. In particular, I wanted to determine whether there was a consistent age at which such windows of openness slammed shut.

As a CD of Wagner highlights played on ukulele boomed outside my office, I decided to try to figure out when we form our musical tastes, and when we stop being open to most new music. My research assistants and I called radio stations that specialize in the music of various periods: contemporary rock, the

"Stairway to Heaven" seventies stations, the fifties doo-wop stations, and so on. In each case, we posed the same two questions to the station manager: When was most of the music that you play first introduced? And what is the average age of your listeners?

After more than forty phone calls around the country, a pattern became clear: not a lot of seventeen-year-olds were tuning in to the Andrews Sisters, not a lot of Rage Against the Machine was being played in retirement communities, and devotees of sixty nonstop minutes of James Taylor were starting to wear relaxed-fit jeans. This can be stated more precisely: Most people are twenty years old or younger when they first hear the popular music they choose to listen to for the rest of their lives. When we combined those results with a measure of how variable the data were, we figured out that if you are more than thirty-five years old when a style of popular music is introduced there's a greater than ninety-five per cent chance that you will never choose to listen to it. The window has closed.

Next, I turned to the sensory realm of food. Psychologists have long studied gustatory novelty in laboratory animals, trying to understand how they choose their food, correct a dietary deficiency, or avoid a toxin. For wildlife zoologists, too, these issues have started to arise—particularly when, as a result of habitat degradation, an animal population is forced into a new ecosystem. The anthropologist Shirley Strum studied a troop of wild baboons in Kenya after a group of farmers forced them off their native grounds, and watched the animals learn what plants in their new home were good to eat. The laboratory and the field studies show the same thing: animals normally shy away from novel foods, and when they finally do get hungry enough to try something new the youngsters are the ones most given to exploration: they're most likely to make a discovery, and most open to changing their behavior when they see that someone else has.

Does the pattern apply to us? To pursue the time-window strategy I used with the radio stations, I needed a type of food that, by Middle American standards, was truly anomalous and that had been introduced during a recent, identifiable time. I thought about pizza or bagels, but both had been too pervasive for too long. There was the shift in Chinese-restaurant food from chop-suey Cantonese to spicy Szechuan, but it was hard to identify any clear transition point.

Sushi worked. Little pieces of raw fish served with horseradish and bits of vegetable carved to look like flowers: here was something that probably remains a bit off-putting to the pot-roast crowd living near the amber waves of grain. Returning to our phones, my research assistants and I called sushi restaurants throughout the Midwest: from Omaha, Nebraska on down to Eden Prairie, Minnesota. When was sushi first introduced into your town? How old is your average non-Asian customer?

In a number of instances, the news that some neurobiology professor wanted information for a survey generated consternation. We also stumbled on what was apparently a nasty feud in Bloomington, Indiana, over which of two sushi places had opened first. But fifty restaurants later we had uncovered a fairly clear pattern. The typical non-Asian Midwestern sushi patron had been less than twenty-eight years old when sushi first arrived in town, and among townspeople who were older than thirty-nine at that time the odds were greater than ninety-five per cent that they would never touch it. Another window closed.

Emboldened further, I looked into one more window. I live near the Haight district in San Francisco, and thanks to this proximity I was dimly aware that what is currently outrageous in fashion has changed since my peers and I were affronting our elders by wearing jeans to high school. Here, surely, was another realm amenable to the time-window approach. Tattoos wouldn't fill the bill, because they have been around for a long while and because their connotations have shifted. Pierced ears for men don't work, either, and for much the same reason: sixty-year-old Republican assemblymen can get away with earrings these days. Soon I had entered the world of tongue studs and navel and genital rings. Retreating to my office, I let my research assistants handle all those phone calls on their own: When did you first start offering this type of body piercing in your town? How old is your average customer?

At these establishments, the news that a neurobiologist wanted information prompted not one raised eyebrow, pierced or otherwise. Thirty-five data points later, we had a remarkably clear answer. The average tongue-stud wearer was eighteen or younger when that sociopolitical deconstructionist fashion statement, or whatever it is, arrived on the scene. And if you were older than twenty-three at the time, the odds are ninety-five per cent that you have passed up tongue studs altogether, probably just trying instead to get a hairdo like Jennifer Aniston's.

Now we had some major scientific discoveries on our hands: for at least one particular fashion novelty, the window of receptivity essentially closed by age twenty-three; for popular music, it closed by thirty-five; for an alien food type, by thirty-nine. These findings seemed reminiscent of work that had been done regarding creativity, where, in study after study, age has emerged as a leading factor. The profession of mathematics, for instance, is built almost entirely upon the creative breakthroughs of wunderkinder, and studies of other creative professions show a less extreme version of the same pattern. Count the number of melodies per year from a composer, poems from a poet, original research findings from a scientist, and, on the average, you'll find a decline after a certain, relatively youthful peak.

These studies also indicate that over time the great creative minds not only are less likely to generate something new but are less open to someone else's novelty—the same phenomenon I was seeing in the sushi bars. Think of Einstein, in his later years, fighting a rear-guard action against quantum mechanics, or of Alfred Mirsky as the last major figure in cell biology to reject the idea that DNA was the molecule of heredity. As the physicist Max Planck once observed, established generations of scientists never accept new theories; they die first. In some cases, the closing mind of a former revolutionary rejects what should have been the logical extension of his revolution. Consider Martin Luther, who spent his final years helping to crush the peasant uprisings gal-

vanized by his own youthful work. There's a consistent trend emerging here. As we age, all of us—the senior scientist flailing against his errant disciples, the commuter twiddling with the radio dial for a familiar tune—becomes less open to someone else's novelty.

What can this be about? The psychologist Dean Keith Simonton has shown that the decline in creativity and openness among great minds isn't predicted by age so much as by how long people have worked in one discipline. Scholars who switch disciplines seem to have their openness rejuvenated. What matters most isn't chronological age but "disciplinary" age.

There are a number of ways you might try to account for this effect. Maybe it's that the same old stodgy tricks seem fresh and original in the new discipline. Maybe it's that an aging individual who is a high achiever in one discipline and switches to another is unusually open to novelty in the first place. Or maybe changing disciplines truly does stimulate the mind to regain some of its youthful openness to novelty; as the neuroscientist Marian Diamond has shown, environmental stimulation can make more elaborate neuronal connections in the adult brain. An alternative explanation finds support in Simonton's recent work. Novel discoveries in a field are, pretty much by definition, the ones that overturn the entrenched ideas of the intellectual élites. The reason that these gray eminences become reactionary, then, is simply that they have the most to lose in the face of novelty.

But I don't think any of this tells us much about the narrowing of taste. When it comes to picking a radio station for the

drive home, our investment in the status quo isn't what's preventing us from listening to music popular with kids twenty years younger than we are. And the eminence idea doesn't tell us much about why old animals are unwilling to try new foods.

You might think that the explanation was neurological—that some novelty center in our brain starts to atrophy with age, losing neurons left and right. In fact, though, in most brain regions there isn't any dramatic neuron loss as we get older. With extreme age, there is a loss of connections between neurons, causing neuronal networks of communication to weaken. That probably has something to do with why it's more difficult for us to absorb new information and apply it in a novel way as we age, while our ability to recall facts and apply them in the habitual way remains intact. But it doesn't explain the declining *appeal* of novelty: I don't think most folks holding out for a good, thick steak do so because they have trouble understanding the raw-fish paradigm of sushi. The real problem with the neurological approach, however, is that there is no such thing as a novelty center in the brain, let alone sub-areas for fashion, music, or food which age at different speeds.

Maybe getting a grip on the phenomenon requires shifting the emphasis. In Tracy Kidder's "Old Friends," a nursing-home resident says about his forgetful roommate, "Heard only twice, Lou's memories could seem monotonous. Heard many times, they were like old friends. They were comforting," I've been asking why, as we get older, novelty becomes unappealing. Maybe we need to try to understand why repetition becomes appealing.

There's a stage of childhood in which kids become mad for repetition, taking pleasure in the realization that they are mastering rules. Maybe the pleasure at the other end of life is the realization that the rules are still there—as are we. Given that aging contracts our neural networks and makes our cognition more repetitive, it would be a humane quirk of evolution if we were reassured by that repetition. As Igor Stravinsky lay dying, he repeatedly banged his ring against the metal railing of his hospital bed, startling his wife each time. Finally, with a touch of irritation, she asked why he was doing that, since he knew she was still there. "But I want to be sure that *I* still exist," he replied.

Why, really, does it matter whether people are open to novelty in their cultural and social choices? Does society really need more eighty-year-olds with tongue studs eating raw eel? Is it a crime if I keep listening to that Bob Marley tape? There may even be some advantage for social groups if their aging members become protective archivists of their cultural inheritance, instead of constantly jettisoning the old in order to soak up the new. The physiologist Jared Diamond has argued that part of the success of Cro-Magnons was that they lived about fifty per cent longer than Neanderthals did, and so when some rare ecological catastrophe hit there was a substantially greater chance that someone would be old enough to remember the last time that it happened and how they got out of the mess then. (Perhaps, in my old age, if there's a locust infestation that devastates food stores at my university I'll be able to save the youngsters by my recollections of which wild plants behind the Student Union are safe to eat, along with an ancillary lecture about how reggae isn't what it used to be.)

But as I hang up the lab coat and actually reflect on some of this, I find it a little dispiriting. When I see the finest of my students ready to run off to the Peace Corps and minister to lepers in the Congo—or teach some kid in the barrio just outside the university how to read—I re- member that, once, it was easier to be that way. An open mind is a prerequisite to an open heart. And then there's simply the impoverishment that comes with this closing of the mind to novelty and glorying in repetition, as years of cultural exploration are likely to give way to banging on a hospital-bed railing. What a shock to discover that at the age of forty you've already been dipped in bronze and placed on a mantelpiece—that there are already societal institutions like oldies radio stations, whose very existence affirms the fact that you are no longer where culture is. If (as my administrative assistant assures me) there's a rich, vibrant world out there, it shouldn't be just for twenty-year-olds to explore for exploration's sake. Whatever it is that fends us off from novelty, I figure maybe it's worth putting up a bit of a fight, even if it means forgoing Bob Marley's greatest hits every now and then.

 **Article Review Form at end of book.**

WiseGuide Wrap-Up

- We can adapt to and compensate for many of the changes associated with aging.

- It is important to recognize and understand the differences between normal aging and common diseases associated with aging.

R.E.A.L. Sites

This list provides a print preview of typical **coursewise** R.E.A.L. sites. There are over 100 such sites at the **courselinks**™ site. The danger in printing URLs is that web sites can change overnight. As we went to press, these sites were functional using the URLs provided. If you come across one that isn't, please let us know via email to: webmaster@coursewise.com. Use your Passport to access the most current list of R.E.A.L. sites at the **courselinks**™ site.

Site name: Ask NOAH about Aging and Alzheimer's Disease
URL: http://www.noah.cuny.edu:8080/aging/aging.html
Why is it R.E.A.L.? NOAH (New York Online Access to Health) is a collaborative effort among City University of New York, Metropolitan New York Library Council, New York Academy of Medicine, and the New York Public Library. The site offers the basics of aging; including physiological changes and common problems; care and treatment, with discussion of general care, coping, housing, and nutrition; and information resources.
Key topics: alzheimer's disease, dementia
Activity: List the causes of Alzheimer's Disease

Site name: Get to Know Your Endocrine System
URL: http://www.healthy.net/hwlibraryarticles/aesoph/endocrinesystem.htm
Why is it R.E.A.L.? Health World Online operates this site. It is the only Internet health network that integrates alternative and conventional health information. This particular article provides an overview of the endocrine system and offers a description of each gland's function as well as beneficial products that each gland produces.
Key topic: endocrine system
Activity: Explain the role of melatonin in the functioning of the body.

Site name: Healthy Aging
URL: http://www.healthy.net/wellness/aging/index.html
Why is it R.E.A.L.? This site is part of Health World Online and provides information on natural life extension, strategies for life extension, and anti-aging medicine.
Key topic: life expectancy
Activity: Identify some of the topics you find in this "alternative" site.

Site name: Nutritional Programs for Healthy Aging & Longevity
URL: http://www.healthy.net/wellness/aging/programs.htm
Why is it R.E.A.L.? This document, also from Health World Online, provides information on some alternative nutritional methods for healthy aging.
Key topics: life expectancy, nutrition
Activity: Suggest a diet plan to counteract the aging process.

section

3

Key Points

- Certain chronic and acute conditions are more prevalent among the elderly.

- Some chronic conditions, such as depression, are misdiagnosed in the elderly.

- Specific populations have a greater incidence of certain conditions.

Chronic and Acute Conditions

WiseGuide Intro

While Section 2 dealt with the normal changes of aging, Section 3 identifies some of the common conditions associated with getting older. Even though these afflictions are not part of the normal aging process, the elderly are more susceptible to them. Just as one can compensate for the normal changes connected to aging, adjustment in lifestyles can help individuals cope with these conditions.

Some of the conditions explored in this section are long-term, chronic conditions. Conditions such as osteoporosis and specific types of blindness are addressed, with information provided about prevention, diagnosis, and treatment. Alzheimer's disease is a major concern and fear of many elderly. One of the readings in this section helps alleviate some of the fears associated with the condition. Another mental health condition explored in this section is depression among the elderly. This overlooked, misdiagnosed condition can often be effectively treated.

Some chronic and acute conditions are more prevalent among the minority elderly. This section also provides an update and overview on special health considerations in African American elders.

Sexually transmitted diseases (STDs)? Among the elderly? Believe it or not, specific risk factors for STDs are unique to the elderly population. This section discusses statistics, diagnosis problems, treatment, and prevention options for this seldom-discussed health concern of senior citizens.

Questions

Reading 12. What are some of the common health conditions that are more prevalent in the African American elderly population? Aside from poor health status, what other factors affect longevity among African American elders?

Reading 13. What is the greatest risk factor for transmission of HIV in the elderly population? What other STDs are prevalent in the elderly?

Reading 14. What is the most common factor associated with depression in the elderly? What are the treatment options for depression in the elderly?

Reading 15. What are the risk factors associated with osteoporosis? How can osteoporosis be treated?

Reading 16. What is the relationship between world population trends and the need for eye care and eye surgery? Describe how avoidable blindness can be eliminated in the future.

Reading 17. What are the warning signs of stroke? What types of treatments are available for stroke victims?

Reading 18. Why do the elderly typically decrease or moderate their drinking habits as they age? What things correlate with heavy drinking among the elderly?

What are some of the common health conditions that are more prevalent in the African American elderly population? Aside from poor health status, what other factors affect longevity among African American elders?

Special Health Considerations in African-American Elders

Charles P. Mouton, M.D.

Charles P. Mouton, M.D. is assistant professor in the Department of Family Medicine at the UMDNJ–New Jersey Medical School, Newark, Dr. Mouton graduated from Howard University College of Medicine. He completed a residency in family practice at Prince Georges Hospital Center in Cheverly, Md. He also completed a fellowship in geriatrics at George Washington University Medical Center in Washington, D.C. Address correspondence to Charles P. Mouton, M.D., Department of Family Medicine, UMDNJ–New Jersey Medical School, 185 S. Orange Ave., MSB B–623, Newark, NJ 07103.

Older African Americans constitute an expanding part of the elderly population in the United States. Although socioeconomic factors affect longevity and functional status more than race, African-American elders, as a whole, show poorer health status, as well as greater levels of financial strain and care-giver burden. Incidence rates of hypertension, heart disease, stroke, end-stage renal disease, dementia and prostate cancer are higher among African Americans than among the white population.

The incidence of depression, however, is lower. Cancer survival rates are also lower, in part because of lower rates of cancer screening in this group. Physicians should carefully choose instruments to assess cognitive and physical status in African-American elders. The Activities of Daily Living scale and the Short Portable Mental Status Questionnaire are two tools that have been specially tested and shown to be reliable and valid in this population group. The Geriatric Depression Scale is a useful diagnostic tool that is quick to use in a busy office practice. Taking the time during an initial visit to understand the patient's values and perceptions of health and illness builds a sense of comfort and trust that will set a positive tone for the entire doctor-patient relationship and may empower the patient to take positive steps to improve health habits.

In daily practice, family physicians are encountering an increasing number of older patients, many of whom are African American. Currently, African Americans make up almost 8 per-cent of the population older than 65, a percentage that is expected to reach 8.6 percent by 2010.[1] Once African Americans reach age 85, their life expectancy is an additional 8.2 years for men and 10.6 years for women, compared with 5.5 and 7.2 years for white men and women, respectively.[2] African-American elders are a heterogeneous group, with backgrounds from north and south of the Mason-Dixon line and both sides of the Mississippi. This population includes people who have migrated from the Caribbean basin and the African continent.

Providing health care for such a varied group requires special attention to some specific concerns. Yet, because of this diversity, no study or series of findings fits every older African American. Emphasis should be placed on evaluating each older African-American patient as an individual. Nonetheless, physicians should use the remarks in this article as "points to consider" when managing health care for

"Special health considerations in African-American elders" by Charles P. Mouton from AMERICAN FAMILY PHYSICIAN, March 1997, Vol. 55, No. 4, pp. 1243–1254. Reprinted by permission of the American Academy of Family Physicians.

older African Americans. This article concentrates on special concerns related to the doctor-patient relationship, socioeconomic issues, care-giving issues, functional health and the assessment of cognitive and emotional health. Special considerations in selected disease conditions are discussed.

Comprehensive Assessment

Comprehensive assessment is an important part of the initial evaluation of older African Americans (*Table 1*)*[3–13] It is helpful in planning recommendations for care, and it serves to establish a strong doctor-patient relationship. Through this assessment, the physician demonstrates her or his interest in the African-American elder as a whole person, as well as his or her clinical competency.

Issues in the Doctor-Patient Relationship

For African-American elders, the initial patient-physician encounter often sets the tone for the entire relationship. African Americans expect a physician to be open and willing to listen. While they may vary in their preference for autonomy, African Americans generally expect to be given information about their illness. Unfortunately, studies show that African Americans are less likely to receive health information than white Americans.[1,2] African-American patients are also less likely to be referred to specialists or to receive surgical and diagnostic procedures.[14]

Furthermore, many older African Americans have adapted to a society in which institutions have been authoritarian and discriminatory. Because of this historical experience, African-American elders may be less likely to adopt or desire a collegial relationship with a non-African-American physician.[15] This tendency may change as "babyboomers" mature, since they are living in a different historical context, largely because of the Civil Rights movement.

To get over this barrier, non-African-American physicians can foster a more collegial doctor-patient relationship by taking extra time to discuss the patient's values, understand the patient's perceptions of health and illness, and develop trust. Asking about end-of-life treatment preferences or obtaining a value history may help in the development of a collegial relationship. If the physician also cares for other members of the patient's family, making inquiries about those family members indicates a level of personal concern. Explaining examinations, diagnoses and procedures, both verbally and with illustrations, can also go a long way toward enhancing communication with older African-American patients.

Socioeconomic Factors

Socioeconomic factors, more than racial factors, have a great impact on longevity and functional decline. In fact, when socioeconomic forces are taken into account, many of the differences between African Americans and other older adults disappear or narrow. As a whole, African-American elders show greater levels of financial strain than their white counterparts.[16] Older African Americans may also face what

some have termed "double jeopardy." Their age and minority status lead to a greater burden of illness and greater limitation on their financial resources.[17] Physicians should consider the financial constraints of their older African-American patients when recommending treatment. While direct questions about finances may be offensive to some older African Americans, others may appreciate the option of using a less expensive treatment with similar effectiveness.

Caregiver Issues

Early studies indicated that African-American families tend to provide the bulk of the care for their older family members.[18,19] More recent research indicates that, over the past decade, this level of personal care-giving has begun to erode.[16] The multiple demands on African-American families caring for both children and aging parents can lead to higher levels of stress. Also, because of crises resulting from human immunodeficiency virus (HIV) infection, incarceration and homicide, more older African Americans are becoming caregivers for orphaned grandchildren.

Physician should be watchful for signs of care-giver stress by screening family members and patients with questionnaire such as the Caregiver Strain Index (*Figure 1*)*[20] Physicians should also be prepared to provide information about respite services and support groups for stressed caregivers. This information can be obtained from local chapters of the Area Agency on Aging or private groups such as the local Alzheimer's Disease Association.

*Table 1 not included in this publication.

*Figure 1 not included in this publication.

Advanced Care Planning

Physicians benefit from developing an understanding of the older African-American patient's health goals and treatment preferences, which play a major role in medical decision making. Also, physicians should encourage clear communication through written advance directives and family discussions. Although African-American elders may be less inclined to complete written advance directives, they are often more willing to discuss their preferences with family members. Appropriately involving family members as informed participants in the decision-making process can help facilitate this discussion. Furthermore, understanding the patient's health preferences is important in developing strategies to maintain health and physical function.

Assessing Function

Maintaining function is one of the main reasons older African Americans seek medical care. As African Americans age, their functional status declines more rapidly than the functional status of whites. Older African Americans are 1.38 times more likely than whites to have trouble getting around and more than 1.5 times more likely to be confined to their homes.[21] However, as they reach their 80s and 90s, older African Americans tend to function better than whites. Because of the importance function plays in the health of older African Americans, several instruments have been adapted, including self-report questionnaires such as the Activities of Daily Living Scale and the Instrumental Activities of Daily Living Scale, as well as other performance-based measures.[3,22]

Assessment of function using the Activities of Daily Living Scale has proved to be fairly reliable and valid in African Americans.[4] The scale evaluates behaviors considered predictive of the independent living ability of older adults. Physicians can use this instrument to identify older African Americans who may benefit from assisted living or a greater level of caregiving. Having a network of home health agencies, social work case management and long-term care placement as resources may help facilitate the care of these frail older adults once they are identified.

Another instrument that assesses a higher level of function is the Instrumental Activities of Daily Living Scale.[5] Although it has been used in African-American populations, data on its reliability and validity in this group are limited.

Since the Activities of Daily Living and Instrumental Activities of Daily Living scales are based on self-report, performance-based assessments of function have been developed to provide a more objective measurement. Performance-based measures include the Gait and Balance evaluation, the Timed Manual Performance test and the Get Up and Go Test.[6-8] No data on the validity of these instruments in African-American elderly are available, but some clinicians find these measures helpful.

Assessing Cognition

In addition to physical function, cognition also declines with age. Instruments that assess cognitive function range from brief forms (taking five to 15 minutes to complete), such as the Mini-Mental State Examination (MMSE) (*Figure 2*)*[9] and the Short Portable Mental Status Questionnaire, to lengthy forms (taking hours to complete), such as formal neuropsychologic batteries.[9,10] The accuracy of brief instruments in older African Americans is a critical issue. For example, usage of the standard cutoff score of 23 on the MMSE leads to an overdiagnosis of dementia in older African Americans.[23] Using a lower cutoff score of 19 corrects for this tendency. The MMSE score also should be adjusted for patients with lower educational levels (less than the eighth grade).

Another instrument, the Short Portable Mental Status Questionnaire, has been used in older African Americans. The Short Portable Mental Status Questionnaire is the only brief cognitive assessment instrument that has been fully validated in African-American elders; however, it is less sensitive to milder deficits in cognitive function.[10] Physicians should choose an appropriate instrument and regularly screen older African Americans for dementia.

Dementia

Dementia, a syndrome characterized by a decline in memory, language and other cognitive functions, affects more than 15 percent of persons over age 65 and almost 50 percent of persons over age 80. Studies show that dementia is more prevalent among African Americans than among whites.[24,25] However, inaccuracy in identifying cognitive impairment resulting from the inflationary effect of race, acculturation and education is a major problem.[26]

*Figure 2 not included in this publication.

Of the irreversible dementias, dementia of the Alzheimer's type is the most prevalent among African Americans. However, Multi-Infarct Dementia tends to occur more frequently in African Americans than in whites.[27] The presentation and use of the modified Haschinski Ischemia Score can help differentiate between these two types of dementia.[28]

Treatment of irreversible dementia is directed toward altering neurophysiology or preventing degeneration. The cholinesterase inhibitors tacrine (Cognex) and donepezil (Aricept) are approved for the treatment of Alzheimer's dementia. The effectiveness of these drugs in African Americans seems to be similar to their effectiveness in whites, but clinical trials have enrolled relatively small numbers of African Americans. In patients with multi-infarct dementia, platelet inhibitors such as aspirin have been recommended to prevent progression of disease. Information on the prevalence of the reversible dementias in African Americans is limited.

Depression

Depression, a disorder manifested by depressed mood and/or loss of interest or pleasure in daily activities occurs commonly in older adults. Unfortunately, no well-designed epidemiologic studies of the prevalence of depressive disorders in older African Americans are available. Available data suggest that major depression is less common in African-American elders than among white elders.[29] In fact, suicide rates for older adults are highest among white men and lowest among African-American women. For screening, the Center for Epidemiologic Studies of Depression Scale (CES-D) is one questionnaire that has been used in both African-American and older populations (*Figure 3*).[12]

Another popular brief assessment scale is the Geriatric Depression Scale (GDS).[11] The GDS is a 15-item scale with a sensitivity of 64 percent and a specificity of 95 percent for depression using a cutoff score of 4 in older African Americans.[30] In comparative studies, the GDS had a sensitivity of only 43 percent compared with a rate of 75 percent for the CES-D.[30] However, the short administration time of the GDS makes it an attractive instrument for use in a busy clinical practice. Once depression is diagnosed, considerations in selecting a treatment are similar in both African-American and white elders.

Arthritis

Osteoarthritis, a degenerative process of articular cartilage, is a major cause of morbidity in both African-American and white elders, leading to more than 7 million office visits annually.[31] In a study of African-American elders, 53 to 66 percent had been diagnosed with osteoarthritis.[31] In older African Americans, special considerations in choosing a treatment should include the risk of drug side effects, especially gastrointestinal hemorrhage and nephrotoxicity, and the degree to which osteoarthritis impairs daily function.

Hypertension

As with younger African-American adults, hypertension is a common problem for older African Americans. In persons who are age 60 years or older, hypertension affects approximately 70 percent of African Americans, 60 percent of Mexican Americans and 60 percent of non-Hispanic whites.

Hypertension is a major contributor to the "60,000 annual excess deaths" suffered by African Americans.[32] Because of hypertension, African Americans have a 1.3-fold greater rate of nonfatal strokes, a 1.8-fold greater rate of fatal strokes, a 1.5-fold greater number of heart disease deaths and a fivefold greater rate of end-stage renal disease.[33] However, if adequate therapy is provided, older African Americans can achieve declines in blood pressure similar to those of whites and a lower incidence of cardiovascular disease.

Guidelines for treating hypertension in older African Americans are extrapolated from the general recommendations for special populations. For patients with stage 1 hypertension, without evidence of end-organ damage, an attempt to control blood pressure with lifestyle modification (weight loss, reduced dietary sodium intake, increased physical activity and moderation of alcohol intake) should be tried for at least six months before initiating pharmacologic therapy. For pharmacologic treatment, diuretic agents are recommended as first-line therapy in both African-American and older adults. Also, African Americans, regardless of age, respond better to calcium channel blockers than do whites.[34] Monotherapy with alpha blockers or alpha-beta blockers seems to be equally effective in African Americans and whites; beta blockers and angiotensin-converting enzyme inhibitors may be less effective among African Americans than among whites.

The Center for Epidemiologic Studies Depression Scale

Instructions for questions: Below is a list of the ways you might have felt or behaved. Please tell me how often you felt this way during the past week.

During the past week:	Rarely or none of the time (less than 1 day)	Some or a little of the time (1 to 2 days)	Occasionally or a moderate amount of the time (3 to 4 days)	Most or all of the time (5 to 7 days)
1. I was bothered by things that usually do not bother me.	0	1	2	3
2. I did not feel like eating; my appetite was poor.	0	1	2	3
3. I felt that I could not shake off the blues even with help from my family or friends.	0	1	2	3
4. I felt that I was just as good as other people.	0	1	2	3
5. I had trouble keeping my mind on what I was doing.	0	1	2	3
6. I felt depressed.	0	1	2	3
7. I felt that everything I did was an effort.	0	1	2	3
8. I felt hopeful about the future.	0	1	2	3
9. I thought my life had been a failure.	0	1	2	3
10. I felt fearful.	0	1	2	3
11. My sleep was restless.	0	1	2	3
12. I was happy.	0	1	2	3
13. I talked less than usual.	0	1	2	3
14. I felt lonely.	0	1	2	3
15. People were unfriendly.	0	1	2	3
16. I enjoyed life.	0	1	2	3
17. I had crying spells.	0	1	2	3
18. I felt sad.	0	1	2	3
19. I felt that people dislike me.	0	1	2	3
20. I could not get "going."	0	1	2	3

Figure 3 is adapted from Radloff, L.S. The CES-D Scale: A self-report depression scale for research in the general population. Appl. Psychol. Measure 1977: 1: 385–401. Used with permission.

Cancer

When matched for age, African Americans have greater incidence rates and mortality for certain cancers. The overall five-year cancer survival rate for African Americans is 12 percentage points below that of whites. For 25 primary cancers, African Americans had lower survival rates in all but three. Breast and prostate cancer are two of the leading cancers for which older African Americans show poorer survival rates.

The five-year breast cancer survival rates between 1978 and 1982 were 73.5 to 76.4 percent for white women compared with 60.5 to 64.1 percent for African-American women, despite the lower incidence rates in the latter group. This survival differential is related to the large number of African-American women presenting with lymph node involvement or direct extension of their cancer (stage IIIB), and their lower rates of screening and poorer socio-economic status.[35] By encouraging early detection through mammographic screening, clinical breast examination and breast self-examination, family physicians can intervene to improve the health of African-American women.

Prostate cancer rates are 30 percent higher in African-American men over 65 years of age, compared with white men. Older African-American men with prostate cancer also have lower survival rates than white men, 64 percent compared with 79 percent, possibly because of a later stage of detection. As for screening, African-American men have higher prostate-specific antigen (PSA) levels across all stages, grades and age categories, and are 2.2 times as likely to have values over 10 ng per mL (confidence interval: 1.3 to 3.6).[36] Although controversial, screening with digital rectal examination and PSA level determination in African-American men over 40 years of age may be appropriate.[37]

Prevention

Besides paying attention to breast and prostate cancer in older African Americans, family physicians should also be aware of the need for cancer prevention in this group. Seventy percent of cancer mortality and morbidity is related to major remediable risk factors such as diet, tobacco use and alcohol abuse. Proportionately more African Americans smoke than whites, although whites proportionately smoke more cigarettes per day. Also, the rate of alcohol consumption in older African Americans is predicted to increase over the next 20 years.

Unfortunately, many investigators feel that urban African Americans are one of the hardest groups to reach using traditional education and behavioral techniques to promote lifestyle changes.[38] One factor may be the sense of powerlessness that older African Americans feel regarding

health improvement. This sense of powerlessness leads to depending on someone else (i.e., the physician) to take responsibility for health and poses a barrier to behavior change. Powerlessness also leads to poorer adherence to treatments that require active behavior changes. Educational efforts addressed at alleviating this sense of powerlessness while simultaneously developing healthy behaviors among African-American elders would strengthen the health of the entire community and make the primary care physician's job easier and more fulfilling.

Final Comment

In caring for the increasing numbers of older African-American patients, family physicians should consider the special characteristics and needs of this group. Understanding the differences in detection of disease and impairment can help the physician avoid unnecessary treatment. Remaining vigilant to conditions that occur more commonly among this population allows for more timely treatment. Essential for both of these tasks is the need for physicians to develop a strong doctor-patient relationship that allows older African-American patients to feel comfortable and empowers them to adapt healthier lifestyles.

References

The author thanks Desiree Manning and Margie Vines for assisting in the preparation of the manuscript.

1. A profile of older Americans, 1990. Washington, D.C.: American Association of Retired Persons, 1990.
2. Harel Z, McKinney EA, Williams M. eds. Black aged: understanding diversity and service needs. Newbury Park, Calif.: Sage Publications, 1990.
3. Katz S, Ford AB, Moskowitz RW, et al. Studies of illness in the aged: the index of ADL: a standardized measure of biological and psychosocial function. *JAMA* 1963; 185(12):914–9.
4. Spector WD. Functional disability scales. In: Spilker B, ed. Quality of life assessments in clinical trials. New York: Raven, 1990.
5. Lawton MP, Brody EM. Assessment of older people: self-maintaining and instrumental activities of daily living. *Gerontologist* 1969; 9:179–86.
6. Williams ME, Hornberger JC. A quantitative method of identifying older persons at risk for increasing long term care services. *J Chronic Dis* 1984; 37:705–11.
7. Tinetti ME. Performance-oriented assessment of mobility problems in elderly patients. *J Am Geriatr Soc* 1986; 34:119–26.
8. Kallman H, Kay AD, Zuckerman JD. Gait evaluation in the elderly. *Patient Care* 1990; 24:129–44.
9. Folstein MF, Folstein SE, McHugh PR. "Mini-mental state." A practical method for grading the cognitive state of patients for the clinician. *J Psychiatr Res* 1975; 12:189–98.
10. Pfeiffer E. A short portable mental status questionnaire for the assessment of organic brain deficit in elderly patients. *J Am Geriatr Soc* 1975; 23:433–41.
11. Sheikh JT, Yesavage JA. Geriatric Depression Scale: recent evidence and development of a shorter version. *Clin Gerontol* 1986; 5:165–72.
12. Radloff LS. The CES-D Scale: a self-report depression scale for research in the general population. *Appl Psychol Measure* 1977; 1:385–401.
13. Beck AT, Ward CH, Mendleson M, Mock J, Erbaugh J. An inventory for measuring depression. *Arch Gen Psychiatry* 1961; 4:53–63.
14. Hall JA, Roter DL, Katz NR. Meta-analysis of correlates of provider behavior in medical encounters. *Med Care* 1988; 26(7):657–75.
15. Mouton CP, Johnson MS, Cole DR. Ethical considerations with African-American elders. *Clin Geriatr Med* 1995; 11(1):113–29.
16. Jackson JS, Chatters LM, Taylor RJ, eds. Aging in black America. Newbury Park, Calif.: Sage Publications, 1993.
17. Ferraro KF. Double jeopardy to health for black older adults? *J Gerontol* 1987; 42(5):528–33.

18. Harper MS, ed. Minority aging: essential curricula content for selected health and allied health professions. United States Department of Health and Human Services, Public Health Service, Health Resources and Services Administration. Rockville, Md.: Government Printing Office, 1990; DHHS publication no. HRS-P-DV 90-4.

19. Brangman S. African-American elders. Implications for health care providers. *Clin Geriatr Med* 1995; 11:15-23.

20. Robinson BC. Validation of a caregiver strain index. *J Gerontol* 1983; 38:344-8.

21. Edmonds MK. Physical health. In: Jackson LS, Chatters LM, Taylor RJ, eds. Aging in African American America. Newbury Park, Calif.: Sage Publications, 1993:151-67.

22. Katz S, Downs TD, Cash HR, Grotz RC. Progress in the development of the index of ADL. Gerontologist 1970; 10:20-30.

23. Bohnstedt M, Fox PJ, Kohatsu ND. Correlates of Mini-Mental Status Examination scores among elderly demented patients: the influence of race-ethnicity. *J Clin Epidemiol* 1994; 47:1381-7.

24. Heyman A, Fillenbaum G, Prosnitz B, Raiford K, Burchett B, Clark C. Estimated prevalence of dementia among elderly black and white community residents. *Arch Neurol* 1991; 48:594-8.

25. Schoenberg BS, Anderson DW, Haerer AF. Severe dementia.

Prevalence and clinical features in a biracial US population. *Arch Neurol* 1985; 42:740-3.

26. Crum RM, Anthony JC, Bassett SS, Folstein MF. Population-based norms for the Mini-Mental State Examination by age and educational level. *JAMA* 1993; 269:2386-91.

27. Advisory Panel on Alzheimer's Disease. Fourth Report of the Advisory Panel on Alzheimer's disease, 1992. Washington, D.C.: United States Department of Health and Human Services, Government Printing Office, 1993.

28. Rosen WG, Terry RD, Fuld PA, Katzman R, Peck A. Pathological verification of ischemic score in differentiation of dementias. *Ann Neurol* 1980; 7:486-8.

29. Robins LN, Reiger DA, eds. Psychiatric disorders in America: the epidemiologic catchment area study. New York: Free Press, 1991.

30. Baker FM. Mental health issues in elderly African Americans. *Clin Geriatr Med* 1995; 11:1-13.

31. Schappert SM. National Ambulatory Medical Care Survey: 1992 summary. Division of Health Care Statistics, National Center for Health Statistics. Advance Data 1994; 253:1-20.

32. Birrer RB. Urban family medicine: lost horizon or last frontier? *Am Fam Physician* 1992; 46:1074-6

33. Wassertheil-Smoller S, Apostolides A, Miller M, Oberman A, Thom T. Recent status of detection, treatment, and control of

hypertension in the community. *J Community Health* 1979; 5:82-93.

34. Hypertension prevalence and status of awareness, treatment, and control in the United States. Final report of the Subcommittee on Definition and Prevalence of the 1984 Joint National Committee. *Hypertension* 1985; 7:457-68.

35. Gordon NH, Crowe JP, Brumberg DJ, Berger NA. Socioeconomic factors and race in breast cancer recurrence and survival. *Am J Epidemiol* 1992; 135:609-18.

36. Moul JW, Sesterhenn IA, Connelly RR, Douglas T, Srivastava S, Mostofi FK, et al. Prostate-specific antigen values at the time of prostate cancer diagnosis in African-American men. *JAMA* 1995; 274:1277-81.

37. Woolf SH, Lawrence RS. The physical examination: where to look for preclinical disease. In: Woolf SH, Jonas S, Lawrence RS, eds. Health promotion and disease prevention in clinical practice. Baltimore: Williams & Wilkins, 1996.

38. Fox SA, Stein JA. The effect of physician-patient communication on mammography utilization by different ethnic groups. *Med Care* 1991; 29:1065-82.

Article Review Form at end of book.

What is the greatest risk factor for transmission of HIV in the elderly population? What other STDs are prevalent in the elderly?

Sexually Transmitted Diseases in the Elderly

Deborah A. DeHertogh, MD

Dr. DeHertogh is Associate Clinical Professor in the Department of Medicine at the University of Connecticut in Farmington.

Abstract

Many elderly persons maintain heterosexual and homosexual activity. Therefore, this age group is at risk for all sexually transmitted diseases (STDs), including AIDS. Blood transfusion has remained the most important risk factor for human immunodeficiency virus (HIV) infection in people over 60 years of age because of the long incubation period of the disease. In the future, however, sexual contact is likely to become an increasingly important risk category in older individuals. Older patients with HIV infection may progress to full-blown AIDS more rapidly and have higher mortality rates than younger patients with the disease. Other STDs, such as primary and secondary syphilis, gonorrhea, and herpes simplex, have also been reported in the elderly. [Infect Urol 8(1):5–7, 11 1995. © 1995 SCP Communications, Inc.]

Introduction

Many physicians who are not geriatricians may be surprised by the existence of sexually transmitted diseases (STDs) in the elderly. Unfortunately, ageist attitudes, widespread both in society and in the medical profession, assume that the elderly are not sexually active. As a result, a sexual history is frequently not obtained from an older person. A diagnosis of acquired immune deficiency syndrome (AIDS) may then be missed because the elderly patient was assumed to have no risk factors in the absence of a blood transfusion history. A missed or delayed diagnosis has obvious impact on the proper care of the patient and on the risk of transmission to any sexual partner.

Human Immunodeficiency Virus Infection

Epidemiology

Although human immunodeficiency virus (HIV) infection remains uncommon in the elderly, epidemiologic data show that approximately 10% of AIDS cases occur in persons over the age of 50, 2.4% occur in those over 60, and 0.7% occur in persons over the age of 70.[1] Despite the availability of HIV testing of the blood supply since 1985, blood transfusion still remains the major risk factor in the 1990s for HIV infection in individuals over 70 years of age. This is likely due to the long incubation period for symptomatic HIV infection in persons who were transfused before 1985. Blood transfusion will continue to be a risk factor in older age groups in the future, because they receive the majority of all blood products, and screening is not 100% sensitive. In the future, however, sexual contact (either homosexual or heterosexual) is likely to become an increasingly important risk factor in older individuals.

In 1988, Peterman and coworkers[2] reported a study of transmission of HIV infection to heterosexual contacts of adults with transfusion-associated HIV infection. Many of the couples were "older." Of 80 spouses who had sexual contact with the index patient, 25 were men and 55 were women. HIV antibody was found in two of 25 husbands (8%) and ten of 55 wives (18%). The HIV-infected wives tended to be older (median age, 62 years; range, 27 to 73 years) than the seronegative wives (median age, 54 years; range, 25 to 72 years) and had fewer sexual contacts per month (2.9 vs. 4.6). However, neither of these differences was statistically significant. The investigators speculated that the older women might have a higher rate of infection despite fewer numbers of sexual contacts because of an increased likelihood of mucosal disruption during vaginal intercourse or because of age-associated increased susceptibility to infection. All spouses reported vaginal sexual contact, and only two women reported occasional anal intercourse. None of the seropositive couples had used condoms, diaphragms, or spermicides, and very few had used any contraceptives because most were beyond their reproductive years.

Several points from this study are worth emphasizing:

- Heterosexual transmission of HIV infection does occur, even in older patients.

- Male-to-female transmission of HIV infection is more common.

- Older women appear somewhat more susceptible to HIV infection, perhaps because of postmenopausal thinning of the vaginal mucosa and greater susceptibility to mucosal tears during coitus.

- Older individuals beyond their reproductive years do not use barrier contraceptives such as condoms and are thus afforded no protection against HIV or other STDs.

Table I	Two Retrospective Studies of Older Patients with HIV	
	New York[3]	**Canada[4]**
No. of patients	26	33
Gender		
Male	20	30
Female	6	3
Mean age	64.9 yrs	60.1 yrs
Age range	60 to 75 years	55 to 72 yrs
Risk factors		
Blood transfusion	58%	21%
Homosexual/bisexual activity	19%	67%
Heterosexual contact	15%	6%
Intravenous drug use	4%	0%
Unknown	4%	6%

Clinical Studies

Two retrospective studies provide perspective on the role of sexual activity in the transmission of HIV infection in the elderly population.[3,4] The first was a retrospective study of 26 patients, 60 years of age or older, from North Shore University Hospital in New York.[3] The second study was from Canada and used a retrospective cohort design to compare 33 HIV-infected patients over the age of 55 with 58 HIV-infected patients under the age of 40.[4] The demographic characteristics and risk factors for the patients in each of these studies are listed in Table I.

In the New York study,[3] blood transfusion was the most frequent risk factor (58% of patients), as has been reported by others.[1] In contrast, homosexual/bisexual activity was the leading risk factor (67% of patients) in the Canadian study.[4] However, the Canadian study also showed that older patients were significantly more likely than younger patients to have acquired HIV infection through blood transfusion ($P. < .005$). Six patients (23%) in the New York study developed

malignancies, and 46% died during a mean follow-up period of 15.2 months. The Canadian study reported that older patients were more likely to have AIDS at presentation ($P. < .001$), progressed to AIDS more rapidly ($P. < .002$), and had higher mortality rates ($P. < .001$) than younger patients.

In 1994, results of the National AIDS Behavioral Surveys (NABS) in the U.S. were published.[5] The NABS was conducted from 1990 to 1991 and included responses from approximately 14,000 adults, of whom 3,188 were 50 years of age or older. Ten percent of Americans 50 years of age or older had at least one risk factor for HIV infection identified in the surveys. These at-risk Americans were one-sixth as likely to use condoms during sex and one-fifth as likely to have been tested for HIV infection as a comparison group of at-risk adults in their 20s.

Clinical Manifestations

Dementia is one of the protean manifestations of HIV infection in both the young and old. Several case reports demonstrate dementia as either the initial presenting feature of HIV infection in the elderly or as a complication that developed in an elderly patient with known HIV infection.[6–9] Although HIV remains a relatively rare cause of dementia in the elderly, differentiating HIV-related dementia from Alzheimer's disease or other causes of dementia in the elderly presents a significant diagnostic challenge. Although routine HIV testing in the evaluation of dementia in the elderly may not be appropriate, taking an accurate history for risk factors (including sexual history) should serve as a guide.

Other Considerations

The diagnosis of HIV infection in an elderly patient presents the physician and family with many difficult decisions. One issue is whether to institute antiretroviral therapy, which has significant toxicities, even in much younger patients. In addition, the elderly spouse of an HIV-infected patient may have considerable difficulty coping with the diagnosis, reacting with both anger and fear. Providing care for the patient as he or she becomes progressively ill from the disease is also a challenge. Many younger AIDS patients are cared for by their parents. For older patients, family support may be difficult to obtain.

Primary and Secondary Syphilis

The usual context of syphilis in the elderly is that of an asymptomatic patient with a positive VDRL (venereal disease research laboratory) test at low titer on routine screening blood tests. The diagnosis is then made of late latent or tertiary syphilis as a result of an infection that may have oc-

curred decades earlier. Whether to perform a lumbar puncture to exclude asymptomatic neurosyphilis is often referred to infectious disease consultants. However, it is important to realize that patients who continue to be sexually active into their seventh and eighth decades are also at risk of acquiring primary and secondary syphilis.

Reports of recently acquired syphilis in this age group are rare. In one retrospective study of recently acquired syphilis in patients 60 years of age and older, 35 patients had either primary syphilis (9), secondary syphilis (12), or early latent syphilis (14) reported between 1986 and 1990.[10] The ages of these patients ranged from 60 to 76 years, with a mean of 64.7 years. All but 2 of the patients were men, and the majority (25 of 35, 71%) were black. A detailed sexual history was available for 24 of the 35 patients. No patients reported homosexual activity. Ten male patients had more than one sexual partner within 2 months of diagnosis. Of these, two had at least one symptomatic partner, and one had a partner previously treated for early latent syphilis. Five of these ten patients reported sexual contact with a prostitute. Ten additional patients had only one sexual partner within 2 months of their diagnosis. Two had a symptomatic partner, and three had partners previously treated for secondary syphilis. Four patients reported only one partner within one year of diagnosis, of which one had a partner treated for early latent syphilis. Remarkably, only four patients had a record of being tested for HIV infection. Two of these four patients had HIV antibodies.

Patients with ulcerative lesions from syphilitic or herpetic infections may be at increased risk of acquiring HIV infection,[11] so it is important to offer HIV testing to anyone, regardless of age, who has another STD.

There are two case reports of recently acquired syphilis in two elderly women who had been sexually abused.[12,13] The possibility of sexual abuse should always be considered when evaluating any STD in an elderly patient.

Other Sexually Transmitted Diseases

There is very little published information about the incidence of other STDs such as gonorrhea, herpes simplex, or chlamydia in older age groups. In a Hartford, Conn., study, 13 of the 35 patients over 60 years of age with recently acquired syphilis also had coexisting gonococcal infections, and one patient had genital herpes.[10] In another study, reported from England, STDs were diagnosed in 22 or 73 patients over 60 years of age who presented to the genitourinary department in 1988.[14] These included cervical gonorrhea (one patient), nongonococcal urethritis (six patients), genital warts (five patients), genital herpes (three patients), and five patients positive for treponemal antibodies.

Conclusion

Many older persons continue to be sexually active well into their seventh, eighth, and even ninth decades. Medical personnel need to be aware of this and to become comfortable about routinely asking older individuals about their sexual activity. Otherwise, treatable STDs will remain undiagnosed.

Older individuals themselves need to be cognizant of the fact that their sexual behavior puts them at risk of acquiring STDs. They should take appropriate precautions such as using condoms and not engaging in risky sexual behaviors. Syphilis, genital herpes, and chlamydial infections do not appear to present any differently or to be more severe in the elderly. However, HIV infection in older individuals appears to progress more rapidly to AIDS and death than in younger patients.

1. Ship J. Wolff A, Selik R: Epidemiology of acquired immune deficiency syndrome in persons 50 years or older. *J Acquir Immune Defic Syndr* 4:84–88, 1991.

2. Peterman T, Stoneburner R, Allen J, et al: Risk of human immunodeficiency virus transmission from heterosexual adults with transfusion-associated infections. *JAMA* 259:55–58, 1988.

3. Lichtman S, Dar S, Shepp D, et al: Clinical manifestations of HIV infection in elderly patients. *Clin Res* 2:44A, 1991.

4. Ferro S, Salit I: HIV infection in patients over 55 years of age. *J Acquir Immune Defic Syndr* 5:348–353, 1992.

5. Stall R, Catania J: AIDS risk behaviors among late middle-aged and elderly Americans. *Arch Intern Med* 154:57–62, 1994.

6. Rosenzweig R, Fillit H: Probable heterosexual transmission of AIDS in an aged woman. *J Am Geriatr Soc* 40:1261–1264, 1992.

7. McBride M., Maw R, Dinsmore W, et al: Acquired immune deficiency syndrome in the elderly: Two case reports. *J Royal Soc Med* 85:240–241, 1992.

8. O'Neill D, Coakley D, Walsh J, et al: HIV seropositivity in a geriatric medical unit. *Postgrad Med J* 64:832–834, 1988.

9. Fillit H, Fruchtman S, Sell L, et al: AIDS in the elderly: A case and its implications. *Geriatrics* 44:65–70, 1989.

10. Berinstein D, DeHertogh D: Recently acquired syphilis in the elderly population. *Arch Intern Med* 152:330–332, 1992.

11. Quinn T, Cannon R, Glasser D, et al: The association of syphilis with the risk of human immunodeficiency virus infection in patients attending sexually transmitted diseases clinics. *Arch Intern Med* 150:1297–1302, 1990.

12. Bierman S: The "terrible" question. *JAMA* 253:641, 1985.

13. Luke E: Syphilis in the elderly. *JAMA* 254:1722–1723, 1985.

14. Rogstad K, Bignell C: Sex and the elderly. *BMJ* 299:1279, 1989.

Article Review Form at end of book.

What is the most common factor associated with depression in the elderly? What are the treatment options for depression in the elderly?

Recognizing and Treating Depression in the Elderly

Mark D. Miller, MD

Mark D. Miller, MD is Assistant Professor of Psychiatry and Medical Director, Late-Life Depression Programs, at the Western Psychiatric Institute and Clinic at the University of Pittsburgh Medical Center in Pennsylvania.

The author would like to recognize the guidance and mentorship of Charles Reynolds, III, MD, and Ellen Frank, PhD, as well as the secretarial assistance of Diana Donnelly. The author's own studies were supported by NIMH Grants MH37869, MH43832, and MH52247, and a NARSAD award.

Abstract

A study of community dwellers estimated that 15% of the elderly showed significant depressive symptoms. A smaller subset (1% to 2%) met criteria for a major depressive disorder. In nursing homes, the prevalence of depression can be as high as 25%. Rates of depression in primary care clinics range from 5% to 37%. Stressors such as chronic pain, medical disability, or the death of one's spouse are more commonly seen in the elderly and can result in a reactive depression. In one study, more than two-thirds of suicides in the elderly took place in the context of depression, and 75% of all geriatric patients who completed suicide had seen their primary care physician in the previous month. Antidepressant medication, psychotherapy, and electroconvulsive therapy have all been successful therapeutic approaches in elderly persons with depression. An overview of geriatric depression is presented, with emphasis on the clinical presentation, associated factors, and newer treatment options. [Medscape Mental Health 2(3), 1997. © 1997 Medscape, Inc.]

Introduction

The majority of elderly persons lead active, independent lives and possess the necessary coping skills to adjust to changes in their lives as they age. Guarding against an ageist bias will allow for the greatest objectivity when treating elderly patients. Nevertheless, chronic pain, medical disability, or the death of one's spouse can result in a depressive reaction in any individual, regardless of age, who finds such stressors overwhelming. These stressors are more commonly seen, however, in the elderly. The presence of multiple stressors or the inability to cope can result in an episode of depression.

A consensus conference on geriatric depression was convened at the National Institute of Mental Health in 1991 to pool research efforts to better understand the problem of geriatric depression and to seek improved treatment strategies.[1] On January 20, 1996, a consensus update was held to report and summarize new findings,[2] many of which will be referred to in this text.

We review depression in the elderly, with emphasis on the clinical presentation, associated factors, and newer treatment options that have become available in recent years, based on broad research efforts and a growing body of experience worldwide.

Overview

Incidence

The Epidemiological Catchment Area study of community dwellers estimated that 15% of the elderly showed significant depressive symptoms.[3] A smaller subset (1% to 2%) met criteria for a major depressive disorder. This sample did not include those in nursing homes, where the prevalence of depression can be as high as 25%.[4] Rates of depression in primary care clinics have ranged from 5% to 37%.[5,6]

Depression Is Disabling

Depression is not a normal response to aging, but it remains underdiagnosed and undertreated in geriatric patients. This may be because health care providers are often more focused on medical problems and frequently have lower functional expectations for elderly patients.[5]

Luber and colleagues[7] found that depressed patients at any age require almost twice as many office visits, are more likely to use multiple medications, and have longer stays when hospitalized.[4] In addition, depression in the geriatric population is a highly recurrent disease, with rates of repeat episodes as high as 40% to 80%.[5] Thus, it appears that it is no longer sufficient to relieve the initial depression. Clinicians must be aware of these high recurrence rates and should understand that long-term management of depression is often required.[8]

Depression Can Be Fatal

Suicide rates are the highest among elderly white males and are higher in general among the elderly than in younger age groups (Fig. 1*). More than two-thirds of suicides in the elderly take place in the context of depression, and 75% of all geriatric patients who complete suicide had seen their primary care physician in the previous month.[5] Depressed elderly persons with suicidal ideation (active or passive) have higher depression ratings than depressed elders without suicidal ideation.[9] Any suicidal ideation should be taken seriously, since the elderly are less prone, compared with other age groups, to use suicide talk as a threat to manipulate others.[10]

Medical Comorbidity

Commonly, the hallmark of depression in the elderly is its comorbidity with medical illness. The increased longevity of the elderly in the U.S. has been accompanied by an increase in the rate of attendant chronic medical problems, such as arthritis, chronic pain, or sensory impairment. Quality of life may be compromised by the morbidity associated with these chronic medical problems which, in turn, can contribute to depression.

Depression makes medical illness or physical disability worse, and an increase in medical problems is a risk factor for depression.[11,12] Depression can also make chronic pain feel more intense, and living with chronic pain can contribute to depression.[13,14] For this reason, antidepressant medications are now commonly used to help manage chronic pain syndromes.

Recognizing the syndrome of depression in an elderly patient's list of medical ailments is not always straightforward. It is,

*Not included in this publication.

therefore, not surprising that the diagnosis of depression is often missed in primary care settings. However, when the diagnosis is made correctly and effective treatment is carried out, studies have shown that patients function better even though their underlying medical condition has not changed. For example, Borson and associates[15] reported on patients with chronic obstructive pulmonary disease (COPD) who were depressed. Half the group was randomly assigned to receive nortriptyline, and the other half received a placebo in a double-blind trial. Depression improved only in the nortriptyline group. In addition, self-ratings of anxiety, physical comfort, and functionality also improved in the nortriptyline group, despite no change in the underlying severity of the COPD in either group (Fig. 2*).

In another study of ambulatory elders treated for recurrent depression, Miller and others[11] found no correlation between rates of response to a standard treatment for depression and the patient's level of medical burden. The patients with the greatest degree of medical problems responded just as frequently as did the medically healthier patients. This finding suggests that depression can and should be adequately treated, regardless of the level of comorbid medical condition. Miller and coworkers[16] also demonstrated in another study that depressed geriatric patients showed improvement in self-rated general health scores when treated to remission of their depression, even though there was no change in their actual medical status.

*Not included in this publication.

Clinical Presentation

Somatic Focus

In addition to the hallmark DSM-IV symptoms of major depression outlined in Table I,[17] most notable difference between the clinical presentation of depression in the elderly and in younger age groups is the high prevalence of somatic complaints. Depressed elderly individuals often present with a chief complaint of increased arthritic, abdominal, or headache pain that usually has a core of real pathology but is now perceived by the patient as intensely exacerbated.

Today's elderly are frequently unfamiliar with the manifestations of "depression" or may be unclear about its meaning. Many elderly depressed patients define their problem as an inability to do their usual housework or a lack of motivation rather than a focus on sadness or low mood, particularly if they see no legitimate reason to be sad. These same patients, described as alexithymic (lex = to know, thymos = to feel; thus, "an inability to know one's feelings"), will often show a complete remission of symptoms when appropriately treated for depression.[18] They may still not comprehend the syndrome of major depression; they just know that they now feel improved. Primary care physicians or ancillary health care staff might consider the use of depression-rating scales to help make the correct diagnosis (Table II).

Corroborating History

Obtaining a corroborating history from confidants or family members is highly recommended. The clinician may have to infer a diagnosis based on the family's de-scription of marked changes consistent with depression. For example, family members might describe their elderly mother as having been active in church affairs and walking regularly for fitness, but now she appears to them as dulled; she declines invitations and sits watching television for hours, with no particular interest in what she watches. This marked change in activity coupled with pervasive negativity and listlessness should raise the possibility of depression in the mind of the clinician even if the patient denies feeling sad.

Educating Those Involved

Educational efforts are often required for patients and families when managing depression at any age, but particularly so with depression in the elderly. Treating geriatric depression often requires addressing the concerns of family members as well as managing the patient. Family stressors can include the need to take time off to escort an ill parent to appointments and to otherwise perform double-duty with their own immediate family needs. Finally, there is the specter of old interpersonal conflicts with parents that can potentially be rekindled by the demands of caregiving.

Comorbid Anxiety

In addition to a somatic focus, anxiety symptoms and irritability are also commonly seen in geriatric depression. Particularly in the elderly, patients with agitated depression can present with symptoms of pacing or hand wringing and sometimes with an obsessional focal point such as worry over adequate finances or the perceived threat of cancer.[19]

Psychotic Symptoms

Psychotic symptoms can also accompany depression in the elderly. These are usually negativistic delusions (false beliefs), such as "I feel that I'm dying," or a guilt-ridden perception that punishment is deserved. Hallucinations are rarely involved in psychotic depression, nor are the more bizarre delusions seen in schizophrenia (e.g., feeling under the control of radio waves).[20] The rapid onset of visual hallucinations suggests the possibility of delirium.[21]

Table I DSM-IV Criteria for Major Depression
>=5 of the following symptoms >=2 weeks. At least 1 symptom is:
• Depressed mood
OR
• Loss of interest or pleasure in nearly all activities
PLUS
• Changes in appetite or weight
• Insomnia or hypersomnia
• Psychomotor agitation or retardation
• Feelings of worthlessness or guilt
• Difficulty thinking, concentrating, or making decisions
• Recurrent thoughts of death or suicidal ideation, plans, or attempts
Accompanied by functional impairment

Data from American Psychiatric Association.[17]

Table II	Geriatric Depression Scale	Yes	No
1.	*Are you basically satisfied with your life?	1	0
2.	Have you dropped many of your activities and interests?	1	0
3.	Do you feel that your life is empty?	1	0
4.	Do you often get bored?	1	0
5.	*Are you hopeful about the future?	1	0
6.	Are you bothered by thoughts you can't get out of your head?	1	0
7.	*Are you in good spirits most of the time?	1	0
8.	Are you afraid that something bad is going to happen to you?	1	0
9.	*Do you feel happy most of the time?	1	0
10.	Do you often feel helpless?	1	0
11.	Do you often get restless and fidgety?	1	0
12.	Do you prefer to stay in your room rather than go out and do new things?	1	0
13.	Do you frequently worry about the future?	1	0
14.	Do you feel you have more problems with memory than most people?	1	0
15.	*Do you think it is wonderful to be alive now?	1	0
16.	Do you often feel downhearted and blue?	1	0
17.	Do you feel pretty worthless the way you are now?	1	0
18.	Do you worry a lot about the past?	1	0
19.	*Do you find life very exciting?	1	0
20.	Is it hard for you to get started on a new project?	1	0
21.	*Do you feel full of energy?	1	0
22.	Do you feel that your situation is hopeless?	1	0
23.	Do you think that most people are better off than you are?	1	0
24.	Do you frequently get upset over little things?	1	0
25.	Do you frequently feel like crying?	1	0
26.	Do you have trouble concentrating?	1	0
27.	*Do you enjoy getting up in the morning?	1	0
28.	Do you prefer to avoid social gatherings?	1	0
29.	*Is it easy for you to make decisions?	1	0
30.	*Is your mind as clear as it used to be?	1	0

To administer: If the respondent is unable to read the questionnaire, the items may be asked verbally. All items must be read verbatim; the interviewer must not interpret any item for the respondent even if directly asked what an item refers to. The total score is derived by totaling the number of answers indicated as a "1" (yes) on the 20 unstarred items plus those scored as a "0" (no) on the 10 starred items (answers indicative of a depressive symptom.) A score > 10 indicates the need to evaluate for significant dysphoria.

Reprinted with permission from T.L. Brink, PhD.

Bipolar Disorder and Mania in the Elderly

The prevalence of bipolar disorder or manic depression in the general population is 1%.[22] The diagnosis is usually made by the third or fourth decade of life, and exacerbations can be seen throughout later life, either as frequent mood swings or hovering at one pole of the bipolar spectrum with chronic symptoms, sometimes despite optimal treatment.

Mania or severe depression can present for the first time late in life. In retrospect, a history can sometimes be pieced together that is highly suggestive of a "bipolar spectrum." That is, these individuals were prone to periods of overactivity, recklessness, or foolhardy spending that may have been undiagnosed hypomania, but because their behavior never clearly crossed lines of social taboos, treatment was never considered. These individuals may have suffered from unrecognized depressions as well. For a variety of reasons, such as the stress of an intercurrent medical illness, a course of prednisone, or a cerebrovascular event, the heretofore smoldering symptoms may appear as classic symptoms of bipolar disorder for the first time in later life. It should also be noted that organic causes of mania—such as poststroke, secondary to head trauma, or drug-induced—do exist (Table III*).[23,24]

Factors Associated with Depression in the Elderly

Prior History and Family History

Genetic vulnerability for depressive disorders has been long recognized, although the exact modes of inheritance are unclear. In an elderly person who has had previous bouts of depression, such as during the postpartum period or after stressful transitions (e.g., leaving home, losing a family member), there is a greater vulnerability to depression later in life. An elderly patient with a vague history of mild depression but clear diagnoses of depression in first-degree relatives has a 1.5 to 3 times greater vulnerability for depression than the general population.[25–27]

Aging

There is some evidence that monoamine oxidase (MAO) levels increase with age. The effect of this phenomenon is to metabolize amine neurotransmitters at a faster rate, resulting in a state of relative neurotransmitter depletion, which could increase the risk for depression.[28]

Dementia and Neurodegenerative Process

Depression is sometimes seen in patients in the early stages of dementia as a psychological reaction to the broad implications of being aware of losing one's cognitive capacity.[29] Dementia associated with vascular disease frequently has a depressive component resulting from disrupted neuronal systems that are necessary for the maintenance of mood. Depression has long been recognized as a common sequelae following stroke (26% to 61%)[29] and is one of the diagnostic criteria for multi-infarct dementia on the Hachinski ischemia scale.[30,31] The associated depression seems to be independent of any physical disability that results from the stroke.

In addition, improvements in imaging technology have shown an association between patients with "silent strokes" (hyperintensities or periventricular white-matter lesions on MRI) an higher rates of depression. Disrupted neuronal systems are the likely mechanism linking the high incidence of depression and atherosclerotic cardiac and cerebrovascular diseases.[31]

Zubenko and Moosey[32] reported that patients with Alzheimer's disease who were also depressed had more hallmark pathologic damage (plaques and tangles) in the norepinephrine-rich locus ceruleus region of the brain at autopsy than Alzheimer's-disease patients who were not depressed. These findings suggest that Alzheimer's-disease patients show a biological risk for depression secondary to the degenerative process. Similarly, patients with Parkinson's disease, Huntington's disease, and multiple sclerosis also show a biological risk for depression because of subcortical degenerative processes.[33]

Metabolic Derangements

A thorough history and physical examination along with screening laboratory tests should be standard procedure when evaluating depression in the elderly. Individuals in this age group are more at risk than those in younger age groups for metabolic derangements, some of which are associated with depression. Cyanocobalamine or vitamin B_{12} deficiency,[34] thyroid imbalance in either direction,[35] and electrolyte disturbances are examples of metabolic disruptions that can show in associated mood changes. Delirium can also result from metabolic derangements, and it may present with mood changes that may be missed if it is accompanied by psychomotor retardation rather than agitation.[36]

Medications Associated with Depression

Many medications are associated with depression, including antimicrobials, antihypertensives, antineoplastics, neuroleptics, steroids, hormones, and other miscellaneous medications. A temporal association between the onset of depressive symptoms and institution of a new medication should prompt the reconsideration of the new medication and a switch to a different class. For example, some patients are vulnerable to depression while taking beta-blockers for the treatment of hypertension. The substitution of an angiotensin-converting enzyme inhibitor might resolve the depressive symptoms.

Substance Abuse

Alcoholism and other substance abuse too often go unrecognized in the elderly, who may have maintained their consumption level as they aged but became unable to metabolize or withstand the agent's depressive effects on the central nervous system. The co-occurrence of substance abuse with other psychiatric diagnoses in anxiety and depressive disorders is well recognized. Alcoholism is also an associatd risk factor for suicide.[37] A family history of alcoholism in first-degree relatives conveys an increased risk for depression.

Bereavement

Bereavement is an obvious stressor commonly seen among the elderly. The stress of losing a spouse outranks all others on the Holmes/Rahe scale for depression,[38] although grieving over the loss of any significant person can, in itself, precipitate depression. Symbolic losses include loss of health, appearance, work-related prestige, financial strength, or cognitive abilities.

Depressive symptoms associated with bereavement are too often overlooked by health care personnel as "normal" for the grieving elder. Zisook and Schucter[39] showed that widows often display depressive symptoms 2 years after their loss. Increased substance abuse among the bereaved can also contribute indirectly to depression.

Uncomplicated bereavement and major depression can have many symptoms in common[40] and might be treated with the same therapies. Research has documented the benefit of nortriptyline in ameliorating the vegetative symptoms of depression, although the intensity of the psychological symptoms of grief do not seem to improve as much with nortriptyline alone.[41] The subjective meanings of the loss might require a psychotherapeutic approach for the relief of grief-related depression.[42] The selective serotonin reuptake inhibitor (SSRI) medications are also showing promise as effective agents in this group (Prigerson HE et al, 1996. Unpublished data.) A combined approach is often the most effective, in our experience.

Predisposing Personality Traits

Personality or character traits are formed early in life and remain as interpretive filters of lifelong experience. Certain personality traits or disorders increase the risk for depression. For example, the obsessional businessman who prided himself as a problem-solver may become depressed when he faces a problem he can not fix—even by redoubling efforts (to seek mastery or regain control)—such as an incurable medical problem or the loss of a spouse. Individuals with excessive dependent traits may decompensate and become depressed upon the loss of the organizing personality in their life.[43,44]

Fear of Impending Death

The fear or anguish connected with impending death is depressing for some. Often a collusion takes place within families and, at times, health care workers, to avoid talking about the obvious when death approaches. Appropriately trained counselors, nurses, clergy, and medical students, as well as increasing experience with hospice teams, have provided more opportunities for the depressed elderly to confront this issue directly. The physician may be the best person to broach the subject of impending death openly; to allay fears of an undermedicated, painful death; and to encourage the completion of wills and "unfinished business." Properly documented advance directives can be drawn up in order to prevent unwanted, artificial life extension and to help relieve the fear of impending death that can be depressing for some elders.

Treatment—Antidepressant Medication

SSRIs

Antidepressant medication is the most common therapy for geriatric depression. The newer SSRIs are effective and generally well tolerated by elderly patients. These drugs have largely supplanted the tricyclic antidepressants (TCAs) as first-line agents due to their comparative cardiac safety, ease of use, tolerability, minimal anticholinergic effects, and low lethality in overdose.[45–47]

Not all patients can tolerate SSRI medications, however, because of gastrointestinal side effects (e.g., nausea, bloating, or diarrhea); headaches; and, less frequently, sexual dysfunction. Caution is required when coadministering SSRIs with certain other medications. For example, the SSRIs are powerful inhibitors of the cytochrome P-450 enzyme system. If they are combined with medications such as phenytoin, tricyclics, neuroleptics, theophylline, or warfarin, the blood levels of these concomitant drugs can rise precipitously.[45]

TCAs

The TCAs are effective agents in depression in the geriatric population with a long record of success.

Nortriptyline is the best tolerated and most studied TCA in this patient group.[47] Electrocardiograms must be obtained prior to beginning TCA therapy in the elderly, and anticholinergic effects such as dry mouth, urinary retention, constipation, and orthostatic hypotension must be monitored.

Measuring serum levels of nortriptyline can be an important guide to an adequate dosage. A serum level at the midpoint of the recommended range of 50–150 ng/mL achieves more stable antidepressant response, in our experience, than levels at the lower end of the range (Perel J, 1994. Verbal communication.). Blood levels should be measured also because approximately 5% of the population are slow metabolizers of nortriptyline. These patients may achieve an adequate serum level of nortriptyline on a dosage as low as 20 mg per day and may show toxic levels at regularly prescribed doses.[46]

Alternatives

First-line antidepressant therapy with SSRIs or TCAs is effective in relieving depression in 60% to 70% of geriatric patients.[47] For patients who are unresponsive or intolerant to this first-line therapy, bupropion, venlafaxine, or an MAO inhibitor can be tried alone or, alternatively, with augmentation strategies that include the combined use of TCAs and SSRIs (reducing the dose of TCA is imperative to avoid toxic levels), or as augmentation with lithium, methylphenidate, or thyroid hormone.[48–50] Anxiety symptoms are managed with concomitant benzodiazepines or buspirone, while psychotic symptoms require combined treatment with antipsychotic medication.[47]

Common Mistakes Using Antidepressants in the Elderly

Excessive Initial Dosage

An excessive initial dose of antidepressant medication can cause intolerable sedation. An initial dose of 50 mg per day of nortriptyline might lead the patient to discontinue treatment due to intense side effects. However, beginning with a dose of 10 mg per day with 10 mg increases every 3 to 7 days thereafter achieves the same final dose of 50 mg/day and can result in an effective regimen and a patient adherent to the regimen. The adage, "start low and go slow" is a prudent guideline for the elderly when the goal is to maximize compliance and minimize rapid onset of side effects.

Inadequate Trials of Antidepressants

It is imperative to allow adequate time for pharmacotherapeutic trials before considering a particular regimen to be a failure. Many patients commonly describe receiving four different medication trials in 4 weeks. None of these drug trials is adequate to judge their potential efficacy. A minimum of 4–6 weeks is required to declare that a medication trial has failed.

Failure to Monitor TCA Blood Levels

TCAs such as nortriptyline show a linear dose/serum-level relationship. Nortriptyline has a therapeutic window of 50–150 ng/mL, and a serum level of 80–120 ng/mL is recommended. Declaring that a trial of nortripty-

line has failed without a documented blood level is pure guesswork. In addition, as mentioned earlier, slow metabolizers may become toxic at low doses of nortriptyline, further justifying the use of serum drug levels.

Inadequate Dosage

Several SSRIs are effective at single daily doses that do not require much, if any, titration. This fact has improved the delivery of an adequate dose. Many patients who "failed" a drug trial and were referred to psychiatrists experienced in treating geriatric patients were often not given an adequate dosage. Dosage recommendations for some common antidepressants are summarized in Table IV*.

Maintenance Pharmacotherapy Is Too Brief

To guard against the high recurrence rate of depression in the elderly, the clinician should avoid withdrawing antidepressant medication too soon. Antidepressant medication should be maintained at therapeutic doses for 6–9 months for the first episode of major depression. For a second lifetime episode, continue the medications for at least 1 year. After 3 or more lifetime episodes, consider lifetime maintenance pharmacotherapy.[51] Frank and colleagues[52] reported that in midlife patients, maintenance pharmacotherapy is clearly protective against future episodes in recurrent depression. Preliminary results for a similar study in elderly patients (Maintenance Therapies for Late-Life Recurrent Major Depression) are shown in Figure 3*[53]

*Not included in this publication.

Treatment— Psychotherapy

The NIMH collaborative study (non-geriatric-age adults) reported that psychotherapy was equivalent in efficacy to antidepressant medication for all but the most severe depressions.[54] Many current case reports and prospective studies have clearly illustrated the willingness and ability of the elderly to benefit from psychotherapy.[55–57] Short-term psychotherapy approaches have also been developed for the elderly.[58,59] It has been our research experience that some elderly who ultimately benefitted greatly from psychotherapy were not clear about the process or the benefits—they just wanted to feel better. Having no prior experience, many elderly persons are not sure what psychotherapy is all about, and it may be necessary to educate them about the process.

If the depression occurs in the context of psychosocial stressors, psychotherapy may be all that is necessary to achieve a remission of depressive symptoms in an older person willing to engage in self-reflection. For those with more severe depression that includes a considerable number of vegetative symptoms, such as disorganized sleep or significant weight loss, an antidepressant is also often required. Since depression is always experienced in a social context, with frequent disruption of interpersonal relationships, combined treatment with antidepressant medication and psychotherapy often seems the most reasonable choice. A psychotherapeutic component to treatment strategies can also help ensure adherence to a medication regimen, as well as educate the patient about the symptoms and mechanisms of depression in order to place the patient's social dysfunction in a rational perspective.

The 3-year follow-up study by Frank and colleagues[52] showed that although psychotherapy (interpersonal psychotherapy in this study) was not as potent a protector as imipramine against future episodes of depression (in nongeriatric adults), it was clearly superior to placebo. A similar study with geriatric patients is under way,[53] and Niederehe[60] has recently reviewed the efficacy of psychosocial treatments for geriatric depression.

Treatment—ECT

Electroconvulsive therapy (ECT) is a very effective treatment for depression; it is usually undertaken after several medication trials have failed or when a patient is severely suicidal. In 1938, the question of inducing a seizure as a treatment for depression was explored after it was noted that epileptic patients who were depressed showed a marked improvement in mood after a seizure. Treatment with ECT for depression was found to be successful.[61]

Typically, 6 to 12 ECT treatments are required for an antidepressant response. Maintenance antidepressant medication is begun upon completion. Unilateral ECT causes less memory loss and confusion compared with bilateral ECT and is attempted first. Patients with coexisting dementia are prone to post-ECT confusion and may require a longer time interval between treatments.

Some centers offer outpatient maintenance ECT for patients who cannot be stabilized on antidepressant medication.

A common myth is that ECT causes permanent memory damage. The seizure induced by ECT certainly causes temporary interference with the laying down of new memory, such that patients often have impaired recall of events experienced immediately prior to their ECT treatment. However, long-term follow-up studies have not demonstrated any difference in memory at 6 months after a completed course of ECT, compared with baseline.[62,63]

When to Hospitalize?

Depressed geriatric patients should be considered for inpatient psychiatric hospitalization if they are suicidal, have complex medical problems, are candidates for ECT, show severe psychotic symptoms, or do not have an adequate social support system.[6] A specialized geriatric psychiatry unit is preferred in order to maximize the benefit of a trained multidisciplinary team of psychiatrists, internists, nurses, and social workers to address the patient's needs.

Conclusion

Research, improved awareness, and treatment advances have revolutionized the care of depressed elderly persons in the last 15 years. With current resources and knowledge, optimism has justifiably replaced therapeutic nihilism. The current task at hand is to educate the public in general, and all health care workers in particular, about the availability of effective treatments. Depression should never be considered normal, neither in childhood nor in later life.

References

1. *Diagnosis and treatment of depression in late-life.* Reprinted from NIH Consensus Development Conference Consensus Statement, Nov 4–5:9(3), 1991.
2. Consensus Update Conference: Diagnosis and treatment of late-life depression. *Am J Geriatr Psychiatry* 4:S1, 1996.
3. Blazer D, Hughes DC: The epidemiology of depression in an elderly community population. *Gerontologist* 27:281–287, 1987.
4. Samuels SC, Katz IB: Depression in the nursing home. *Psychiat Ann* 25:419–424, 1995.
5. Lebowitz BD: Diagnosis and treatment of depression in late-life: An overview of the NIH consensus statement. *Am J Geriatr Psychiatry* 4:S1, S3–S6, 1996.
6. Gurland BJ, Cross PS, Katz S: Epidemiological perspectives on opportunities for treatment of depression. *Am J Geriatr Psychiatry* 4:S1, S7–S13, 1996.
7. Luber MP, Alexopoulos GS, Charlson M: *Recognition, treatment, comorbidity and resource utilization of depressed patients in a general medical practice.* Presented at the Annual Meeting of the Society of General Internal Medicine, 1996.
8. Conwell Y: Suicide in elderly patients, in Schneider LS, Reynolds CF, Lebowitz BD, et al (eds): *Diagnosis and Treatment of Depression in Late Life.* Washington, D.C., American Psychiatric Press, 1994, pp 397–418.
9. Szanto K, Reynolds CF, Frank E, et al: Suicide in elderly depressed patients: Is active vs passive suicidal ideation a clinically valid distinction? *Am J Geriatr Psychiatry* 4:197–207, 1996.
10. Osgood NJ: Prevention of suicide in the elderly. *J Geriatr Psychiatry* 24:293–305, 1991.
11. Miller MD, Paradis CF, Houck PR, et al: Chronic medical illness in patients with recurrent major depression. *Am J Geriatr Psychiatry* 4:281–290, 1996.
12. Lyness JM, Caine ED, Consell Y, et al: Depressive symptoms, medical illness, and functional status in depressed psychiatric inpatients. *Am J Psychiatry* 150:910–915, 1993.
13. Williamson GM, Schulz R: Pain, activity restriction, and symptoms of depression among community-residing elderly adults. *J Gerontol* 47:P367–P372, 1992.
14. Parmelee PA, Katz IR, Lawton MP: The relation of pain to depression among institutionalized aged. *J Gerontol* 46:15–21, 1991.
15. Borson S, McDonald GJ, Gayle T, et al: Improvements in mood, physical symptoms, and function with nortriptyline for depression in patients with chronic obstructive pulmonary disease. *Psychosomatics* 33:190–201, 1992.
16. Miller MD, Schulz R, Paradis C, et al: Changes in perceived health status in depressed elders treated to remission of recurrent major depression. *Am J Psychiatry* 153:1350–1352, 1996.
17. American Psychiatric Association: *Diagnostic and Statistical Manual,* ed 4. Washington, D.C., American Psychiatric Association, 1994.
18. Nemiah JC, Sifneos PC: Affect and fantasy in patients with psychosomatic disorders, in Hill O (ed): *Modern Trends in Psychosomatic Medicine.* London, Butterworth, 1970, p. 126.
19. Alexopoulos GS, Meyers BS, Young RC, et al: Anxiety in geriatric depression: Effects of age and cognitive impairment. *Am J Geriatr Psychiatry* 3:108–118, 1995.
20. Lehmann HE, Cancro R: Schizophrenia: Clinical features, in Kaplan HI, Sadock BJ (eds): *Comprehensive Textbook of Psychiatry/IV.* Baltimore, Williams & Wilkins, 1985, pp. 680–746.
21. Lipowski ZJ. Delirium in the elderly patient. *N Engl J Med* 320:578–582, 1989.
22. Weissman JM, Boyd JH: Affective disorders: Epidemiology, in Kaplan HI, Saddock BJ (eds): *Comprehensive Textbook of Psychiatry/IV.* Baltimore, Williams & Wilkins, 1985, pp. 764–833.
23. Greenberg DB, Brown GL: Mania resulting from brain stem tumor. *J Nerv Ment Dis* 173:434–436, 1985.
24. Harsch HH, Miller M, Young LD: Introduction of mania by L-dopa in a nonbipolar patient. *J Clin Psychopharmacol* 5:338–339, 1985.
25. Andreasen NC, Rice J, Endicott J, et al: Familial rates of affective disorder: A report from the National Institute of Mental Health Collaborative Study. *Arch Gen Psychiatry* 44:461–469, 1987.
26. Gershon ES, Berettini W, Nurnberger J Jr, et al: Genetics of affective illness, in Meltzer HY (ed): *Psychopharmacology: The Third Generation of Progress.* New York, Raven Press, 1987, pp. 481–491.
27. Weissman MM, Wickramaratne P, Merikangas KR, et al: Onset of major depression in early adulthood: Increased familial loading and specificity. *Arch Gen Psychiatry* 41:1136–1143, 1984.
28. Robinson DS, Davies JM, Nies A, et al: Relation of sex and aging to monoamine oxidase activity of human plasma and platelets. *Arch Gen Psychiatry* 24:536–541, 1971.
29. Miller MD: Opportunities for psychotherapy in the management of dementia. *J Geriatr Psychiatry Neurol* 2:11–17, 1989.
30. Krishnan KRR, Gadde KM: The pathophysiologic basis for late-life depression: Imaging studies of the aging brain. *Am J Geriatr Psychiatry* 4:S1, S22–S33, 1996.
31. Hachinski VC, Lassen NA, Marshall J: Multi-infarct dementia: A cause of mental deterioration in the elderly. *Lancet* 2:207, 1984.
32. Zubenko G, Moosey J: Major depression in primary dementia: Clinical and neuropathological correlates. *Arch Neurol* 45:1182–1186, 1988.
33. Cassem NH: Depression, in Hackett TP, Cassem NH (eds): *Handbook of General Hospital Psychiatry.* Littleton, Mass., PSG Publishing, 1987, pp. 227–260.
34. Hector M, Burton JR: What are the psychiatric manifestations of Vitamin B12 deficiency? *J Am Geriatr Soc* 36:1105–1112, 1988.
35. Blazer DG: Affective disorders in late-life, in Busse EW, Blazer DG (eds): *Geriatric Psychiatry.* Washington, D.C., American Psychiatric Press, 1989, pp. 369–401.
36. Raskind MA: Organic mental disorders, in Busse EW, Blazer DG (eds): *Geriatric Psychiatry.* Washington, D.C., American Psychiatric Press, 1989, pp. 313–368.
37. Miller, NS: Alcohol and drug dependence, in Sadavoy J, Lazarus LW, Jarvik LF (eds): *Comprehensive Review of Geriatric Psychiatry.* Washington, D.C., American Psychiatric Press, 1991, pp. 387–401.
38. Linn L: Clinical manifestations of psychiatric disorders, in Kaplan HI, Saddock BJ (eds): *Comprehensive Textbook of Psychiatry/IV.* Baltimore, Williams & Wilkins, 1985, pp. 550–590.

39. Zisook S, Schucter SR: Depression through the first year after the death of a spouse. *Am J Psychiatry* 148:1346–1352, 1991.

40. Zisook S (ed): *Biopsychosocial aspects of bereavement (Progress in Psychiatry Series, vol 8).* Washington, D.C., American Psychiatry Press, 1987.

41. Pasternak RE, Reynolds CF, Schlernitzauer M, et al: Acute open-trial nortriptyline therapy of bereavement-related depression in late life. *J Clin Psychiatry* 53:307–310, 1991.

42. Miller MD, Frank E, Cornes C, et al: Applying interpersonal psychotherapy to bereavement-related depression following loss of a spouse in late life. *J Psychother Prac Res* 3:149–162, 1994.

43. Agronin ME: Geriatric personality disorders: Diagnosis, course, and treatment. *Clin Adv Treat Psychiatr Disorders* 10:1, 1996.

44. Kunik ME, Mulsant BH, Rifai AH, et al: Personality disorders in elderly inpatients with major depression. *Am J Geriatr Psychiatry* 1:38–45, 1993.

45. DeVane LC: Pharmacokinetics of the newer antidepressants: Clinical relevance. *Am J Med* 97(suppl 6A):6A–23S, 1994.

46. Pollock BG: Recent developments in drug metabolism of relevance to psychiatrists. *Harvard Rev Psychiatry* 2:204–213, 1994.

47. Schneider LS: Pharmacologic considerations in the treatment of late-life depression. *Am J Geriatr Psychiatry* 4:S1, S51–S65, 1996.

48. Debatista C, Schatzberg AF: An algorithm for the treatment of depression and its subtypes. *Psychiatric Annals* 24(7):341–347, 1994.

49. Flint AJ, Rifat SL: A prospective study of lithium augmentation in antidepressant-resistant geriatric depression. *J Clin Psychopharmacol* 14(5):353–356, 1994.

50. Zimmer B, Rosen, J, Thornton J, et al: Adjunctive lithium carbonate in nortriptyline-resistant elderly depressed patients. *J Clin Psychopharmacol* 11(4):254–256, 1991.

51. Guideline: Continuation and maintenance treatment options: Objectives and indications for continuation treatment, in *Depression in Primary Care: Treatment of Major Depression*, vol 2. US Department of Health and Human Services, Clinical Practice Guideline 5, 1993.

52. Frank E, Kupfer DJ, Perel JM, et al: Three-year outcomes for maintenance therapies in recurrent depression. *Arch Gen Psychiatry* 47:1093–1099, 1990.

53. Reynolds CF, Frank E, Perel JM, et al : Maintenance therapies for late-life recurrent major depression: Research and review circa 1995. *Int Psychogeriatr* 7(suppl):S27–S39, 1995.

54. Elkin E, Tracie SH, Watkins JT, et al: National Institute of Mental Health treatment of depression collaborative research program: General effectiveness of treatments. *Arch Gen Psychiatry* 46:971–982, 1989.

55. Thompson LW, Davies R, Gallagher D, et al: Cognitive therapy with older adults. *Clin Gerontol* 5(3/4):245ff, 1986.

56. Gallagher D, Thompson LW: Effectiveness of psychotherapy for both endogenous and nonendogenous depression in older adult outpatients. *J Gerontol* 38(6):707–712, 1983.

57. Frank E, Frank N, Cornes C, et al: Interpersonal psychotherapy in the treatment of late-life depression, in Klerman GL, Weissman MM (eds): *New Applications of Interpersonal Psychotherapy*. Washington, DC, American Psychiatric Press, 1993.

58. Miller MD, Silberman RL: Using interpersonal psychotherapy with depressed elders, in Zarit SH, Knight B (eds): *A Guide to Psychotherapy and Aging: Effective Clinical Interventions in a Life-Stage Context*. Washington, D.C., American Psychological Association, 1996.

59. Miller MD, Cornes C, et al: Applying interpersonal psychotherapy to bereavement-related depression following loss of a spouse in late life. *J Psychother Prac Res* 3:150–162, 1994.

60. Niederehe G: Psychosocial treatments with depressed older adults. *Am J Geriatr Psychiatry* 4:S1,S66–S78, 1996.

61. Weiner RD: The role of electroconvulsive therapy in the treatment of depression in the elderly. *J Am Geriatr Soc* 30:710–712, 1982.

62. Zorumski CF, Rubin EH, Burke WI: Electroconvulsive therapy for the elderly: A review. *Hosp Community Psychiatry* 39:643–647, 1988.

63. Hay DP: Electroconvulsive therapy, in Sadavoy J, Lazarus LW, Jarvik LF (eds): *Comprehensive Review of Geriatric Psychiatry*. Washington, D.C., American Psychiatric Press, 1991, pp. 469–485.

Article Review Form at end of book.

What are the risk factors associated with osteoporosis? How can osteoporosis be treated?

Update on Primary Osteoporosis

Daniel L. Hurley, M.D., and Sundeep Khosla, M.D.

From the Division of Endocrinology, Metabolism. Nutrition and Internal Medicine Mayo Clinic Rochester, Rochester, Minnesota.

Osteoporosis is the most common bone disorder encountered in clinical practice. It is also one of the most important diseases facing our aging population. The United States alone, an estimated 1.5 million fractures that occur annually are attributed to osteoporosis, and they account for an estimated $13 billion annually. With the projected increase in life expectancy for the global population, osteoporosis and osteoporosis-related fractures have the potential to become an even larger health-care problem in the future. This article focuses on the evaluation and treatment of primary osteoporosis women.

(Mayo Clin Proc 1997;72:943–949)

Osteoporosis is characterized by a decrease in bone mass and microarchitectural deterioration of the skeleton that leads to increased bone fragility and fracture. Common fracture sites are those with pronounced amounts of trabecular bone, including the vertebrae (43%), the hip (17%), and the distal part of the forearm (13%). Other skeletal sites, however, are not immune to bone loss and account for 27% of all osteoporosis-related fractures. The lifetime risk of a white woman sustaining a fracture of the spine, hip, or distal aspect of the forearm is 40%. This incidence is as great as the combined risks of breast, endometrial, and ovarian cancer. The lifetime risk of similar fractures in men is 13%, equivalent to that of prostate cancer.[1]

In the United States, a substantial amount of the estimated $13 billion spent annually for direct medical expenses for osteoporosis-related fractures is for the care of patients with hip fracture. In the geriatric population, hip fracture leads to death in 25% of patients, inability to walk without the aid of some assistance in half the survivors, and long-term confinement to a health-care facility in another 25%. Assessing the indirect expenses and morbidity due to osteoporosis-related fractures relative to time lost from work and functional impairment is difficult.[2]

Pathophysiology

Bone remodeling is a dynamic process that is necessary to provide calcium for extracellular function, to repair and remove old bone, and to maintain skeletal elasticity. The etiology of osteoporosis is multifactorial and is related to factors affecting two distinct bone processes: the acquisition of maximal bone density or peak bone mass that occurs at the end of the third decade of life and the loss of bone beginning during perimenopause and extending into old age (Fig. 1*). Bone loss may occur in either trabecular or cortical bone and results from an imbalance of skeletal remodeling that favors bone resorption. Cortical bone predominates in the shafts of long bones, whereas trabecular bone is concentrated in the vertebrae, ends of long bones, pelvis, and other flat bones.

The less bone mass accumulated during skeletal growth, the greater the risk of fracture later in

Address reprint requests to Dr. D. L. Hurley, Division of Endocrinology, Metabolism, and Nutrition, Mayo Clinic Rochester, 200 First Street SW, Rochester, MN 55905.

*Not included in this publication.

life as bone loss ensues. Important factors that may affect peak bone mass are genetic influences, race, gender, calcium intake, sexual maturation, and exercise. Bone density is greater among black than among Asian or white population groups, and women have less bone mass than men in all three groups.[3] Adequate calcium intake is important during bone growth and consolidation; it can help achieve maximal bone mass and result in fewer fractures with aging.[4,5] Of note, however, recent studies of twins and mother-daughter pairs have shown that heredity may be responsible for up to 70% of peak bone mass and may help to explain the familial aggregation of osteoporosis.[6]

After peak bone mass has been obtained, orderly remodeling ensures that the amount of bone resorbed by osteoclasts is balanced by the amount of new bone formed by osteoblasts.[7] A net loss in bone mass occurs when changes in bone turnover result in increased bone resorption or decreased bone formation. With aging, a protracted slow phase of bone loss occurs in both men and women (type II osteoporosis). For most women entering menopause, trabecular bone loss is approximately 1% per year.[8] A subset of women, however, may have an accelerated phase of bone loss of up to 5% per year beginning at menopause, which may continue for 15 to 20 years (type I osteoporosis). Thus, women have an increased predisposition to osteoporosis with aging, not only because of lower peak bone mass than men but also because of menopause-related accelerated bone loss.[9]

Type I osteoporosis is a syndrome that characteristically affects women early after meno-pause. It results from a disproportional loss of trabecular bone that leads to an increase in painful "crush"-type vertebral fractures, fractures of the distal part of the forearm, ankle fractures, and, occasionally, loss of teeth. Trabecular bone has a greater surface area than cortical bone and is therefore metabolically more active. During accelerated bone loss after menopause, trabecular bone loss is increased threefold, whereas cortical bone loss is only slightly more than normal. All postmenopausal women are relatively deficient in estrogen and have similar sex steroid levels; however, only a small proportion of women have development of type I osteoporosis. Thus, in these women, additional factors may be acting in conjunction with estrogen deficiency. The possibilities include a diminished peak bone mass, increased local cytokine production that enhances bone resorption, impaired bone formation, or some combination of these factors.[10]

In vitro studies have confirmed the importance of estrogen in modulating cytokine activity. The role of cytokines likely varies according to their capacity to either recruit premature osteoclasts (through interleukin [IL]-1, IL-6, and colony-stimulating factor) or stimulate existing osteoclasts (through IL-1 and tumor necrosis factor α). After oophorectomy in rodents, an immediate and pronounced increase is noted in the number of osteoclasts in trabecular bone.[11] This is closely linked with an increase in osteoblast IL-6 production.[12] Murine stromal cells also produce higher amounts of macrophage colony-stimulating factor during a state of estrogen deficiency.[13] Although some studies have suggested that, in humans, estrogen deficiency is associated with increased IL-1 and tumor necrosis factor α production by circulating mononuclear cells,[14] circulating cytokine levels do not seem to differ in normal women versus those with osteoporosis.[15] Thus, in humans, the precise role of cytokines in mediating postmenopausal bone loss remains unresolved. In the past, estrogen was believed to have only an indirect effect on bone tissue; however, a study conclusively demonstrated that human bone cells contain sex steroid receptors and respond directly to the administration of estrogen.[16] Thus, although the precise mediators of bone turnover have not yet been elucidated, evidence is strong that estrogen directly regulates bone turnover and that estrogen deficiency may be associated with alteration in cytokine production.

Age is the most important determinant of bone mass. During the slow phase of age-related bone loss, men and women lose a similar amount of trabecular and cortical bone, an estimated 35% and 25%, respectively. Women lose an additional 25% of trabecular bone and 10% of cortical bone during the accelerated phase of postmenopausal bone loss.[9] Age-related bone loss begins by age 40, occurs at approximately 0.6 to 0.7% yearly, and continues throughout life. Type II osteoporosis, a syndrome characteristically affecting women 70 years of age and older, results from a loss of both trabecular and cortical bone. Its usual manifestation is a deformity of the spine that leads to dorsal kyphosis ("dowager's hump"), multiple "wedge"-type vertebral fractures, hip fractures, and, commonly, fractures of the pelvis, proximal aspect of the humerus, and tibia.

Recent studies indicate that age-related factors may lead to bone loss through impaired renal calcium conservation and secondary hyperparathyroidism.[17] A well-known fact is that postmenopausal women require a higher calcium intake than do premenopausal women to maintain calcium balance.[18] The primary regulator of intestinal calcium absorption is 1,25-dihydroxyvitamin D, the biologically active metabolite of vitamin D. Evidence shows that aging decreases both the renal production of 1,25 dihydroxyvitamin D and the intestinal responsiveness to this metabolite.[19,20] Impaired calcium conservation is the likely explanation for the secondary hyperparathyroidism seen in elderly persons,[20-22] which may lead to functional hyperplasia,[23] parathyroid gland enlargement,[24] and increased bone loss.[25] Recent studies indicate that both the abnormalities of parathyroid hormone secretion and the increased bone resorption are reversible with sufficient calcium intake.[26] An increasingly clear fact is that estrogen deficiency is associated with impaired intestinal and renal tubular calcium absorption that contributes to the negative calcium balance after menopause.[27-30] Finally, an age-related impairment in osteoblast function may also contribute to bone loss in elderly persons.

Diagnosis and Evaluation

The major diagnostic advance in recent years has been the development of practical methods for measuring bone density at clinically important fracture sites. Of the available techniques, dual-energy x-ray absorptiometry is increasingly being used because of its excellent reproducibility (1 to 2%), low radiation exposure (less than 3 mrem), and brief scan time (5 to 10 minutes). A rationale for measuring bone density is to predict the risk of future fracture (Table 1*). Each standard deviation (SD) decrease in bone density approximately doubles the risk of fracture. The World Health Organization convened an expert panel to define osteoporosis on the basis of bone mass measurements. The definition is based on T scores, defined as the number of SD units of the bone density in a specific person that is lower than the reference mean value for a young adult (Table 2*). On the basis of these criteria, bone mineral density measurements can now be used to diagnose osteoporosis even in the absence of fragility fractures. Two bone density measurements would be needed over time to predict a person's rate of untreated bone loss or response to therapy.

Biochemical markers for bone resorption and formation have recently become available (Table 3*) and have the potential to provide prognostic information on rates of bone loss.[31] Several studies suggest that increased levels of biochemical markers indicate accelerated bone turnover and may predict an increased risk of fracture independent of the level of bone mineral density. Currently, however, the ability of these markers to predict the rate of bone loss accurately in an individual patient remains to be established, and the most practical use of biochemical markers is to monitor response to therapy. The enthusiasm generated by the potential usefulness of bone resorp-

*Not included in this publication.

tion markers in clinical practice stems from the fact that changes occur within weeks to a few months after therapy has been initiated, whereas changes in bone density may not be discernible for up to 2 years.

Clinical Manifestation

The development of osteoporosis is insidious. Thus, the clinical manifestation of acute pain associated with fracture is often the first symptom, and it is noted long after significant bone loss has occurred. Patients may misinterpret acute back pain as a muscle or ligament strain rather than as an osteoporosis-related fracture. Fractures may occur with minimal and non-weight-bearing activity; thus, the patient's impression that the pain is not related to a fracture is erroneously reinforced. This is especially true if the pain gradually subsides over time. Chronic back pain can be another feature of osteoporosis, and it also may be incorrectly interpreted as muscle strain or arthritis. Radiographs will help detect deformities due to vertebral, pelvic, and hip fractures, but they are not sensitive enough to diagnose early bone loss in the absence of fracture. As much as 30% of a patient's bone mass may be lost before osteopenia can be diagnosed radiographically.

With the advent of methods to measure bone mass accurately, osteoporosis is no longer a diagnosis established only in older women. Physicians can now identify persons who not only have diminished bone density in the absence of fracture but also have an increased risk for the development of osteoporosis later in life. Nevertheless, the diagnosis of primary osteoporosis as the cause of bone loss is a diagnosis of exclusion. The physician must have a high index of suspicion for certain medical diseases, surgical procedures, and medications that may be associated with the development of osteoporosis. One or more factors causing secondary osteoporosis (Table 4*) can be identified in approximately 20% of women and 40% of men who have vertebral or hip fractures.[32] These patients may have earlier and more severe bone loss due to secondary factors in addition to bone loss associated with aging and postmenopausal estrogen deficiency.

Treatment

The best treatment for osteoporosis is prevention. Bone toxins associated with osteoporosis, such as tobacco smoking and excessive alcohol consumption, should be eliminated. Sufficient intake of calcium and vitamin D is important. A regular weight-bearing physical activity program is encouraged to increase muscle mass and improve balance. Several studies have now shown bone gain in postmenopausal women who are enrolled in a regular exercise program in comparison with bone lost in sedentary control subjects.[33] Finally, estrogen replacement therapy should be considered at the time of menopause (see subsequent discussion).

After a vertebral fracture, skilled physiotherapy and analgesics may help to alleviate acute back pain. Early mobilization is important and can be assisted by gentle massage, heat, and ice to diminish muscle spasm. Although the use of an orthotic device may be helpful when pain limits back movement and ambulation, the use of an orthopedic back brace is rarely needed. Rest may be neces-

sary for patients with extreme back pain but should not be prescribed routinely. Chronic back pain is often caused by repetitive vertebral fracture, muscle strain, and osteoarthritis. Chronic back pain may be substantially alleviated with instruction in proper posture, gait-assisting devices as necessary, and regular back extension exercises to strengthen paravertebral muscles. Although calcitonin therapy (see subsequent discussion) has a reported analgesic effect in the treatment of an acute vertebral fracture, we do not recommend its use before a trial of more conventional analgesic medication and physiotherapy.

Drug therapy for osteoporosis consists of agents that decrease bone resorption and increase bone formation. The only drugs currently approved by the United States Food and Drug Administration (FDA) for the treatment of osteoporosis are the antiresorptive agents, calcium, estrogen, calcitonin, and the bisphosphonate alendronate. Calcium is safe, well tolerated, and inexpensive and may act by decreasing parathyroid hormone secretion. A National Institutes of Health Consensus Development Conference on calcium recently provided recommendations for optimal calcium intake: 800 to 1,000 mg per day during childhood, 1,200 to 1,500 mg per day from age 12 to 24 years, 1,000 mg per day from age 25 to time of menopause or age 65 if estrogen replete, and 1,500 mg per day after age 65 or after menopause if estrogen deplete.[34]

Adequate vitamin D intake is also important. This is especially true for elderly persons who may be housebound or unable to synthesize vitamin D in the skin and who have decreased

intestinal absorption of vitamin D. In the United States, 10% of an unselected group of elderly patients with his fracture and 20% of a group of elderly patients admitted to a nursing home were found to have subclinical osteomalacia.[35] At least 400 IU of vitamin D should be ingested daily. This is the amount in a daily multivitamin and is the standard recommended daily allowance to prevent nutritional rickets in children. A recent French study noted a significant reduction in hip fractures in a large number of elderly women treated with 800 IU of vitamin D and 1,200 mg of elemental calcium daily,[36] although this effect was not seen in a subsequent study when 400 IU of vitamin D was administered to an elderly population that may not have been deficient in vitamin D.[37]

Estrogen has long been the mainstay for preventing and treating osteoporosis. Estrogen receptors are present in bone, and estrogen directly affects bone cell function by inhibiting osteoclastic bone resorption. The effect of estrogen on bone may be mediated by decreasing the production of bone-resorbing cytokines, increasing the production of factors inhibiting bone resorption, or decreasing skeletal responsiveness to circulating parathyroid hormone (or some combination of these factors). Numerous studies have established the effectiveness of estrogen. In general, estrogen increases the mean vertebral bone density by more than 5% and reduces the vertebral fracture rate by 50%.[38,39] Long-term estrogen use reduces the rate of hip fracture by 25% and decreases overall mortality due to osteoporosis-related fractures. Estrogen has been shown to be effective in

*Not included in this publication.

reducing vertebral and hip fractures in women studied up to the age of 75 years.[39, 40] These benefits, however, may be realized only with long-term estrogen use. Bone loss accelerates when use of estrogen is discontinued,[41] and the risk of hip fracture may return to almost baseline after 10 or more years without estrogen therapy. Both oral and transdermal administration of estrogen have proved beneficial in preventing bone loss, and a dose of 0.625 mg of conjugated equine estrogen or its equivalent is effective. The use of lower doses of estrogen may act in synergy with sufficient calcium intake to prevent bone loss, but too few studies have been done to recommend this approach routinely. In addition to reducing fracture rates, long-term estrogen use may also decrease the occurrence of coronary artery disease by as much as 50%.[42,43] Further-more, estrogen use in postmenopausal women improves vasomotor tone,[44] decreases low-density lipoprotein cholesterol, and increases high-density lipoprotein cholesterol.[45,46] The decision-making process for hormone replacement therapy must consider all the risks and benefits of estrogen use, especially each patient's unique risk profile for the development of osteoporosis, ischemic heart disease, and breast cancer.[47] Although risk of uterine cancer is associated with unopposed use of estrogen in postmenopausal women, this risk can be negated with use of a progestational agent in conjunction with estrogen. A progestational agent is unnecessary if a woman has had a hysterectomy.

Bisphosphonates, carbon-substituted analogues of pyrophosphate, are potent inhibitors of bone resorption. These drugs have the potential to become alternatives to estrogen for women in whom hormone therapy is either contraindicated or not well tolerated. Studies of the first-generation biphosphonate etidronate initially indicated that intermittent use of this drug (400 mg daily for 2 weeks every third month) in conjunction with calcium supplementation decreased the rate of vertebral fractures;[48,49] however, these data were not confirmed in follow-up studies. For this reason and because of the potential for impaired mineralization and possible hip fracture with long-term use, etidronate has not been approved by the FDA for the treatment of osteoporosis. Second- and third-generation biphosphonates such as alendronate, tiludronate, and residronate are much more potent and have a greater therapeutic window between the desired inhibition of bone resorption and the unwanted inhibition of mineralization. Alendronate is the first of these newer bisphosphonates to be approved by the FDA for the treatment of osteoporosis. In a large-scale clinical trial, 10 mg of alendronate daily increased bone density in the spine by 8.8% and in the hip by 5.9% over 3 years in comparison with placebo.[50] These findings were associated with a 48% reduction in vertebral fracture rates, and recent data indicate that alendronate therapy can also significantly decrease the rate of hip fracture.[51] Alendronate is generally well tolerated, although some patients have a low but significant rate of gastrointestinal side effects, including gastroesophageal discomfort and, of greater concern, extensive esophageal ulcerations.[52] Thus, preexisting or new gastrointestinal symptoms are a relative contraindication to the use of alendronate. Gastrointestinal absorption of alendronate is extremely poor, and the drug must be administered with water only at least 30 minutes before breakfast or other medications are ingested. In addition, the patient must remain upright after the drug has been taken.

The FDA has also approved the use of alendronate as a 5-mg daily dose for the prevention of bone loss in patients with osteopenia (Table 2*). Nonetheless, until further data are available regarding this treatment strategy, we believe that it may be prudent to reserve the 5-mg dose of alendronate therapy for patients with osteopenia who are not candidates for estrogen replacement therapy and who have significant and ongoing bone loss, as documented by bone density measurements over time.

Calcitonin has been approved in two forms for treating osteoporosis, subcutaneous injection and nasal spray. The nasal form is less expensive, but symptoms of nasal rhinitis may compromise its use. The subcutaneous form may be associated with local skin irritation at the injection site, and systemic effects include nausea and flushing. Some patients may have development of neutralizing antibodies and secondary resistance to calcitonin over time. Calcitonin has been shown to be effective in decreasing biochemical markers of bone turnover and in preventing bone loss in post-menopausal osteoporosis.[53,54] Nasal calcitonin, however, seems to be less effective in preventing bone loss at the hip than estrogen and alendronate. Calcium supplementation should always be provided with calcitonin therapy to prevent the pos-

---

*Not included in this publication.

sibility of inducing secondary hyperparathyroidism.

Sodium fluoride is the only bone formation-stimulating drug that has been widely studied. In two major controlled clinical trials, fluoride at a dose of 75 mg per day substantially increased bone mass but did not significantly decrease the rate of vertebral fractures.[55,56] In contrast, a recent study that used 50 mg daily in a sustained-release form indicated a reduction in vertebral fracture rates over 4 years.[57] Further direct studies of bone in patients receiving 50 mg of fluoride daily in a non-sustained release form indicated increased bone fragility.[58] Thus, the future role of sodium fluoride in the treatment of osteoporosis remains unclear.

Discussion

At menopause, all women should be counseled about the overall risks and benefits of estrogen replacement therapy. Women with premature surgical or early natural menopause have an increased risk of accelerated bone loss and should receive estrogen replacement therapy at least until the usual age of menopause. Treating all perimenopausal women with estrogen to prevent osteoporosis is probably unwise because of the potential side effects of treatment and the high cost of follow-up care. In selecting women who would benefit the most from estrogen treatment, the physician must thoroughly discuss all the potential benefits and risks of hormone replacement therapy. For women who do not choose estrogen therapy for other benefits, such as for the treatment of vasomotor or genitourinary symptoms, measurement of bone mineral density of the hip or lumbar spine will help to determine those at greater risk for future fracture; such women would benefit the most from estrogen treatment. In women with bone densities in the normal range (T score within 1 SD of the normal mean for young adults), estrogen therapy is unnecessary for osteoporosis protection. Those with bone densities in the osteoporosis range (T score more than 2.5 SD lower than the normal mean for young adults) have a high risk of future fracture and should receive estrogen therapy unless contraindications are present. If the bone density is in the low-normal range (T score between 1 and 2.5 SD below the normal mean for young adults), estrogen therapy should be offered. If such women decline estrogen therapy, the bone mineral density should be remeasured in 1 or 2 years, and these women should be counseled about antiresorptive treatment if substantial additional bone loss ensues.

Conclusion

During the past decade, enormous strides have been made in our understanding of the physiology of bone turnover and bone loss, in the development of new techniques to diagnose osteoporosis and predict risk of future fracture, and in the approval of new pharmacologic agents to help prevent bone loss and fracture. Expectations are high for future progress in the prevention and treatment of osteoporosis to help control this major public health problem.

References

1. Melton LJ III., Thamer M, Ray NF, Chan JK, Chesnut CH III, Einhorn TA, et al. Fractures attributable to osteoporosis: report from the National Osteoporosis Foundation. *J Bone Miner Res* 1997;12:16–23.

2. Ray NF, Chan JK, Thamer M, Melton LJ III. Medical expenditures for the treatment of osteoporotic fractures in the United States in 1995: report from the National Osteoporosis Foundation. *J Bone Miner Res* 1997; 12:24–35.

3. Silverman SL. Madison RE. Decreased incidence of hip fracture in Hispanics, Asians, and blacks: California Hospital Discharge Data. *Am J Public Health* 1988; 78:1482–1483.

4. Matkovic V, Kostial K, Simonovic I, Buzina R. Brodarec A. Nordin BE. Bone status and fracture rates in two regions of Yugoslavia. *Am J Clin Nutr* 1979; 32:540–549.

5. Johnston CC Jr, Miller JZ, Slemenda CW. Reister TK, Hui S, Christian JC, et al. Calcium supplementation and increases in bone mineral density in children. *N Engl J Med* 1992; 327:82–87.

6. Slemenda CW, Turner CH, Peacock M, Christian JC, Sorbel J, Hui SL, et al. The genetics of proximal femur geometry, distribution of bone mass and bone mineral density. *Osteoporos Int* 1996; 6:178–182.

7. Rodan GA. Coupling of bone resorption and formation during bone remodeling. In: Marcus R, Feldman D, Kelsey J, editors. Osteoporosis. San Diego: Academic Press; 1996. pp 289–299.

8. Ravn P, Hetland ML, Overgaard K, Christiansen C. Premenopausal and postmenopausal changes in bone mineral density of the proximal femur measured by dual-energy x-ray absorptiometry. *J Bone Miner Res* 1994; 9:1975–1980.

9. Riggs BL, Melton LJ III. Involutional osteoporosis. *N Engl J Med* 1986; 314:1676–1686.

10. Riggs BL, Melton LJ III. Clinical heterogeneity of involutional osteoporosis: implications for preventive therapy. *J Clin Endocrinol Metab* 1990; 70:1229–1232.

11. Parfitt AM, Mathews CH, Villanueva AR, Kleerekoper M, Frame B, Rao DS. Relationship between surface, volume, and thickness of iliac trabecular bone in aging and in osteoporosis: implications for the microanatomic and cellular mechanisms of bone loss. *J Clin Invest* 1983; 72:1396–1409.

12. Manolagas SC, Jilka RL. Cytokines, hematopoiesis, osteoclastogenesis,

and estrogens [editorial]. *Calcif Tissue Int* 1992; 50:199–202.

13. Tanaka S, Takahashi N, Udagawa N, Tamura T, Akatsu T, Stanley ER, et al. Macrophage colony-stimulating factor is indispensable for both proliferation and differentiation of osteoclast progenitors. J Clin Invest 1993;91:257–263

14. Pacifici R, Brown C, Puscheck E, Friedrich E, Slatopolsky E, Maggio D, et al. Effect of surgical menopause and estrogen replacement on cytokine release from human blood mononuclear cells. Proc Natl Acad Sci U S A 1991;88:5134–5138

15. Khosla S, Peterson JM, Egan K, Jones JD, Riggs BL. Circulating cytokine levels in osteoporotic and normal women. J Clin Endocrinol Metab 1994;79:707–711

16. Eriksen EF, Colvard DS, Berg NJ, Graham ML, Mann KG, Spelsberg TC, et al. Evidence of estrogen receptors in normal human osteoblast-like cells. Science 1988;241:84–86

17. Ledger GA, Burritt MF, Kao PC, O'Fallon WM, Riggs BL, Khosla S. Role of parathyroid hormone in mediating nocturnal and age-related increases in bone resorption. J Clin Endocrinol Metab 1995; 80:3304–3310

18. Heaney RP, Recker RR, Saville PD. Menopausal changes in calcium balance performance. J Lab Clin Med 1978;92:953–963

19. Eastell R, Yergey AL, Vieira NE, Cedel SL, Kumar R, Riggs BL. Interrelationship among vitamin D metabolism, true calcium absorption, parathyroid function, and age in women: evidence of an age-related intestinal resistance to 1,25-dihydroxyvitamin D action. J Bone Miner Res 1991;6:125–132

20. Epstein S, Bryce G, Hinman JW, Miller OH, Riggs BL, Hui SL, et al. The influence of age on bone mineral regulating hormones. Bone 1986;7:421–426

21. Forero MS, Klein RF, Nissenson RA, Nelson K, Heath H III, Arnaud CD, et al. Effect of age on circulating immunoreactive and bioactive parathyroid hormone levels in women. J Bone Miner Res 1987;2:363–366

22. Young G, Marcus R, Minkoff JR, Kim LY, Segre GV. Age-related rise in parathyroid hormone in man: the use of intact and midmolecule antisera to distinguish hormone

secretion from retention. J Bone Miner Res 1987;2:367–374

23. Ledger GA, Burritt MF, Kao PC, O'Fallon WM, Riggs BL, Khosta S. Abnormalities of parathyroid hormone secretion in elderly women that are reversible by short term therapy with 1.25-dihydroxyvitamin D$_3$. J Clin Endocrinol Metab 1994;79:211–216

24. Akerstrom G, Rudberg C, Grimelius L, Bergstrom R, Johansson H, Ljunghall S, et al. Histologic parathyroid abnormalities in an autopsy series. Hum Pathol 1986;17:520–527

25. Riggs, BL, Melton LJ III. The prevention and treatment of osteoporosis. N Engl J Med 1992;327:620–627

26. McKane WR, Khosla S, Egan KS, Robins SP, Burritt MF, Riggs BL. Role of calcium intake in modulating age-related increases in parathyroid function and bone resorption. J Clin Endocrinol Metab 1996;81:1699–1703

27. Gennari C, Agnusdei D, Nardi P, Civitelli R. Estrogen preserves a normal intestinal responsiveness to 1,25-dihydroxyvitamin D$_3$ in oophorectomized women. J Clin Endocrinol Metab 1990;71:1288–1293

28. McKane WR, Khosla S. Burritt MF, Kao PC, Wilson DM, Ory SJ, et al. Mechanism of renal calcium conservation with estrogen replacement therapy in women in early postmenopause—a clinical research center study. J Clin Endocrinol Metab 1995;80:3458–3464

29. McKane WR, Khosla S, Risteli J, Robins SP, Muhs JM, Riggs BL. Role of estrogen deficiency in pathogenesis of secondary hyperparathyroidism and increased bone resorption in elderly women. Proc Assoc Am Physicians 1997;109:174–180

30. Khosla S, Atkinson EJ, Melton LJ III, Riggs BL. Effects of age and estrogen status on serum parathyroid hormone levels and biochemical markers of bone turnover in women: a population-based study. J Clin Endocrinol Metab 1997;82:1522–1527

31. Delmas PD. Biochemical markers for the assessment of bone turnover. In: Riggs BL, Melton LJ III, editors. Osteoporosis: Etiology, Diagnosis, and Management. 2nd ed. Philadelphia: Lippincott-Raven; 1995. pp 319–333

32. Khosla S, Riggs BL, Melton LJ III. Clinical spectrum. In: Riggs BL, Melton LJ III, editors. Osteoporosis: Etiology, Diagnosis, and Management. 2nd ed. Philadelphia: Lippincott-Raven; 1995. pp 205–223

33. Kohrt WM, Snead DB, Slatopolsky E, Birge SJ Jr. Additive effects of weight-bearing exercise and estrogen on bone mineral density in older women. J Bone Miner Res 1995;10:1303–1311

34. Optimal calcium intake [Consensus Conference]. JAMA 1994;272:1942–1948

35. Komar L, Nieves J, Cosman F, Rubin A, Shen V, Lindsay R, Calcium homeostasis of an elderly population upon admission to a nursing home. J Am Geriatr Soc 1993;41:1057–1064

36. Chapuy MC, Arlot ME, Duboeuf F, Brun J, Crouzet B, Arnaud S, et al. Vitamin D$_3$ and calcium to prevent hip fractures in elderly women. N Engl J Med 1992;327:1637–1642

37. Lips P, Graafmans WC, Ooms ME, Bezemer PD, Bouter LM. Vitamin D supplementation and fracture incidence in elderly persons: a randomized, placebo-controlled clinical trial. Ann Intern Med 1996;124:400–406

38. Ettinger B, Genant HK, Cann CE. Long-term estrogen replacement therapy prevents bone loss and fractures. Ann Intern Med 1985;102:319–324

39. Lufkin EG, Wahner HW, O'Fallon WM, Hodgson SF, Kotowicz MA, Lane AW, et al. Treatment of postmenopausal osteoporosis with transdermal estrogen. Ann Intern Med 1992;117:1–9

40. Weiss NS, Ure CL, Ballard JH, Williams AR, Daling JR. Decreased risk of fractures of the hip and lower forearm with postmenopausal use of estrogen. N Engl J Med 1980;303:1195–1198

41. Christiansen C, Christiansen MS, Transbol I. Bone mass in postmenopausal women after withdrawal of oestrogen/gestagen replacement therapy. Lancet 1981;1:459–461

42. Grady D, Rubin SM, Petitti DB, Fox CS, Black D, Ettinger B, et al. Hormone therapy to prevent disease and prolong life in postmenopausal women. Ann Intern Med 1992;117:1016–1037

43. Grodstein F, Stampfer MJ, Manson JE, Colditz GA, Willett WC, Rosner B, et al. Postmenopausal estrogen and progestin use and the risk of

cardiovascular disease. N Engl J Med 1996;335:453–461

44. McCrohon JA, Adams MR, McCredie RJ, Robinson J, Pike A, Abbey M, et al. Hormone replacement therapy is associated with improved arterial physiology in healthy post-menopausal women. Clin Endocrinol 1996;45:435–441

45. Kim CJ, Min YK, Ryu WS, Kwak JW, Ryoo WH. Effect of hormone replacement therapy on lipoprotein(a) and lipid levels in postmenopausal women: influence of various progestogens and duration of therapy. Arch Intern Med 1996;156:1693–1700

46. Paganini-Hill A, Dworsky R, Krauss RM. Hormone replacement therapy, hormone levels, and lipoprotein cholesterol concentrations in elderly women. Am J Obstet Gynecol 1996;174:897–902

47. Grodstein F, Stampfer MJ, Colditz GA, Willett WC, Manson JE, Joffe M, et al. Postmenopausal hormone therapy and mortality. N Engl J Med 1997;336:1769–1775

48. Watts NB, Harris ST, Genant HK, Wasnich RD, Miller PD, Jackson RD, et al. Intermittent cyclical etidronate treatment of postmenopausal osteoporosis. N Engl J Med 1990;323:73–79

49. Storm T, Thamsborg G, Steiniche T, Genant HK, Sorensen OH. Effect of intermittent cyclical etidronate therapy on bone mass and fracture rate in women with postmenopausal osteoporosis. N Engl J Med 1990;322:1265–1271

50. Liberman UA, Weiss SR, Broll J, Minne HW, Quan H, Bell NH, et al (Alendronate Phase III Osteoporosis Treatment Study Group). Effect of oral alendronate on bone mineral density and the incidence of fractures in postmenopausal osteoporosis. N Engl J Med 1995;333:1437–1443

51. Black DM, Cummings SR, Karpf DB, Cauley JA, Thompson DE, Nevitt MC, et al (Fractures Intervention Trial Research Group). Randomized trial of effect of alendronate on risk of fracture in women with existing vertebral fractures. Lancet 1996;348:1535–1541

52. de Groen PC, Lubbe DF, Hirsch LJ, Daifotis A, Stephenson W, Freedholm D, et al. Esophagitis associated with the use of alendronate. N Engl J Med 1996;335:1016–1021

53. Reginster JY, Denis D, Deroisy R, Lecart MP, De Longueville M, Zegels B, et al. Long-term (3 years) prevention of trabecular postmenopausal bone loss with low-dose intermittent nasal salmon calcitonin. J Bone Miner Res 1994;9:69–73

54. Overgaard K, Hansen MA, Jensen SB, Christiansen C. Effect of salcatonin given intranasally on bone mass and fracture rates in established osteoporosis: a dose-response study. BMJ 1992;305:556–561

55. Riggs BL, Hodgson SF, O'Fallon WM, Chao EYS, Wahner HW, Muhs JM, et al. Effect of fluoride treatment on the fracture rate in postmenopausal women with osteoporosis. N Engl J Med 1990;332:802–809

56. Kleerekoper M, Peterson EL, Nelson DA, Phillips E, Schork MA, Tilley BC, et al. A randomized trial of sodium fluoride as a treatment for postmenopausal osteoporosis. Osteoporos Int 1991;1:155–161

57. Pak CY, Sakhaee K, Piziak V, Peterson RD, Breslau NA, Boyd P, et al. Slow-release sodium fluoride in the management of postmenopausal osteoporosis: a randomized controlled trial. Ann Intern Med 1994;120:625–632

58. Sogaard CH, Mosekilde L, Richards A, Mosekilde L. Marked decrease in trabecular bone quality after five years of sodium fluoride therapy—assessed by biomechanical testing of iliac crest bone biopsies in osteoporotic women. Bone 1994;15:393–399

Article Review Form at end of book.

What is the relationship between world population trends and the need for eye care and eye surgery? Describe how avoidable blindness can be eliminated in the future.

Blindness and Visual Disability

Seeing ahead— Projections into the next century

Worldwide, there are close to 150 million people with significant visual disability of whom almost 38 million are blind. Many of the major avoidable (preventable and treatable) and unavoidable causes of blindness are ageing-related. This means that the older a person is, the greater the chance of developing such conditions.

The major age-related causes of blindness and visual disability include cataract (which accounts for around 16 million blind people) glaucoma (5.2 million), diabetic retinopathy (around 2 million) and age-related macular degeneration (around 3 million).

These diseases have come to the forefront as the number of people affected by trachoma (about 6 million blind), xerophthalmia (blindness due to vitamin A deficiency) and "river blindness" (onchocerciasis) have been gradually reduced. However, the latter conditions will remain important causes of preventable blindness in some regions of the world. Where they have been endemic in the past, blindness and visual impairment may persist or even increase with ageing, as in trachoma-related blindness.

The number of people who become blind each year is estimated to be in the region of 7 million. Over 70% of these people receive treatment and their vision is restored. Thus, the number of blind persons worldwide is currently increasing by up to 2 million per year. Eighty percent of these new cases are ageing-related.

Demographic trends indicate that the global population will increase from 5.8 billion in 1996 to an estimated 7.9 billion by 2020. While changes in fertility rates over the next two decades may influence these projections, the estimates for the older age groups are expected to be accurate. By 2020, the number of elderly persons (60 years of age and above) will almost double and reach 1.2 billion, of whom more than three-quarters will be in developing countries.

If no additional resources become available, it is projected that, by the year 2020, there will be about 54 million blind people aged 60 and over living in the world, 50 million of them in developing countries. It follows that population ageing presents a major challenge to eye health care providers. This is true globally, but particularly important in the middle and low income countries where demographic changes are likely to outstrip economic progress.

Spiralling Needs and Demands

In view of the demographic and epidemiological transition, the burden of disabling eye diseases and the consequent need and demand for eye care services will increase in absolute terms. The challenge for governments and health care providers will be to meet this demand.

Better education and awareness among communities would break down some of the current barriers to greater utilization of existing services. Available and affordable technologies that provide better quality of eye care will further induce more patients to seek treatment and often at an earlier stage.

Types of treatment such as day surgery, which reduces costs and minimizes patient inconvenience, are also likely to enhance demand, particularly for cataract surgical services.

Finally, due to rapid urbanization, 60% of the populations in developing countries is expected to live in cities or large towns by the year 2020. This will increase the demand for urban-based services. However, in rural areas, a marginalised elderly population may still remain with their needs unmet.

Increasing Costs

Because of increased demand and as a result of the introduction of new technologies, the costs for eye care and surgery are expected to escalate. "Fee for service" and other payment schemes may become common practice in most countries, given the limited national health budgets that will be available. It may, therefore, be necessary to contain costs in developing countries through the transfer of new technologies and adaptation of existing ones.

Equity and Accessibility of Services

One of the future challenges will be to tackle the twin issues of equity and inequality of services. With the growth of market economies, and health care becoming market-oriented, wide disparities in income levels could still be a feature in many parts of the world. It is well known that the burden of visual disability is greatest in economically deprived populations; women and the elderly are generally in the most disadvantaged positions.

Access to eye care for these populations could be ensured through appropriate technological development that renders such care affordable. Some of these cost-effective technologies have already been identified and are currently being applied. The use of low-cost intra ocular lenses (IOL) in cataract surgery is one such example. Because of the transfer of technology to developing countries, the IOL cost has now decreased some thirty fold. Greater efforts will be made to develop and evaluate new low-cost preventive and curative options.

Human Resources and Technology Development

A major challenge in eliminating avoidable blindness in the future will be that of ensuring an appropriately trained and skilled workforce. At present, there is a wide disparity in eye care provider/population ratios between and within countries. With more widespread economic development, this ratio is likely to decrease.

By 2020, a global challenge will be to provide full coverage and improved quality of services for the prevention of blindness and the alleviation of low vision.

Such a challenge calls for a global response from a wide constituency—governments that are convinced that there is much to be gained from investment in eye health, professionals who are conscious of their societal responsibility, as well as nongovernmental organizations and the private sector who are committed to meet this challenge.

It is an opportunity for bilateral, multilateral and intergovernment organizations and institutions to contribute to development through improved health, enhanced wellbeing and economic productivity. To make it happen, informed individuals and their communities need to become active and committed partners in the global response.

For further information, please contact Health Communications and Public Relations, WHO, Geneva (41 22) 791 2532/2584. Fax (41 22) 791 4858.

All WHO Press Releases, Facts Sheets and Features can be obtained on Internet on the WHO home page http://www.who.ch/

Article Review Form at end of book.

What are the warning signs of stroke? What types of treatments are available for stroke victims?

New Success Against Stroke

Prevention, improved therapies help fight this devastating condition.

John Henkel

John Henkel is a staff writer for FDA Consumer.

Rusty Van Sickle considers herself one of the lucky ones.

A victim of two massive strokes in 1993, one of which left her in a three-week coma, the Florida resident has, in her words, "come back." She's at the point where, with some accommodations, she can hold down a job in her field of social work.

"I can drive now," says Van Sickle, 43. "I cook and do home chores. I do many of the things I used to do." But, she adds, hinting at the long road she's had to recovery, "I've had to relearn all of them."

She has lingering effects such as a lack of visual sharpness and skewed spatial judgment. Paralysis on the left side of her body and damage to her brain's balance center keep her confined to a wheelchair most of the time.

But she keeps a positive outlook and admits that her stroke was "not really that bad when you compare it with what others have been through."

Stroke ranks as the third leading killer in the United States, behind heart disease and cancer. More than a half million Americans have a stroke each year, according to the National Institute of Neurological Disorders and Stroke (NINDS). Following a 25-year decline, stroke deaths are now on an upswing. Figures from the American Heart Association show that 158,061 Americans died of stroke in 1995, the latest year for which statistics are available—a 10 percent jump over the 143,769 deaths in 1992.

Some professionals have explanations. "The increase in stroke deaths is linked to the aging of the population and may also be the result of a decrease in the detection and treatment of high blood pressure," says Russell Luepker, M.D., director of epidemiology at the University of Minnesota. He adds that high blood pressure is one of the primary risk factors for stroke, and that about one-third of the

Stroke ranks as the third leading killer in the United States, behind heart disease and cancer.

Americans who have it are unaware.

Stroke also is the most common cause of adult disability. "Millions of people are challenged by the devastating aftermath of stroke," says Jan Breslow, M.D., president of the American Heart Association, adding that up to one-third of stroke survivors need help caring for themselves, 20 percent need help walking, and 70 percent are not able to perform the same job tasks they did before the stroke.

Amid these grim statistics, however, hope is emerging that the devastating effects of stroke can be lessened, possibly reversed, in many cases. Activase (alteplase), a genetically engineered version of the body's own tissue plasminogen activator (t-PA) that can dissolve clots, was approved by the Food and Drug Administration in 1996 for treating the most common type of stroke. It had been approved earlier for treating heart attacks. In clinical trials, Activase boosted recovery odds significantly in selected stroke patients treated within the first three hours of the onset of symptoms.

FDA also has approved the anticoagulant drug Coumadin

"New Success Against Stroke" by John Henkel from FDA CONSUMER, March-April 1998.

(warfarin) for treating patients at high risk of having a stroke, such as those with a heart valve defect or who have suffered a heart attack. Doctors also prescribe low-dose aspirin to their patients who have had previous heart attacks or strokes because studies have shown that aspirin can prevent repeat heart attacks and strokes in these patients. Aspirin is an "antiplatelet" that can prevent the "clumping" of blood platelets that creates clots and triggers heart attacks and strokes. Last November, FDA approved another antiplatelet drug for treating stoke, Plavix (clopidogrel), and for several years, doctors have prescribed the drug Ticlid (ticlopidine hydrochloride), also approved as an antiplatelet.

Several drug treatments, including one designed to stop the rapid death of brain cells following a stroke, are in clinical trials now. Also under study is a spring-like device used to prop open blood vessels after blockages are removed, a therapy that may reduce the chance of stroke.

Medical professionals emphasize that there are at least five risk factors (see box on page 98) that, when treated, can decrease the possibility of stroke. Knowing stroke's warning signs (see box above) and seeking emergency help immediately if they appear can reduce the risk of death or disability significantly.

What Is a Stroke

Sometimes called a "brain attack," a stroke occurs when blood circulation to the brain fails. This cuts off oxygen and can kill brain cells, affecting neurological functions such as speech, vision, coordination, and thought.

Strokes fall into two broad categories: those caused by

Heed Stroke's Warning Signs

From the onset of stroke symptoms, time is precious. Getting emergency help within three hours can mean the difference between severe brain damage and full or partial recovery.

If you have *any* of the following warning signs, call, or have someone call, 911 immediately:

- sudden weakness or numbness in the face, arm or leg
- sudden dimness or loss of vision, particularly in one eye
- sudden difficulty speaking or understanding speech
- sudden severe headache with no known cause
- unexplained dizziness, unsteadiness, or sudden falls, especially in conjunction with the other warning signs.

Occasionally, strokes cause double vision, drowsiness, nausea, or vomiting. Also, because warning signs sometimes may last only a few minutes and disappear, it may be tempting to ignore them. But these "mini-strokes," or transient ischemic attacks (TIAs), could be your body's warning of a future full-blown stroke. So even if the symptoms go away quickly, seek medical help right away.

—J.H.

blood-flow blockage and those caused by bleeding. An *ischemic stroke*, which occurs when a blood vessel in the brain or neck is blocked, is the most common stroke, responsible for about 80 percent of cases. Such blockages may form within a blood vessel of the brain or neck (thrombosis), may migrate to the brain or neck as a clot from another part of the body (embolism), or may result from severe narrowing of an artery in or leading to the brain (stenosis).

Less common is *hemorrhagic stroke*, in which a blood vessel bursts, causing bleeding into the brain or in the spaces surrounding the brain.

Stroke is an equal threat to men and women. It occurs in all age groups and races, though African Americans suffer more severe strokes and have a death rate nearly double that of whites. Scientists have identified a "stroke belt" in the Southeastern states, especially in the coastal plain areas of the Carolinas and Georgia. A study in the May 1997 issue of the journal *Stroke* showed

High blood pressure is one of the primary risk factors for stroke.

that stroke deaths in this Southern region are more than double those of the nation overall in ages 35 to 54. For ages 55 to 74, deaths in the belt are 1.7 times greater. Why? "It could be a wide range of things," says George Howard, professor of epidemiology at Bowman Gray School of Medicine in Winston-Salem, N.C., and lead author of the *Stroke* study. He says possible factors include the region's lifestyle choices such as smoking more or eating more fat and salt.

Though most strokes occur in adults over 40, children also have strokes, though these are typically caused by underlying conditions such as congenital heart disease or sickle cell anemia.

Sometimes young adults between 20 and 40 fall victim. Bill McGarry was a 22-year-old engineer in 1977 when a stroke plunged him into a three-month coma on advanced life-support machines. More than 20 years later, he still has paralysis, blindness, and nagging problems such as greatly reduced mathematical and analytical abilities. Speech therapy allowed him to regain control of his vocal cords. In 1989, he received a master of education degree from the University of New Orleans and began working as a career counselor in 1990. He now lives independently in his own home in Austin, Texas.

The key to this kind of recovery, he says, is to stay focused on getting better and to not lose faith when rehabilitation reaches a plateau. Support from family and friends also is crucial. "Improvement is almost glacial at times," he says. "But it adds up . . . a step here and a second there and eventually you can walk across the room or down to the corner."

Turning the Tide

While strokes like McGarry's continue to cause devastating effects, new treatments now offer the potential for reversing or lessening stroke effects. The conclusion of a December 1996 symposium sponsored by NINDS that brought together experts from medical centers nationwide was that stroke is always a medical emergency. To survive or recover from it requires immediate care and effective responses from everyone in the "chain of care": medical technicians, emergency departments, and doctors. Public education also is crucial so stroke victims and those around them will recognize stroke symptoms and seek help quickly.

Before 1995, the medical community viewed stroke mainly as an "unfortunate medical problem requiring only supportive care and monitoring," writes Paul E. Pepe, M.D., of Pittsburgh's Allegheny General Hospital, in an overview of the NINDS sym-

Control Stroke Risk Factors

The National Institute of Neurological Disorders and Stroke has identified five *treatable* risk factors associated with stroke. Agency officials emphasize that having a risk factor doesn't mean you'll have a stroke. And not having a risk factor doesn't mean you'll avoid a stroke. But your likelihood of having a stroke grows as the number and severity of risk factors increase. Risk factors that can be controlled by medical treatment include:

- **High blood pressure.** This is by far the most important risk factor. Have your blood pressure checked by a qualified professional, and if it is high, seek medical attention to bring it into the normal range. Some over-the-counter (OTC) drugs may cause high blood pressure. For example, phenylpropanolamine (PPA), a widely used ingredient in OTC cough, cold, and weight-loss drugs, is under review because of concerns that the compound, especially in doses beyond those recommended, may elevate blood pressure and increase the risk of stroke. The Nonprescription Drug Manufacturers Association, at FDA's request, is sponsoring a study of PPA in OTC drugs and its possible relationship to an increased risk of stroke.

- **Cigarette smoking.** Studies have linked smoking to the buildup of fatty substances in the carotid artery, the main neck artery supplying blood to the brain. Blockage of this artery is the main cause of strokes in Americans. Nicotine in cigarettes can raise blood pressure, and smoke can make blood thicker and more likely to clot.

- **Heart disease.** Disorders such as coronary artery disease, valve defects, irregular heartbeat, and enlargement of one of the heart's chambers can create clots that may break loose and cause a stroke. Regular physicals will pinpoint treatable problems.

- **History of stroke.** If you experience a "mini-stroke," or transient ischemic attack (TIA), with symptoms that quickly subside, seek emergency help. If you have had a stroke, consult with your doctor about what you can do to avoid a second stroke.

- **Diabetes.** This causes destructive changes in blood vessels throughout the body, including the brain. If blood glucose levels are high at the time of a stroke, brain damage is usually more severe than when glucose is well controlled. Treating diabetes can delay complications that increase stroke risk. (See "Diabetes Demands a Triad of Treatments" in the May–June 1997. FDA Consumer.)

—J.H.

posium. Unless a patient had passed out or was having trouble breathing, the case often was not handled urgently.

Now the stroke-care landscape is changing—albeit slowly—as more emergency rooms adopt policies of treating appropriate stroke patients with the bioengineered clot-dissolving drug Activase. In a dramatic five-year clinical trial sponsored by the National Institutes of Health and concluded in 1995, 624 patients received either intravenous Activase or a placebo within three hours of stroke symptoms' onset. The re-

sult was that 11 percent more of the Activase-treated patients had few or no signs of disability compared to the placebo group.

"One of the keys to the success of [the NIH study] was treating stroke as the true emergency that it is," says Thomas Brott, M.D., clinical investigator at the University of Cincinnati Medical Center, one of the study sites. "The concept that stroke is every bit as serious as heart attack is one that physicians must recognize in order for this new treatment to have widespread benefit."

Activase is indicated only for treating ischemic strokes. So before the drug is used, medical professionals must rule out hemorrhagic stroke by various tests, including a computerized axial tomography (CT) scan, which can indicate hemorrhages through sectional views of the brain.

Despite Activase's promise, it has been slow to catch on as a stroke treatment. In a November 1997 American Heart Association conference, researchers presented findings estimating that of 200,000 stroke patients who might have benefited from the drug, only 6,000 received it. Though some of these patients reached the emergency room too late to get the drug, others were not treated because emergency personnel were not trained or prepared to administer it, the researches say.

Another drug, Coumadin (warfarin), can cut in half the 80,000 strokes that occur each year due to the rapid and erratic heartbeat condition called atrial fibrillation. But it too is underused, according to a study by the Agency for Health Care Policy and Research (AHCPR). Atrial fibrillation makes people more prone to form blood clots in the heart that can lodge in the brain and cause strokes. Though Coumadin can thin blood and keep clots from forming, only a quarter of atrial fibrillation patients undergo the therapy. AHCPR researchers say 50 to 75 percent of all atrial fibrillation patients over 60 should receive this blood-thinning therapy.

AHCPR also has reported on carotid endarterectomy, a surgical procedure that removes fatty plaque from the arteries that carry blood from the heart to the brain. Because carotid artery blockage is a major cause of stroke, the surgery can be beneficial and cost-effective for patients with stroke-related symptoms and a high-degree of blockage. But AHCPR stresses that surgery benefits diminish when applied to patients without symptoms but with known blockages. Identifying blockages in asymptomatic patients can involve expensive and invasive diagnostic methods such as angiography, which carries its own risk of stroke and other complications. For that reason, AHCPR does not advocate large-scale screening of asymptomatic people.

Though stroke occurrence overall is on a slight upswing, there's reason to be hopeful. Medical professionals say it is unlikely that stroke will ever be eliminated completely. But medical weapons such as Activase and Coumadin hold promise to at least help curb the disorder's destructive path.

Article Review Form at end of book.

Why do the elderly typically decrease or moderate their drinking habits as they age? What things correlate with heavy drinking among the elderly?

Alcohol Consumption among the Elderly in a General Population, Erie County, New York

Amy L. Mirand, PhD,
and John W. Welte, PhD

Amy L. Mirand is with Roswell Park Cancer Institute, and John W. Welte is with the Research Institute on Addictions, Buffalo, NY.

Abstract

Objectives. Relatively few studies of drinking among the elderly have been completed despite the growing proportional representation of the elderly in the US population. This study sought to estimate the prevalence of and to observe whether active or health-oriented lifestyles are asso-

Requests for reprints should be sent to Amy L. Mirand, PhD, Roswell Park Cancer Institute, Cancer Information Service, RSC, Corner of Carlton and Elm Sts, Buffalo, NY 14263. This paper was accepted September 19, 1995.

ciated with heavy drinking among the elderly.

Methods. Random-digit dialing telephone interviews were conducted with 2325 Erie County, New York, general population residents aged 60 years or older.

Results. The prevalence of heavy drinking was 6%. Adjusted analyses showed positive associations between heavy drinking and being male, having suburban residency, and currently using cigarettes. Negative relationships were observed between heavy drinking and socioeconomic status, rural residency, and degree of health orientation. Age and level of active lifestyle were not significant contributors to the model.

Conclusions. Of the studied variables, health orientation offers the greatest opportunity to address heavy

drinking among the elderly. (Am J Public Health. 1996; 86:978–984).

Introduction

By the year 2020, the elderly will account for 52 million people in the United States and, with the aging of the baby boomers, about 66 million by the year 2030.[1] The increasing proportion of persons 60 years and older in the population and the trend in increasing life expectancies warrant attention to alcohol problems among the elderly. Yet despite the documented economic impact of such behavior, relatively few studies of problem drinking among this population have been completed.[2]

The longitudinal and cross-sectional studies that have investigated elderly respondents generally show a decline in alcohol consumption with increasing age.[3-11] Various reasons have been advanced to explain this decline.[12] A differential mortality effect may partially explain the declining percentage of drinkers, particularly heavy drinkers, with age seen in cross-sectional studies. However, the observed drinking decline appears in most longitudinal studies as well and thereby supports the proposition that most drinkers indeed lower their consumption with age. It has been offered that the declining prevalence of heavy drinking with age may reflect antialcohol attitudes of Americans influenced by Prohibition. However, the stability of age patterns of drinking since the 1940s depreciates the explanatory value of a Prohibition cohort effect. Also, the drinking decline with age occurs in Western countries that did not experience Prohibition.[12,13]

Elderly respondents commonly cite poor health as a reason for their decreased drinking.[14-16] Also, the Alameda County Aging Study found that good physical functioning in elders is associated with moderate drinking.[17] Yet other researchers have observed that elders who retain their physical capabilities are the most likely to be heavy drinkers.[18,19]

Other frequently given reasons for decreased drinking are changes in socializing patterns owing to maturation, social affiliation with persons who drink less and [14,15] lessened exposure to alcohol-encouraged social circumstances.[10] The antithesis is that an active or leisure-oriented lifestyle may be associated with heavy drinking among the elderly.[20]

An increased concern about health may contribute to reduced alcohol consumption. The Centers for Disease Control's Behavioral Risk Factor Surveys showed that health-enhancing behaviors tend to cluster together; for example, women who exercise and fasten their seat belts are less likely to smoke or drink heavily.[21]

Some studies that have examined drinking among the elderly were based on small samples, clinical samples, convenience or volunteer samples, or samples restricted to men.[3-7,22] Often the elderly were not the major focus of the study, and measurement of study factors was not adapted for use among them. The current study addresses some of these methodological issues while seeking to (1) demographically characterize elderly drinkers, (2) determine the prevalence of heavy drinking among them, and (3) observe whether active and health-oriented life-styles are associated with heavy drinking among the elderly.

Methods

The probability sample of 2325 Erie County, New York, residents aged 60 years and older was interviewed between May 1990 and July 1991 using computer-assisted telephone interviewing[23] The sample was identified by the random-digit dialing of telephone numbers that were stratified into 10 geographic districts within the county by proportional allocation. The sample was generated by attaching a random four-digit suffix to the designated central office code numbers specific to the county. The percentage of completed interviews in each stratum was approximately equal to that of the total telephone numbers in the frame from each district.

Only one elderly resident per household could be included. When a household contained two or more age-eligible persons, one person was randomly selected by means of a random selection chart. Once the selection of an eligible household resident was made, calls were continued until an interview or two direct refusal calls were obtained.

Out of the 8614 households containing an age-eligible potential respondent, 6419 (75%) respondents cooperated sufficiently to make it to the screening question. The main screening question defined a drink as 12 oz of beer, 4 oz of wine, one shot of liquor, or one mixed drink.[24] The respondents were asked if there was ever a time in their lives when they drank, on average, more than two drinks per day. All persons who answered affirmatively were eligible for study participation. Of the 6419 respondents who were screened, 1566 were screened positive, 1189 (76%) of whom granted an interview. Among the 4853 negative screens, one third were selected for participation on the basis of random selection tables. Thus, 3397 were randomized out; of the remainder, 1136 granted an interview and 320 refused. This produced a response rate of 78% (i.e., 1136/[1136 + 320]) for negative screens. The overall response rate was 66% ([1189 + 1136 + 3397]/8614).

The average daily ethanol intake within the past 12 months was estimated by summing the beverage-specific products of the following equation: frequency of intake × number of drinks × ounces per drink × percentage of alcohol by volume.[24] The percentage of alcohol by volume was 5% for beer, 14% for wine, and 45% for liquor. A drink equivalent was defined as 0.5 oz of ethanol. Respondents who drank alcohol beyond just a taste during their lives were termed ever drinkers. Current drinkers drank alcohol during the 12 months before the interview. Heavy drinking was defined as a mean daily intake of more than 1.0 oz of ethanol (more than two drinks per day). This definition is in agreement with that used in a study of men and women aged 60 through 86 in which heavy intake was designated as more than 30 g of ethanol per day, the equivalent of more than two drinks per day.[7] A non-heavy drinker drank an average of no more than 1 oz of ethanol per day during the 12 months before the interview. Abstainers were those who reported no alcohol intake during the 12 months prior to the interview.

Active lifestyle, health-oriented life-style, and socioeconomic status (SES) were composite variables. The active lifestyle variable, which indicated the respondent's degree of social activity and interaction, was adapted from the work of the Rehabilitation Indicators Project.[25] The items were frequency measures of activity, socializing and attendance of various events (e.g., working on a hobby or craft, visiting with a friend or relative, going to a movie). Health orientation, adapted from Walker et al.,[26] measured the extent of engaging in good health practices, with a concentration on exercise, nutrition, and health responsibility (e.g., exercising vigorously, including fiber in the diet, checking oneself for signs of poor health).

SES was derived as a composite of (1) average yearly household income; (2) the highest occupational prestige score (based on "usual lifelong" occupation), designed by the 1980 census occupation classifications,[27] between the respondent and the respondent's partner; and (3) the highest educational level attained between the respondent and the respondent's partner. Ninety-five percent of this sample reported ever being married, and two thirds of the sample were women. Thus, the contribution of the partner to the participant's SES was acknowledged to provide a rational SES assignment, particularly for the generations of women in this elderly sample. The *Health and Daily Living Form Manual* was the source of the medical conditions scale.[28] Respondents indicated whether they were currently experiencing certain illnesses (e.g., diabetes, chronic liver trouble, cancer).

Logistic regression analyses were used to clarify the relationship between heavy drinking and the independent variables observed in bivariate analyses. The independent variables included sex (0 = female, 1 = male), age, race (0 = African American, 1 = White), religion, marital status, place of residence, employment status, church attendance, smoking (0 = no, 1 = yes), number of persons in household, health-oriented lifestyle, active lifestyle, and number of current medical conditions. Dummy variables were used for categorical variables. The odds ratio (OR), an estimate of the relative risk for the dependent variable, was the multiplier for the change in risk for 1 unit of change in the independent variable. To ensure an accurate representation of the population from which the sample was de-

rived, a weight inversely proportional to the selection probability was calculated for each case. The weighted sample size was equal to the true sample size.

Results

Table 1 provides a description of the 2325 elderly Erie County current residents interviewed in the survey. These individuals constituted a representative sample of the county's population aged 60 and older, with minor exceptions.[29] The sample was 66% female whereas the actual population of the county aged 60 and older was 59% female. The census race distribution of the county in the 60+ age range was 6.1% African American, 0.2% American Indian, and 0.2% Asian, compared with the study's 5% African American, 0.3% Native American, and 0.3% Asian. The study's Hispanic designation (1.6%) did not correspond to the census's "Spanish Origin" designation and thus could not be compared with census figures. To avoid numerous empty cells, all subsequent analyses that included race were restricted to African American and Whites. Study members ranged in age from 60 to 94, the mean being 69.5 years.

The demographics by drinking patterns are also shown in Table 1. Seventy-seven percent of the total sample reported ever drinking. Sixty-two percent of the sample—72% of the men and 57% of the women—were current drinkers, and 13% of the men and 2% of the women were current heavy drinkers. The overall prevalence of heavy drinking was 6% and did not vary with race.

A significant decline was observed in the percentage of current drinkers with age (x^2

Table 1

Sample Demographics, by Drinking Status: Erie County, NY, Residents Aged 60 or Older

	Total Sample[a]	Current Drinkers		Current Heavy Drinkers/Total Sample	
		No.	%	No.	%
Total sample	2325	1440	62	135	6
Sex					
Male	779	557	72	101	13
Female	1543	883	57	34	2
Age, y					
60–64	550	370	67	32	6
65–69	669	454	68	39	6
70–74	471	301	64	29	6
75–79	279	154	55	15	5
80+	208	98	47	7	3
Race					
White	2056	1326	64	116	6
African American	102	43	42	6	6
Religion					
Jewish	48	36	75	2	4
Catholic	1171	808	69	67	6
Protestant, evangelical or fundamentalist	332	185	56	20	6
Protestant, not evangelical or fundamentalist	414	248	60	22	5
Other	112	64	57	5	4
None	53	33	62	7	13
Church attendance					
Often/routinely	1541	980	64	71	5
Never/sometimes	780	461	59	66	8
Marital status					
Married	1294	885	68	81	6
Widowed	627	347	55	29	5
Divorced/separated	145	81	56	8	6
Never married	100	62	62	4	4
Socioeconomic status					
High	569	439	77	28	5
Upper middle	567	371	65	33	6
Lower middle	562	323	57	42	7
Low	572	310	54	33	6
Employment status					
Employed	357	263	74	22	6
Retired	1378	901	65	90	7
Disabled	106	47	44	5	5
Homemaker	233	131	56	4	2
Other	54	35	65	1	2

trend = 34.20, $P. < .0001$); however, a concurrent decline in the percentage of heavy drinkers with age was not seen (x^2 trend = 1.03, $P. < .31$). SES was positively associated with current drinking (x^2 trend = 72.61, $P. < .0001$) although no relationship was observed for heavy drinking (x^2 trend = 0.892, $P = .34$). Analysis showed heavy drinking to be negatively associated with level of health-oriented lifestyle (x^2 trend = 9.35, $P = .002$), but likelihood of current drinking was not differentiated by level of health orientation (x^2 trend = 0.65, $P = .42$). An active lifestyle was correlated with current drinking (x^2 trend = 70.80, $P = .002$) but not with heavy drinking (x^2 trend = 2.52, $P = .11$).

The results of the logistic regression analyses are in Table 2*. Main effects with a significant positive association with heavy drinking were being male, having suburban residency, and currently using cigarettes. Negative relationships with heavy drinking were seen with SES, rural residency, and health orientation. Age was not a significant contributor to the model. Comparison of all current drinkers with abstainers revealed the inverse relationship between age and drinking observed by other researchers.[6,7,10,15] Current and heavy drinking shared a negative association with level of health orientation. Unlike heavy drinking, however, current drinking was also associated with religion variables, employment status, and level of active lifestyle. Although an inverse relationship was observed between heavy drinking and SES, a positive association was seen for current drinking.

The presented model reduced the chi-square of the likeli-

*Not included in this publication.

Table 1 continued on next page.

hood of the observed results for heavy drinking by 14% and for current drinkers by 11%, although the chi-square values for comparison with hypothetical perfect models (2384 with 2043 *df* for drinkers; 790 with 2038 *df* for heavy drinkers) remained statistically significant. This report, however, limited its independent variables to demographics and active and health-oriented lifestyles. An analysis reported elsewhere, which included a broader assortment of predictor variables, found drinking patterns earlier in life to be significantly explanatory of current drinking.[30]

Discussion

Because this sample was restricted to persons 60 years of age and older, it was appropriate to use measures of drinking and other behaviors developed for elderly respondents. Generally, studies have not focused on elders and have applied to all participants measures, case definitions, and classifications standardized on the nonelderly. Also, variance in the definition of heavy drinking has made it difficult to state clearly the comparability of study findings. These methodological factors offer a partial explanation for the range of reported prevalence of current drinking among the elderly; that range is between 53% and 96% for men and between 43% and 88% for females.[7,31–33] Moreover, whereas previous literature indicates that 2% to 10% of the elderly population drinks heavily,[7,32,34–36] the current study reports 6% of the total sample to be heavy drinkers. As with the current drinking estimates, the prevalence rates of heavy drinking among men and women are

Table I Continued					
	Total Sample[a]	**Current Drinkers**		**Current Heavy Drinkers/Total Sample**	
		No.	%	No.	%
Residence					
Urban	1114	655	59	68	6
Suburbs	877	588	67	45	5
Rural	196	138	70	10	5
Health orientation					
Low	635	399	63	53	8
Medium	889	561	63	50	6
High	747	484	65	33	4
Active lifestyle					
Low	731	374	51	52	7
Medium	786	525	67	45	6
High	753	544	72	39	5
Medical conditions					
0	371	255	69	19	5
1	605	420	69	39	6
2	544	362	67	37	7
3	325	195	60	18	6
≥ 4	302	154	51	11	4
Persons sharing household					
0	638	354	55	32	5
1	1117	797	71	73	7
2	257	150	58	14	5
≥ 3	116	72	62	3	3
Current cigarette smoker					
Yes	371	257	69	37	10
No	1821	1128	62	87	5

[a]The numbers in each total category and the corresponding percentages represent weighted numbers. Because of rounding errors, the weighted numbers in the status categories do not always equal the total number of cases.

comparable to those reported in a population-based survey similar in design and sample source to the present study.[32]

The observed decrease in percentage of current drinkers with age coincides with findings in previous reports.[11,37,38] However, age was not correlated with the probability of heavy drinking, a finding that has been observed by other researchers as well.[4,39] Persons who continue heavy drinking through old age may be the remainder population exhibiting a survivor phenomenon.[18] Unless these survivors are experiencing a type of threshold phenomenon, a decreasing proportion of heavy drinking due to mortality or morbidity would still be expected across advancing age categories. However, this trend was not observed. Also, in adjusted analyses, the number of current medical conditions did not discriminate heavy drinkers from the remainder of the sample. These findings suggest that heavy drinking is attributable to factors that affect the development and maintenance of drinking habits throughout life and that age is concomitant with these factors rather than a cause in itself.

Just as Smart and Liban[40] observed no significant association between religious participation and probability of alcohol problem symptoms or dependency among the elderly, this study found no significant association between church attendance and heavy drinking. Frequency of church attendance is undoubtedly affected by factors that preclude physical attendance. The presence of a number of current medical conditions and age in the logistic models, however, did not alter the finding. The study did not measure the degree of assimilation of religious structure in the respondents' lives.

The number of current medical conditions was not correlated with heavy or current drinking. The enumeration of these conditions is not a direct measure of quality of life or degree of health, factors that may provide a more accurate assessment of the effect of health status on drinking behaviors of the elderly than do current medical conditions.

Adjusted analyses showed that the likelihood of heavy drinking increased as SES decreased, a relationship that has been reported by other researchers. Glynn et al.[4] reported that lower SES men were twice as likely to drink three or more drinks per day than were higher SES men. Inverse relationships have also been observed between elderly problem or heavy drinking and components of the SES variable such as education.[41]

Present employment was associated with an increased likelihood of current drinking. It is probable that the relationship between current employment status and drinking is a correlate of health and quality of life. Some proportion of the elderly population is excluded from current employment because of illness or disablement, reasons observed in this study to be associated with a decreased likelihood of drinking. The elder subgroup that continues working may be experiencing lower rates of mortality and morbidity than those elders not employed. This "healthy worker effect" coincides with the Alameda County Aging Study, which, as previously noted, found good physical functioning in elders to be associated with moderate drinking.[17]

Previous investigations of health-related practices and health-status outcome have identified low-level alcohol use to be an independent predictor of decreased mortality and morbidity rates.[42–44] Also, low alcohol intake tends to cluster with health-oriented behaviors.[21] On the basis of this clustering effect, it was not unexpected to observe the inverse probability of current or heavy drinking.

Level of active lifestyle is not a significant determinant of heavy drinking. Alexander and Duff[20] found that an active or leisure-oriented lifestyle was associated with current and heavy drinking among the residents of three retirement communities, almost 20% of whom were defined as heavy drinkers who drank an average of at least two drinks per day. The populations of retirement communities, however, are self-selected in that the residents choose a particular environment and assume lifestyles inherent to that environment. Thus, observations drawn from such a sample may not be readily generalizable. Yet, a prosocial tone connected with an active lifestyle, as well as church attendance and current employment, appears to be involved in an explanation of current drinking. In the current study, removal of abstainers from the denominator to distinguish heavy drinkers from nonheavy drinkers revealed an inverse relationship between active lifestyle and heavy drinking (OR = 0.85; 95% confidence interval = 0.47, 1.55).

Adjusted analyses showed urban residency to be associated with an increased probability of heavy drinking while rural residency was negatively related to heavy drinking. The relationship between residence and heavy drinking may reflect the physical availability of alcohol, with urban environments offering greater access to alcohol. Supposition about the effect of residence on drinking, however, is presented cautiously because of the small number of rural heavy drinkers.

Multiple persons in a household may prompt the expectation of increased levels of social factors related to alcohol consumption. Bivariate analyses, however, revealed that respondents living with three or more persons were more apt to report smaller numbers of close friends and relatives, lower SES, and lower active lifestyle levels than respondents living with one or two persons. The current study did not investigate circumstances of living arrangements or quality of relationships. However, the negative relationships seen between the number of persons currently living in the respondent's household and the respondent's drinking patterns suggest that elderly individuals might have multiple housemates for practical rather than social reasons. The lessened emphasis on social aspects may translate into fewer opportunities or encouragement's to imbibe.

The relationship between cigarette and alcohol use is well documented; therefore, it was not surprising to find heavy drinking associated with current cigarette use.[31,41,45] However, no significant association was seen for current drinkers. A probable explanation for this lack of association lies in the nondifferentiation between never and former smokers. The inclusion of questions about lifetime cigarette use would have provided a more accurate assessment of the effect of cigarette use on the probability of current and heavy drinking. Also, a mortality differential by cigarette use within the sample's cohort could result in spurious conclusions about the association between cigarette use and drinking.

Although the population sample was derived from a single geographic area, the county is not so distinct as to severely limit the generalizability of the findings. Erie County is the 13th largest county in the United States.[46] It is principally urban and suburban, dominated by the cities and surrounding suburbs of Buffalo, Tonawanda, and Lackawanna. The distribution of the respondents' usual occupation throughout life (20% managerial/professional, 33% nonprofessional white collar, 11% service, 26% blue collar, 10% lifelong homemaker) reflects the county's history of a diversified economy. The per capita income of Buffalo is similar to that of cities such as Baltimore, Philadelphia, and St. Louis.[46]

Criticisms concerning the validity of questionnaire self-report of alcohol consumption have largely stemmed from comparisons between respondent diary and recall self-reports of alcohol intake. The strength of the criticism about recall reports are tempered, however, by diary study limitations, such as the use of subjective rather than objective assessments of alcohol use, small sample sizes, and samples restricted to alcoholics in a clinical environment.[47–49] In the current study, the use of diaries would have been impractical owing to the accompanying increased cost and time expenditures and the high degree of respondent compliance required over time. In addition, the hypotheses of the study were addressed at the group level of data analysis and did not require the level of individual detail obtained through diaries. Moreover, although concerns have been expressed about the applicability of recall measurements of alcohol use among elderly samples,[50] recall reports have been shown to provide adequate validity and reliability at the group level of analysis when comparative evaluations between recall and diary methods were done among the general population elderly.[51,52]

The use of random-digit dialing to recruit the sample was supported by the fact that elderly persons are more likely to have a telephone than are younger persons.[53] Despite increased random-digit dialing coverage, however, the elderly are less likely to participate in telephone surveys than are other age groups.[54,55] The reported average response rates among the elderly, about 50% to 63%, are significantly lower than those for other age groups.[55–57] In this regard, the study response rate of 66% proved to be above average. There are substantial reasons to believe that nonresponse bias was not a severe biasing factor in this study. As a pilot study for a proposed longitudinal follow-up, we attempted reinterviews with 179 of our original respondents and completed reinterviews with 123 of them. A comparison of the demographics and drinking patterns (from the original survey) of those who were available for a second interview with comparable data of those who were not available showed no statistically detectable differences except that the nonresponders were on average, 2 years older. Moreover, methodological research conducted by the National Institute of Drug Abuse[58] has tended to show that nonresponse is not a serious problem in drinking or drug surveys. When the institute's researchers located and interviewed (using a monetary incentive) a sample of those who had refused to participate in their annual national survey, the refusers proved to be almost identical on demographics and alcohol or drug use patterns to those who had granted an interview initially.

Telephone surveys also tend to over-represent those elderly individuals who are more likely to be highly educated, relatively healthy, and in the younger age groups.[56] Multivariate analyses controlled for the effects of these variables so that slight biases will not effect the statistical significance of other risk factors. Prevalence rates, however, will reflect these biases if they exist in the data.

Empirical research of data quality reveals no large-scale differential response effect by mode of collection (e.g., telephone call, face-to-face interview) that can be attributed to age. Mode differences that have been observed have generally been distributed equally across all age ranges; the elderly are no more susceptible than anyone else to mode effects in terms of level of missing data, response distributions, and number of answers to open-ended questions.[56] The evidence supports the use of telephone interviewing as a viable means of collecting data among the general population elderly.

In conclusion, the profile differences between current and heavy drinkers suggest different etiological mechanisms. However, measurement of current factors may not coincide with the presence or level of factors important in the development, maintenance, and adaptation of drinking patterns before age 60. Of the variables included in this report, level of health orientation offers the greatest opportunity to address heavy drinking among the elderly.

References

1. US Senate Special Committee on Aging, the American Association of Retired Persons, the Federal Council on Aging, and the US Administration on Aging. *Aging America: Projections and Trends, 1991 Edition*. Washington, DC: US Dept of Health and Human Services; 1991; DHHS publication FCoA 91–28001.
2. Adams WL, Yuan Z, Barboriak JJ, Rimm AA. Alcohol-related hospitalizations of elderly people. *JAMA* 1993;270:1222–1225
3. Vaillant GE. *The Natural History of Alcoholism*. Cambridge, Mass: Harvard University Press; 1983.
4. Glynn R, Bouchard G, LoCastro J, Hermos J. Changes in alcohol consumption behaviors among men in the normative aging study. In: Maddox G, Robins LN, Rosenberg N, eds. *Nature and Extent of Alcohol Problems among the Elderly*. Washington, DC: US Dept of Health and Human Services; 1984:101–116. NIAAA Research Monograph 14.
5. Stall R. Change and stability in quantity and frequency of alcohol use among aging males: a 19-year follow-up study. *Br J Addict*. 1986;81:537–544.
6. Fillmore KM. Prevalence, incidence and chronicity of drinking patterns and problems among men as a function of age: a longitudinal and cohort analysis. *Br J Addict*. 1987;82:77–83.
7. Adams WL, Garry PJ, Rhyne R, Hunt WC, Goodwin JS. Alcohol intake in the healthy elderly: changes with age in a cross-sectional and longitudinal study. *J Am Geriatr Soc*. 1990;38:211–216.
8. Mishara BL, Kastenbaum R. *Alcohol and Old Age*. New York, NY: Grune & Straton; 1980.
9. Holzer CE III, Robins LN, Myers JK, et al. Antecedents and correlates of alcohol abuse and dependence in the elderly. In: Maddox G, Robins LN, Rosenberg N, eds. *Nature and Extent of Alcohol Problems among the Elderly*. Washington DC: US Dept of Health and Human Services; 1983:217–244. NIAAA Research Monograph 14.
10. Christopherson VA, Escher MC, Bainton BR. Reasons for drinking among the elderly in rural Arizona. *J Stud Alcohol* 1984;45:417–423.
11. Barnes GM. Patterns of alcohol use and abuse among older persons in a household population. In: Wood WG, Elias MF, eds. *Alcoholism and Aging: Advances in Research?* The Chemical Rubber Co, CRC Press, Inc; 1982:4–15.
12. Stall R. Research issues concerning alcohol consumption among aging populations. *Drug Alcohol Depend*. 1987;19:195–213.
13. Edwards G, Chandler J, Hensman C, Peto J. Drinking in a London suburb: II. correlates of trouble with drinking among men. *QJ Stud Alcohol*. 1972;6:94–119.
14. Cahalan D, Cisin IH, Crossley HM. American drinking practices. New Brunswick, NJ: Rutgers Center of Alcohol Studies; 1969, Monograph 6.
15. Stall R. Respondent-identified reasons for change and stability in alcohol consumption as a concomitant of the aging process. In: Janes CR, Stall R, Gifford SM, eds. *Anthropology and Epidemiology. Interdisciplinary Approaches to the Study of Health and Disease*. Boston, Mass: D. Reidel Publishing Co; 1986:275–301.
16. Johnson LA. *Use of Alcohol by Persons 65 Years and Over. Upper East Side of Manhattan*. Washington, DC: National Institute on Alcohol Abuse and Alcoholism; 1974.
17. Guralnik JM, Kaplan GA. Predictors of healthy aging: prospective evidence from the Alameda County Study. *Am J Public Health*. 1989;79:703–708.
18. Nakamura CM, Molgaard CA, Stanford EP, et al. A discriminant analysis of severe alcohol consumption among older persons. *Alcohol Alcohol*. 1990;25:75–80.
19. Kivela SL, Nissinen A, Punsar S, Puska P, Karvonen M. Determinants and predictors of heavy alcohol consumption among aging Finnish men. *Compr Gerontol [B]*. 1988;2:103–109.
20. Alexander F, Duff RW. Drinking in retirement communities. *J Am Soc Aging*. 1988;12(4):58–62.
21. Bradstock K, Forman MR, Binkin NJ, et al. Alcohol use and health behavior lifestyles among US women: the Behavioral Risk Factor Surveys. *Addict Behav*. 1988;13:61–71.
22. Hurt RD, Finlayson RE, Morse RM, Davis LJ. Alcoholism in elderly persons: medical aspects and prognosis of 216 inpatients. *Mayo Clin Proc*. 1988;63:753–760.
23. Welte JW, Mirand AL. *Alcohol Use by the Elderly: Patterns and Correlates. A Report on the Erie County Elder Drinking Survey*. Buffalo, NY: Research Institute on Addictions; 1992.
24. Russell M, Welte JW, Barnes GM. Quantity-frequency measures of alcohol consumption: beverage-specific vs global questions. *Br J Addict*. 1990;86:409–417.
25. Brown M, Diller L, Fordyce W, Jacobs D, Gordon W. Rehabilitation indicators; their nature and uses for assessment. In: Bolton B, Cook DW. eds. *Rehabilitation Client Assessment*. Baltimore, Md: University Park Press; 1980:102–117.
26. Walker SN, Sechrist KR, Pender NJ. The health-promoting lifestyle profile: development and psychometric characteristics. *Nurs Res*. 1987;36:76–81.

Acknowledgement: This work was supported by grant #90–AR–0122 from the Administration on Aging, US Dept of Health and Human Services.

27. Stevens G, Cho JH. Socioeconomic indexes and the new 1980 census occupational classification scheme. *Soc Sci Res.* 1985;14:142–168.

28. Moos RH, Cronkite RC, Billings AG, Finney JW. *Health and Daily Living Form Manual.* Veterans Administration and Stanford University Medical Centers; 1983.

29. *1980 Census of Population and Housing: Census Tracts, Buffalo, NY, Standard Metropolitan Statistical Area.* Washington DC: US Bureau of the Census; 1983. PHC 80–2–106.

30. Welte JW, Mirand AL. Lifetime drinking patterns of elders from a general population survey. *Drug Alcohol Depend.* 1994;35:133–140.

31. Suisky SI, Jacques PF, Otradovec CL, Hartz SC, Russell RM. Descriptors of alcohol consumption among noninstitutionalized nonalcoholic elderly. *J Am Coll Nutr.* 1990;9:326–331.

32. Barnes GM. Alcohol use among older persons: findings from a western New York State general population survey. *J Am Geriatr Soc.* 1979;27:244–250.

33. Bridgewater R, Leigh S, James OFW, Potter JF. Alcohol consumption and dependence in elderly patients in an urban community. *Br Med J.* 1987;295:884–885.

34. Molgaard CA, Nakumura CM, Stanford EP, Peddecord KM, Morton DJ. Prevalence of alcohol consumption among older persons. *J Community Health.* 1990;15:239–251.

35. Schuckit MA, Pastor PA. The elderly as a unique population: alcoholism. *Alcohol: Clin Exp Res.* 1978;2:31–38.

36. Jinks MJ, Raschko RR. A profile of alcohol and prescription drug abuse in a high-risk community-based elderly population. *DICP, Ann Pharmacother.* 1990;24:971–975.

37. Hilton ME. Trends in US drinking patterns: further evidence from the past 20 years. *Br J Addict.* 1988;83:269–278.

38. Johnson P, Armor DJ, Polich S, Stambul H. *US Adult Drinking Practices: Time Trends, Social Correlates and Sex Roles.* Santa Monica, Calif: Rand Corp; 1977.

39. Temple MT, Leino EV. Long-term outcomes of drinking: a 20-year longitudinal study of men. *Br J Addict.* 1989;84:889–899.

40. Smart RG, Liban CB. Predictors of problem drinking among elderly, middle-aged and youthful drinkers. *J Psychoactive Drugs.* 1981;13:153–163.

41. Klatsky AL, Friedman GD, Siegelaub AB, Gerard MJ. Alcohol consumption among White, Black, or Oriental men and women: Kaiser Permanente multiphasic health examination data. *Am J Epidemiol.* 1977;105:311–323.

42. Wingard DL, Berkman LF, Brand RJ. A multivariate analysis of health-related practices—a nine-year mortality follow-up of the Alameda County Study. *Am J Epidemiol.* 1982;116:765–775.

43. Belloc NB, Breslow L. Relationship of physical health status and health practices. *Prev Med.* 1972;1:409–421.

44. Benfante R, Reed D, Brody J. Biological and social predictors of health in an aging cohort. *J Chronic Dis.* 1985;38:385–395.

45. *Smoking and Health: A Report of the Surgeon General.* Washington, DC: US Dept of Health and Human Services, Public Health Service; 1979:12–39.

46. *County and City Data Book*, 1988. Washington, DC: US Bureau of the Census; 1988.

47. Redman S, Sanson-Fisher RW, Wilkinson C, Fahey PP. Gibberd RW. Agreement between two measures of alcohol consumption. *J Stud Alcohol.* 1987;48:104–108.

48. Uchalik DC. A comparison of questionnaire and self-monitored reports of alcohol intake in a nonalcoholic population. *Addict Behav.* 1979;4:409–413.

49. Watson CG, Tilleskjor C, Hoodecheck-Schow EA, Pucel J, Jacobs L. Do alcoholics give valid self-reports? *J Stud Alcohol.* 1984;45:344–348.

50. Graham K. Identifying and measuring alcohol abuse among the elderly: serious problems with existing instrumentation. *J Stud Alcohol.* 1986;47:322–326.

51. Tucker JA, Gavornik MG, Vuchinich RE, Rudd EJ, Harris CV. Predicting the drinking behavior of older adults from questionnaire measures of alcohol consumption. *Addict Behav.* 1989;14:655–658.

52. Samo JA, Tucker JA, Vuchinich RE. Agreement between self-monitoring, recall, and collateral observation measures of alcohol consumption in older adults. *Behav Assess.* 1989;11:391–409.

53. Thornberry OT. Methodological issues in random digit dialed surveys of the elderly. Paper presented at the 110th Annual Meeting of the American Public Health Association, November 1982; Montreal, Canada. Cited by: Herzog AR, Kulka RA. Telephone and mail surveys with older populations: a methodological overview. in: Lawton MP, Herzog AR, eds. *Special Research Methods for Gerontology.* Amityville, NY: Baywood Publishing Co, Inc: 1989:63–89.

54. Friedman M, Wasserman IM. Characteristics of respondents and non-respondents in a telephone survey study of elderly consumers. *Psychol Rep.* 1978;42:714.

55. Weaver CN, Holmes SL, Glenn ND. Some characteristics of inaccessible respondents in a telephone survey. *J Appl Psychol.* 1975;60:260–262.

56. Herzog AR, Rodgers WL, Kulka RA. Interviewing older adults: a comparison of telephone and face-to-face modalities. *Public Opinion Q.* 1983;47:405–418.

57. Massey JT, Barker PR, Hsiung S. An investigation of response in a telephone survey. *Proceedings of the Section on Survey Research Methods.* American Statistical Association; 1981:426–431.

58. Turner CF, Lessler JT, Gfroerer JC. *Survey Measurement of Drug Use—Methodological Studies.* Washington, DC: US Dept of Health and Human Services; 1992.

Article Review Form at end of book.

WiseGuide Wrap-Up

- Some conditions prevalent among the elderly will have a vast impact on society due to the increase in numbers of elderly.

- Some conditions not typically associated with the elderly include STDs and depression.

- Prevention is just as important with the elderly as it is with younger people.

R.E.A.L. Sites

This list provides a print preview of typical **coursewise** R.E.A.L. sites. There are over 100 such sites at the **courselinks**™ site. The danger in printing URLs is that web sites can change overnight. As we went to press, these sites were functional using the URLs provided. If you come across one that isn't, please let us know via email to: webmaster@coursewise.com. Use your Passport to access the most current list of R.E.A.L. sites at the **courselinks**™ site.

Site name: Alzheimer's Disease Education and Referral Center (ADEAR)

URL: http://www.alzheimers.org/

Why is it R.E.A.L.? ADEAR is a service of the National Institute on Aging that supplies information on Alzheimer's and related dementias. This site includes specific Alzheimer's disease publications including those online and a list of many free publications that can be ordered by mail.

Key topics: Alzheimer's disease, dementia

Activity: Go to the "Calendar of Events" page. Suggest conferences to attend.

Site name: American Cancer Society

URL: http://www.cancer.org/

Why is it R.E.A.L.? This is a reliable place to go for cancer information. The cancer information section is very thorough and includes information on specific cancers, statistics, patient and family information, alternative therapies, and guidelines for prevention and detection. You can also access information on research and progress, donations and memorials to the Cancer Society, and media services.

Key topic: immune system

Activity: Type in "aging" in the "Search our Site" box. What information is provided?

Site name: American Lung Association

URL: http://www.lungusa.org/index2.html

Why is it R.E.A.L.? You can find information in the American Lung Association's "Diseases A to Z" that covers respiratory-related diseases from asthma to tuberculosis. Data and statistics also are included.

Key topic: cardio-respiratory system

Activity: Identify a topic in the "Special Focus" section that relates to aging.

Site name: American Academy of Neurology

URL: http://www.aan.com/public/fact.html

Why is it R.E.A.L.? The American Academy of Neurology posts fact sheets on a range of neurological disorders, including Alzheimer's disease, Parkinson's, essential tremor, tremor, and stroke. Each fact sheet includes a brief background on the disorder, symptoms, causes, treatment, and experimental treatments.

Key topics: Alzheimer's disease, nervous system

Activity: Look up "Parkinson's Disease" and identify the age group most affected by the condition.

section

4

Key Points

- Lifestyle choices can make a difference in the quality of life as we age.

- Sexuality and the elderly is often a taboo topic.

- Exercise and nutrition are key components to healthy aging.

- Diet can play a role in longevity.

- The elderly, on the average, take more prescriptions than younger individuals.

Healthy Aging

WiseGuide Intro

In previous sections, some of the mysteries of aging were highlighted, along with expected, and not-so-expected, changes that accompany the aging process. Section 4 takes a positive look at some of the ways we can increase the likelihood of experiencing healthy aging. One way is to examine the use of medications in the lives of the elderly.

A reading in this section provides an excellent overview of problems associated with polymedication among the elderly, with suggestions on how to reduce the incidences of adverse drug reactions.

The role of exercise and nutrition as major contributors to healthy aging has been well documented in the literature. Guidelines, recommendations, and encouragement are offered in several readings in this section. Exercise and nutrition habits of people from other cultures help support the role of these components in longevity and quality of life.

Sexuality and the elderly is a topic often avoided because of the number of myths and misconceptions associated with it. But as more has been learned about aging, sexual activity has been identified as an integral component of the normal aging process. The readings in this section will help dispel some of the misconceptions and misunderstandings concerning aging and sexuality.

? Questions ?

Reading 19. What is the average number of prescriptions taken by each elderly person in the United States? Why do the elderly typically take more prescriptions?

Reading 20. What is an unrealized potential of exercise in old age? What is the overall aim of exercise and the elderly?

Reading 21. How does the life expectancy in Japan differ from that in the United States? What are some of the factors

associated with long life in Okinawa?

Reading 22. Aerobic exercise is recommended for the treatment and prevention of what chronic diseases associated with old age? What are some practical guidelines for implementing an exercise program for the elderly?

Reading 23. What is the most general age-related change in the sexual response cycle? What is the average age of menopause?

What is the average number of prescriptions taken by each elderly person in the United States? Why do the elderly typically take more prescriptions?

Aging Well with Fewer Medications

Gordon A. Ireland

St. Louis College of Pharmacy

Successful aging is a term that has appeared frequently in both medical and lay press during the last few years. The social sciences community has embraced this concept and the Aging 2000 program has received, at least, cautious support from the medical community. The United States federal government, in its attempt to overhaul the country's health care system, has successful aging as one of its primary goals. It would seem that to successfully age is the politically correct desire of all human beings. If it isn't, then it should be! At least that is the message we are hearing.

If asked, many people would likely admit the desire to age successfully, although our individual conceptions of what this means would differ along several dimensions. To some it would mean remaining healthy and productive until death. To others it would mean living within adequate financial means all their lives. Still others would think it means not having to become dependent on others. Despite the various interpretations of successful aging, the majority seem to expect the health care system to provide a long life free from physical and mental ailments as part of aging. This attitude has led a large percentage of our elderly population into a lifestyle that is dependent on the health care system to maintain their successful aging mode. They believe the system has an answer for every malady and that answer comes in the form of medication.

This belief results from years of seeking immediate gratification and a quick fix for undesirable conditions. Medication has become a means to fulfill the quick fix expectations when health problems are the concern (Honig & Cantilena, 1994; Michocki, Lamy, Hooper, & Richardson, 1993; Stewart & Cooper, 1994). Medication seeking behavior is enhanced by a society that, up to this point in time, supports the adage, "For every health problem there is a medicinal cure." The general public is regularly informed of chemical substances that "melt away fat" with neither a change in diet nor physical activity required; permit the consumption of fatty foods without increasing cholesterol blood levels; increase energy; improve outlook on life; mellow personality; increase life expectancy; allow consumption of food that previously caused gastric irritation; and claim a myriad of other remedies. This information is provided for both prescription and nonprescription medications by manufacturers, merchants, and health care practitioners on billboards, in newspapers, in magazines, in books, on television, through direct mail advertising, and even at movie theaters.

Publicity on such a scale has caused patients to expect medication as *the* appropriate treatment for a medical problem. Patient expectation is thus one of the leading reasons for health care practitioners prescribing medications not only for treatment of an existing ailment but also for prevention of a potential one (Miller, 1974).

Polymedication

The population older than age 65, which in the United States composes 12% of the population, consumes 25% to 30% of prescription medications (Lamy, 1993). Many reasons for older individuals taking multiple medications are identified in Figure 1.

The result is an average of 4 prescriptions per person (Hale, May, Marks, & Stewart, 1987; Pulliam, Hanlon, & Moore, 1989; Stewart & Cooper, 1994). In Long-term care facilities, the average is about 7.5 prescriptions per patient (Lamy, 1993). These figures do not include nonprescription medications or alternative medicines (homeopathic and health food substances).

There are legitimate reasons for the elderly population to be taking more medications than younger people. Individuals older than the age of 65 report an average of about four health problems per individual, whereas the average in the total population aged 20 to 65 years is approximately two (Fleming, Pulliam, & Perfetto, 1994; Kleinfeld & Corcoran, 1988). Not only do members of the older population have a greater average number of health problems, but the problems manifest themselves differently than in the younger population. A greater percentage of these illnesses are diseases of a chronic nature, such as arthritis, emphysema, diabetes, and hypertension, that may require continuous medication therapy (Pulliam et al., 1989). This leads to a greater number of baseline medications on which other medications are added as therapy for new ailments or treatment for adverse reactions produced by previous medicines (Pulliam et al., 1989).

Aging well concerns choices. It concerns those choices that enable the individual to overcome limitations and obstacles presented during the aging process. An older person who shuns the "magic pill" dependency, who uses medications with knowledgeable care in maintaining a desirable quality of life despite age-related infirmities, is aging well. As with the general population, "use not abuse" should guide medication compliance among older persons. Medications can assist a person to successfully age, but wise use of medication potentiates aging well. There are several methods of minimizing medication use and there are also methods of using medications wisely.

Many in our elderly population attempt to maintain a healthy lifestyle through good diet, adequate hydration, regular exercise, and an invigorating psychological and physical environment. Data collected from national senior Olympians reveals that among these physically fit, athletic individuals, there is less use of medications than among the general older population as well as an apparent increase in quality of life (Fontane & Hurd, 1992; Stewart & Cooper, 1994). The reasons for this observation are probably multifaceted. Although the data to elaborate this assertion remain to be specifically analyzed, we do know that these individuals seem to take an active personal interest and exercise control of their health condition. They communicate regularly with health professionals and therefore are knowledgeable regarding factors that produce and maintain good health. They usually have established a healthy lifestyle early in life and continue this practice into their older years. They monitor their health regularly and if a health problem occurs, they seek a professional health care provider to learn about the problem. Because they are knowledgeable about medica-

Figure 1	Reasons for Polymedicating

A. Multiple Disease States
1. Average of 2.3 diseases/person
2. Diseases increase with age
3. Diseases change with age
4. Expectations change with age

B. Multiple Providers
1. Specialization in health care
2. Specialists' medication familiarity
3. Health care communications
4. Practitioner shopping
5. Attempt for cure

C. Legal Implications
1. Fear of litigation
2. "Cover all bases"

D. Patient Experimentation
1. Home remedies
2. Sharing medications
3. Medication collecting

E. Nonprescription Medications
1. Not considered medications
2. Increased interest in self-care
3. Cheaper than prescription medications

F. Search for Total Therapy
1. Quick fix
2. Patient education

G. Patient Communication
1. Dishonest about medication taking
2. Deny symptoms

H. Cognitive Impairment
1. Decreased memory
2. Slow mental-function
3. Altered vision
4. Altered taste
5. Altered hearing

I. Economic Status
1. Medicaid medication availability
2. Cost-effective choices
3. Generic medications
4. Mail-order medications

tions with indications and adverse effects, they are reluctant to take medication without considering the benefits and risks of the chemical therapy. Although sufficient analysis of senior Olympians data has not been completed, I believe the desire to be in control of their health condition causes them to critically appraise their health care. To evaluate before undergoing therapy is one of the most important factors in their ability to age well compared to their age peers.

Considerations When Medicating

Medication use, in response to health problems, can improve the ability of an individual to age well. However, this end point can be achieved only by the older person being well informed regarding the rationale for taking medication, the physiological changes that occur due to the aging process, how these changes may affect medication action, the potential problems associated with taking medication, and methods of making correct decisions involving the use of medications.

The cornerstone principle for rational medication use in the elderly population should be to improve the mental and/or physical quality of life of the individual. Therefore, if the individual does not experience improvement, then continuation of the chemical should be questioned. This rationale applies to all chemical intervention whether using prescription, nonprescription, or alternative medicines.

Simply because no apparent detriment has been identified while taking a chemical does not necessarily mean the chemical is benefiting the user. One of the most common arguments for continuing medications in an elderly patient is that "the patient has been taking them for a long time and he or she seems to be doing alright." This type of observation does not allow for changes in the progression of a specific disease, the necessity of treatment at this time of life, or the fact that the patient might do better without multiple medications.

As humans age, they undergo changes in their physiological activity, which may change the severity of disease, the need for chemical therapy, the activity of a chemical, the results of the chemical's activity, and how the body reacts to the chemical substance (Honig & Cantilena, 1994); for example, Digoxin is effective in treating congestive heart failure in young patients but may cause more detrimental effects than benefits in older patients. These factors should be taken into consideration before a chemical is taken into the body, whether it's a prescription, over-the-counter (nonprescription), or alternative medication. The consideration to take or not to take a chemical is ultimately the individual's. Persons in control of their health care assimilate the information provided by both health care practitioners and other sources, contemplate the choices, and make their own informed decision. This decision is made within the framework of maintaining their own quality of life as they grow older.

Physiological changes of aging occur insidiously. These changes are usually not apparent until they cause a problem with mental or physical function, or medication use. Many physiological changes have the capability of affecting medication use in older adults. Changes in body composition may cause a change in the size of an effective dose; for example, lower dose of high blood pressure medicines. Changes in neurological function—for example, decreased coordination—may cause the chemical to produce a greater coordination deficit, for example, antianxiety agents. The decreased thirst mechanism may cause dehydration, which could lead to decreased absorption of a chemical through the gastrointestinal tract and increased potential for detrimental effects. Endocrine system changes may affect how long a chemical remains active in the body. The changes in gastrointestinal activity usually cause a slowing of the rate of absorption in the older individual. This would cause a longer time between taking the dose and experiencing the therapeutic effect, that is, aspirin would take longer to decrease pain. The decrease in hepatic metabolism could cause the activity of a chemical to last for a longer time than it would in a younger person. This effect is especially true for chemicals that are metabolized in the liver by the oxidation pathway, that is, Diazepam (Valium) may last up to 6 times longer. Renal (kidney) function also decreases during the aging process and may also cause the activity of a chemical to last longer than usual (Honig & Cantilena, 1994; Ireland, 1993; Kleinfeld & Corcoran, 1988; Pulliam et al., 1989).

Because all these physiological changes occur naturally during aging, it is important to evaluate the extent of these changes prior to an older person using any chemical including alternative medications. Older individuals can minimize the problems physiological changes may produce by knowing the changes and investigating how these changes may negatively interact with the chemical they are about to take. Then they can make an informed decision to produce the best possible result. Not all of these changes occur to the same degree or at the same rate in each older person. Persons who exercise regularly, maintain a good diet, stimulate their mental function, and maintain good body hydration seem to decrease the rate and severity at which the physiological changes occur. It is, therefore, very important for older individuals to maintain a good exercise program, a good diet, mental stimulation, and good hydration.

Potential problems associated with the use of chemicals in the elderly individual are the adverse reactions (unwanted detrimental toxic or side effects) that may occur. Adverse reactions in older persons occur more often and are frequently more severe than seen in younger individuals (Beard, 1992; Cooper, 1989; Ireland, 1993). Body systems in which adverse reactions most commonly occur are listed in Figure 3.

Different types of medications may cause unwanted effects in the central nervous system function; for example, histamine-2 blockers and digoxin may cause mental function compromise and caffeine may cause increased stimulus sensitivity and insomnia. Many high blood pressure medications may cause depression, and medications to treat epilepsy may cause problems with balance. An excess decrease in blood pressure and a dizzy feeling on standing may be caused by too much high blood pressure medication or diuretic. Increase in blood pressure may occur from caffeine or ginseng.

Figure 3* Systems Most Affected

1. Central Nervous System
   a. Mental compromise
   b. Depression
   c. Excitation
   d. Cognitive function
   e. Amnesia
   f. Ataxia
2. Cardiovascular System
   a. Hypotension
   b. Orthostatic hypotension
   c. Hypertension
   d. Dysrrhythmias
   e. Angina
3. Gastrointestinal System
   a. Gastritis
   b. Gastroesophageal reflux
   c. Constipation
   d. Diarrhea
   e. Ulceration

Abnormal heart rhythms and angina may be produced from antipsychotic medications and also caffeine or ginseng. Gastritis may be produced by the use of nonsteroidal anti-inflammatory medications, such as aspirin and ibuprofen. The incidence of gastrointestinal bleeding secondarily to these medications used in the treatment of inflammation is greater in the older population than in younger individuals. Constipation, diarrhea, and gastroesophageal reflux (heartburn) are commonly caused by a wide variety of chemicals. Again, the individual's knowledge of these possible detrimental effects, how they are caused, and the necessity of avoiding them is the older person's means to age well while using medications.

As medications are added to medications already in use by the person, and as older individuals

*Note: Figure 2 has not been included in this publication.

treat themselves with nonprescription medications and alternative medications, the chances of the occurrence of adverse reactions increase. As the number of medications older persons take increases, the number of patients experiencing adverse reactions also increases (Cooper, 1989; Ireland, 1993). Because adverse effects usually make patients feel worse, the rationale for the continuation of any chemical that might be implicated in causing the adverse effect should be questioned.

Older patients taking multiple medications have the potential of experiencing many problems (Beers & Ouslander, 1989). Multiple medication use is associated with a greater number of potential and actual adverse effects. Increased medication interactions may occur between prescription, nonprescription, and alternate medications. These interactions may increase or decrease the rate of absorption, increase or decrease the strength of the effect, and increase or decrease the length of activity of the medication in the body, that is, aspirin containing products may increase the effect of warfarin (an anticoagulant medication).

Many problems of polymedication may be avoided by the older person demanding full disclosure of the reason each specific medication is being prescribed, the desired beneficial effect, and the potential unwanted effects, and insisting on a complete review of medications currently prescribed before another medication is added. The following is a list of 15 items that older individuals need answered prior to taking any medication.

1. Medication name
2. Medication form

3. Dosing schedule

4. Action if dose is missed

5. Medication purpose

6. Therapeutic goal

7. Time to effect

8. Self-monitoring for therapeutic effect

9. Medication interactions

10. Food interactions

11. Common adverse reactions

12. Self-monitoring for adverse reactions

13. Actions to minimize adverse reactions

14. Action if adverse reaction occurs

15. Consequences of stopping medication

The individual, when fully informed, can discuss the merits of chemical therapy with the practitioner to determine the most beneficial plan. By taking an assertive role in the determination of medication therapy, the older person assumes some responsibility for decreasing the number of medications that person will be taking. The frequent outcome of this assertiveness regarding medicines is a decrease in the potential for adverse drug interactions.

All patients, both young and old, become less compliant (adherence to directions of use) to medication scheduling as the number of medications increases. The greater the number of medications or doses, the greater the noncompliance (Beers & Ouslander, 1989). By the time 4 medications are on the list, about 2 doses of one of them are missed per week. Therefore, when patients are attempting to take 11 or 12 medications, the decrease in compliance may become extremely significant.

Polymedicating also results in increased cost to patients in almost every case. In fact, sometimes the expense causes noncompliance in that patients will take a medication two times a day rather than four times a day so that it will last twice as long and they will have to buy it only half as many times.

Increased health care costs due to the need for treating adverse effects and medication interaction problems have been documented (Beard, 1992; Stewart & Cooper 1994). Part of health care costs could be lessened if patients are adequately instructed on the taking and monitoring of their many medications. However, it is very difficult to adequately instruct any patient who is taking multiple medications. Many older individuals taking medications may have poor short-term memory and thus have difficulty remembering some of the instructions. If multiple medications are absolutely necessary, it is imperative that the patient seek both verbal and written instruction in an attempt to avoid potential drug administration and monitoring errors.

The most significant problem, however, is what polymedicating can do to the patient's quality of life. Most elderly who are being polymedicated state that they would rather be taking less medications. Patients who are aging well should establish good communication with their health care practitioner and voice their desire to take fewer medications. Many times this is a sufficient catalyst to stimulate the practitioner into attempting medication reduction.

With all these potential and actual problems associated with taking multiple medications, it should not be hard to prove that

our elderly population could be aging well on fewer medications. Studies have determined that the average elderly patient in the health care system is receiving too many medications (Honig & Cantilena, 1994). Others have shown that patients can have their medication numbers reduced at significant medication cost savings (Karki, Mott, & Rosato, 1991). Still others have demonstrated that a more judicious use of sedatives, antianxiety agents, and antipsychotic agents in long-term care facilities produce a better quality of life for the patients and staff (Lamy, 1993). Volumes have been written on the potential benefits of medication reduction in the elderly population.

No large study has attempted to show the effect of medication reduction on total health care costs. Various studies have been undertaken to evaluate the appropriateness of the medications given to elderly patients, only to show that there is an appropriate diagnosis recorded to support the use of each medication. This research, however, has not questioned the rationale for continuing multiple medications in stable older patients or in patients exhibiting signs of adverse reactions. One factor contributing to this problem is difficulty encountered by a health care practitioner trying to separate an adverse medication reaction from abnormalities associated with the aging process. Often new medications are started to treat adverse effects of a current medication under the assumption that the problem is disease or age related.

Reports from several studies in progress should give us some answers to the effect of medication reduction on the cost of health care for elderly

	Questions to Ask Regarding Medications

Figure 5*

1. Does the patient feel better on the medication?
2. Is the medication producing adverse effects?
3. Does the medication have a solid indication?
4. Does the medication have a questionable indication?
5. Does the medication have correct pharmacokinetics?
6. Can a more cost-effective medication be substituted?
7. Has the patient been adequately instructed?
8. Does the patient have an avenue of response if a problem should develop?

persons. For example, during the past 4 years we have been conducting a medication reduction clinic at the Veterans Administration Medical Center in St. Louis. Patients older than the age of 65 taking 10 or more medications are evaluated with the purpose of discontinuing any medications that are not absolutely necessary. Preliminary data suggest we can achieve a 50% reduction in medication numbers without negatively affecting the patient's quality of life. The data also suggest that subsequent hospitalizations may be decreased among patients who had their number of medications reduced (Ireland, Morley, Powers, Perry, & Miller, 1995). Medication reduction may be achieved and polymedicating avoided if correct questions are asked and if appropriate responses to those questions are taken by the medical practitioner each time the patient is seen. The answers to these questions, if de-

*Note: Figure 4 has not been included in this publication.

termined with an inquisitive and open mind, can result in the discontinuation of medications for many older patients taking multiple medications.

"Aging well with fewer medications" is a slogan whose time has come. Older individuals can assume more responsibility for their own health condition. Whether taking prescribed medications or self-medicating, they can increase their knowledge of how age is affecting their bodies and how these changes influence the chemicals they take for health maintenance or the treatment of disease. They can critically question the need for any medication, prescription, nonprescription, or alternative. If they feel worse after giving the medication an adequate trial, they should question the need for continuing the therapy. A direct line of honest, forthright communication is essential between the patient aging well and the health care practitioner.

As a society, we cannot continue looking for quick fixes in life, especially in the field of health care. Medication is only as good as the underlying nonpharmacological base to which it is applied. Regular physical and mental exercise, good diet, and good hydration are the foundation stones to aging well. Upon this foundation, the addition of the knowledge of aging physiology, medication-use principles, a questioning mind, and the determination to assume responsibility for health care will develop the structure for aging well with appropriate medication use.

References

Beard, K. (1992). Adverse reactions as a cause of hospital admission in the aged. *Drugs & Aging, 2,* 356–367.

Beers, M. H., & Ouslander, J. G. (1989). Risk factors in geriatric drug prescribing, a practical guide to avoiding problems. *Drugs, 37,* 105–112.

Cooper, J. W. (1989). Reviewing geriatric concerns with commonly used drugs. *Geriatrics, 44,* 79–86.

Fleming, B. B., Pulliam, C. C., & Perfetto, E. M. (1994). Medication use by home health patients. *Journal of Geriatric Drug Therapy, 7,* 33–45.

Fontane, P. E., & Hurd, P. D. (1992). Self-perceptions of national senior Olympians. *Behavior Health Aging, 2,* 101–111.

Hale, W. E., May, F. E., Marks, R. G., & Stewart, R. B. (1987). Drug use in an ambulatory elderly population: A five year update. *Drug Intelligence and Clinical Pharmacy, 21,* 530–535.

Honig, P. K., & Cantilena, L. R. (1994). Polypharmacy: Pharmacokinetic perspectives. *Clinical Pharmacokinetics, 26,* 85–90.

Ireland, G. A. (1993). Principles of prescribing medications. In T. Yoshikawa (Ed.), *Ambulatory geriatric care.* St. Louis, MO: Mosby.

Ireland, G. A., Morley, J. E., Powers, D., Perry, M., & Miller, D. K. (1995). *The effect of medication reduction on the healthcare of elderly ambulatory patients.* Manuscript submitted for publication.

Karki, S. D., Mott, P., & Rosato, L. (1991). Impact of a team approach on reducing polypharmacy. *Consulting Pharmacist, 6,* 133–137.

Kleinfeld, M., & Corcoran, A. J. (1988). Medicating the elderly. *Geriatrics, 14,* 14–23.

Lamy, P. P. (1993). Institutionalization and drug use in older adults in the US. *Drugs & Aging, 3,* 232–237.

Michocki, R. J., Lamy, P. P., Hooper, F J., & Richardson, J. P. (1993). Drug prescribing for the elderly. *Archives of Family Medicine, 2,* 441–444,

Miller, R. R. (1974). Prescribing habits of physicians: Parts IV–VI. *Drug Intelligence and Clinical Pharmacy, 8,* 81–91.

Pulliam, C. C., Hanlon, J. T., & Moore, S. R. (1989). Contemporary issues in geriatric drug therapy. *Journal of Geriatric Drug Therapy, 4,* 43–86.

Stewart, R. B., & Cooper. J. W. (1994). Polypharmacy in the aged. *Drugs & Aging, 4,* 449–461.

Article Review Form at end of book.

What is an unrealized potential of exercise in old age? What is the overall aim of exercise and the elderly?

Resist Old Age
Exercise!

Jerry Morris

Professor J. N. Morris is in the Health Promotion Sciences Unit at the London School of Hygiene and Tropical Medicine. He was awarded the new international Olympic medal and prize for research in exercise sciences at the Atlanta Games, USA, in July 1996. His address is: London School of Hygiene & Tropical Medicine, Health Promotion Sciences Unit, Department of Public Health & Policy, Keppel Street, London WCIE 7HT, United Kingdom.

Abstract

Death rates in old age are falling, life expectancy is rising. Will these additional years be in sickness or will they be active, useful, and independent for growing numbers of older adults?

Good news: across the world, death rates in old age are falling, life expectancy is rising. The grand question now is whether this increasing longevity will be accompanied by a fall in sickness during old age. That would mean additional years of active, useful, independent well-being for growing numbers of longer-lived survivors. Otherwise, there will be more infirm old people, with their physical, mental and social disadvantages worsening over a longer span.

Already affecting sizeable minorities, these infirmities commonly progress as age advances leading to increasing frailty with waning faculties, diminishing vigour and capacity for physical effort, weaker muscles, slower gait, joint stiffness, and postural instability. Later, more often in the "old old" (the 75 plus) than in the "young old" (aged 65–74) and frequently precipitated by disease or injury, disability supervenes. This can restrict the essential activities of daily living, is liable to lead to depression as well as physical hazards and social isolation, and risks burdening individuals, their families and the health and welfare services till the end.

Can this progression be prevented? The answer at present is fragmentary—but encouraging. The prevalent infirmities of age are a compound of biological ageing (a decline in physical fitness begins as early as the 20s); the effects of inactivity and disuse (often stretching back for decades); and disease.

The key questions are: can the ageing processes be slowed at all by exercise? Can the consequences of inactivity be rectified?

And can the major diseases be reduced, postponed or attenuated? Positive evidence is accumulating on all these fronts from research, including controlled trials.

Thus, brisk walking has been shown to improve cardiovascular performance and muscular work in people in their 70s by as much proportionately as comparable exercise in the young. Such a rise in "fitness" will counter frailty in getting about, for example crossing a busy road. It is typically assumed that "brisk" means walking at about four kilometers an hour—today's typical healthy woman aged 75 to 80 finds about three kilometers an hour comfortable. Trials focused specifically on strengthening muscles in frail subjects aged over 90 have been similarly successful.

Rejuvenation Effect

These measures are achieving a "rejuvenation" effect of many years. There is a bonus too in terms of increased capacity for independence and for playing a social role (including caring for others). With the renewed ability to get about freely, the elderly can enjoy more stimulating environments and keep their minds more active. All this is a reminder of the waste of potential health and well-being that stems from the modern preference for physical inactivity.

Exercise certainly can play its part in preventing coronary heart disease, the common diabetes of later life, osteoporosis, and falls and fractures. But perhaps the more obvious unrealized potential of exercise in old age is in the treatment and rehabilitation of the many people with diseases and disabilities of heart, lungs and joints. It is vital to make the most of the general and local capabilities of these patients so that they can cope more effectively. Improving the walking capacity of people with chronic bronchitis and so relieving their breathlessness, or building up the muscles serving osteoarthritic knees are good examples of this. There are plenty of opportunities here for primary health care teams.

The overall aim is to encourage the elderly to exercise the large muscles regularly, working up gradually to a moderate intensity—feeling warm and breathing a little harder—and sustaining the exercise for half-an-hour or so on most days. Brisk walking and swimming are the most enjoyable and popular activities, and are virtually risk-free. They should preferably be undertaken in company and arranged to give structure to the daily routine.

Stair-climbing is another beneficial activity. Like walking and swimming it should be habitual in middle age, and should then be continued without question into old age. Gardening and home maintenance and repair are excellent psychologically and physically; they contribute to muscle strength and joint flexibility, to balance and dexterity, and to weight control, although less to cardiovascular fitness. Overall, increased activity will also help to assure optimal nutrition.

Some elderly people will wish to join classes and groups, while the many very old who are in residential and nursing homes must not be forgotten. Such group sessions can build confidence, promote sociability and help establish a routine; guidance may be provided on exercises to stimulate the pelvic floor for bladder control, and to strengthen bones. Before joining such a class, or if there are any doubts on any aspect, a doctor should be consulted about what exercise is most appropriate for the particular individual. Lower levels of exercise than those described here will still be beneficial, even quite minimal activity for people who are immobilized by their disability or are housebound.

Enterprising local health and leisure services are increasingly engaging in such health promotion. Unfortunately, a lot of apathy must be anticipated in response and, judging by past experience, this will be especially true among the less educated and the poor. Special facilities and low prices may not be enough to attract the target groups. Local trials are likely to be necessary to determine how best to attract those who will benefit most, for example, frail elderly women.

Improving physical fitness, and enhancing the capabilities that this activates, are a crucial part of the answer to the problem of increasing longevity. The cultural shift that is needed involves the whole of society—and must engage old people themselves. The Roman author Cicero saw this as a matter of mortality, writing more than 2000 years ago: "It is our duty to resist old age; to compensate for its defects by a watchful care; to fight against it as we would fight against disease; to adopt a regimen of health; to practice moderate exercise."

Article Review Form at end of book.

How does the life expectancy in Japan differ from that in the United States? What are some of the factors associated with long life in Okinawa?

The Healthiest Women in the World

Deborah Franklin

Abstract

The people of Okinawa live a long time because of their unique diet. Okinawa is an island off Japan, and was a trade route stop. Its people incorporated pork and sweet potatoes, less salt, and more fresh vegetables into the Japanese diet to give it more protein and fat, and less salt.

Long, long ago, or so Japanese parents have told beguiled children for generations, there lived in a coastal village a young man named Urashima, who was clever and kind and wise beyond his years. Sometimes Urashima is said to have been a wealthy and handsome prince; in other tellings, a master fisherman, whose nets bulged and glistened even when those less gifted caught nary a squid. However the edges of this age-old fable are embroidered, Urashima's fortunes always take their most dramatic turn on the day that he pauses on the beach to rescue a huge and hunkering turtle from a circle of nasty children who are pounding it with sticks.

The turtle rewards Urashima's compassion by inviting him to dive with it, deep beneath the waves, to an iridescent palace of coral and foam. In this enchanted and enchanting land, known as the Turtles' Paradise, life is joyful and gentle, full of music and good friends. No one hungers or is lonely. And no one ever grows old.

These days Japan's most beloved fairy tale has a new twist, confirmed by scientists seeking keys to long life. The Turtles' Paradise really exists, researchers say. It's a cluster of subtropical islands located 400 saltwater miles southwest of mainland Japan. This coral archipelago, as close to Hong Kong as to Tokyo, has for centuries been an outpost of blended cultures and cuisines. Long before its annexation by Japan in 1879, it was the place where that stranger-shy nation came to do the dance of trade with the rest of Asia and, 50 years ago, to do battle with the United States. The Turtles' Paradise, researchers say, is Okinawa.

Consider this: American men now live an average of nearly 72 years; American women, a respectable 79. Meanwhile, the average life span in Japan has, in recent decades, stretched to nearly 76 years for men and 83 for women. And no region of Japan, or the world, enjoys greater longevity than Okinawa, where a woman's age at death averages 84-plus years. What's more, unlike the oldest old in the formerly Soviet Republic of Georgia, who are now suspected of exaggerating their age, people aged 100 or older in Okinawa have the paperwork to prove their claims, thanks both to a Japanese culture that places great value on certain birthdays, and to a bureaucracy efficient enough to keep track.

But elderly Okinawans aren't just old, records show, they are remarkably healthy. Many manage to postpone for decades, or avoid altogether, the osteoporosis, prostate and breast cancer, diabetes, clogged arteries, stroke, and other diseases that elsewhere tend to sap life before stealing it. Researchers who study these most senior of seniors say it's as though

Okinawans have managed to stretch the middle of their lives, instead of the end.

The reasons aren't all—or even mostly—genetic. Okinawans who move to mainland Japan, California, or Brazil eventually adapt the lifestyle and shortened life span of their new homes. Okinawa's secrets apparently have more to do with how you live than who you are, and that means the islands' life-enhancing magic should work just as well in Wichita or Warsaw as in the Turtles' Paradise.

Okinawa is Japan with salsa—a hybrid culture where formal kimonos are streaked with bold geometrics, breezy palm trees grow alongside the fluttering cherry, and Japanese precision and punctuality are tempered by an easygoing cadence known locally as "Okinawan time." Just as in Tokyo, businessmen in Okinawa greet each other with formal bows and young women hide bashful giggles with their hands. Removing one's shoes before entering any home is considered not merely good manners but good hygiene. Still, despite its status as a full-fledged Japanese prefecture (the equivalent of a U.S. state), Okinawa is now and always has been a place apart, beginning with food.

"The first key to long life here is pork," Kazuhiko Taira explains one afternoon in a coastal cafe, over a savory one-pot lunch of noodles, seaweed, and spareribs in broth. It's a couple of hours past the noon rush, but at least half the red-checked tables in the neighborhood shop are still occupied by locals lingering over steamy noodles and catching up.

Slim and handsome at age 50, Taira makes his living studying old people as a gerontologist and epidemiologist in Nishihara, Okinawa, at the University of the Ryukyus. (For the 400 years before Japanese rule, the islands were sovereign, known as the Kingdom of the Ryukyus.) At least a few days each week Taira travels the length of the island, taking tea at village senior centers and in family homes with people who have lived this century's history.

On his rounds, Taira takes the seniors' blood pressure and asks about diet, sleep, and hobbies, but he is just as interested, he says, in the stories they tell. A 97-year-old fishmonger, for example, ascribes her long life to her morning ritual: a cold-water massage and a handful of toasted soybeans washed down with a can of Coca-Cola. ("She tells me she prefers beer," Taira says, "but recently switched to Coke because it's half the price.") A 101-year-old grandmother, who kept her family together through the lean war years by selling rice, tells her 70-year-old daughter that she must eat plenty of fish and many vegetables if she, too, wants to live a long time. "But always keep one-fifth of the stomach empty," the older woman advises. "Never, never be too full." Sound advice, perhaps, but Taira points out that whenever he shows up at their house, both women fill the table with delectables and insist that he eat and eat. "Grandmother . . . ," he says, and shrugs and smiles.

Though long-life advice from the elders never ends with food, it always seems to start there, Taira says. A meticulous scientist, he also manages the deadpan delivery of a comedian who knows better than to rush his punch line. "Okinawan cuisine," he says, "is very healthy—and very, very greasy."

Tonic of lard, hunk of rejuvenating ham? Step this way, into the Ryukyuan Kingdom, where secrets to long life are rarely what they seem. The pork that Taira touts does indeed seem to dominate the pink plastic menu of the little cafe, as it has Okinawan cuisine for the six centuries since domestic pigs first trotted down the gangways of Chinese trading ships. In addition to the mouth-watering noodle soup, or pork "soba," that Taira chooses for himself, and the tenderloin medallions coated in toasted sesame that he recommends to a tourist, the menu offers boiled pigs' feet, entrail soup, and a vinegared slaw of shredded ears; bold testament to an old saying used to tweak squeamish tourists from the mainland: "Pigs can be eaten from nails to tail—everything but the voice." Still, with the scant quantities of meat used in any single dish, and fat-stripping cooking methods, the cuisine can be considered greasy only relative to Japan's historically spartan diet.

In 1964 Taira left Okinawa's main island for college in war-scarred Nagasaki. At the time, Okinawa was still recovering from its own date with death: three horrific months in 1945, when more than 200,000 soldiers and civilians were killed in the bloodiest Pacific battle of World War II. Less well-known, except to locals like Taira, was Okinawa's tenacious claim to life—extremely long life. That obscurity was about to end.

In the United States, health officials had turned up evidence linking heart disease, America's number one killer then and now, to a diet high in fat, and had launched their now-familiar diatribe against the all-American cheeseburger-and-fries cuisine. Meanwhile, in Japan, the dietary problems were different.

Like the United States, postwar Japan had reaped the benefits of antibiotics, clean water, and widespread refrigeration of food; death from infectious disease was way down from even a generation before. Nonetheless, the Japanese were still dropping dead in their early sixties, not so much from heart disease as from their number one killer, stroke. The problem: too much salt and not enough protein and fat.

That fact surprises most Americans, so accustomed have we become to painting fat and its daughter cholesterol as angels of death. But the truth is that fat is the mortar to protein's brick when it comes to building and maintaining the outer membrane of every cell in the body. Most Americans have to work hard to get their blood cholesterol levels down to the American Heart Association's recommended cap of 200 milligrams per deciliter of blood. But when a person's cholesterol levels are too low— below 100 or so, as they were among those eating the traditional Japanese diet before the 1970s—it is a sign that he or she probably isn't eating enough fat.

What's more, high salt consumption adds to the risk. The Japanese still average about 12 to 14 grams of salt a day, almost 50 percent more than most Americans. A diet with that much sodium can exacerbate dangerously high blood pressure, particularly in genetically susceptible people, or if combined with a shortfall of calcium, potassium, and magnesium.

High blood pressure and weakened cell membranes were the main diet-linked devils of pre-1970s Japan. Tiny blood vessels in aging brains fatally leaked or burst, prompting the internal bleeding known as hemorrhagic stroke. Twice as many people died from fatal strokes as from the next most prominent killer, cancer. (Although strokes afflict many Americans, too, the cause in the United States is usually different: a fat-related clogging of the blood vessels that feed the brain.)

As Japanese health officials pondered all this, they noticed that Okinawans were somehow outwitting the medical scourges of both East and West, achieving a rate of hemorrhagic stroke much lower than mainland Japan's and a rate of heart disease far below that of the United States and most of Europe.

Kazuhiko Taira was among those who investigated, and one of the first things he and the others scrutinized was the Okinawans' diet. "The differences we found," he says, "were quite striking."

In the decades before 1960, Japanese adults typically ate seven to nine bowls of rice each day, supplemented by six to nine bowls of fermented soybean (miso) soup and a few small servings of seaweed or salty pickled vegetables. Fresh vegetables were much less common. Whatever animal protein people got came from fish, and it wasn't much—a bit of hard herring roe, say, or dried fish flakes to flavor the rice, or a bite of broiled or salt-cured fish with dinner a few times a week.

In some circles of overfed America today, a passion has arisen for the virtues of an Asian "peasant" diet—rice-based, fat-free, mostly meatless meals. But Japanese researchers, less romantic about their dietary past, warn that, just as there are diseases of excess, it is possible for a society to eat too simply. Japan's National Institute of Health and Nutrition recently noted that most Japanese had "made too much of the staple food, steamed rice," even in the peaceful decades before World War II, relying on it for as much as 80 percent of their calories.

Okinawa was certainly no wealthier than Japan. Most people were subsistence farmers, foresters, or fishermen. But even in those days before jets brought a wealth of fresh produce, the Okinawan diet, while still built around fish and rice, was more varied than Japan's. And it was varied in ways that turned out to be life lengthening, offering lessons not just to the Japanese of 30 years ago but to modern Americans as well.

For hundreds of years, Okinawa has been a crossroads, where traders from Asia and beyond couldn't help but swap recipes along with their luxury goods. Pigs weren't the only import from China; fibrous, vitamin-rich root crops, such as taro and sweet potatoes, have long been as fundamental to an Okinawan meal as rice. Pork, the staple meat, is simmered for hours to a melt-in-the-mouth tenderness, with fat repeatedly skimmed off the top. It's then soaked in a marinade of brown sugar and strong rice brandy (awamori) to add flavor. Chunks are added sparingly to soups or noodles, or to rice that is then fried with carrots, white radish, and greens. The leftover lard is used, in amounts much greater than in Japan but sparing by U.S. standards, in a regional specialty called champuru, a light stir-fry of tofu and whatever fresh vegetables are at hand. Southeast Asia is the likely source of the ginger and brown sugar combination that lends many local dishes a smoky-sweet, molasses flavor. Okinawans enjoy strong flavorings—fiery chili oil in their noodles, the wicked bite of bitter melon—to a degree not found in Japanese cuisine.

Through all this mixing and matching of tastes and textures, the Okinawans were eating three times more meat (and accompanying fat) than were Japanese mainlanders, 50 percent more tofu, and 40 percent less salt. This small tweaking of a dietary style that is still distinctly Asian enabled the Okinawans to retain the virtues of the Japanese fish-and-rice meals while avoiding the vices that lead to deadly strokes. By eating more fresh vegetables than pickled, Taira says, the Okinawans have always taken in more vitamins and fiber and less salt than their mainland counterparts. This also helps account for their historically much lower rates of stomach and colon cancer.

Yukio Yamori, a pathologist at Kyoto University who collaborates with Taira, has for the last 15 years headed a World Health Organization study of the links between diet and longevity in 25 regions around the world. Yamori thinks many aspects of the Okinawan diet—beyond, fat, fiber, and protein—should interest Americans.

"Tofu and other soybean products are particularly rich in isoflavonoids—estrogen-like compounds that we now believe may help deter osteoporosis by aiding in calcium absorption," Yamori says. "They may also help account for the lower rates of breast and prostate cancer found in Japan relative to the United States." He notes that his most recent study, of postmenopausal women in Japan and Hawaii, showed that women who ate the most soy had the densest bones. If the finding holds up, he says, it might help explain why elderly Japanese—and especially Okinawan—women seem to suffer far fewer bone fractures than American women, though the Japanese consume far less calcium.

The seafood and seaweed that Japanese—as well as Okinawans—now eat virtually every day, Yamori says, are excellent sources of not only protein but omega-3 fatty acids, which help keep arteries unclogged and reduce the risk of heart disease. "Over and over again, around the world," he says, "we have found that people who eat fish several times a week were much less likely to suffer heart disease than those who eat fish only rarely."

The implications for Americans, he says, are simple—and developing a taste for kelp or shredded pigs' ears isn't required. Striving to reduce fat in the diet to around 25 or 30 percent of daily calories will match what the Okinawans and modern Japanese eat. It's fine to go ahead and eat meat if you want to, Yamori says. Just not so much. Even today, with pasta and salad edging out meat loaf and steak, Americans eat an average of 12 ounces of meat daily—more than three times the average eaten by Okinawans. As you cut back on meat, Yamon suggests, try to eat fish at least four times a week, and toss a few chunks of tofu into the fresh veggie stir-fry. Both the fish and the soybean curd, he says, have benefits meat can't provide. And at least some of the same anticancer agents plentiful in dark green seaweeds are found in dark, leafy, landlocked vegetables such as bok choy and bitter greens; these will taste not only authentic but delicious in the champuru.

Kazuhiko Taira enjoys fish and champuru as much as the next fellow, and he takes pride in Okinawan cuisine, but he's also certain that simply eating right—a bit of seaweed here, a sand dab there—won't get you to the Turtles' Paradise. "We have a saying here that 'food is medicine,'" Taira says, "but that is only part of the answer. The second and maybe more important secret to a long and healthy life in Okinawa is what we call yuimaru."

Hiroko Sho, a friend of Taira's, is happy to explain. The warm and elegant 63-year-old widow of the heir to the last Ryukyuan emperor, Sho is a former vice governor of health and education for Okinawa. She has traveled the world and also knows well the ways of her island's tiniest villages. Yuimaru, she says, which comes from the Japanese words for "circle" and "connection," makes those villages run.

"Work and independence have always been very important to us," she says. "When people get older, even if their children no longer live in the village, they want to stay in their own homes for as long as possible and to keep working, if only a little every day." In Okinawa, she says, that sort of work, whether it's farming, weaving, managing a market or a fish store, is possible even for 80- or 90-year-old men and women.

"An older lady, for instance," Sho says, "may have had a fish store for a long time. In her younger years, she gets up early and goes to the wholesaler herself to buy the fish. But as she gets older, some neighbor, perhaps a younger one, goes to the wholesaler and picks up fish and brings it over for her. You see? So she can still sell fish, still make a business, if on a smaller scale. The amount she sells maybe goes down gradually.

"What's just as important is that some people come over and buy what she sells. Even if the fish she sells is no longer so fresh, or maybe she doesn't wash her hands, we go over, we enjoy conversation, and we buy a little from her.

"We may not eat it," Sho hastens to add. "We may buy the fish we eat from somebody else. But we don't tell her that, and we continue to buy a little fish from her. That's yuimaru."

It is that sense of belonging, of being necessary, Sho believes, that makes people want to wake up and unlock the fish store at age 103.

The concept started, Sho says, on the farm. "Today yuimaru is a pretty word we cling to," says 63-year-old farmer Hiroichi Yonamine. "But when my father was young, yuimaru was so crucial to survival that people didn't talk about it—they lived it." Hiroichi's father is 103-year-old Takejo, a straight-backed man who by 1947 had lost seven children to war and sickness. With the help of his remaining family, Takejo rebuilt a thriving sugarcane farm in south-central Okinawa. Hiroichi, who visits often, speaks with tender admiration of the way Takejo scraped together provisions for the family during the war, when the Yonamines were reduced to moving nightly from cave to cave to find shelter from tanks and grenades.

Those hard times are long gone, if not forgotten. On a springtime Sunday, the family's two generations of elders gather, laughing and joking, around a low table spread with fritters, fruit, and brown sugar candy. Hiroichi sits cross-legged at his father's side, pausing every few minutes to refill Takejo's cup with hot jasmine tea. In Okinawa, Hiroichi says, neighbors are like family. As in America, farming rewards neither the lazy nor the fiercely independent; all hands must come together, whether the task is bringing in a crop, raising a barn, or—in Okinawa—building the family tomb.

Just as the aged are greatly respected on the island, Hiroichi explains, so are the dead, and every family has an elaborate mausoleum. When Takejo Yonamine was a young man, tombs were built of limestone bricks, each weighing more than a thousands pounds and cut by hand from ancient coral cliffs. "There's no way a single family could build a tomb," Hiroichi says. "So after a long day in the fields, neighbors would get together to cut and haul these stones. They would tie ropes around the rocks, a few men in front, several to each side, with someone up ahead banging a gong, so that they could all pull at the same stroke, and they would drag these stones miles up the hill to the site of the tomb." Takejo nods his assent. "That," the older man says, "is yuimaru."

Now that more and more people in Japan are living past 80 and 90 years old, the government, like that of the United States, is suddenly, urgently, interested in figuring out how to keep these people vital. To that end, Taira has begun a new study comparing the lives of elderly residents of three places: Akita, a northern village on the Japanese mainland that has many descendants of Okinawan immigrants; Naha, the capital city in south-central Okinawa; and Ogimi, a northern Okinawan village that time forgot.

While the south was ravaged in 1945, the war hardly touched northern Okinawa, and much of Ogimi looks as it must have when the Turtles' Paradise story was first told. Houses are small and wooden, capped by red, Chinese-style tile roofs; every morning, doors, windows and oiled-paper walls slide away in a frictionless second to welcome the air and light.

And what air, what light. The mountains, thick with native pine, drop almost directly to the ocean, giving seaside Ogimi a craggy backdrop like the shores of Maine. But unlike Maine, Ogimi's waters are turquoise and warm, the climate gentle year-round, and the elderly residents—the average age in the village is 72—able to spend much of the year outdoors, walking, gardening, shopping for a few groceries, or just gathering over the backyard fence to talk over old and new times.

So far Taira's study has turned up some differences he expected. Naha and Ogimi villagers eat less salt and more meat, vegetables, and tofu than their Akita counterparts. The lower rates of cancer, hypertension, and hip fractures in Naha and Ogimi, he says, probably reflect those eating habits. But what interests him most are the differences in social and physical activity.

Winters in Akita are long, frosty, and damp. So it's not surprising, Taira says, that its elderly residents are sedentary much of the year. What is less easily explained is why the elderly in Ogimi village are much more physically active than those in Naha, though they share the same mild climate. When Taira asked healthy seniors in both places to wear pedometers for several days, to get a sense of how active they were, he found that the people of Ogimi took almost twice as many steps. Questionnaires confirmed that Ogimi residents also seemed happier. Taira suspects yet another effect of yuimaru.

Without much arable land, and with very little industry, Ogimi has for generations sent her children away to be educated or to seek jobs. The elders left behind, Taira says, have forged particularly strong bonds with neighbors and friends. "When they wake up in the morning in Ogimi," Taira says, "the first thing everyone does is throw open the doors. If they look down the block and see that a friend's door isn't open, everyone rushes over to see what is wrong.

"It is true that we greatly respect the elderly all over Okinawa," Taira continues. "But in the city, if you live alone or even with your children it is easier to withdraw from social activity, to stop going to the community center, to stop seeing friends—and to stop getting exercise. Socializing is good for the body as well as the soul."

That, of course, is just as true in the United States, where many studies have shown that elderly people with strong connections to at least one other person live longer, and are more resilient to injury, illness, and emotional loss, than people who are isolated.

Ushi Okushima is living proof. Tanned and wiry from 95 years of working the Ogimi soil, Okushima is, at 4 foot 8, a tiny but commanding woman. Though all but one of her children, in addition to her 13 grandchildren and 20 great-grandchildren, live in the distant city, Okushima is content to let them come visit her. If she left

Ogimi for more than a day or two, she says, who would care for her farm?

Stepping lightly through her ten or so rows of beans, carrots, tomatoes, radishes and papayas, Okushima stoops to pick a beetle off a leaf of Chinese cabbage. "Never would I live in Naha," she says. "I have friends and neighbors here. On summer evenings we walk along the beach until after seven or eight at night. We dance, we drink awamori, we talk and talk and talk for hours. All this enjoyment. . . . If I went to Naha I would die, I think."

It is late afternoon when Okushima finishes in her garden, brushes the dust from her hands, and turns for the half-block walk home. She stops for a minute to share a joke with an 82-year-old neighbor who is parking her bike. Overhead, birds circle, gathering up stragglers as they, too, head home to roost. The sea looks peaceful and empty; even late-going fishing boats have long since pulled in their nets.

Near the beach, where visitors enter Ogimi, stands a limestone welcome marker, a tribute to the villagers' renowned longevity. Carved into the dark rock in Japanese characters are the words of another old Okinawan saying: "At 70 you are still a child, at 80 a young man or woman. And if at 90 someone from Heaven invites you over, tell him, '0h, just go away, and come back when I am 100.' "

Take a hint from the men and women of Okinawa, who live longer than everyone else on earth: The best diet is anything but austere and fat-free. What's more, any American with a well-seasoned skillet and a sharp knife can get the benefits the Okinawans do. Here's how:

Pile on the Rice: It's the base of all Asian eating and the foundation of the Okinawans' healthful diet. For the sake of variety, shop around—try fragrant basmati, delicate jasmine, or nutty brown rice.

Shell out for Seafood: Granted, it's more expensive than red meat or chicken—but it's much better for you. Grilled, steamed, poached, or baked, fish and shrimp deliver omega-3 fatty acids, which help keep your arteries clear.

Try Cooking with Tofu: Dice it into stir-fries; crumble it into soups. Tofu's mild flavor and pleasing texture make it adaptable to many dishes. Best of all, its soy compounds seem to fend off breast and other cancers.

Use Meat as a Condiment: Pork is popular in Okinawan cuisine, but the portions are small by American standards, and it's not served every day. Linguine with tomato sauce and a handful of diced pancetta? That's the idea.

Vary Your Vegetables: Most American supermarkets now carry mustard greens, Chinese cabbage, bok choy, and more. Toss them into stir-fries at the last minute (they cook rapidly), or add them to soups. The Okinawans owe their longevity in part to their taste for fresh, brightly colored vegetables.

Reach for the Spices: Never mind the evidence that garlic, ginger, and hot peppers all have disease-fighting powers. They add savor and soul to any dish.

Article Review Form at end of book.

Aerobic exercise is recommended for the treatment and prevention of what chronic diseases associated with old age? What are some practical guidelines for implementing an exercise program for the elderly?

Nutrition, Exercise and Healthy Aging

William J. Evans and Deanna Cyr-Campbell

W. J. Evans (corresponding author) is a professor of nutrition and applied physiology and D. Cyr-Campbell is a research dietitian with the Noll Physiological Research Center, Pennsylvania State University, University Park, PA 16802.

Abstract

Advancing age is associated with a remarkable number of changes in body composition, including reduction in lean body mass and increase in body fat, which have been well documented. Decreased lean body mass occurs primarily as a result of losses in skeletal muscle mass. This age-related loss in muscle mass has been termed "sarcopenia". Loss in muscle mass accounts for the age-associated decreases in basal metabolic rate, muscle strength, and activity levels, which, in turn are the cause of the decreased energy requirements of the elderly. In sedentary persons, the main determinant of energy expenditure is fat-free mass, which declines by about 15% between the third and eighth decade of life. It also appears that declining energy needs are not matched by an appropriate decline in energy intake, with the ultimate result being increased body fat content. Increased body fatness and increased abdominal obesity are thought to be directly linked to the greatly increased incidence of non-insulin-dependent diabetes mellitus among the elderly. In this review we will discuss the extent to which regularly performed exercise can affect nutrition needs and functional capacity in the elderly. We will also discuss a variety of concerns when prescribing exercise in the elderly, such as planning for a wide variability in functional status, medical status, and training intensity and duration. Finally, we will attempt to provide some basic guidelines for beginning an exercise program for older men and women and establishing community-based programs.

Sarcopenia, the age-associated loss of muscle mass[1], is a direct cause of an age-related decrease in muscle strength. Our laboratory[2] examined muscle strength and mass in 200 healthy 45- to 78-year-old men and women, and concluded that muscle mass (not function) is the major determinant of age- and sex-related differences in strength. This relationship is independent of muscle location (upper vs lower extremities) and function (extension vs flexion). Reduced muscle strength in the elderly is a major cause of their increased prevalence of disability. With advancing age and very low activity levels seen in the very old, muscle strength and power are critical components of walking ability[3]. The high prevalence of falls among the institutionalized elderly may be a consequence of their lower muscle strength.

The question that we have been attempting to address is: To what extent are these changes inevitable consequences of aging? Our data suggest that changes in body composition and aerobic capacity that are associated with increasing age may not be age related at all. By examining endurance-trained men, we saw that body fat stores and maximal aerobic capacity were not related to age, but rather to the total number of hours these men were exercising per week[4]. Even among sedentary persons, energy spent in daily activities explains more than 75% of the variability in body fatness among young and older men[5]. These data and the results of other investigations indicate that levels of physical activity are important in determining energy expenditure and, ultimately, body fat accumulation.

Aerobic Exercise

Aerobic exercise has long been an important recommendation for the prevention and treatment of many of the chronic diseases typically associated with old age. These include non-insulin-dependent diabetes mellitus (NIDDM) (and impaired glucose tolerance), hypertension, heart disease, and osteoporosis. Regularly performed aerobic exercise increases the maximum capacity to take in and use oxygen during exercise (VO_2 max) and insulin action. Meredith et al[6] examined the responses of initially sedentary young (aged 20 to 30 years) and older (aged 60 to 70 years) men and women to 3 months of aerobic conditioning (70% of maximal heart rate, 45 minutes/day, 3 days/week). They found that the absolute gains in aerobic capacity were similar between the two age groups. However, the mechanism for adaptation to regular submaximal exercise appears to be different between old and young people. Muscle biopsies taken before and after training showed a more than twofold increase in oxidative capacity of the muscles of the older subjects, whereas the young subjects showed smaller improvements. In addition, skeletal muscle glycogen stores in the older sub-

jects, significantly lower than those of the young men and women initially, increased significantly. The degree to which the elderly demonstrate increases in maximal cardiac output in response to endurance training is still largely unanswered. Seals and coworkers[7] found no increases after 1 year of endurance training whereas, more recently, Spina et al[8] observed that older men increased maximal cardiac output and healthy older women demonstrated no change in response to endurance exercise. If these gender-related differences in cardiovascular response are real, it may explain the lack of response in maximal cardiac output when older men and women are included in the same study population.

Exercise and Carbohydrate Metabolism

The fact that aerobic exercise has substantial effects on skeletal muscle may help explain its importance in the treatment of glucose intolerance and NIDDM. Seals and coworkers[9] found that a high-intensity training program resulted in greater improvements in the insulin response to an oral glucose load than lower-intensity aerobic exercise. However, their subjects began the study with normal glucose tolerance. Kirwan and coworkers[10] found that 9 months of endurance training at 80% of the maximal heart rate (4 days/week) resulted in reduced glucose-stimulated insulin levels; however, no comparison was made to a lower-intensity exercise group. Hughes and coworkers[11] demonstrated that regularly performed aerobic exercise without weight loss resulted in improved glucose tolerance, rate of insulin-

stimulated glucose disposal, and increased skeletal muscle GLUT-4 levels in older subjects with glucose intolerance. In this investigation, a moderate intensity aerobic exercise program was compared with a higher-intensity program (50% vs. 75% of maximal heart rate reserve, 55 minutes/day, 4 days/week for 12 weeks). No differences in effect were seen between the moderate- and higher-intensity aerobic exercise on glucose tolerance, insulin sensitivity, or muscle GLUT-4 (the glucose transporter protein in skeletal muscle) levels, indicating, perhaps, that a prescription of moderate aerobic exercise should be recommended for older men or women with NIDDM or at high risk for NIDDM to help to ensure compliance to the program.

Endurance training and dietary modifications are generally recommended as the primary treatment for persons with NIDDM. Cross-sectional analysis of dietary intake supports the hypothesis that a low-carbohydrate/high-fat diet is associated with the onset of NIDDM[12]. This evidence, however, is not supported by prospective studies where dietary habits have not been related to the development of NIDDM.[13,14] The effects of a high-carbohydrate diet on glucose tolerance have been equivocal.[15,16] Hughes et al[17] compared the effects of a high-carbohydrate (60% carbohydrate and 20% fat)/high-fiber (25 g dietary fiber/1,000 kcal) diet with and without 3 months of high intensity (75% maximum heart rate reserve, 50 minutes/day, 4 days/week) endurance exercise in older men and women with glucose intolerance. Subjects were fed all of their food on a metabolic ward during the 3-month study and were not allowed to lose weight. These investigators observed no improvement in glucose tolerance or insulin-stimulated glucose uptake in either the diet or the diet-plus-exercise group. The diet-plus-exercise group demonstrated a significant and substantial increase in skeletal muscle glycogen content, and at the end of the training their muscle glycogen stores were considered to be saturated. Because the primary site of glucose disposal is skeletal muscle glycogen stores, the extremely high muscle glycogen content associated with exercise and a high-carbohydrate diet likely limited the rate of glucose disposal. Thus, when combined with exercise and a weight-maintenance diet, a high-carbohydrate diet had a counter-regulatory effect. It is likely that the value of a high-carbohydrate/high-fiber diet is in the treatment of excess body fat, which may be an important cause of the impaired glucose tolerance. Recently, Schaefer and co-workers[18] demonstrated that older subjects consuming an ad libitum high-carbohydrate diet lost weight.

There appears to be no attenuation of the response of elderly men and women to regularly performed aerobic exercise compared with the response seen in young subjects. Increased fitness levels are associated with reduced mortality and increased life expectancy. Fitness has also been shown[19] to prevent the occurrence of NIDDM in those who are at the greatest risk for developing this disease. Thus, regularly performed aerobic exercise is an important way for older people to improve their glucose tolerance.

Aerobic exercise is generally prescribed as an important adjunct to a weight loss program. Aerobic exercise combined with weight loss has been demonstrated to increase insulin action to a greater extent than weight loss through diet restriction alone. In a study by Bogardus et al[20], diet therapy alone improved glucose tolerance, mainly by reducing basal endogenous glucose production and improving hepatic sensitivity to insulin. Aerobic exercise training, on the other hand, increased carbohydrate storage rates; therefore, "diet therapy plus physical training produced a more significant approach toward normal"(22, p. 316) p. 316). However, aerobic exercise (as opposed to resistance training) combined with a hypocaloric diet has been demonstrated to result in a greater reduction in resting metabolic rate than diet alone[21]. Heymsfield and coworkers[22] found that aerobic exercise combined with caloric restriction did not preserve fat-free mass and did not further accelerate weight loss compared with diet alone. This lack of an effect of aerobic exercise may have been due to a greater decrease in resting metabolic rate in the exercising group. In, perhaps, the most comprehensive study of its kind, Goran and Poehlman[23] examined components of energy metabolism in older men and women engaged in regular endurance training. They found that endurance training did not increase total daily energy expenditure because there was a compensatory decline in physical activity during the remainder of the day. In other words, when elderly subjects participated in a regular walking program, they rested more, so activities outside of walking decreased and, thus, 24-hour energy expenditure was unchanged. Ballor et al[24] compared the effects of resistance training to that of diet restriction alone in obese women. They found that resistance exercise training resulted in increased strength and gains in muscle size as well as a preservation of fat-free mass during weight loss. These data are similar to the results of Pavlou et al.[25] who used both aerobic and resistance training as an adjunct to a weight loss program in obese men.

Strength Training

Although endurance exercise has been the more traditional means of increasing cardiovascular fitness, strength or resistance training is currently recommended by the American College of Sports Medicine as an important component of an overall fitness program.[26] This is particularly important in the elderly in whom loss of muscle mass and weakness are prominent deficits.

Strength conditioning or progressive resistance training is generally defined as training in which the resistance against which a muscle generates force is progressively increased over time. Progressive resistance training involves few contractions against a heavy load. The metabolic and morphologic adaptations resulting from resistance and endurance exercise are quite different. Muscle strength has been shown to increase in response to training between 60% and 100% of the one repetition maximum (1RM). 1RM is the maximum amount of weight that can be lifted with one contraction. Strength conditioning will result in an increase in muscle size and this increase in size is largely the result of increased contractile proteins. The mechanisms by which the mechanical events stimulate an increase in RNA synthesis and subsequent protein synthesis are not well understood. Lifting weight requires that a muscle shorten as it produces force. This is called a concentric contraction, Lowering the weight, on the other hand, forces the muscle to lengthen as it produces force. This is an eccentric muscle contraction. These lengthening muscle contractions have been shown to produce ultrastructural damage that may stimulate increased muscle protein turnover.[27]

Our laboratory examined the effects of high-intensity resistance training of the knee extensors and flexors (80% of 1RM, 3 days/week) in older men (aged 60 to 72 years). The average increases in knee flexor and extensor strength were 227% and 107% respectively. Computed tomography (CT) scans and muscle biopsies were used to determine muscle size. Total muscle area as determined by CT analysis increased by 11.4%, whereas the muscle biopsies showed an increase of 33.5% in Type I fiber area (slow twitch) and a 27.5% increase in Type II fiber area (fast twitch). In addition, lower body VO$_2$max increased significantly while upper body VO$_2$max did not, indicating that increased muscle mass can increase maximal aerobic power. It appears that the age-related loss in muscle mass may be an important determinant in the reduced maximal aerobic capacity seen in elderly men and women.[28] Improving muscle strength can enhance the capacity of many older men and women to perform activities such as climbing stairs, carrying packages, and even walking.

We applied this training program to a group of frail, institutionalized elderly men and women (mean age = 90 [+ or −] 3 years, range = 87 to 96 years).[29] After 8 weeks of training, the 10 subjects in this study increased muscle strength by almost 180% and muscle size by 11%. A similar intervention on frail nursing home residents demonstrated not only increases in muscle strength and size, but increased gait speed, stair-climbing power, and balance.[30] In addition, spontaneous activity levels increased significantly, whereas the activity of a nonexercising control group was unchanged. In this study, the researchers also examined the effects of exercise combined with a protein-energy supplement (240-mL liquid supplying 360 kcal in the form of carbohydrate [60%], fat [23%], and soy-based protein [17%]) designed to augment energy intake by about 20% and provide one third of the Recommended Dietary Allowance (RDA)[31] for vitamins and minerals (see Figure 1*). Although no interaction was seen with muscle strength, functional capacity, or muscle size (no differences in improvements between the supplemented group and a nonsupplemented control group), the men and women who consumed the supplement and exercised gained more weight than the three other groups examined (exercise-control, nonexercise supplemented, and nonexercise control). The nonexercising subjects who received the supplement reduced their habitual dietary energy intake so that total energy intake was unchanged. It should be pointed out that this was a very old, very frail population with diagnoses of multiple chronic diseases. The increase in

*Not included in this publication.

overall levels of physical activity has been a common observation in our studies.[30,32,33] Because muscle weakness is a primary deficit in many older persons, increased strength may stimulate more aerobic activities like walking and cycling.

In addition to its effect on increasing muscle mass and function, resistance training can also have an important effect on the energy balance of elderly men and women[34]. Men and women participating in a resistance training program of the upper and lower body muscles required approximately 15% more energy to maintain body weight after 12 weeks of training compared with their pretraining energy requirements. This increase in energy needs came about as a result of an increased resting metabolic rate, the small energy cost of the exercise, and what was presumed to be an increase in activity levels. Although endurance training has been demonstrated to be an important adjunct to weight loss programs in young men and women by increasing their daily energy expenditure, its usefulness in treating obesity in the elderly may not be great. This is because many sedentary older men and women do not spend much energy when they perform endurance exercise because of their low fitness levels. Thirty to 40 minutes of exercise may increase energy expenditure by only 100 to 200 kcal with very little residual effect on energy expenditure. Aerobic exercise training will not preserve lean body mass to any great extent during weight loss. Because resistance training can preserve or even increase muscle mass during weight loss, this type of exercise for those older men and women who must lose weight may be of genuine benefit.

Bone Health

The increased energy need resulting from strength training may be a way for the elderly to improve their overall nutritional intake when the energy is derived from nutrient-dense foods. In particular, calcium is an important nutrient to increase because calcium intake was found to be one of the only nutrients consumed at a level below the RDA in the diet of free-living elderly men and women in the Boston Nutritional Status Survey[35], which assessed free-living and institutionalized elderly men and women. Careful nutrition planning is needed to reach the recommended calcium levels of 1,500 mg/day for postmenopausal women with osteoporosis or using hormone replacement therapy, and 1,000 mg/day for postmenopausal women taking estrogen. Increased energy intake from calcium-containing foods is one method to help achieve this goal.

In one of the few studies to examine the interaction of dietary calcium and exercise, we studied 41 postmenopausal women consuming either high-calcium (1,462 mg/day) or moderate-calcium (761 mg/day) diets. Half of these women participated in a year-long walking program (45 minutes/day, 4 day/week, at 75% of heart rate reserve). Independent effects of the exercise and dietary calcium were seen. Compared with the moderate-calcium group, the women consuming a high-calcium diet displayed reduced bone loss from the femoral neck, independent of whether the women exercised. The walking prevented the loss of trabecular bone mineral density seen in the nonexercising women after 1 year. Thus, it appears that calcium intake and aerobic exercise are both independently beneficial to bone mineral density at different sites. The effects of 52 weeks of high-intensity resistance exercise training was examined in a group of 39 postmenopausal women.[32] Twenty were randomly assigned to the strength training group (2 days/week, 80% of IRM for upper and lower body muscle groups). At the end of the year significant differences were seen in lumbar spine and femoral bone density between the strength-trained and sedentary women (Figure 2*). However, unlike other pharmacologic and nutritional strategies for preventing bone loss and osteoporosis, resistance exercise affects more than just bone density. The women who participated in strength training improved their muscle mass, strength, balance, and overall levels of physical activity. Thus, resistance training can be an important way to decrease the risk of osteoporotic bone fractures in postmenopausal women.

Protein Needs and Aging

Inadequate dietary protein intake may be an important cause of sarcopenia. Previous estimates of dietary protein needs of the elderly using nitrogen balance have ranged from 0. 59 g to 0. 8 g per kilogram per day.[36–38] However, the low value was reported by Zanni et al[38] who preceded their 10-day dietary protein feeding with a 17-day protein-free diet, which was likely to improve nitrogen retention during the 10-day balance period. Recently, we[39] reassessed the nitrogen-balance studies mentioned above using the currently accepted, 1985 World Health Organization[40] nitrogen-balance formula. These newly recalculated data were combined with nitrogen-balance data collected on 12 healthy older men and women (8 men and 4 women, age range = 56 to 80 years) consuming the current RDA for protein or double this amount (0.8 g per kilogram per day and 1.6 g per kilogram per day, respectively) in our laboratory. Our subjects consumed the diet for 11 consecutive days and nitrogen balance (milligrams of nitrogen per kilogram per day) was measured during days 6 to 11. The estimated mean protein requirements from the three retrospectively assessed studies and the current study[39] can be combined by weighted averaging to produce an overall protein requirement estimate of 0.9 ± 0.043 g per kilogram per day. The combined estimate, excluding the data from our 12 subjects, is 0.894 ± 0.048 g protein per kilogram per day.

The current RDA of 0.8 g per kilogram per day is based on data collected, for the most part, on young subjects. The RDA includes an upward adjustment based on the coefficient of variability (CV) of the average requirement established in these studies (0.6 g per kilogram per day). According to the CV previously established for nitrogen-balance studies, an adequate dietary protein level for 97.5% of the elderly population would be provided by an intake of 25% (twice the standard deviation) above the mean protein requirement. Our data suggests that safe protein intake for elderly adults is 1.25 g per kilogram per day. On the basis of current and recalculated short-term nitrogen-balance results, a safe recommended protein intake for older men and

*Not included in this publication.

women should be set at 1.0 g to 1.25 g high-quality protein per kilogram per day. Sahyoun[35] reported that approximately 50% of 946 healthy free-living men and women above the age of 60 years living in the Boston, Mass., area consume less than this amount of protein. The same study showed that 25% of the elderly men and women consume < 0.86 g and < 0.81 g protein per kilogram per day, respectively. A large percentage of homebound elderly people consuming their habitual dietary protein intake (0.67 g mixed protein per kilogram per day) have been shown[41] to be in negative nitrogen balance.

High-intensity resistance training appears to have profound anabolic effects in the elderly. Data from our laboratory demonstrate a 10% to 15% decrease in nitrogen excretion at the initiation of training that persists for 12 weeks. That is, progressive resistance training improved nitrogen balance; thus, older subjects performing resistance training have a lower mean protein requirement than do sedentary subjects. These results are somewhat at variance to the results of Meredith et al.[42], which demonstrated that regularly performed aerobic exercise causes an increase in the mean protein requirement of middle-aged and young endurance athletes. This difference likely results from increased oxidation of amino acids during aerobic exercise that may not be present during resistance training.

Muscle Strength Training in the Elderly

Muscle strength training can be accomplished by virtually anyone. Many health care professionals have directed their patients away from strength training in the mistaken belief that it can cause undesirable elevations in blood pressure. The systolic pressure elevation during aerobic exercise is far greater than that seen during resistance training performance with proper technique. Muscle-strengthening exercises are rapidly becoming a critical component of cardiac rehabilitation programs as clinicians realize the need for strength and endurance for many activities of daily living.

Guidelines for Resistance Exercise Prescription in Elderly People

The following are some practical suggestions for implementing an exercise program for the elderly. We have included guidelines for resistance exercise training, a medical screening questionnaire used for a community-based fitness program, and recommendations on how to begin a community-based program.

Candidates

Adults of all ages are candidates for involvement in an exercise program. However, elderly patients or patients with hypertension should be carefully evaluated before beginning a strength training program. Instead of a treadmill stress test, we use a weight-lifting stress test. Have the patient perform three sets of eight repetitions at approximately 80% of 1RM. Monitor electrocardiogram and blood pressure responses during the exercise. Patients with rheumatoid or osteoarthritis may participate. Patients with a limited range of motion should train within the range of motion that is relatively pain free. Most patients will see a dramatic improvement in the pain-free range of motion as a result of resistance training.

Exercises

Resistance training should be directed at the large muscle groups that are important in everyday activities, including those in the shoulders, arms, spine, hips, and leg. Each repetition should be performed slowly through a full range of motion, allowing 2 to 3 seconds to lift the weight (concentric contraction) and 4 to 6 seconds to lower the weight (eccentric contraction). Performing the exercise more quickly will not enhance strength gains and may increase the risk of an injury.

Training Intensity and Duration

A high-intensity resistance training program has been shown to have the most dramatic effects at all ages. This is a training intensity that will approach or result in muscular fatigue after the muscle has been lifted and lowered with proper form 8 to 12 times. A weight that you can lift 20 or more times will increase your muscular endurance, but not result in much of a gain in strength or muscle mass. The amount of weight that is lifted should increase as strength builds. This should take place about every 2 to 3 weeks. In our studies, we have seen a 10% to 15% increase in strength per week during the first 8 weeks of training. We have seen substantial gains in muscle strength and mass as well as an improvement in bone density with only 2 days/week of training.

Breathing Technique

For proper breathing technique, inhale before a lift, exhale during the lift, and inhale as the weight is lowered to the beginning position. Avoid performing the Valsalva maneuver (i.e., holding your breath during force production). With proper breathing technique, the cardiovascular stress of resistance exercise is minimal and heart rate and blood pressure should rise only slightly above resting values.

Equipment

Any device that provides sufficient resistance to stress muscles beyond levels usually encountered may be used. Weight stack or compressed-air resistance machines may be found at many community fitness facilities or purchased for home use. Simple weight-lifting devices might include Velcro-strapped wrist and ankle bags filled with sand or lead shot, or heavy household objects such as plastic milk jugs filled with water or gravel, or food cans of various sizes.

Increasing Levels of Physical Activity in the Elderly

Initial Health Assessment

Community-based exercise programs for men and women over the age of 50 years are growing in popularity. For such programs, physician screening for every participant may be either impractical or a barrier to participation. However, the American College of Sports Medicine recommends a physician-supervised stress test for anyone over the age of 50 who wants to begin a vigorous training program.[43] If the general recommendation is for an older person to simply walk or participate in a resistance training program, this test is probably not necessary.

The questions presented in Figure 3* may be helpful in determining which persons should be carefully examined by a physician. This questionnaire was developed by Maria Fiatarone, MD, for use in a statewide, community-based exercise program for men and women over the age of 50. Persons who answered yes to any of the questions were strongly encouraged to speak to a physician before participating. However, participation in the exercise program was not prevented if a person did not have a physician's statement. The reason for many of these questions should be obvious. Clearly, the biggest concern is that a person with cardiovascular disease will experience myocardial infarction during exercise. These questions are designed in an attempt to determine who may be at greatest risk.

In our experience, this sort of questionnaire is effective in identifying persons who may be at a higher risk than the general population of men and women over the age of 50 years. Our Massachusetts-wide program—"Keep Moving—Fitness After Fifty"—was a community-based walking program for men and women over the age of 50 years. At its peak, between 7,500 and 8,000 men and women (mean age = 67 ± 5 years) had registered and participated. Walking clubs were located throughout the state in nursing homes, retirement communities, hospitals, and Councils on Aging (buildings that housed many of the activities provided by the Massachusetts Executive Office of Elder Affairs). The questionnaire was approved by a medical advisory board for this program. During the 8 years of the program, there were no reports of a myocardial infarction, cardiac arrest, or other cardiovascular event during the exercise training session.

Warm-Up and Cool-Down

Advancing age results in increased muscle stiffness and reduced elasticity of connective tissue. For this reason proper warm-up and stretching can have a greater effect in reducing the risk of an orthopedic injury in the elderly than in young men and women. A 5-minute warm-up (exercise at a reduced intensity) followed by 5 to 10 minutes of slow stretching is highly recommended. Cool-down after exercise is also important in older persons. One should never finish a workout by immediately jumping into a hot shower. End an exercise session with a slow walk and more stretching. Postexercise stretching will be more effective than the stretching done before the exercise. This is because the muscles have warmed up and, along with tendons and ligaments, are much more elastic. Find a friend to exercise with. The more people one exercises with, the more likely it is that one will stay with the exercise. This is a perfect opportunity for sons and daughters to spend time with their older parents, to the benefit of both generations.

Community-Based Programs

With interest in the establishment of community-based exercise programs for the elderly increasing, the following recommendations may be helpful.

*Not included in this publication.

- Work with local or state agencies. Often, state agencies for aging have a small amount of resources set aside for health-related activities. The persons working in these agencies have access to the elderly population in your area.
- Use an already developed infrastructure. Councils on Aging may have a facility specifically designated for programs that serve the elderly. Contact your local hospital, YMCA, or university.
- Promote and advertise your program as a social exercise program. Often, older women and men will join programs because of increased opportunity for socialization, not necessarily for fitness benefits.
- More women than men will join. Use strategies to increase your recruitment of men.
- Plan for a wide variability in functional status. Highly fit and very frail persons are likely to join. For example, if you establish a walking program, plan to have at least two groups, slow and fast.
- Form a medical advisory group of local physicians.
- Attempt to incorporate some resistance exercise in any newly established program.

Conclusion

There is no group in our society that can benefit more from regularly performed exercise than the elderly. Although both aerobic and strength conditioning are highly recommended, only strength training can stop or reverse sarcopenia. Increased muscle strength and mass in the elderly can be the first step toward a lifetime of increased physical activity and a realistic strategy for maintaining functional status and independence.

References

1. Evans WJ. What is sacropenia? *J Gerontal.* 1995; 50A (special issue):5–8.
2. Frontera WR, Hughes VA, Evans WJ. A cross-sectional study of upper and lower extremity muscle strength in 45–78 year old men and women. *J Appl Physiol.* 1991; 71:644–650.
3. Bassey EJ, Fiatarone MA, O'Neill EF, Kelly M, Evans W J, Lipisitz LA. Leg extensor power and functional performance in very old men and women. *Clin Sci.* 1992; 82:321–327.
4. Meredith CN, Zackin MJ, Frontera WR, Evans WJ. Body composition and aerobic capacity in young and middle-aged endurance-trained men. *Med Sci Sports Exerc.* 1987; 19:557–563.
5. Roberts SB, Young VR, Fuss P, Heyman MB, Fiatarone MA, Dallal GE, Cortiella J, Evans WJ. What are the dietary energy needs of adults? *Int J Obesity.* 1992; 16:969–976.
6. Meredith CN, Frontera WR, Fisher EC, Hughes VA, Herland JC, Edwards J, Evans WJ. Peripheral effects of endurance training in young and old subjects. *J Appl Physiol.* 1989; 66:2844–2849.
7. Seals DR, Hagberg JM, Hurley BF, Ehsani AA, Holloszy JO. Endurance training in older men and women: cardiovascular responses to exercise. *J Appl Physiol: Respirat Environ Exercise Physiol.* 1984; 57(4):1024–1029.
8. Spina RJ, Ogawa T, Kohrt WM, Martin WH III, Holloszy JO, Ehsani AA. Differences in cardiovascular adaptation to endurance exercise training between older men and women. *J Appl Physiol.* 1993; 75(2):849–855.
9. Seals DR, Hagberg JM, Hurley BF, Ehsani AA, Holloszy JO. Effects of endurance training on glucose tolerance and plasma lipid levels in older men and women. *JAMA.* 1984; 252:645–649.
10. Kirwan JP, Kohrt WM, Wojta DM, Bourey RE, Holloszy JO. Endurance exercise training reduces glucose-stimulated insulin levels in 60- to 70-year-old men and women. *J Gerontol.* 1993; 48(3):M84–M90.
11. Hughes VA, Fiatarone MA, Fielding RA, Kahn BB, Ferrara CM, Shepherd P, Fisher EC, Wolfe RR, Elahi D, Evans WJ. Exercise increases muscle GLUT 4 levels and insulin action in subjects with impaired glucose tolerance. *Am J Physiol.* 1993; 264:E855–E862.
12. Marshall JA, Hamman RF, Baxter J. High-fat, low-carbohydrate diet and the etiology of non-insulin-dependent diabetes mellitus: the San Luis Valley Diabetes Study. *Am J Epidermiol.* 1991; 134:590–603.
13. Feskens EJM, Kromhout D. Cardiovascular risk factors and the 25-year incidence of diabetes mellitus in middle-aged men. *Am J Epidemiol.* 1989; 130:1101–1108.
14. Lundgren J, Bengtsson C, Blohme G, Isaksson B, Lapidus L, Lenner RA, Saaek A, Winther E. Dietary habits and incidence of noninsulin-dependent diabetes mellitus in a population study of women in Gothenburg, Sweden. *Am J Clin Nutr.* 1989; 49:708–712.
15. Garg A, Grundy SM, Unger RH. Comparison of effects of high and low carbohydrate diets on plasma lipoprotein and insulin sensitivity in patients with mild NIDDM. *Diabetes.* 1992; 41:1278–1285.
16. Borkman M, Campbell LV, Chisholm D J, Storlien LH. Comparison of the effects on insulin sensitivity of high carbohydrate and high fat diets in normal subjects. *J Clin Endocrinol.* 1991; 72:432–437.
17. Hughes VA, Fiatarone MA, Fielding RA, Ferrara CM, Elahi D, Evans WJ. Long term effects of a high carbohydrate diet and exercise on insulin action in older subjects with impaired glucose tolerance. *Am J Clin Nutr.* 1995; 62:426–433.
18. Schaefer EJ, Lichtenstein AH, Lamon-Fava S, McNamara JR, Schaefer MM, Rasmussen H, Ordovas JO. Body weight and low-density lipoprotein cholesterol changes after consumption of a low-fat ad libitum diet. *JAMA.* 1995; 274:1450–1455.
19. Helmrich SP, Ragland DR, Leung RW, Paffenbarger RS Jr. Physical activity and reduced occurrence of non-insulin-dependent diabetes mellitus. *N Engl J Med.* 1991; 325:14–52.
20. Bogardus C, Ravussin E, Robbins DC, Wolfe RR, Horton ES, Sims EAH. Effects of physical training and diet therapy on carbohydrate

metabolism in patients with glucose intolerance and non-insulin-dependent diabetes mellitus. *Diabetes.* 1984; 33:311–318.

21. Phinney SD, LaGrange BM, O'Connell M, Danforth E Jr. Effects of aerobic exercise on energy expenditure and nitrogen balance during very low calorie dieting. *Metabolism.* 1988; 37:758–765.

22. Heymsfield SB, Casper K, Hearn J, Guy D. Rate of weight loss during underfeeding: relation to level of physical activity. 1989; 38(3):215–223.

23. Goran MI, Poehlman ET. Endurance training does not enhance total energy expenditure in healthy elderly persons. *Am J Physiol* 1992; 263:E950–E957.

24. Ballor DL, Katch VL, Becque MD, Marks CR. Resistance weight training during caloric restriction enhances lean body weight maintenance. *Am J Clin Nutr* 1988; 47:19–25.

25. Pavlou KN, Steffee WP, Lerman RH, Burrows BA. Effects of dieting and exercise on lean body mass, oxygen uptake, and strength. *Med Sci Sports Exerc.* 1985; 17:466–471.

26. ACSM position stand—the recommended quantity and quality of exercise for developing and maintaining cardiorespiratory and muscular fitness in healthy adults. *Med Sci Sports Exerc.* 1990; 22:265–274.

27. Evans WJ, Cannon JG. The metabolic effects of exercise-induced muscle damage. In: Holloszy JO, ed. *Exercise and Sport Sciences Reviews.* Baltimore, Md: Williams & Wilkins; 1991:99–126.

28. Flegg JL, Lakatta EG. Role of muscle loss in the age-associated reduction in VO$_2$max *J Appl Physiol.* 1988; 65:1147–1151.

29. Fiatarone MA, Marks EC, Ryan ND, Meredith CN, Lipsitz LA, Evans WJ. High-intensity strength training in nonagenarians. Effects on skeletal muscle. *JAMA.* 1990; 263:3029–3034.

30. Fiatarone MA, O'Neill EF, Ryan ND, Clements KM, Solares GR, Nelson ME, Roberts SB, Kehayias JJ, Lipsitz LA, Evans WJ. Exercise training and nutritional supplementation for physical frailty in very elderly people. *N Engl J Med* l994; 330:1769–1775.

31. Food and Nutrition Board. *Recommended Dietary Allowances.* 10th ed. Washington, DC: National Academy Press; 1989.

32. Nelson ME, Fiatarone MA, Morganti CM, Trice I, Greenberg RA, Evans WJ. Effects of high-intensity strength training on multiple risk factors for osteoporotic fractures. *JAMA.* 1942; 272:1909–1914.

33. Frontera WR, Meredith CN, O'Reilly KP, Evans WJ. Strength training and determinants of VO$_2$max in older men. *J Appl Physiol.* 1990; 68:329–333.

34. Campbell WW, Crim MC, Young VR, Evans WJ. Increased energy requirements and body composition changes with resistance training in older adults. *Am J Clin Nutr.* 1994; 60:167–175.

35. Sahyoun N. Nutrient intake by the NSS elderly population. In: Hartz SC, Russell RM, Rosenberg IH, eds. *Nutrition in the Elderly: The Boston Nutritional Status Survey.* London, England: Smith-Gordon and Company; 1992:31–44.

36. Gersovitz M, Munro H, Scrimshaw N, Young V. Human protein requirements: assessment of the adequacy of the current recommended dietary allowance for dietary protein in elderly men and women. *Am J Clin Nutr.* 1982; 35:6–14.

37. Uauy R, Scrimshaw N, Young V. Human protein requirements: nitrogen balance response to graded levels of egg protein in elderly men and women. *Am J Clin Nutr.* 1978; 31:779–785.

38. Zanni E, Calloway D, Zezulka A. Protein requirements of elderly men. *J Nutr.* 1979; 109:513–524.

39. Campbell WW, Crim MC, Dallal GE, Young VR, Evans WJ. Increased protein requirements in the elderly: new data and retrospective reassessments. *Am J Clin Nutr.* 1994; 60:167–175.

40. World Health Organization, Food and Agriculture Organization, United Nations University. Energy and protein requirements. *World Health Organ Tech Rep Ser.* 1985:724.

41. Bunker V, Lawson M, Stansfield M, Clayton B. Nitrogen balance studies in apparently healthy elderly people and those who are housebound. *Br J Nutr.* 1987; 57:211–221.

42. Meredith CN, Zackin MJ, Frontera WR, Evans WJ. Dietary protein requirements and body protein metabolism in endurance-trained men. *J Appl Physiol.* 1989; 66:2850–2856.

43. Kenney WL, ed. *ACSM's Guidelines for Exercise Testing and Prescription.* 5th ed. Media, Pa: Williams & Wilkins; 1995.

44. Saltin B. Physical training in patients with intermittent claudication. In: *Physical Conditioning and Cardiovascular Rehab.* New York, NY: Cohen, Mock and Ringquist; 1981:181–196.

Article Review Form at end of book.

What is the most general age-related change in the sexual response cycle? What is the average age of menopause?

Aging and Sexuality

Cindy M. Meston, PhD

Seattle, Washington

Recent research suggesting that a high proportion of men and women remain sexually active well into later life refutes the prevailing myth that aging and sexual dysfunction are inexorably linked. Age-related physiological changes do not render a meaningful sexual relationship impossible or even necessarily difficult. In men, greater physical stimulation is required to attain and maintain erections, and orgasms are less intense. In women, menopause terminates fertility and produces changes stemming from estrogen deficiency. The extent to which aging affects sexual function depends largely on psychological, pharmacological, and illness-related factors. In this article I review the physiological sex-related changes that occur as part of the normal aging process in men and women. I also summarize the effects on sexual function of age-related psychological issues, illness factors, and medication use. An understanding of the sexual changes that accompany normal aging may help physicians give patients realistic and encouraging advice on sexuality. Although it is important that older men and women not fall into the psychosocial trap of expecting (or worse, trying to force) the kind and degree of sexual response characteristic of their youth, it is equally as important that they not fall prey to the negative folklore according to which decreased physical intimacy is an inevitable consequence of the passage of time.

(Meston CM. Aging and sexuality. In: *Successful Aging. West J Med* 1997; 167:285–290)

> [My] . . . Age is as a lusty winter.
> Frosty, but Kindly.
> WILLIAM SHAKESPEARE
> *As You Like It*[1]

Sexual desire and activity continue well into later life for both men and women but can be affected in various ways by aging. I begin by discussing these effects in men.

Men

Although an age-related decline in sexual activity and desire among men has been reported in numerous studies, maintaining a healthy interest in sexual activity is not uncommon among 70-, 80-, and even 90-year-old men. Pfeiffer and associates[2] reported that 95% of men aged 46 to 50 years and 28% of men aged 66 to 71 years have intercourse on a weekly basis. Diokno and co-workers[3] have reported that nearly 74% of married men older than 60 remain sexually active, and Bretschneider and McCoy[4] found that 63% of men aged 80 to 102 years continue to be sexually active. In view of the fact that sexuality in the literature is often defined exclusively in terms of intercourse, these estimates would probably be even higher if noncoital acts such as touching, caressing, fantasy, and masturbation were taken into account.

The age-related decrease in libido noted among men is most frequently attributed to a decline

From the Reproductive and Sexual Medicine Clinic, University of Washington School of Medicine, Seattle.

This research was supported by a Social Sciences and Humanities Research Council of Canada postdoctoral fellowship.

Reprint requests to Cindy M. Meston, PhD. Reproductive and Sexual Medicine Clinic. University of Washington School of Medicine. Psychiatry Outpatient Center, 4225 Roosevelt Way, NE, Suite 306, Seattle, WA 98105. E-mail: meston@u.washington. edu.

in testosterone levels and to changes in receptor site sensitivity to androgen. The sex hormone status of a healthy man remains relatively stable from puberty until the fifth decade of life, at which time androgen production gradually declines. The first sign of an alteration endocrine function is a small increase in pituitary-stimulating hormone levels (gonadotropins), which signals the relative inability of the aging testes to efficiently produce testosterone.[5] Serum testosterone levels gradually decline as a consequence, and by age 80 they may be only a sixth those of a younger man.[6] Although the drop in serum testosterone levels clearly parallels the decline in sexual libido noted with age, there is little evidence to suggest that testosterone replacement therapy augments sexual drive in men with normal baseline testosterone levels. That is, administering massive doses of androgen to an 80-year-old will not restore his libido to what it was when he was 18.[5]

There appears to be a minimal level of testosterone necessary for adequate sexual functioning, above and beyond which additional amounts have no effect. This probably reflects limitations set by the number and sensitivity of functional testosterone receptors. Because most older men apparently have these receptors in numbers above the "critical" level, it is generally assumed that exogenous testosterone would be superfluous and would not restore age-related decreases in sexual drive. Using a placebo-controlled design, Morales and associates[7] examined the effects of exogenously administered adrenal androgen dehydroepiandrosterone (DHEA) on a number of age-related factors in 13 men aged 40 to 70 years. When levels were restored to those of a younger age group, DHEA had no direct effect on sexual interest. Replacement DHEA did, however, have a beneficial effect on general measures of well-being. Such measures may, in turn, have a positive effect on sexual satisfaction and function. Further studies of the effects of DHEA on male sexual function and well-being are required before treatment considerations are warranted.

Women

A decline in sexual interest and desire is frequently reported to be more severe in aging women than aging men. Such assertions are often based on studies that compare the incidence of sexual activity in aging men with that in aging women. For example, recent research indicates that approximately 56% of married women older than 60 (compared with 75% of married men) are sexually active,[3] as are approximately 30% of women aged 80 to 102 years (compared with 63% of men).[4] As noted earlier, sexual interest and activity in studies of this nature are too often measured solely according to frequency of intercourse. Given that by the age of 80 or older there are 39 men for every 100 women,[8] lack of opportunity may well account for a large portion of such gender differences. More importantly, gender differences in the incidence of intercourse and masturbation are apparent in adolescence and throughout adulthood,[9] not only among older people. Hence, age-related changes in sexual activity may best be understood by examining change across a person's total lifespan rather than comparing incidence between genders. To this end, the Janus report[10] indicated surprisingly little change in sexual activity across the average woman's lifespan. In this report, 68% of women aged 39 to 50 engaged in sexual activity at least once a week, as did 65% of women aged 51 to 64 and 74% of women older than 65. As is the case in men, masturbation frequency in women has been noted to decline with age, but it continues to be practiced by approximately half of the healthy female population over the age of 60.[12] In contrast to research indicating that sexual desire declines with age, 9% of women interviewed for a Danish study[13] reported an increase in sexual desire during or after menopause.

One of the primary causes of decreased sexual desire in postmenopausal women is decreased vaginal lubrication or a thinning of the vaginal lining, both of which may lead to pain during vaginal intercourse. In such cases, sexual desire generally returns once some form of treatment (for example, estrogen or lubricants) has relieved the symptoms.[14] A lack of bioavailable testosterone may also reduce sexual desire in women. Although there is no absolute level of testosterone necessary for sexual desire, it has been suggested that there is a threshold level of circulating androgen below which the intensity of desire is affected.[15] It is not clear why some menopausal women experience a sharp decline in testosterone production,[14] nor has it been proved that androgen replacement therapy is of more than marginal therapeutic value in such cases.[15] More importantly, the safety of prescribing testosterone is currently controversial. Testosterone may affect cholesterol and liver protein levels; at high doses, it may also cause masculinizing effects such as facial hair or lowered vocal pitch.[14] Researchers have recently examined the effect of the adrenal androgen DHEA on the sexuality of women aged 40 to 70 years.[7,16] Although neither circulating nor replacement levels of DHEA were directly linked to measures of sexuality in women, DHEA was significantly associated with measures of overall well-being.[7,16] Well-being in turn was shown to be predictive of the quality of sexual relationships.[16] Further studies of this nature are required before suggestions for treatment can be made.

The less frequent reports of increased sexual desire among older women may also be explained by hormonal changes that occur following menopause. When estrogen levels decline, levels of follicle-stimulating hormone and luteinizing hormone increase in an effort to stimulate estrogen production. The increase in these two hormones stimulates certain cells in the ovarian stromal tissue to produce testosterone. Women vary widely with regard to efficiency in producing testosterone in this manner.[14] Women who have an increase in testosterone production during or after menopause may possibly have increased sexual desire. Psychological factors such as elimination of the fear of conception may also play a role in increasing sexual desire after menopause.[14]

Physiologic Aspects of Aging and Sexuality in Men

With regard to actual physiologic changes that occur with age and affect sexual functioning, much individual variation exists. It has been estimated that 55% of men experience impotence by the age of 75.[17] This should not be taken to mean that erectile failure is a normal stage in the aging process. The alterations that lead to decreased sexual functioning, particularly erectile failure, are multifactorial, made up of elements that may be both organic (such as the effects of disease or medication) and psychological (for example, anxiety and guilt). It is clear that all stages of the human sexual response cycle, as defined by Masters and Johnson,[18] are influenced by age-related factors, but there is no evidence to suggest that erectile failure is inevitable among aging men who are psychologically and physiologically healthy.

The Sexual Response Cycle

Normal age-related changes that accompany the excitement stage of sexual response in men include a decrease in, or lack of, elevation in testosterone levels; a decrease in scrotal vasocongestion; reduced tensing of the scrotal sac; and delayed erection. Where a young man may achieve a full erection in seconds, an older man may require several minutes to attain a similar response. Age-related changes in adrenergic and cholinergic mechanisms may partly explain these changes. The process of erection is a vascular event mediated by the autonomic nervous system. Corporeal smooth-muscle tone plays a primary role in erectile ability; gap junctions and ion channel mechanisms, in turn, are largely responsible for determining the degree of smooth-muscle tone.[19] With advancing age, there is evidence that a decline occurs in the number of β-adrenergic and cholinergic receptors, which may lead to increased dominance of α^1-adrenergic activity (that is, increased corporeal smooth-muscle tone). This in turn may interfere with the corporeal smooth-muscle relaxation necessary for initiation and maintenance of the erectile response.[19] Age-related cellular changes may also negatively affect the erectile response through an increased deposition of connective tissue, causing a decrease in penile distensibility.[19] This loss of corporeal elasticity may lead to lowered compression among emissary veins, resulting in venous leakage and consequent difficulty achieving erection.

Penile sensitivity also decreases with age.[20] Attaining and maintaining an erection, therefore, becomes more dependent on direct physical stimulation and less dependent on, or responsive to, centrally controlled visual, psychological, or nongenital excitation.[19] As a result, partners may need to facilitate the erectile response by providing manual or oral stimulation before intromission and possibly at periods throughout the sexual act to help sustain erection until orgasm. Penile rigidity declines gradually, beginning in most men at age 60.[19] Generally, rigidity remains adequate for vaginal intercourse, but couples may need to experiment with different coital positions or supplement intercourse with manual stimulation.

The plateau stage of sexual response is prolonged with age, and pre-ejaculatory secretions and emissions are reduced or cease to occur. Prior difficulties with pre-mature ejaculation may be resolved in older men because of the increase in stimulation and time required to reach orgasm. The duration of orgasm decreases with age, there are fewer and less intense spastic prostate and urethral muscle contractions, and there is a decrease in expulsive ejaculatory force. The period of inevitability before ejaculation is reduced from between 2 to 4 seconds in younger men to approximately 1 second in older men, and there is a slow but gradual decline in semen volume per ejaculation.[19] Occasionally orgasm may occur without ejaculation. The final postorgasmic or resolution stage of sexual response is marked by more rapid loss of vasocongestion and an increase in the length of the refractory period. For a man in his 20s the refractory period may last only minutes; for a man in his 80s it may extend to several days— probably the amount of time required for ionic and neurotransmitter concentrations to be restored to normal levels.[19]

Physiologic Aspects of Aging and Sexuality in Women

Effects of Menopause

Menopause, which occurs in most women at about age 50, is associated with substantial reductions in estrogen, progesterone and androgen levels. Following menopause, estrogen is almost exclusively derived from the peripheral conversion of adrenal androgens. Around age 65, there is a further decrease in adrenal androgen production, often referred to as adrenopause.[15] The decline in estrogen that accompanies menopause leads to a number of normal age-related changes in genital appearance. Such changes include a reduction in pubic hair, loss of fat and subcutaneous tissue from the mons pubis, atrophy of the labia majora, and shortening and loss of elasticity of the vaginal barrel. Vaginal secretions decrease in quantity as a result of

both atrophy of the Bartholin glands and a decrease in the number and maturity of vaginal cells. The vaginal epithelium, which is highly estrogen dependent, becomes flattened and loses glycogen: this leads to a decrease in *Lactobacillus* species and lactic acid and an increase in vaginal pH.[21] These alterations affect the vaginal microbial population and put aging women at greater risk for developing bacterial infections.[22] Together with decreased vaginal lubrication, the reduction in thickness of the epithelium from approximately eight to ten cell layers to three to four may lead to postcoital bleeding, mild burning sensations during intercourse, and pain.[22] For such reasons, dyspareunia is the most common sexual complaint older women seeking gynecologic consultation.[23] With decreased estrogenic stimulation, the uterus is reduced in size and the total collagen and elastic content decreases by 30% to 50%.[24] The uterine cervix also atrophies and loses fibromuscular stroma, and the ovaries, with no remaining follicles, become reduced in size and weight and the ovarian stromal tissue becomes fibrotic and sclerotic.[22] Estrogen replacement therapy, when given systemically at high doses, has a beneficial effect on urogenital tissue[23] but is associated with an increased risk of breast and endometrial cancer.[25] In the absence of other postmenopausal symptoms, vaginal estrogen cream administered a few times per week may be equally effective.

The Sexual Response Cycle

A number of age-related changes affect the female sexual response cycle. During the excitement phase, vaginal blood flow and genital engorgement are less in-

tense than in younger women and take longer to occur. This phenomenon may be less pronounced in women who continue to be sexually active than in those who are celibate, although its mechanism is not well understood.[15] Vaginal lubrication is delayed and reduced in quantity. Whereas in younger women the excitement stage with lubrication may take only 10 to 15 seconds, in postmenopausal women it may take as long as 5 minutes or longer.[26] The decrease in vaginal vasocongestion and lubrication may contribute to dryness of the vagina and may make intercourse painful. A variety of topical lubricants have been used successfully to compensate for insufficient vaginal lubrication. For women who prefer not to use a lubricant during intercourse, nonhormonal preparations such as Replens or oil from a vitamin E capsule, applied vaginally every other day, may greatly alleviate vaginal dryness, as may taking zinc orally.[14] Despite these age-related physiologic changes, several studies have reported that postmenopausal women report little or no change in the subjective experience of sexual arousal.[27]

The plateau phase of sexual response is prolonged in older women, uterine elevation is reduced, the labia majora do not elevate to the same degree as in younger years, the breasts become less vasocongested, and nipple erection is less likely to occur.[1,15] The orgasmic response does not appear to be substantially affected by age. Women retain multiorgasmic capacity, although the number and intensity of vaginal and rectal contractions are reduced.[5] While younger women average five to ten vaginal contractions with orgasm, older women average two or three.[5] As is the case in men, the resolution stage of sexual response in older women is characterized by a rapid loss of vasocongestion.

Illness, Medication Use, and Sexuality Among Older Persons

Physical illness can affect sexual function directly by interfering with endocrine, neural, and vascular processes that mediate the sexual response, indirectly by causing weakness or pain and psychologically by provoking changes in body image and self-esteem. The scope of this article precludes a comprehensive discussion of the effects of medical illness on sexuality; accordingly, only the most prevalent age-related medical illnesses, prescribed medications, and their effects on sexuality will be mentioned here (for a review, see Badeau[28]).

Men

Medical or surgical therapy for a number of age-related diseases can affect erectile function by interfering with the neurologic innervation of the penis. Interventions that may have this effect include lower abdominal surgery, pelvic irradiation, and certain types of prostate surgery.[5] Transurethral resection of the prostate has been reported to cause erectile failure in 4% to 12% of cases.[2] Radical prostatectomy for prostate cancer, cystectomy for bladder cancer, and colerectal surgery may all damage the neuromuscular bundle of the penis. Although increasing attention has been paid to preservation of the neurovascular bundle, men with aberrant cavernous arteries more

often than not suffer erectile dysfunction from such procedures.[19] A number of age-related disease states may interfere with erectile function directly. The atherosclerosis associated with cardiovascular disease may involve the penile arteries as well as the coronary arteries. Occlusion of the abdominal aorta or the iliac arteries may also be associated with the failure to attain erection.[5] Because the act of intercourse increases heart rate and blood pressure, fear of chest pain during intercourse may further impede sexual relations. Diabetes mellitus is commonly associated with erectile failure. Within only five years after the onset of type II disease, 60% of male patients have some form of sexual dysfunction.[19] The causes of erectile failure in diabetic men are largely neurogenic and vascular, but also include alterations in corporeal smooth-muscle reactivity and microangiopathy, which may cause arterial insufficiency.[19] Somatic and autonomic neuropathy may produce neurogenic impotence in older diabetic men. Other endocrine or metabolic disorders associated with erectile problems include hypothyroidism, hyperthyroidism, hypogonadism, hyperprolactine-mia, and Cushing's disease. Systemic disorders known to impair erection include renal failure, chronic obstructive pulmonary disease, cirrhosis, and myotonia dystrophia. Among the neurologic disorders that may inhibit erection are spinal cord injury, cerebrovascular accidents, temporal lobe epilepsy, multiple sclerosis, and sensory neuropathy.[1,5]

A wide variety of drugs have been reported to impair erectile ability, particularly among older persons. The aging process influences physiologic

drug distribution, metabolism, and excretion and renders older persons more vulnerable to the side effects of medication.[19] Among medications, antihypertensive agents that act either centrally (for example, methyldopa and clonidine) or peripherally (for example, reserpine, guanethidine), β-blockers (such as propranolol or labetalol), α-blockers (including prazocin and terazocin), and diuretics (for example, thiazide and spironolactone) appear to be the primary offenders in causing impaired erection.[19] In addition, cardiovascular drugs (such as disopyramide), cancer chemotherapy agents, anxiolytics (benzodiazepines), antipsychotics (for example, haloperidol, thioridazine, and chlorpromazine), a wide range of antidepressants (such as imipramine, amitriptyline, trazodone, and fluoxetine), lithium, and numerous drugs of abuse (including cocaine, alcohol, narcotics, and amphetamines) have all been linked to impaired erectile function (for reviews, see Schiavi and Rehman[19] and Meston and Gorzalka[30]). With diseases such as depression, hypertension, and atherosclerosis, it is difficult to determine the extent to which the sexual dysfunction is a result of the prescribed medication or the disease per se, given that both may negatively affect the sexual response.

Women

Surgical treatment of gynecologic and breast cancer often has a deleterious effect on sexual function in women by assaulting body image. Although breast or vulvovaginal surgery undoubtedly affects self-esteem in women of all ages, the psychological damage may be further compounded in older women whose body image is perhaps already affected by age-related body changes. Urinary incontinence occurs in up to 25% of older women during intercourse.[31] This disorder commonly leads to dissatisfaction with the sexual relationship or withdrawal from sexual contact because of embarrassment. Renal failure has been reported to cause anorgasmia, decreased libido, and impaired vaginal lubrication in women on dialysis.[1]

Hysterectomy is the most commonly performed operation in women: more than a third of women in the United States have had a hysterectomy by age 60. This procedure has not been shown to have a direct effect on sexual function, some women, however, report a decline in orgasmic pleasure following hysterectomy because of the absence of uterine contractions. For women who view hysterectomy as a further loss of femininity, self-esteem and body image may be damaged by this type of surgery. Conversely, for women who experience relief from pain, abnormal bleeding, or cramping, hysterectomy may result in improved sexual function.[1]

In contrast to an abundance of research on diabetes and male sexual function, there is a paucity of studies examining the effects of diabetes on female sexual function. Decreased sexual desire, anorgasmia, and difficulty obtaining sufficient vaginal lubrication during sexual arousal have been identified in some women with type II diabetes mellitus.[5,15] The duration of diabetes, age, or insulin dosage does not appear to be correlated with sexual function among women with diabetes,[32] and there is no evidence that peripheral or autonomic neuropathies directly affect the female sexual response.[15]

Research into the effects of medication use on sexual function in women has lagged considerably behind that in men. Antidepressant drugs are commonly reported to affect sexual functioning in women. Side effects associated with antidepressant medications include decreased sexual desire, impaired arousal and lubrication, vaginal anesthesia, delayed orgasm, and anorgasmia (for a review, see Meston and Gorzalka[30]). Serotonergic systems are frequently implicated in antidepressant-induced sexual side effects, although data are inconsistent as to whether the role of serotonin in sexual behavior is inhibitory, excitatory, or both.[30] Antipsychotic and neuroleptic medications have also been linked to impaired sexual function in women. Most recently, the antihypertensive drug clonidine has been shown to impair physiologic sexual response in women by decreasing vaginal blood volume and pressure pulse responses.[33] Clearly, there is a need for further research in this area.

Psychological Aspects of Aging and Sexuality

Not surprisingly, a number of psychological factors that influence the sexuality of younger persons also affect older men and women. Of particular importance is the nature of the interpersonal relationship. Marital conflict, relationship imbalances, commitment issues, intimacy and communication problems, lack of trust, mismatches in sexual desire, boredom, and poor sexual technique are just some of the common sources of sexual dissatisfaction noted among couples of all ages.[5,34] In older people these factors may be amplified by anger and resentment that may have built over the years, as well as by feelings of entrapment and resignation if the option to leave the relationship no longer seems viable. As with younger couples, marital satisfaction is closely linked to sexual satisfaction in older couples.[34]

Increases in psychosocial stresses, such as the death of a spouse, loss of a job or social status, deterioration of support networks, and health- and finance-related family problems, are common experiences among the aged. These life changes may contribute to sexual difficulties in older people by increasing the likelihood of depression or anxiety. "Widower's syndrome" refers to the onset of sexual difficulties in older persons who resume sexual interactions after a period of celibacy following the death of a spouse. Sexual difficulties in this situation are generally attributable to unresolved feelings of grief, guilt, anger, or even relief in cases in which the partner had been ill for a long period before death.[5] Performance anxiety related to beginning a new sexual relationship may be a problem for both men and women, but may play a particularly detrimental role in male sexual function because of the well-known adverse effects of anxiety on erectile function.

Because women generally marry men older than themselves, and are likely to outlive men by an average of seven to eight years, women are more likely than men to experience the death of a spouse in old age. Given the shortage of available older male partners, women are also more likely than men to spend the later years of life alone.

Many older women report feeling sexually frustrated at the lack of an available sexual partner. Although masturbation is a viable option, older persons may have been brought up to believe that masturbation is unnatural or even unhealthy. Education and permission from a health care professional may help to alter such misconceptions.[5] Also common among older people are false expectations regarding the effects of aging on sexuality. Self-critical anxieties about one's sexual abilities or physical imperfections can be distracting or even destructive to sexual pleasure and excitement. The societal emphasis that has linked sexuality almost exclusively to young people may lead some older people to feel ashamed of their continued sexual interest and may consequently discourage them from seeking sexual advice. Information from physicians regarding normal age-related changes in sexuality and encouragement, together with advice on how to continue meaningful sexual relations, may play a key role in altering such negative attitudes.

References

1. Kaiser FE. Sexuality in the elderly. *Geriatr Urol* 1996; 1:99–109
2. Pfeiffer E, Verwoerdt A, Want HS. Sexual behavior in aged men and women. *Arch Gen Psychiatry* 1968; 19:735–758
3. Diokno AC, Brown MB, Herzog AR. Sexual function in the elderly. *Arch Intern Med* 1990; 150:197–200
4. Bretschneider JG, McCoy NL. Sexual interest and behavior in healthy 80 to 102 year olds. *Arch Sex Behav* 1988; 17:109–129
5. Leiblum SR, Rosen RC, editors. *Principles and practice of sex therapy. Update for the 1990s.* New York: Guilford Press; 1989.
6. Schover LR. *Prime time: sexual health for men over fifty.* New York: Holt, Rinehart & Winston; 1984
7. Morales AJ, Nolan JJ, Nelson JC, Yen SS. Effects of replacement dose of dehydroepiandrosterone in men and women of advancing age. *J Clin Endocrinol Metab* 1994; 78:1360–1367
8. *Current Population Reports Series.* US Bureau of the Census 1057:25, 1990
9. Meston CM, Trapnell PD, Gorzalka BB. Ethnic and gender differences in sexuality: Variations in sexual behavior between Asian and non-Asian university students. *Arch Sex Behav* 1996; 25:33–72
10. Janus SS, Janus CL. *The Janus Report on sexual behavior.* New York: John Wiley & Sons; 1993
11. Christenson CV, Gagnon JH. Sexual behavior in a group of older women. *J. Gerontal* 1965; 20:351
12. Ludeman K. The sexuality of the older person: review of the literature. *Gerontologist* 1981; 21:203
13. Koster A. Change-of-life anticipations, attitudes, and experiences among middle-aged Danish women. *Health Care Women Int* 1991; 12:1
14. Barbach L. Sexuality through menopause and beyond. *Menopause Management* 1996; 5:18–21
15. Roughan PA, Kaiser FE, Morley JE. Sexuality and the older woman. *Care Older Woman* 1993; 1:87–106
16. Cawood EHH, Bancroft J. Steroid hormones, the menopause, sexuality and well-being of women. *Psychol Med* 1996; 26:925–936
17. Kinsey AC, Pomeroy WB, Martin CE. *Sexual behavior in the human male.* Philadelphia (Pa): WB Saunders; 1948
18. Masters WH, Johnson VE. *Human sexual response.* Boston (Mass): Little, Brown; 1966
19. Schiavi RC, Rehman. Sexuality and aging. *Urol Clin North Am* 1995; 22:711–726
20. Edwards AE, Husted J. Penile sensitivity, age and sexual behavior. *J Clin Psychol* 1976; 32:697–700
21. Semens JF, Wagner G. Estrogen deprivation and hormonal function in postmenopausal women. *JAMA* 1982; 445:248–253
22. Bachmann GA. Influence of menopause on sexuality. *Int J Fertil* 1995; 40:16–22
23. Bachmann G, Leiblum S. Grill J, Brief sexual inquiry in gynecologic practice. *Obstet Gynecol* 1989; 73:425–427
24. Woessner JP. Age-related changes of the human uterus: its connective tissue framework. *J Gerontal* 1963; 18:220–224
25. Dupont WD, Page DL. Menopausal estrogen replacement therapy and breast cancer. *Arch Intern Med* 1991; 151:67–72
26. Gupta K. Sexual dysfunction in elderly women. *Urol Care Elderly* 1990; 6:197–203
27. Myers L, Morokoff P. *Physiological and subjective sexual arousal in pre and postmenopausal women.* Paper presented at the American Psychological Association Meeting, 1985
28. Badeau D. Illness, disability and sex in aging. *Sex Dis* 1995; 13:219–237
29. Bolt JW, Evans C, Marshall UR. Sexual dysfunction after prostatectomy. *Br J Urol* 1986; 58:319
30. Meston CM, Gorzalka BB. Psychoactive drugs and human sexual behavior: The role of serotonergic activity. *J Psychoactive Drugs* 1992; 24:1–40
31. Hilton P. Urinary incontinence during sexual intercourse: a common but rarely volunteered symptom. *Br J Obstet Gynaecol* 1988; 95:377–381
32. Meston CM, Gorzalka BB, Wright JM. Inhibition of physiological and subjective sexual arousal in women by clonidine. *J Psychosom Med* 1997; 59:399–407
33. Schreiner-Engel P, Schiavi RC, Vietorisz D. et al. The differential impact of diabetes type on female sexuality. *J Psychosom Res* 1987; 31:23–33
34. Brecher E. *Love, sex and aging: a Consumer's Union survey.* Boston (Mass): Little, Brown; 1984

Article Review Form at end of book.

WiseGuide Wrap-Up

- It's never too late to make lifestyle adjustments to improve the quality of life.

- An active, independent old age is more important than long life expectancy.

- Limiting the number of medications one is exposed to can reduce the incidence of adverse drug reactions.

- Sexual activity among the elderly is both normal and necessary.

R.E.A.L. Sites

This list provides a print preview of typical **coursewise** R.E.A.L. sites. There are over 100 such sites at the **courselinks**™ site. The danger in printing URLs is that web sites can change overnight. As we went to press, these sites were functional using the URLs provided. If you come across one that isn't, please let us know via email to: webmaster@coursewise.com. Use your Passport to access the most current list of R.E.A.L. sites at the **courselinks**™ site.

Site name: Nutrition Analysis Tool

URL: http://www.ag.uiuc.edu/~food-lab/nat

Why is it R.E.A.L.? This site is a nutrition analysis site. Enter food ingested and receive a breakdown of nutrient content. Also gives suggestions of what foods to eat to balance the diet, and offers a way to keep track of everything eaten in a day.

Key topic: nutrition

Activity: Use the Energy Calculator at this site to determine how many calories you should be eating based on your daily activities.

Site name: 50's Fitness: The Basics for the Mature Adult

URL: http://www.fitlife.com/fitness/fit50s.shtml

Why is it R.E.A.L.? This page is part of Fitlife, an electronic resource of fitness, health promotion, wellness, and lifestyle. It offers fundamental fitness information including setting goals, training (frequency, intensity and duration guidelines), target heart rates for each decade over 50, phases of training (warm-up, training, and cool-down), flexibility, and muscular strength and endurance.

Key topic: exercise

Activity: What is the goal for most individuals in this age group?

Site name: Nutrition, Health, and Aging

URL: http://www.usc.edu/dept/gero/nutrition

Why is it R.E.A.L.? This is part of the Andrus Gerontology Center at the University of Southern California in Los Angeles. Visitors to the site can take a quiz on "What Is Your Nutritional Score?", determine if your medications are interfering with what you eat, determine if you are drinking enough water, and learn about the relationship between diet and the diseases of hypertension, cancer, osteoporosis, Parkinson's, and Alzheimer's disease.

Key topics: nutrition, Alzheimer's disease, and medications

Activity: Take the YOU ARE WHAT YOU EAT!!! quiz to determine your nutritional score.

section

5

Key Points

- As the population ages, more stress will be placed upon the health care delivery system.

- There are differences in the way subcultures view medical care providers.

- Innovative programs dealing with both the social needs and physical needs of the elderly are needed.

Aging and Society

WiseGuide Intro

So far, the focus of *Perspectives: Aging* has mainly been on the impact of aging on the body. Section 5 approaches aging from a different perspective and focuses on the impact of aging on *society*. As the aging population continues to increase, the social needs of the elderly must be considered, as well as their physical and psychological needs.

Medical care and long-term care are two critical issues facing today's elderly. As the cost of medical care continues to increase, society is faced with some perplexing problems. Several readings in this section look at options for dealing with these issues. One selection specifically details a model program dealing with managed care and Alzheimer's disease, while another describes an innovative approach to services for the elderly that involves the entire community.

The social discrepancies involving health care and minorities are examined in reading about the historical Tuskegee incident. Another reading reveals the tragedies surrounding elder abuse, another social concern of the aged that is often referred to as the hidden crime. The readings in this section will help open your eyes to the important social issues impacting the elderly of today, as well as future senior citizens. It also describes the positive impact of an intergenerational program that brings together the elderly and children in a mutually beneficial way.

Questions

Reading 24. According to Eric Erikson, what is successful aging related to? What is the most important element of successful aging?

Reading 25. What are the most significant problems facing the elderly today? Does the current social insurance system direct more money to acute or chronic conditions?

Reading 26. What is a Medicare managed care organization? Can an MMCO work with a condition like Alzheimer's disease?

Reading 27. What was the Tuskegee Syphilis Study? What are other reasons African Americans might distrust the medical care system?

Reading 28. What are the relational dynamics of the family involved in elder abuse? What may cause elder abuse?

Reading 29. What are the benefits of bringing the elderly into the classroom? What are some ways seniors can be incorporated in the classroom?

According to Eric Erikson, what is successful aging related to? What is the most important element of successful aging?

Building Communities That Promote Successful Aging

Linda P. Fried, MD, MPH

Baltimore, Maryland

Marc Freedman, MS

Berkeley, California

Thomas E. Endres

Washington, D.C.

Barbara Wasik, PhD

Baltimore, Maryland

Despite the fact that, in a few years, a fifth of the U.S. population will be older than 65 years and people will be living a third of their lives after retirement, we have developed few avenues that would permit older adults to play meaningful roles as they age and few institutions to harness the experience that older adults could contribute to society. In fact, older adults constitute this country's only increasing natural resource— and the least used one. In this article we consider the rationale for developing institutions that harness the abilities and time of older adults, rather than focusing solely on their needs. *Such an approach would decrease the structural lag between a social concept of retirement as unproductive leisure and an aging population that is larger, healthier, and with a need for more productive opportunities. Gerontologically designed opportunities for contribution on a large social scale could well provide a national approach to primary prevention to maintain health and function in older adults.*

(Fried LP, Freedman M, Endres TE, Wasik B. Building communities that promote successful aging. In: Successful Aging. West J Med 1997; 167:216–219)

The end of the 20th century is rife with major social fluxes. We live in an aging society in which, at birth, people can expect to live into their 70s and 80s, compared with their 40s at the beginning of the century. People are living longer, and they are living more of these years in good health. In the postretirement years, more than half of people aged 65 and older are now without disability, although 80% have one or more chronic diseases. Despite the much increased likelihood of living long lives, our society has not evolved its vision of what old age entails. Our social vision of aging no longer involves poverty and deprivation to the degree it did even 30 years ago. The prevailing social images of old age offer two major alternatives: fear of decrepitude, dependency, and relegation to a rocking chair, or at the other extreme, idealized images of limitless recreational time in a retirement community, often segregated from other age groups and the vicissitudes of daily life. In contrast to our social images,

From the Welch Center for prevention, Epidemiology and Clinical Research and the Center for Social Organization of Schools. John Hopkins University, Baltimore, MD (Drs Fried and Wasik); Public/Private Ventures, Berkeley. Ca (Mr Freedman); and the Corporation for National Service, Washington, DC (Mr Endres).

This work was supported in part by funding from the Retirement Research Foundation and the Corporation for National Service.

Reprint requests to Linda P. Fried. MD, MPH 2024 E Monument St., Ste. 2-600, Baltimore, MD 21205. E-mail: lfried@welchlink,welch.jhu.edu.

Eric Erikson and others have posited that the major developmental task that underlies successful aging is generativity—that is, defining one's life contributions and ensuring one's legacy through active participation in meaningful, contributory roles: the chance to "give back." And yet, there are few opportunities for older adults to engage in such meaningful roles or leave such a legacy in the postretirement years, and even fewer designed for having an effect at a scale beyond one-on-one interaction. This has been described as "structural lag,"[1,2] where the "norms, policies and practices are out of step with the demographic realities and policies of an aging society." To decrease this structural lag, we need to re-envision what successful aging in an aging society could mean.

Thus, there are few opportunities for older adults to serve their own developmental needs, and they are, in the main, marginalized from productivity while having a surfeit of time. In fact, retirement is occurring earlier and lasting longer than ever before, as more people, men especially, are retiring in their 50s. Among those aged 55 to 64, only 53% worked for pay in 1989, along with 22% of those aged 65 to 74 and 4% of those 75 and older.[3] During this period of retirement, older adults are, to a large degree, marginalized from productivity while having a surfeit of time. And yet, being able to make a contribution has been described as an essential element of "successful aging."[4] Consistent with this, it has been reported that women who participated in a voluntary organization or activity had greater longevity over a 30-year period than those who did not, controlling for age, their own education, and their husband's occupational status.[5] In a 2.5-year follow-up of the MacArthur Successful Aging study, participation in volunteer activities was predictive of improved functioning in older adults, with 32% lower risk of poor physical function in those so involved, independent of the effect of being active physically.[6] Casual or low-intensity involvements in such activities, however, may not confer these benefits. There is some preliminary evidence from this same study that the amount of time that one is involved in formal volunteering activities is important in conferring health benefits, with greater time involvement predictive of the level of physical functioning two years later (T. Seeman PhD, Department of Gerontology, University of Southern California, Los Angeles, written communication, July 1997). In addition, there is evidence that organized behavior is among the best predictors of survival.[7]

Thus, in concordance with the theories of Eric Erikson,[8] it may be that successful aging is related to the opportunity to accomplish the adult development tasks of late life: integration and generativity. Defining and ensuring one's legacy is a core part of this task. According to Erikson, this is essential to psychological well-being in late life and, thus, to successful aging. It also appears that meeting these developmental needs, in some circumstances, may also confer health and functional benefits.

It is known that remaining active has health benefits important to successful aging. Physical and cognitive activity, along with social engagement (supports and networks), are related to improved health and function with aging. Regular physical activity, both of moderate and high intensity, are associated in older adults with lower frequencies of heart disease and diabetes mellitus, maintenance of weight, more beneficial levels of other cardiovascular disease risk factors, better physical function, and lower likelihood of disability and dependency.[4,6,9-11] Positive social supports and social networks are also independently protective of health and functioning as people age.[6] Social activity has also been related to improved health, functioning, and happiness.[12]

Some early research supports the "use it or lose it" admonition for cognition, as well as for physical activity: it may be that staying cognitively active helps protect memory as people age.[13,14] Therefore, remaining active physically, cognitively, and socially and making a contribution all appear important to health and well-being in late life. Some of these types of activities that are associated with better health may be difficult to accomplish in a retirement community setting or in isolation and, yet, may be highly important for successful aging in their own right. The consistency and intensity of involvement in such activities may also be necessary to affect the well-being of older persons.

This aging society is increasingly conscious of the need to find ways to help a population that is living longer also be healthier. Population-based and clinical methods are needed to develop optimal prevention and treatment modalities and thus reduce the number of years of late life lived sick and disabled. Such efforts should also help to decrease resulting health care costs and care needs. Researchers in clinical medicine and public health are actively engaged in defining the prevention and health promotion practices that will reduce the incidence of disease and prevent disability and dependency in older adults. In addition. we need to develop approaches for health promotion and primary prevention that might be available to older adults on a broad social scale. In part, this could be accomplished by creating widely accessible opportunities for older adults to remain active and productive.

This country has many other pressing social needs in addition to its aging society. One is the need to improve the outcomes of children in our society: their literacy, education, and personal well-being. In fact, the educational levels of children will be predictive of their future health outcomes as they become the next generation of older adults. Public schools, providing the education of most of the children in this country, are underfunded and overworked, needing more human capital to serve increasingly needy children while having less available for this important mission. Research data identify a particularly high-risk period: the progress of children to the third grade is a major predictor of their subsequent educational and occupational outcomes. Children who do not learn to read by the third grade are at risk for failure in school.[15] Undereducated families are ill equipped to support literacy activities in the home. Older adults could provide this support and the attention needed to teach young children to read. Also, many families with working parents have been faced with the problem of time famine. As a result of this, they have less time to work on literacy activities in the

home. Many children would benefit from the presence and support of more adults and from more stability in their lives. Older adults could possibly offer some of this stability, caring, and consistency, which is essential to learning, as well as the richness of their experience and presence as role models. Older adults could provide social capital needed to directly support the educational needs and the outcomes of children. At the same time, older adults could be investing in the development of the well-educated workforce essential to the future stability of their own entitlement programs, Social Security and Medicare.

Thus, a possible area for creating generative opportunities for older adults is through creating meaningful roles for their serving in schools. This could provide a way to enhance successful aging through social programs, through generative institutions. Such an approach could also provide a new societal image of the opportunities and roles of people as they age, in this case playing unique and much-needed roles supporting, the educational outcomes of children. If such roles were developed at a large enough scale and were designed for maximum effects on the needs of children in schools, the aggregate effect of a large number of older adults participating nationally could be to support educational improvement on a population basis. The visibility of new, mature human capital supporting the well-being and learning of children in schools—through nurturing and enriching roles that do not displace paid workers but support their effectiveness—could offer an image for a positive, successful aging and a new, synergistic

intergenerational social contract of the future. This contract is one in which the older generation are looked to, after retirement, to leave their legacy through strengthening the abilities of the younger generation. Such cultural generativity is developmentally appropriate for those who have completed their own child-rearing responsibilities.[16]

The key to having a substantial effect, simultaneously, in meeting unmet needs while improving the well-being of older adults on a population basis is to design programs that are attractive to older adults, support their effectiveness and maximize both their contribution and the health benefits and that are available on a large scale. One approach to this is currently being assessed in a pilot demonstration program entitled the "Experience Corps." This pilot program, in five US cities, places older adults in elementary schools to serve the needs of the schools and children using a unique gerontologic design to meet the goals described earlier. The elements of the model were drawn from gerontologic theory of what would produce maximum recruitment, retention, and effectiveness of older adults; from public health research of what would provide the greatest benefit of health and well-being of participants; from 30 years of experience in the most effective elements of existing senior service programs; and from the experience of small programs around the country in which older adults are assisting in schools. In the Experience Corps, older adults serve at least 15 to 20 hours a week to receive maximal health benefits and to allow them to take on meaningful roles in the schools and to ensure stability in those roles. Roles developed in this pilot program range as follows: from tutoring individual or groups of children in reading, mathematics, or computers and supporting the ability of teachers to meet children's needs by reading to small groups within the class, to developing enrichment programs for the children ranging from a people's court for conflict resolution or teaching socialized play during recess, to reviving and staffing unused school libraries, to programs that enhance attendance.

Roles are designed based on what a principal and teachers consider are their greatest needs and in collaboration with the school. To attract older adults to such intensive service, the adults receive an incentive of either a small stipend or in-kind benefits. The other essential, gerontologically supportive aspects of the program are that participants receive extensive training to extend their effectiveness in their roles. There is a supportive infrastructure for ongoing problem solving. Participants work in teams of six to ten for the greatest effectiveness and to augment their ability to solve problems too big for any one person to change by themselves. This arrangement also helps to develop positive social networks and support, and the members are able to fill in for one another in the event of illness. Enough teams are placed in a single school to make a visible difference in the school environment and to affect school outcomes. This pilot program, jointly developed and sponsored by the Corporation for National Service, Johns Hopkins University (Baltimore, Maryland) and Public/Private Ventures, with funding from the Corporation and the Retirement Research Foundation, is currently under

evaluation to assess its feasibility and the short-term effect on the well-being of participating older adults. It has been successful in recruiting older adults, often from the neighborhoods the schools are in, with a commitment to improving the outcomes for the children in their communities. Retention and enthusiasm by both the participants and schools are high. Ongoing maturation of the model will, it is hoped, offer successful methods for generative roles that enhance outcomes for both the participating older adults and children that can be brought to a larger scale.

There is substantial validity to developing programs that would permit older adults on a large scale to help improve the educational outcomes of the next generation. Children in our society could benefit from a greater presence of older adults in their lives. The model of creating new, generative roles for older adults could be expanded to other areas of needs, as well—for example, in public health, the environment, or supporting independent living of other older persons. Meeting these needs could provide opportunities for increased activity, engagement, generativity, and social support for older adults, as well as opportunities to use their skills and gain new ones. Successful aging could well be enhanced by increased opportunity for "work that will outlive the self" and that "creates a legacy."[6]

Conclusion

We have an aging society that marginalizes older adults, limiting their ability to contribute their skills and time to our society. At the same time, the health and adult development needs of older adults include maintaining

activity levels and engagement with others and having opportunities to "give back" and leave a legacy. With a declining support-dependency ratio and rising costs of entitlement programs for older adults, our society is becoming restive about the current social contract of entitlements without return contributions. These two strands of social change, along with unmet social needs, provide not just problems. They offer an opportunity for revising our social contract toward one of mutual benefit and engagement. We propose that health promotion efforts for older adults can meet social policy in the creation of meaningful service programs for older adults on a large social scale. One such demonstration, of a gerontologic model for high-intensity, critical-mass, senior service on behalf of children, is described above. This deserves replication. It could provide the backbone for making less intensive service more effective. It could also offer a model that could be extended to large-scale programs in which older adults can help meet other social needs in public health, independent living, and the environment. Such generative institutions could facilitate the ability of older adults to leave a collective, as well as individual, legacy. Ultimately, large-scale opportunities for older adults to remain engaged in society and productive should enhance the health and function of our aging population.

References

1. Moen P. Changing age trends: the pyramid upside down? In Bronfenbrenner U, McClelland P, Wethington, Moen P. Cici S. editors. *The state of Americans: this generation and the next.* New York: The Free Press; 1996, pp. 208–258

2. Riley MW, Riley JW. Age integration and the lives of older people. *Gerontologist* 1994; 34:110–115

3. Herzog AR, Kahn RL, Morgan JN, Jackson JS, Antonucci TC, Age differences in productive activities. *J Gerontol: Soc Sci* 1989; 44:S129–S138.

4. Glass TA, Seeman TE, Herzog AR, Kahn R, Berkman LF. Change in productive activity in late adulthood: MacArthur Studies of Successful Aging. *J Gerontol: Soc Sci* 1995; 50B:S65–S76

5. Moen P, Dempster-McClain D, Williams R. Social integration and longevity: an event history analysis of women's roles and resilience. *Am Sociol Rev* 1989: 54:635–647

6. Seeman TE, Berkman LF, Charpentier PA, Blazer DG, Albert MS, Tinetti ME. Behavioral and psychosocial predictors of physical performance: MacArthur Studies of Successful Aging. *J Gerontol: Med Sci* 1995: 50A:M177–M183

7. Granick S, Patterson RD. *Human aging II: an eleven-year follow up biomedical and behavioral study.* US Department of Health, Education and Welfare, Public Health Service, Alcohol, Drug Abuse and Mental Health Administration, National Institute of Mental Health: 1971

8. Erikson EH, Erikson JM, Kivnick HQ. *Vital involvement in old age.* New York: W.W. Norton and Company, 1986

9. Guralnik JM, LaCroix AZ, Abbott RD, Berkman LF, Satterfield S, Evans DA, et al. Maintaining mobility in late life. *Am J Epidermiol* 1993; 137:845–857

10. Siscovick DS, Fried L, Mittelmark M, Butan G. Bild D, O'Leary DH. Exercise intensity and subclinical cardiovascular disease in the elderly. The Cardiovascular Health Study. *Am J Epidemiol* 1997; 145:977–986

11. Paffenbarger RS Jr, Hyde RT, Wing AL, Lee IM, Jung DL, Kampert JB. The association of changes in physical-activity level and other lifestyle characteristics with mortality among men. *N Engl J Med* 1993; 328:538–545

12. Palmore E, Erdman B. *Social patterns in normal aging: findings from the Duke Longitudinal Study.* Durham (NC): Duke University Press; 1981

13. Craik FI, Byrd M, Swanson, JM. Patterns of memory loss in three elderly samples. *Psychol Aging* 1987; 2:79–86

14. Arbuckle TY, Gold D, Andres D, Cognitive functioning of older people in relation to social and personality variables. *Psychol Aging* 1986; 1:55–62

15. Lloyd DN. Prediction of school failure from third grade data. *Educ Psychol Measurement* 1978; 38:1193–1200

16. Kotre J. *Outliving the self.* Dearborn (MI): Norton Press: 1996

Article Review Form at end of book.

What are the most significant problems facing the elderly today? Does the current social insurance system direct more money to acute or chronic conditions?

Long-Term Care
The new risks of old age

Robert Hudson

Robert Hudson is professor of social welfare policy, Boston University School of Social Work. He currently serves as editor of the Public Policy and Aging Report, the quarterly publication of the National Academy on Aging.

Abstract

Public long-term-care insurance should be developed to answer the growing medical needs of the elderly. However, launching a social-insurance program for long-term care and getting rid of the means-testing required by Medicaid would create legitimate cost issues. It is also feared that the introduction of a public long-term-care insurance would increase improper demand for formal services and reduce informal caregiving by family members.

This social policy expert says we are not adequately addressing the new risks of chronic illness and disability that plague older populations, especially as they live longer. He argues that there is a pressing need for public long-term-care insurance and that if any programs are to be priva-

tized, they should be in the income-support arena rather than in health care.

Until twenty-five years ago, pervasive needs among the aged accorded them a high and non-controversial, place on the social-policy agenda. In the years since, however, the aggregate well-being of the aged has improved markedly in both absolute and relative terms. Widespread agreement that "you cannot do enough for the elderly" has been supplanted by a political debate centered on whether today's policy on aging represents success or excess.

Those touting the success of current policy toward elder care point to several facts: Poverty among the elderly (those over age 65) is now 12 percent (down from 40 percent at the time of John F. Kennedy's inauguration); virtually all older people have health insurance (instead of the less than half before Medicare's enactment); and families now are responsible for less than 2 percent of the income needs of their older relatives (instead of an estimated 50 percent at the time of the New Deal). Those citing excesses find

that not only are older people doing very well, they are doing better than some middle-aged adults, many younger adults, and most children. Programs for the aged are enormous and are growing. Some critics contend that their current consumption at public expense endangers future generations by sucking investment capital out of the economy. These views extend farther across the political landscape than one would have dared imagine a decade or two ago. As Neil Howe of the National Taxpayers Union suggests, while conservatives want to rein in government social-welfare activity across the board, today's liberals wish to shift the emphasis from the old to the young.

An alternative view is that, relatively speaking, we have done well—maybe even too well—in assuring that the aged have sufficient incomes to meet ordinary consumption needs; however, we have failed to address the new risks associated with chronic illness and disability that are increasingly plaguing the older population. Before debating the broader question of whether the

"Long-Term Care: The New Risks of Old Age" by Robert Hudson from CHALLENGE, May–June 1997, v. 40, n. 3. Reprinted by permission of M. E. Sharpe, Inc. and the author.

elderly get too much or too little, policy-makers should explore two other questions: How well does current policy address new risks faced by the older population of today and tomorrow, and when is public-policy provision to be preferred to private auspices?

Misaligned Allocations for the Old

The interactions of demographic trends, economic growth, and policy expansion have yielded a mixed bag of successes and failures where older people are concerned. We have done well in maintaining incomes among the old, despite their growing numbers and their advancing age. The fear of outliving one's income has been seriously mitigated over the past quarter-century. Yet, while income security is obviously important, it is not the only determinant of economic insecurity in old age. In addition to being able to meet current consumption needs, economic well-being in old age also requires holdings that, in the words of the economists Karen Holden and Timothy Smeeding, "can be drawn upon to cover the costs of uncertain contingencies."[1] In dealing with these other risks, largely involving health and functional well-being, we have been markedly less successful.

In protecting income in old age, our policy successes has been confined to an event— retirement—which today is widely predictable (health considerations aside) and sufficiently cushioned as to be non-catastrophic for large numbers of older people. Old Age and Survivors Insurance (OASI) and, where necessary, Supplemental Security Income provide very considerable income protections;

Medicare (and its supplements) do nearly as well in the case of acute health-care needs, although as the ethicist Bart Collopy notes, even Medicare coverage can be occasionally faulted for "hiding individual calamity under aggregate comfort."[2]

The daunting problems facing the elderly today center on chronic-care needs, protections against which continue to be largely confined to Medicaid and one's own out-of-pocket expenditures. Yet, the likelihood of and costs for such care are considerable: 43 percent of persons over age 69 will enter a nursing home at least once in their lives.[3] More than 40 percent of nursing home costs are paid for out of pocket (in contrast to only 5 percent in the case of acute health-care needs),[4] and more than 35 percent of community-based residents aged 75 or older face out-of-pocket costs exceeding 20 percent of total income.[5]

Finally, there are differential exposures to these risks among easily identifiable populations. Even where we have been most successful—promoting income security—much of our success has been in elevating large numbers of older persons from "poor" to "near-poor" status. While that accomplishment is not to be dismissed, the near-poor remain vulnerable to any needs that extend beyond basics such as food and shelter. Such individuals, labeled by Smeeding some years ago as the "tweeners," have neither personal assets nor public programs to rely on for needed support at critical junctures. In short, our relative success in boosting most older people above an income threshold is seriously eroded by that income's failure to offer adequate protection against incapac-

ities that growing numbers of individuals are falling victim to in old age. With its relatively heavy emphasis on income maintenance and the low priority given to the potentially severe vagaries associated with chronic illness and functional incapacity, U.S. social insurance denies needed benefits to a precarious but protectable population. The inefficiencies in our social-insurance system lie not so much in whom we protect—the usual argument raised against the well-off Palm Springs set—as in what we protect—reasonable income in the face of potentially overwhelming events. In the case of non-income-based risks, our otherwise successful income-maintenance policies are found to be too little and too late.

Risk and Response: Righting the Balance

The critical question arising from this line of reasoning is how we might better assign responsibilities for different late-life risks. The lion's share of public insurance is directed toward the large beneficiary pool represented by retirement: a highly likely event with low variability. A somewhat smaller but rapidly growing proportion of public funds targeted on the elderly are Medicare (not to be confused with Medicaid) expenditures directed to acute health-care conditions. Relatively few social-insurance dollars are directed toward long-term care needs associated with chronic illness and disability. This pattern of governmental activity is deficient for mutually reinforcing reasons: The public sector is better suited to dealing with relatively infrequent and potentially catastrophic events, and individuals may be considered better prepared to ready themselves for highly likely and the most manageable circumstances, including those associated with conventional retirement from the work force.

Government's heavy role in the retirement income picture and its limited role in chronic care brings with it two notable problems. First, in the late twentieth century, retirement is no longer, actuarially speaking, an insurable event. If insurance is understood as making a claim for an event against which insurance has been taken out, in the case of retirement, the vast majority of the pool make the claim; for many the insured probability of retirement is coming increasingly close to unity. Expressed in more sociological terms, the evolution of old age from a residual to an institutional status also means that social security is increasingly about ensuring that status as much as it is about insuring against an old risk.

Second, the result of government's heavy emphasis on income security precludes the development of needed insurance for more severe, less predictable, highly variable, and unevenly distributed risks—notably those associated with chronic illness and functional incapacity. The irony is that it is in this arena, where the principles of social insurance most clearly pertain, that the social-insurance presence is currently weakest. Its value over individual responsibility through savings and investment is seen both in the unwillingness of most individuals to plan for such exigencies and in the impossibility for those of modest or moderate means to be able to save for long-term related expenses that can easily run $40,000 or more annually.

A strong case can also be made that, in the case of long-term care, social insurance is preferable to private insurance. By being able to mandate the creation of a risk pool far larger than could be created through private insurance mechanisms, social insurance overcomes—although at a cost some might consider prohibitive—the adverse selection problem than often besets private insurance markets. As the economist Nicholas Barr notes, the same compulsory feature also allows a breaking of the "link between premium and individual risk."[6] While, again, it introduces serious cost issues, the social insurance contract can be drawn up in less specific terms than is possible with private insurance mechanisms, most notably by shifting risks over extended periods of time.

Proposals for Righting the Balance

Several analysts have addressed these points in recent years. On the income maintenance front, Robert Haveman has called for markedly curtailing OASI while maintaining its risk-sharing and intergenerational transfer features. All earners would continue to participate in the system, and all would receive a standard OASI benefit pegged at some point in excess of the poverty line.[7] Arguing that there is no need for forced savings for individuals with significant existing or potential additional income flows, Haveman proposes education and incentives to encourage individuals to save for meeting consumption needs and preferences above the basic amount. Ken Judge has made essentially the same argument in the case of

Great Britain, and he uses predictability as a basis for promoting private involvement.[8] Judge argues that demands for many social-care services are contingent upon some highly predictable risks and this holds especially true with respect to the elderly. He goes on to argue that, in principle, provision for such services could be organized through private insurance markets.

Today, there are several proposals emanating from the Social Security Advisory Council that would partially privatize the OASI portion of the system.[9] Council member Sylvester Schieber and five colleagues have suggested moving toward a two-tiered OASI system, in which more than 50 percent of current contributions to the system would be placed in individuals' own personal savings accounts—not as part of social security's long-standing intergenerational pay-as-you-go scheme.

Council members Edward Gramlich and Marc Twinney have proposed mandating an additional 1.6 percent payroll tax toward individual retirement accounts. Proponents of these plans claim that this would promote an increase in national savings, a fairer rate of return for different generations, greater control over individuals' own assets, and formal recognition of the costs and burdens of funding future retirement benefits. The remaining six members of the council, led by Robert Ball, support a plan to maintain benefits in keeping with the present structure. (There are also areas of agreement among the three groups.)

As to the long-term care needs of the elderly, policy proposals must focus on ways to incorporate chronic illness and functional impairment into social insurance. It is a situation that virtually cries out for an insurance presence—potentially private but conceivably public. Of course, any proposal to expand government's role in long-term care faces daunting political obstacles—how to do even more for older people when the future of younger generations, our ability to reduce the federal deficit, and the legitimacy of government's domestic presence are each very much in question. But substantial funding for such a new initiative need not come from new taxes or insurance-related charges. Instead, one I could earmark a portion of social security benefits for long-term-care purposes—that is, trim benefits from a frequently occurring, low-variability event (retirement) and dedicate them to a potentially severe, more episodic and variable event (chronic-care coverage).

Yung-Ping Chen of the University of Massachusetts at Boston argued that the social insurance approach to long-term care blends individual effort and collective assistance.[10] Chen notes that if 5 percent of OASI benefits, some $16 billion annually, were placed in a long-term-care insurance pool, it would amount to roughly 40 percent of current public long-term-care service expenditures. Scaling the earmarked contribution could raise considerably more, depending on the break points. At the individual level, Chen estimates that the 5 percent set-aside could be expected to provide one year of nursing home coverage at 85 percent of customary charges after a ninety-day waiting period and perhaps for as much as two years for coverage in the community.

Moving in the direction of a public-insurance program yields additional advantages. An insurance fund devoted to long-term care would drain the ethical swamp associated with the need to hide or exhaust one's assets and income in order to be eligible for Medicaid long-term-care coverage. It would also eliminate both the role of "elder-care" attorneys to assist such individuals in protecting assets and the invasive and expensive presence of state governments in devising and enforcing "family responsibility" strictures directed at the adult children of frail elders. The greater legitimacy afforded long-term-care services through a public insurance mechanism would also advance the development of non-institutional community-based alternatives to nursing homes, options that are preferred by older people, their families, advocates, and many providers. And because benefits paid for through the social security earmark would, in fact, largely be an intragenerational transfer, such a program would provide some solace to those concerned with looming intergenerational inequities.

Introducing a social-insurance program for long-term care and eliminating the means-testing now tied to Medicaid creates legitimate cost issues. Of great concern is the degree to which introduction of such insurance would induce inappropriate demand for formal services and a corresponding reduction in the provision of caregiving by informal (family) caregivers.[11] Yet recent years have seen considerable advances in the development of case-management protocols and managed long-term care systems, which are centrally designed to

deal with these "moral hazard" problems. Multiple research and demonstration projects are now under way around the country testing systems' abilities to provide needed services, improve equity among similarly situated clients, and contain costs within predetermined boundaries.[12] Results are both tentative and mixed, and no one denies that an aging population will lead to overall expenditure increases. It is now possible, however, to design and introduce eligibility and service monitors into long-term-care systems that can meaningfully constrain cost increases.

This kind of earmarking need not represent the sole source of long-term care revenue—the pool is too small and the aged, whatever the aggregate improvement in their well-being, should not be asked to self-insure completely against events that remain tightly tied to very advanced age. Private long-term care options are growing, and some of the most interesting developments occurring today combine private and public benefits (the latter currently being tied to Medicaid) in ways that encourage the purchase of private policies by guaranteeing an offsetting amount of asset protection when one becomes eligible for public benefits. Today, there is a very limited, private long-term-care insurance market and considerable concern that only those of means and with the luxury of long-term time horizons will avail themselves of such products. That, of course, disproportionately exposes the already-more-vulnerable to this most recent threat to well-being in old age and, in so doing, reveals the need for the mandatory pool only government can create.

Conclusion

By various counts, the United States directs nearly 30 percent of its cash and in-kind benefits toward older people. Because old age has long held both a marginal and sympathetic status, this allocation is not surprising (although we might want to focus on how little we do for others, not how much we do for the elderly). Advanced age has long been one of "the contingencies of modern life," whose consequences social-insurance programs were put in place to address. And those programs, most notably social security, have had and continue to have an enormous positive impact.

More than the amount of money involved, the problem with age-related public benefits today is that they are becoming increasingly independent of selected risks, notably those relatively infrequent, potentially catastrophic, and highly variable ones to which the public sector brings particular strengths. For all its social contributions, the income-maintenance protections of OASI only partially meet this test. And the little-noted passage of legislation liberalizing the earnings test under social security—increasing the earnings exemption for OASI benefit purposes from $11,000 to $30,000 over seven years—further vitiates this linkage. Social security becomes a significant subsidy, for relatively high-income older persons who choose to stay in the labor force rather than a resource for those who have chosen to or have been forced to leave it.

Sorting out age-related risks improves efficiencies and equity in these matters. Public programs can assign weights to different risks and can establish large bene-ficiary pools in which the rich cannot opt out and the poor cannot be excluded. Social historian Theda Skocpol's "targeting within universalism" captures this idea by suggesting more appropriate targeting of benefits and reassessment of how protected groups should be constituted.[13] The most successful instance of targeting within universalism has been in retirement income. The benefit formula favors lower-income workers, and program financing now includes, in addition to the payroll tax revenues from future retirees, partial taxation of higher-income retirees' benefits.

Yet, laudable as these features may be from a social-insurance perspective, such weighing is more imperative in the instances of acute and especially long-term care than it is in that of retirement income. Severe, unpredictable events that can destroy people financially demand both the most broad-based group and the most progressive financing formula. In the particular case of long-term care, a new endeavor might combine mandatory earmarked contributions, a truncated Medicaid long-term-care presence, and incentives for enrolling in private plans.

The balance-of-risk approach suggested here is also responsive to growing opposition to the size and distribution of current old-age entitlements and, to a point, could avoid the means-testing alternative most commonly put forth by critics of universal programs. Those who have not been affected by a "negative outcome" receive nothing; those who have been affected are protected before they slip into poverty. In these and less extreme cases, the risk-based approach represents something of an optimal course between residual, non-contributory; and stigmatizing means-tested programs, on the one hand, and target-inefficient, morally hazardous, and horizontally inequitable universal or citizenship-based programs on the other.

Clearly, we must initiate a major debate about negative outcomes—especially how to assess responsibility for different outcomes. In addition to acute health-care costs, risk-pooling in long-term care is essential, and the social-insurance approach has distinct advantages. Ironically, this analysis also suggests that the area in which social insurance has made the greatest difference—retirement income—is where some reassessment may be in order. There is no need to further privatize retirement income coverage in order to further this long-term care agenda, but, if contemporary circumstances force such unraveling of social-insurance principles, better that it should happen in income maintenance than in health or long-term-care. If privatization carries the day, 401k plans and personal savings accounts addressed to consumption needs are far preferable to health-care reimbursement and medical savings accounts directed at health- and long-term-care needs. It is in the latter areas that encompassing insurance provisions are now required.

Notes

1. K.C. Holden and T.M. Smeeding, "The Poor, the Rich, and the Insecure Elderly Caught in Between," *Milbank Quarterly* 68 (1990): 191–220.
2. B. Collopy, "Medicare: Ethical Issues in Public Policy for the Elderly," *Social Thought* (1985): 5–14.

3. P. Kemper and C.M. Murtaugh, "Lifetime Use of Nursing Home Care," *New England Journal of Medicine* 324 (1991): 595–600.

4. T. Rice and J. Gabel, "Protecting the Elderly Against High Health Care Costs," *Health Affairs* 5 (1986): 5–21.

5. K. Liu, M. Perozek, and K. Manton, "Catastrophic Acute and Long-Term Care Costs: Risks Faced by Disabled Elderly Persons," *Gerontologist* 33 (1993): 299–307.

6. N. Barr, "Economic Theory and the Welfare State," *Journal of Economic Literature* 30 (1992): 741–803.

7. R. Haveman, *Starting Even: An Equal Opportunity Program to Combat the Nation's New Poverty* (New York: Simon and Schuster, 1988).

8. K. Judge, "The British Welfare State in Transition," in *Modern Welfare States*, ed. R.R. Friedmann, N. Gilbert, and M. Scherer (New York: New York University Press, 1987).

9. V. Reno and K. Olson, "Advisory Council on Social Security to Report Soon," *Social Insurance Update* 1, no. 3 (December 1996): 1–4.

10. Y.-P. Chen, "A 'Three-Legged Stool': A New Way to Fund Long-Term Care?" in *Care in the Long Term: In Search of Community and Security* (Washington, DC: Institute of Medicine, 1993).

11. R.J. Hanley, J.M. Wiener, and K.M. Harris, "Will Paid Home Care Erode Informal Support?" *Journal of Health Politics, Policy, and Law* 16 (1991): 507–21; and Tennstedt, S.S. Crawford, and J. McKinlay, "Is Family Care on the Decline?" *Milbank Quarterly* 71 (1993): 601–24.

12. R.L. Kane and R.A. Kane et al., *Managed Care: Handbook for the Aging Network* (Minneapolis: Institute for Health Services Research, University of Minnesota and the National Academy of State Health Policy, 1996).

13. T. Skocpol, "Targeting Within Universalism: Politically Viable Policies to Combat Poverty in the United States," in *The Urban Underclass*, ed. C. Jencks and P. Peterson (Washington, DC: Brookings Institution, 1991).

Article Review Form at end of book.

What is a Medicare managed care organization? Can an MMCO work with a condition like Alzheimer's disease?

Medicare Managed Care Partnership

Kaiser Permanente and the Alzheimer's Association

Richard D. Della Penna, M.D.

Dr. Della Penna, is Regional Coordinator, Elder Care, Department of Clinical Services, Southern California Permanente Medical Group, Pasadena, Calif.

Mona F. Rosenthal, MPH, Elder Care

Ms. Rosenthal is Clinical Strategy Consultant, Department of Clinical Services, Southern California Permanente Medical Group.

Abstract

In a collaborative project, Kaiser Permanente–Southern California and the Los Angeles Alzheimer's Association established a model program for persons with dementia and their families. The program is designed to improve care from the time of diagnosis to the end of life by increasing accuracy in the diagnosis of dementia, improving provider and caregiver satisfaction, and enhancing the continuity of care. Although the program will be implemented at Kaiser Permanente, the model is designed so that it can be used in other managed care settings. It includes development of a guideline for the diagnosis and management of dementia, a provider training program, member education and support, and provision of care coordination. Implementation began in early 1998. Outcome data, based on formal evaluation, will not be available for 3 years. A preliminary outcome, however, is the successful collaboration between an MCO and a voluntary health organization. [Drug Benefit Trends 10(3): 40–43, 1998. © 1998 SCP Communications, Inc.]

Introduction

A recent Los Angeles Times article declared "Ill Elderly and Poor Fare Worse in HMOs." The headline was referring to a study by Ware and colleagues,[1] which reported that the physical health of elderly Medicare beneficiaries and the chronically ill, non-elderly poor was twice as likely to decline over time in a managed care setting as compared with a fee-for-service setting. While the debate continues about the study's methodology, present relevance, and general applicability, a commonly asked question is whether managed care is good or bad. It is, in concept, neither. The challenge for a Medicare managed care organization (MMCO) is to blend the fragments of fee-for-service health care into programs that demonstrate value by coordinating care and meeting the medical, social, and functional needs of the population it serves.

Medicare Managed Care

MMCOs receive a fixed monthly rate for each member from the Health Care Financing Administration (HCFA). The actual amount, called the AAPCC (average-area-per-capita cost) varies greatly throughout the U.S., and represents 95% of the average cost of caring for a Medicare beneficiary in a fee-for-service setting in a given county. Health plans must offer all Medicare Part A and Part B services to all their Medicare managed care enrollees. The plans, however, typically go beyond Medicare's usual benefit structure, adding such enhancements as prescription medications, eyeglasses, dental care, medical coverage outside the U.S., and more recently, hearing aids. These supplemental benefits are not provided arbitrarily; market research has shown that seniors highly value these added benefits and are more readily attracted to MMCOs that offer them.

MMCOs are searching for better ways to meet the diverse needs of their older members as efficiently as possible. Many efforts are focusing on the management of specific complex diseases associated with high utilization and cost, such as chronic obstructive lung disease, diabetes mellitus, and congestive heart failure. Fewer efforts concentrate on integrating the care of vulnerable populations with lower medical costs, for example, patients with dementia.

As of June 1996, the national penetration of Medicare managed care was 12.5%. Penetration in the Los Angeles area, however, was 40.3%.[2] As the number of Medicare beneficiaries enrolling in MMCOs continues to grow, the need for MMCOs to demonstrate their value becomes more critical if they are to survive in the highly competitive marketplace.

Kaiser Permanente and the LA Alzheimer's Association

Kaiser Permanente, one of the oldest MCOs in the U.S., entered the Medicare managed care arena in 1987. Approximately 3000 physicians of the Southern California Permanente Medical Group (SCPMG) provide medical care to the 2.4 million members in Kaiser Permanente's Southern California (KPSC) region's six service areas. Approximately 10% of Kaiser's membership is over 65 years old, of which 80% are enrolled in Senior Advantage, its Medicare managed care program. Of those who are not Senior Advantage enrollees, 10% remain in fee-for-service Medicare and 10% are not Medicare beneficiaries. Most of KPSC's medical services fall within the traditional medical model of service delivery (i.e., physicians providing care to patients in medical offices or hospital settings).

The Alzheimer's Association is a national voluntary health organization dedicated to the development of services for patients and their family caregivers, advocacy toward improved public policy, and research for the prevention, treatment, and cure of Alzheimer's Disease (AD) and related disorders. The Los Angeles chapter is the largest of 220 chapters nationwide. Its activities include a telephone information and referral line, a program to identify and safely return people who wander, financial assistance to families providing care to Alzheimer's patients at home, caregiver support groups, professional training programs, community education, and a federally funded program to develop culturally sensitive support services for Latino caregiving families.

Dementia

Dementia is a clinical syndrome characterized by the acquired loss of cognitive and intellectual function, impairing a person's ability to think clearly, remember, communicate, and in the final stages, to perform even the most basic activities of daily living. There are many kinds of irreversible, progressive dementia. In the U.S., AD and the dementia associated with vascular disease are the most common. Diseases such as Pick's and Creutzfeldt-Jakob are uncommon types. There are some forms of dementia that may be arrested or reversed, such as the dementia of depression and medication use-associated dementia. These must be distinguished from the others so that they can be treated.[3,4]

AD affects 10% of the population aged 65 years or older, and as many as 47% of those 85 and over.[5] Longer survival and the large cohort of aging baby boomers will significantly increase the number of cases.

The definitive diagnosis of AD is usually made at autopsy; however, mental status and other types of testing can distinguish an irreversible dementia, such as AD, from those that may be temporary. Unfortunately, many people are mislabeled as having an irreversible dementia due to a lack of either physician knowledge or use of tools to distinguish it from reversible forms. As a result, there can be unnecessary referrals to specialists, delayed diagnosis, and consequent distress for patient, family, and provider.

Once diagnosed, the medical management of dementia often focuses on behavioral problems (e.g., hallucinations, paranoia, combativeness) and intermittent medical problems such as infection. Drug therapy—such as reversible acetylcholinesterase inhibitors (e.g., tacrine and donepezil)—is now available for a small number of patients with dementia. This treatment does not slow or halt the progression of AD, but it has been associated with a statistically significant improvement as measured by the Alzheimer's Disease Assessment Scale.[6] But it is unclear to what extent these changes translate into clinical improvement.

The cost of the disease is borne by the affected individuals, their families, and society. In the U.S., approximately $80 billion to $100 billion is spent annually on AD, most of which is paid out of pocket.[7] Dementia is a major cause of long-term nursing care facility stays and associated private and public financial cost. In nursing care facilities, over 70% of the residents may meet diagnostic criteria for dementia.[8]

A recent study demonstrated that psychological support for caregivers delayed institutionalization,[9] but the crushing social and emotional burdens carried by informal caregivers strain the traditional health care system to which they turn for relief. Often what those caregivers require is respite, education, or psychosocial support, which typically have not been provided by managed care. As a

result, the physician becomes the contact to manage problems that can be more suitably addressed by other professionals. This compounds the attendant frustration of families and physicians.

Project Planning Process

The Alzheimer's Association, in recognition of the increasing role of Medicare managed care in Los Angeles, approached SCPMG about working collaboratively to improve the care and services received by Kaiser members with dementia. Four areas of concern surrounding this population were noted: (1) identification of the cognitively impaired, (2) accuracy of diagnosis, (3) management after diagnosis, and (4) overall coordination of care. The goal of the collaboration is to develop a sustainable program that will address these concerns across the continuum of care. The focus is not only on those with dementia, but also on their families and the SCPMG providers who care for them. Another goal of the collaboration is to establish a program that will be replicated throughout the Kaiser Permanente system as well as in other MCOs. A program such as this is also consistent with the accreditation requirements for MMCOs to demonstrate continuity of care.

The work group that was formed is composed of SCPMG geriatricians, neurologists, social workers, health educators, psychiatrists, and Alzheimer's Association staff and consultants. Together, they developed a guideline for the diagnosis and management of dementia, an educational program for providers and caregivers, and a care management program for members in the metropolitan Los Angeles

service area—comprising nearly 400,000 Kaiser members, of whom approximately 50,000 are elderly. It was assumed that in this service area, 4500 members have AD; assuming one caregiver for each person with the illness doubles the number of members affected.

Clinical Practice Guideline Development

Imprecise terms describing varying and various cognitive states are regularly encountered in the medical record notations of professionals caring for older people. The use of terms such as organic brain syndrome (OBS), confused, confusional state, chronic confusion, and senile dementia appear, in some situations, to be used interchangeably. The misapplication of the diagnosis of AD to a wide range of different dementing illnesses also speaks to this issue. The development of a clinical practice guideline for the diagnosis and management of dementia was essential to the development of the remainder of the program. The literature and existing guidelines and efforts were reviewed, including those of the American Academy of Neurology, the Agency for Health Care Policy and Research, and the American Association of Mental Retardation Work Group on Practice Guidelines for Care Management of Alzheimer's Disease Among Adults With Mental Retardation.[10–14] The goal of the work group was to tailor these guidelines to the Kaiser Permanente system.

The guideline, like all clinical practice guidelines, is intended to provide direction, but allows for independent physician judgment. According to the guideline, the primary care physician begins the diagnostic process with a history and the Folstein Mini-Mental Status Examination (MMSE).[15] If a dementing process is suggested, laboratory tests and neuroimaging are recommended. Neurologic, psychiatric, or geriatric consultation may also be considered. Once a diagnosis is established, the patient would be referred to a care manager who would develop and implement a plan of care in concert with the family and physician.

Education and Training

The development of the educational program focuses on both members and providers.

Member Education

As a MCO, a major focus of KPSC is health education, which is provided in each of its medical centers. In addition to classes and brochures, there is a Health Phone for members offering prerecorded information on a number of health topics, including dementia. In addition, the work group collaborated with a national publisher of health education materials to revise an existing brochure on dementia for use by and outside of KPSC.

Advocacy and support groups for caregivers of KPSC members and dementia will be jointly coordinated by KPSC and the Alzheimer's Association. A similar group for KPSC members with HIV/AIDS, called People With Kaiser, has been effective for both the members and the organization.

Providers

A 3-hour didactic and interactive training session was designed for physicians, nurse practitioners, physician assistants, and social workers in the primary care, neurology, psychiatry, home health, hospice, and emergency departments. Learning objectives include the ability to: (1) list the signs and symptoms of dementia, (2) make a differential diagnosis of dementia per the developed guideline, and (3) appropriately manage a patient's course of illness to meet biopsychosocial needs—i.e., address comorbidities; use or refer to internal KPSC and external community resources; and manage behavioral problems, family issues, safety issues, and quality of life/end of life issues.

An extensive community resource guide, created by the Alzheimer's Association, will be distributed throughout the primary care network. It will serve as a reference for both providers and family members.

Care Coordinators

Case management or care coordination has multiple definitions and levels of intensity. Two basic models have very different emphases. One concentrates on managing utilization and cost; the other is client focused and is primarily concerned with brokering for services available within the medical care system and the community.

The project's proposed care-coordination model will provide information, support, and referral to caregivers through one-on-one and group interaction. Care coordinators or dementia specialists will also facilitate adherence to the guideline and the established plan of care.

The service area in which the project will be implemented has two medical centers with separate medical and support staffs. Each of them contains a hospital and outlying medical offices for primary care. In one service area, social worker care coordinators will be outplaced to primary care physician offices. In the other area, they will be centrally located and available to physicians on an on-call basis. The care coordinators will receive special training from the Alzheimer's Association.

Outcomes

Early managed care program outcome analyses focused heavily on utilization and cost. As programs have evolved and matured, the emphasis has begun to shift to measure provider and member satisfaction and quality of care. In keeping with this trend, the evaluation of this program will concentrate on improved coordination of care through compliance with the guideline, enhanced provider knowledge, and increased member and provider satisfaction. This will be accomplished by chart reviews, focus groups, and questionnaires. Three different KPSC medical centers with similar demographic characteristics to the pilot area will be control sites.

Discussion

This project will serve as a model for collaboration between MCOs and advocacy groups. It will be a benchmark for other MCOs in diagnosing, managing, and supporting those with dementia and their families. It is anticipated that educating providers on the diagnosis and management of dementia and using specially trained social workers to provide care coordination will significantly increase provider and member satisfaction. Furthermore, it is expected that increased awareness of the different types of dementia and the tools used to distinguish them will improve diagnostic accuracy.

References

1. Ware JE Jr, Bayliss MS, Rogers WH, et al: Differences in 4-year health outcomes for elderly and poor, chronically ill patients treated in HMO and fee-for-service systems: Results from the Medical Outcomes Study. *JAMA* 276:1039–1047, 1996.
2. Health Care Financing Administration: Office of Prepaid Health Care Operations and Oversight: Managed Care. *Managed Care Market Penetration Reports.* http://www.hcfa.gov/medicare/mpsct1.
3. Lendon CL, Ashall F, Goate AL: Exploring the etiology of Alzheimer disease using molecular genetics. *JAMA* 277(12):825–831, 1997.
4. Morrison-Bogorad M, Phelps C. Buckholtz N: Alzheimer disease research comes of age: The pace accelerates. *JAMA* 277:837–840, 1997.
5. Evans DA, Funkenstein HH, Albert MS, et al: Prevalence of Alzheimer's disease in a community population of older persons. *JAMA* 262:2551–2556, 1989.
6. Rogers SL, Friedhof LT, Donepezil Study Group: The efficacy and safety of donepezil in patients with Alzheimer's disease: Results of a US multicentre randomized, double blind, placebo-controlled trial. *Dementia* 7:293–303, 1996.
7. Snow C: Special report: Medicare HMOs develop plan for future of Alzheimer's programming. *Modern Healthcare* September 23, 1996:67–68,70.
8. Rovner BW, German PS, Broadhead J, et al: Prevalence and management of dementia and other psychiatric diagnoses in nursing homes, *Int Psychogeriatr* 2:13–24, 1990.
9. Mittelman MS, Ferris SH, Shulman E, et al: A family intervention to delay nursing home placement of patients with Alzheimer disease. *JAMA* 276:1725–1731, 1996.
10. Agency for Health Care Policy and Research: Guideline Overview No. 19: Early Alzheimer's Disease: Recognition and Assessment. September 1996, AHCPR Pub. No. 96–0704.
11. Quality Standards Subcommittee of the American Academy of Neurology: Practice parameter for diagnosis and evaluation of dementia (summary statement). *Neurology* 44:2203–2206, 1994.
12. Corey-Bloom J, Thal LJ, Galasko D, et al: Diagnosis and evaluation of dementia. *Neurology* 45:211–218, 1995.
13. McDermott J, Dluzen D: The value of routine neuroimaging in the evaluation of dementia in the elderly. *Clin Geriatr* 5(2):72–80, 1997.
14. Geldmacher DS, Whitehouse PJ: Evaluation of dementia. *N Engl J Med* 335:330–336, 1996.
15. Folstein MD, Folstein SE, McHugh PR: Mini Mental State Examination: A practical method for grading the cognitive state of patients for the clinician. *J Psychiatr Res* 12:189–198, 1975.

Article Review Form at end of book.

What was the Tuskegee Syphilis Study? What are other reasons African Americans might distrust the medical care system?

Under the Shadow of Tuskegee

African Americans and health care

Vanessa Northington Gamble, MD, PhD

The author is with the History of Medicine and Family Medicine Departments and the Center for the Study of Race and Ethnicity in Medicine, University of Wisconsin School of Medicine, Madison.

Abstract

The Tuskegee Syphilis Study continues to cast its long shadow on the contemporary relationship between African Americans and the biomedical community. Numerous reports have argued that the Tuskegee Syphilis Study is the most important reason why many African Americans distrust the institutions of medicine and public health. Such an interpretation neglects a critical historical point: the mistrust predated public revelations about the Tuskegee study. This paper places the syphilis study within a broader historical and social context to demonstrate that several factors have influenced—African Americans attitudes toward the bio-medical community. (Am J Public Health. 1997; 87:1773–1778)

Introduction

On May 16, 1997, in a White House ceremony, President Bill Clinton apologized for the Tuskegee Syphilis Study, the 40-year government study (1932 to 1972) in which 399 Black men from Macon County, Alabama, were deliberately denied effective treatment for syphilis in order to document the natural history of the disease.[1] "The legacy of the study at Tuskegee," the president remarked, "has reached far and deep, in ways that hurt our progress and divide our nation. We cannot be one America when a whole segment of our nation has no trust in America."[2] The president's comments underscore that in the 25 years since its public disclosure, the study has moved from being a singular historical event to a powerful metaphor. It has come to symbolize racism in medicine, misconduct in human research, the arrogance of physicians, and government abuse of Black people.

The continuing shadow cast by the Tuskegee Syphilis Study on efforts to improve the health status of Black Americans provided an impetus for the campaign for a presidential apology.[3] Numerous articles, in both the professional and popular press, have pointed out that the study predisposed many African Americans to distrust medical and public health authorities and has led to critically low Black participation in clinical trials and organ donation.[4]

The specter of Tuskegee has also been raised with respect to HIV/AIDS prevention and

Requests for reprints should be sent to Vanessa Northington Gamble, MD, PhD, University of Wisconsin School of Medicine, 1300 University Ave, Madison, WI 53706.

This paper was accepted July 24, 1997.

treatment programs. Health education researchers Dr. Stephen B. Thomas and Dr. Sandra Crouse Quinn have written extensively on the impact of the Tuskegee Syphilis Study on these programs.[5] They argue that "the legacy of this experiment, with its failure to educate the study participants and treat them adequately, laid the foundation for today's pervasive sense of black distrust of public health authorities."[6] The syphilis study has also been used to explain why many African Americans oppose needle exchange programs. Needle exchange programs provoke the image of the syphilis study and Black fears about genocide. These programs are not viewed as mechanisms to stop the spread of HIV/AIDS but rather as fodder for the drug epidemic that has devastated so many Black neighborhoods.[7] Fears that they will be used as guinea pigs like the men in the syphilis study have also led some African Americans with AIDS to refuse treatment with protease inhibitors.[8]

The Tuskegee Syphilis Study is frequently described as the singular reason behind African-American distrust of the institutions of medicine and public health. Such an interpretation neglects a critical historical point: the mistrust predated public revelations about the Tuskegee study. Furthermore, the narrowness of such a representation places emphasis on a single historical event to explain deeply entrenched and complex attitudes within the black community. An examination of the syphilis study within a broader historical and social context makes plain that several factors have influenced, and continue to influence, African

Americans' attitudes toward the biomedical community.

Black Americans' fears about exploitation by the medical profession date back to the antebellum period and the use of slaves and free Black people as subjects for dissection and medical experimentation.[9] Although physicians also used poor Whites as subjects, they used Black people far more often. During an 1835 trip to the United States, French visitor Harriet Martineau found that Black people lacked the power even to protect the graves of their dead. "In Baltimore the bodies of coloured people exclusively are taken for dissection," she remarked, "because the Whites do not like it, and the coloured people cannot resist."[10] Four years later, abolitionist Theodore Dwight Weld echoed Martineau's sentiment. "Public opinion," he wrote, "would tolerate surgical experiments, operations, processes, performed upon them [slaves], which it would execrate if performed upon their master or other whites."[11] Slaves found themselves as subjects of medical experiments because physicians needed bodies and because the state considered them property and denied them the legal right to refuse to participate.

Two antebellum experiments, one carried out in Georgia and the other in Alabama, illustrate the abuse that some slaves encountered at the hands of physicians. In the first, Georgia physician Thomas Hamilton conducted a series of brutal experiments on a slave to test remedies for heatstroke. The subject of these investigations, Fed, had been loaned to Hamilton as repayment for a debt owed by his owner. Hamilton forced Fed to sit

naked on a stool placed on a platform in a pit that had been heated to a high temperature. Only the man's head was above ground. Over a period of 2 to 3 weeks, Hamilton placed Fed in the pit five or six times and gave him various medications to determine which enabled him best to withstand the heat. Each ordeal ended when Fed fainted and had to be revived. But note that Fed was not the only victim in this experiment; its whole purpose was to make it possible for masters to force slaves to work still longer hours on the hottest of days.[12]

In the second experiment, Dr. J. Marion Sims, the so-called father of modern gynecology, used three Alabama slave women to develop an operation to repair vesicovaginal fistulas. Between 1845 and 1849, the three slave women on whom Sims operated each underwent up to 30 painful operations. The physician himself described the agony associated with some of the experiments.[13] "The first patient I operated on was Lucy. . . . That was before the days of anaesthetics, and the poor girl, on her knees, bore the operation with great heroism and bravery." This operation was not successful, and Sims later attempted to repair the defect by placing a sponge in the bladder. This experiment, too, ended in failure. He noted:

The whole urethra and the neck of the bladder were in a high state of inflammation, which came from the foreign substance. It had to come away, and there was nothing to do but to pull it away by main force. Lucy's agony was extreme. She was much prostrated, and I thought that she was doing to die; but by irrigating the parts of the bladder she recovered with great rapidity.

Sims finally did perfect his technique and ultimately repaired the fistulas. Only after his experimentation with the slave women proved successful did the physician attempt the procedure, with anesthesia, on White women volunteers.

Exploitation after the Civil War

It is not known to what extent African Americans continued to be used as unwilling subjects for experimentation and dissection in the years after emancipation. However, an examination of African-American folklore at the turn of the century makes it clear that Black people believed that such practices persisted. Folktales are replete with references to night doctors, also called student doctors and Ku Klux doctors. In her book, *Night Riders in Black Folk History*, anthropologist Gladys-Marie Fry writes, "the term 'night doctor' (derived from the fact that victims were sought only at night) applies both to students of medicine, who supposedly stole cadavers from which to learn about body processes, and [to] professional thieves, who sold stolen bodies—living, and dead—to physicians for medical research."[14] According to folk belief, these sinister characters would kidnap Black people, usually at night and in urban areas, and take them to hospitals to be killed and used in experiments. An 1889 *Boston Herald* article vividly captured the fears that African Americans in South Carolina had of night doctors. The report read, in part:

The negroes of Clarendon, Williamsburg, and Sumter counties have for several weeks past been in a state of fear and trembling. They claim that there is a white man, a doctor, who at will can make himself invisible, and who then approaches some unsuspecting darkey, and having rendered him or her insensible with chloroform, proceeds to fill up a bucket with the victim's blood, for the purpose of making medicine. After having drained the last drop of blood from the victim, the body is dumped into some secret place where it is impossible for any person to find it. The colored women are so worked up over this phantom that they will not venture out at night, or in the daytime in any sequestered place.[15]

Fry did not find any documented evidence of the existence of night riders. However, she demonstrated through extensive interviews that many African Americans expressed genuine fears that they would be kidnapped by night doctors and used for medical experimentation. Fry concludes that two factors explain this paradox. She argues that Whites, especially those in the rural South, deliberately spread rumors about night doctors in order to maintain psychological control over Blacks and to discourage their migration to the North so as to maintain a source of cheap labor. In addition, Fry asserts that the experiences of many African Americans as victims of medical experiments during slavery fostered their belief in the existence of night doctors.[16] It should also be added that, given the nation's racial and political climate, Black people recognized their inability to refuse to participate in medical experiments.

Reports about the medical exploitation of Black people in the name of medicine after the end of the Civil War were not restricted to the realm of folklore. Until it was exposed in 1882, a grave robbing ring operated in Philadelphia and provided bodies for the city's medical schools by plundering the graves at a Black cemetery. According to historian David C. Humphrey, southern grave robbers regularly sent bodies of southern Blacks to northern medical schools for use as anatomy cadavers.[17]

During the early 20th century, African-American medical leaders protested the abuse of Black people by the White-dominated medical profession and used their concerns about experimentation to press for the establishment of Black-controlled hospitals.[18] Dr. Daniel Hale Williams, the founder of Chicago's Provident Hospital (1891), the nation's first Black-controlled hospital, contended that White physicians, especially in the South, frequently used Black patients as guinea pigs.[19] Dr. Nathan Francis Mossell, the founder of Philadelphia's Frederick Douglass Memorial Hospital (1895), described the "fears and prejudices" of Black people, especially those from the South, as "almost proverbial."[20] He attributed such attitudes to southern medical practices in which Black people, "when forced to accept hospital attention, got only the poorest care, being placed in inferior wards set apart from them, suffering the brunt of all that is experimental in treatment, and all this is the sequence of their race variety and abject helplessness."[21] The founders of Black hospitals claimed that only Black physicians possessed the skills required to treat Black patients optimally and that Black hospitals provided these patients with the best possible care.[22]

Fears about the exploitation of African Americans by White physicians played a role in the establishment of a Black veterans hospital in Tuskegee, Ala. In 1923, 9 years before the initiation of the Tuskegee Syphilis Study, racial tensions had erupted in the town over control of the hospital. The federal government had pledged that the facility, an institution designed exclusively for Black patients, would be run by a Black professional staff. But many Whites in the area, including members of the Ku Klux Klan, did not want a Black-operated federal facility in the heart of Dixie, even though it would serve only Black people.[23]

Black Americans sought control of the veterans hospital, in part because they believed that the ex-soldiers would receive the best possible care from Black physicians and nurses, who would be more caring and sympathetic to the veterans' needs. Some Black newspapers even warned that White southerners wanted command of the hospital as part of a racist plot to kill and sterilize African-American men and to establish an "experiment station" for mediocre white physicians.[24] Black physicians did eventually gain the right to operate the hospital, yet this did not stop the hospital from becoming an experiment station for Black men. The veterans hospital was one of the facilities used by the United States Public Health Service in the syphilis study.

During the 1920s and 1930s, Black physicians pushed for additional measures that would battle medical racism and advance their professional needs. Dr. Charles Garvin, a prominent Cleveland physician and a member of the editorial board of the Black medical publication *The Journal of the National Medical Association,* urged his colleagues to engage in research in order to protect Black patients. He called for more research on disease such as tuberculosis and pellagra that allegedly affected African Americans

disproportionately or idiosyncratically. Garvin insisted that black physicians investigate that racial diseases because "heretofore in literature, as in medicine, the Negro has been written about, exploited and experimented upon sometimes not to his physical betterment or to the advancement of science, but the advancement of the Nordic investigator." Moreover, he charged that "in the past, men of other races have for the large part interpreted our diseases, often tinctured with inborn prejudices."[25]

Fears of Genocide

These historical examples clearly demonstrate that African Americans' distrust of the medical profession has a longer history than the public revelations of the Tuskegee Syphilis Study. There is a collective memory among African Americans about their exploitation by the medical establishment. The Tuskegee Syphilis Study has emerged as the most prominent example of medical racism because it confirms, if not authenticates, long-held and deeply entrenched beliefs within the Black community. To be sure, the Tuskegee Syphilis Study does cast a long shadow. After the study had been exposed, charges surfaced that the experiment was part of a governmental plot to exterminate Black people.[26] Many Black people agreed with the charge that the study represented "nothing less than an official, premeditated policy of genocide."[27] Furthermore, this was not the first or last time that allegations of genocide have been launched against the government and the medical profession. The sickle cell anemia screening programs of the 1970s and birth control

programs have also provoked such allegations.[28]

In recent years, links have been made between Tuskegee, AIDS, and genocide. In September 1990, the article "AIDS: Is It Genocide?" appeared in *Essence,* a Black woman's magazine. The author noted; "As an increasing number of African-Americans continue to sicken and die and as no cure for AIDS has been found some of us are beginning to think the unthinkable: Could AIDS be a virus that was manufactured to erase large numbers of us? Are they trying to kill us with this disease?"[29] In other words, some members of the Black community see AIDS as part of a conspiracy to exterminate African Americans.

Beliefs about the connection between AIDS and the purposeful destruction of African Americans should not be cavalierly dismissed as bizarre and paranoid. They are held by a significant number of Black people. For example, a 1990 survey conducted by the Southern Christian Leadership Conference found that 35% of the 1056 Black church members who responded believed that AIDS was a form of genocide.[30] A *New York Times*/WCBS TV News poll conducted the same year found that 10% of Black Americans thought that the AIDS virus had been created in a laboratory in order to infect Black people. Another 20% believed that it could be true.[31]

African Americans frequently point to the Tuskegee Syphilis Study as evidence to support their views about genocide, perhaps, in part, because many believe that the men in the study were actually injected with syphilis. Harlon Dalton, a Yale Law School professor and a former member of the National

Commission on AIDS, wrote, in a 1989 article titled, "AIDS in Black Face," that "the government [had] purposefully exposed Black men to syphilis."[32] Six years later, Dr. Eleanor Walker, a Detroit radiation oncologist, offered an explanation as to why few African Americans become bone marrow donors. "The biggest fear, she claimed, is that they will become victims of some misfeasance, like the Tuskegee incident where Black men were infected with syphilis and left untreated to die from the disease."[33] The January 25, 1996, episode of *New York Undercover*, a Fox Network police drama that is one of the top shows in Black households, also reinforced the rumor that the U.S. Public Health Service physicians injected the men with syphilis.[34] The myth about deliberate infection is not limited to the Black community. On April 8, 1997, news anchor Tom Brokaw, on "NBC Nightly News," announced that the men had been infected by the government.[35]

Folklorist Patricia A. Turner, in her book *I Heard It through the Grapevine: Rumor and Resistance in African-American Culture*, underscores why it is important not to ridicule but to pay attention to these strongly held theories about genocide.[36] She argues that these rumors reveal much about what African Americans believe to be the state of their lives in this country. She contends that such views reflect Black beliefs that White Americans have historically been, and continue to be, ambivalent and perhaps hostile to the existence of Black people. Consequently, African-American attitudes toward biomedical research are not influenced solely by the Tuskegee Syphilis Study. African Americans' opinions

about the value White society has attached to their lives should not be discounted. As Reverend Floyd Tompkins of Stanford University Memorial Church has said, "There is a sense in our community, and I think it shall be proved out, that if you are poor or you're a person of color, you were the guinea pig, and you continue to be the guinea pigs, and there is the fundamental belief that Black life is not valued like White life or like any other life in America."[37]

Not Just Paranoia

Lorene Cary, in a cogent essay in *Newsweek*, expands on Reverend Tompkins' point. In an essay titled "Why It's Not Just Paranoia," she writes:

We Americans continue to value the lives and humanity of some groups more than the lives and humanity of others. That is not paranoia. It is our historical legacy and a present fact; it influences domestic and foreign policy and the daily interaction of millions of Americans. It influences the way we spend our public money and explains how we can read the staggering statistics on Black Americans' infant mortality, youth mortality, mortality in middle and old age, and not be moved to action.[38]

African Americans' beliefs that their lives are devalued by White society also influence their relationships with the medical profession. They perceive, at times correctly, that they are treated differently in the health care system solely because of their race, and such perceptions fuel mistrust of the medical profession. For example, a national telephone survey conducted in 1986 revealed that African Americans were more likely than Whites to report that their physicians did not inquire sufficiently

about their pain, did not tell them how long it would take for prescribed medicine to work, did not explain the seriousness of their illness or injury, and did not discuss test and examination findings.[39] A 1994 study published in the *American Journal of Public Health* found that physicians were less likely to give pregnant Black women information about the hazards of smoking and drinking during pregnancy.[40]

The powerful legacy of the Tuskegee Syphilis Study endures, in part, because the racism and disrespect for Black lives that it entailed mirror Black people's contemporary experiences with the medical profession. The anger and frustration that many African Americans feel when they encounter the health care system can be heard in the words of Alicia Georges, a professor of nursing at Lehman College and a former president of the National Black Nurses Association, a she recalled an emergency room experience. "Back a few years ago, I was have excruciating abdominal pain, and I wound up at a hospital in my area," she recalled. "The first thing that they began to ask me was how many sexual partners I'd had. I was married and owned my own house. But immediately, in looking at me, they said, 'Oh, she just has pelvic inflammatory disease.'"[41] Perhaps because of her nursing background, Georges recognized the implications of the questioning. She had come face to face with the stereotype of Black women as sexually promiscuous. Similarly, the following story from the *Los Angeles Times* shows how racism can affect the practice of medicine:

When Althea Alexander broke her arm, the attending resident at Los Angeles County–USC Medical Center told her to "hold your arm like you usually hold your can of beer on Saturday night." Alexander who is Black, exploded. "What are you talking about? Do you think I'm a welfare mother?" The White resident shrugged: "Well aren't you?" Turned out she was an administrator at USC medical school.

This example graphically illustrates that health care providers are not immune to the beliefs and misconceptions of the wider community. They carry with them stereotypes about various groups of people.[42]

Beyond Tuskegee

There is also a growing body of medical research that vividly illustrates why discussions of the relationship of African Americans and the medical profession must go beyond the Tuskegee Syphilis Study. These studies demonstrate racial inequities in access to particular technologies and raise critical questions about the role of racism in medical decision making. For example, in 1989 *The Journal of the American Medical Association* published a report that demonstrated racial inequities in the treatment of heart disease. In this study, White and Black patients had similar rates on hospitalization for chest pain, but the White patients were one third more likely to undergo coronary angiography and more than twice as likely to be treated with bypass surgery or angioplasty. The racial disparities persisted even after adjustments were made for differences in income.[43] Three years later, another study appearing in that journal reinforced these findings. It revealed that older Black patients on Medicare received coronary artery bypass grafts only about a fourth as often as comparable

White patients. Disparities were greatest in the rural South, where White patients had the surgery seven times as often as Black patients. Medical factors did not fully explain the differences. This study suggests that an already-existing national health insurance program does not solve the access problems of African Americans.[44] Additional studies have confirmed the persistence of such inequities.[45]

Why the racial disparities? Possible explanations include health problems that precluded the use of procedures, patient unwillingness to accept medical advice or to undergo surgery, and differences in severity of illness. However, the role of racial bias cannot be discounted, as the American Medical Association's Council on Ethical and Judicial Affairs has recognized. In a 1990 report on Black–White disparities in health care, the council asserted:

Because racial disparities may be occurring despite the lack of any intent or purposeful efforts to treat patients differently on the basis of race, physicians should examine their own practices to ensure that inappropriate considerations do not affect their clinical judgment. In addition, the profession should help increase the awareness of its members of racial disparities in medical treatment decisions by engaging in open and broad discussions about the issue. Such discussions should take place as part of the medical school curriculum, in medical journals, at professional conferences, and as part of professional peer review activities.[46]

The council's recommendation is a strong acknowledgment that racism can influence the practice of medicine.

After the public disclosures of the Tuskegee Syphilis Study, Congress passed the National

Research Act of 1974. This act, established to protect subjects in human experimentation, mandates institutional review board approval of all federally funded research with human subjects. However, recent revelations about a measles vaccine study financed by the Centers for Disease Control and Prevention (CDC) demonstrate the inadequacies of these safeguards and illustrate why African Americans' historically based fears of medical research persist. In 1989, in the midst of a measles epidemic in Los Angeles, the CDC, in collaboration with Kaiser Permanente and the Los Angeles County Health Department, began a study to test whether the experimental Edmonston-Zagreb vaccine could be used to immunize children too young for the standard Moraten vaccine. By 1991, approximately 900 infants, mostly Black and Latino, had received the vaccine without difficulties. (Apparently, 1 infant died for reasons not related to the inoculations.) But the infants' parents had not been informed that the vaccine was not licensed in the United States or that it had been associated with an increase in death rates in Africa. The 1996 disclosure of the study prompted charges of medical racism and of the continued exploitation of minority communities by medical professionals.[47]

The Tuskegee Syphilis Study continues to cast its shadow over the lives of African Americans. For many Black people, it has come to represent the racism that pervades American institutions and the disdain in which Black lives are often held. But despite its significance, it cannot be the only prism we use to examine the relationship of African Americans with the medical and public health communities. The problem we must face is not just the shadow of Tuskegee but the shadow of racism that so profoundly affects the lives and beliefs of all people in this country.

Endnotes

1. The most comprehensive history of the study is James H. Jones, *Bad Blood*, new and expanded edition (New York: Free Press, 1993).
2. "Remarks by the President in Apology for Study Done in Tuskegee," Press Release, the White House, Office of the Press Secretary, 16 May 1997.
3. "Final Report of the Tuskegee Syphilis Study Legacy Committee," Vanessa Northington Gamble, chair, and John C. Fletcher, co-chair, 20 May 1996.
4. Vanessa Northington Gamble, "A Legacy of Distrust: African Americans and Medical Research," *American Journal of Preventive Medicine* 9 (1993): 35–38; Shari Roan, "A Medical Imbalance," *Los Angeles Times*, 1 November 1994; Carol Stevens, "Research: Distrust Runs Deep; Medical Community Seeks Solution," *The Detroit News*, 10 December 1995; Lini S. Kadaba, "Minorities in Research," *Chicago Tribune*, 13 September 1993; Robert Steinbrook, "AIDS Trials Shortchange Minorities and Drug Users," *Los Angeles Times*, 25 September 1989; Mark D. Smith, "Zidovudine: Does It Work for Everyone?" *Journal of the American Medical Association* 266 (1991): 2750–2751; Charlise Lyles, "Blacks Hesitant to Donate; Cultural Beliefs, Misinformation, Mistrust Make It a Difficult Decision," *The Virginian-Pilot*, 15 August 1994; Jeanni Wong, "Mistrust Leaves Some Blacks Reluctant to Donate Organs," *Sacramento Bee*, 17 February 1993; "Nightline," ABC News, 6 April 1994; Patrice Gaines, "Armed with the Truth in a Fight for Lives," *Washington Post*, 10 April 1994; Fran Henry, "Encouraging Organ Donation from Blacks," *Cleveland Plain Dealer*, 23 April 1994; G. Marie Swanson and Amy J. Ward, "Recruiting Minorities into Clinical Trials: Toward a Participant-Friendly System," *Journal of the National Cancer Institute* 87 (1995):

1747–1759; Dewayne Wickham, "Why Blacks Are Wary of White MDs," *The Tennessean*, 21 May 1997, 13A.
5. For example, see Stephen B. Thomas and Sandra Crouse Quinn, "The Tuskegee Syphilis Study, 1932 to 1972: Implications for HIV Education and AIDS Risk Education Programs in the Black Community," *American Journal of Public Health* 81 (1991): 1498–1505; Stephen B. Thomas and Sandra Crouse Quinn, "Understanding the Attitudes of Black Americans," in *Dimensions of HIV Prevention. Needle Exchange*, ed. Jeff Stryker and Mark D. Smith (Menlo Park, Calif.: Henry J. Kaiser Family Foundation, 1993), 99–128; and Stephen B. Thomas and Sandra Crouse Quinn, "The AIDS Epidemic and the African-American Community: Toward an Ethical Framework for Service Delivery," in *"It Just Ain't Fair": The Ethics of Health Care for African Americans*, ed. Annette Dula and Sara Goering (Westport, Conn.: Praeger, 1994), 75–88.
6. Thomas and Quinn, "The AIDS Epidemic and the African-American Community," 83.
7. Thomas and Quinn, "Understanding the Attitudes of Black Americans," 108–109; David L. Kirp and Ronald Bayer, "Needles and Races," *Atlantic*, July 1993, 38–42.
8. Lynda Richardson, "An Old Experiment's Legacy: Distrust of AIDS Treatment," *New York Times*, 21 April 1997, A1, A7.
9. Todd L. Savitt, "The Use of Blacks for Medical Experimentation and Demonstration in the Old South," *Journal of Southern History* 48 (1982): 331–348; David C. Humphrey, "Dissection and Discrimination: The Social Origins of Cadavers in America, 1760–1915," *Bulletin of the New York Academy of Medicine* 49 (1973): 819–827.
10. Harriet Martineau, *Retrospect of Western Travel*, vol. 1 (London: Saunders & Ottley; New York: Harpers and Brothers; 1838), 140, quoted in Humphrey, "Dissection and Discrimination," 819.
11. Theodore Dwight Weld, *American Slavery As It Is: Testimony of a Thousand Witnesses* (New York: American Anti-Slavery Society, 1839), 170, quoted in Savitt, "The Use of Blacks," 341.
12. F. N. Boney, "Doctor Thomas Hamilton: Two Views of a

Gentleman of the Old South, *Phylon* 28 (1967): 288–292.
13. J. Marion Sims, *The Story of My Life* (New York: Appleton, 1889), 236–237.
14. Gladys-Marie Fry, *Night Riders in Black Folk History* (Knoxville: University of Tennessee Press, 1984), 171.
15. "Concerning Negro Sorcery in the United States," *Journal of American Folk-Lore* 3 (1890): 285.
16. Ibid., 210.
17. Humphrey, "Dissection and Discrimination," 822–823.
18. A detailed examination of the campaign to establish Black hospitals can be found in Vanessa Northington Gamble, *Making a Place for Ourselves: The Black Hospital Movement, 1920–1945* (New York: Oxford University Press, 1995).
19. Eugene P. Link, "The Civil Rights Activities of Three Great Negro Physicians (1840–1940)," *Journal of Negro History* 52 (July 1969): 177.
20. Mossell graduated, with honors, from Penn in 1882 and founded the hospital in 1895.
21. "Seventh Annual Report of the Frederick Douglass Memorial Hospital and Training School" (Philadelphia, Pa.: 1902), 17.
22. H.M. Green, *A More or Less Critical Review of the Hospital Situation among Negroes in the United States* (n.d., circa 1930), 4–5.
23. For more in-depth discussions of the history of the Tuskegee Veterans Hospital, see Gamble, *Making a Place for Ourselves*, 70–104; Pete Daniel, "Black Power in the 1920's: the Case of Tuskegee Veterans Hospital," *Journal of Southern History* 36 (1970): 368–388; and Raymond Wolters, *The New Negro on Campus: Black College Rebellions of the 1920s* (Princeton, NJ: Princeton University Press, 1975), 137–191.
24. "Klan Halts March on Tuskegee," *Chicago Defender*, 4 August 1923.
25. Charles H. Garvin, "The 'New Negro' Physician," unpublished manuscript, n.d., box 1, Charles H. Garvin Papers, Western Reserve Historical Society Library, Cleveland, Ohio.
26. Ronald A. Taylor, "Conspiracy Theories Widely Accepted in U.S. Black Circles," *Washington Times*, 10 December 1991, A1; Frances Cress Welsing, *The Isis Papers: The Keys to the Colors* (Chicago: Third World Press, 1991), 298–299.

Although she is not very well known outside of the African-American community, Welsing, a physician, is a popular figure within it. *The Isis Papers* headed for several weeks the best-seller list maintained by Black bookstores.

27. Jones, *Bad Blood*, 12.
28. For discussions of allegations of genocide in the implementation of these programs, see Robert G. Weisbord, "Birth Control and the Black American: A Matter of Genocide?" *Demography* 10 (1973): 571–590; Alex S. Jones, "Editorial Linking Blacks, Contraceptives Stirs Debate at Philadelphia Paper," *Arizona Daily Star,* 23 December 1990, F4; Doris Y. Wilkinson, "For Whose Benefit? Politics and Sickle Cell," *The Black Scholar* 5 (1974): 26–31.
29. Karen Grisby Bates, "Is It Genocide?" *Essence,* 1990, 76.
30. Thomas and Quinn, "The Tuskegee Syphilis Study," 1499.
31. "The AIDS 'Plot' against Blacks," *New York Times,* 12 May 1992, A22.
32. Harlon L. Dalton, "AIDS in Blackface," *Daedalus* 118 (Summer 1989): 220–221.
33. Rhonda Bates-Rudd, "State Campaign Encourages African Americans to Offer Others Gift of Bone Marrow," *Detroit News,* 7 December 1995.
34. From September 1995 to December 1995, New York Undercover was the top-ranked show in Black households, It ranked 122nd in White households. David Zurawik, "Poll: TV's Race Gap Growing," *Capital Times* (Madison, Wis), 14 May 1996, 5D.
35. Transcript, "NBC Nightly News," 8 April 1997.
36. Patricia A. Turner, *I Heard It through the Grapevine: Rumor in African-American Culture* (Berkeley: University of California Press, 1993).
37. "Fear Creates Lack of Donor Organs among Blacks," *Weekend Edition,* National Public Radio, 13 March 1994.
38. Lorene Cary, "Why It's Not Just Paranoia: An American History of 'Plans' for Blacks," *Newsweek,* 6 April 1992, 23.
39. Robert J. Blendon, "Access to Medical Care for Black and White Americans: A Matter of Continuing Concern," *Journal of the American Medical Association* 261 (1989): 278–281.
40. M.D. Rogan et al., "Racial Disparities in Reported Prenatal Care Advice from Health Care Providers," *American Journal of Public Health* 84 (1994): 82–88.
41. Julie Johnson et al., "Why Do Blacks Die Young? *Time,* 16 September 1991, 52.
42. Sonia Nazario, "Treating Doctors for Prejudice: Medical Schools Are Trying to Sensitize Students to 'Bedside Bias.'" *Los Angeles Times,* 20 December 1990.
43. Mark B. Wenneker and Arnold M. Epstein, "Racial Inequities in the Use of Procedures for Patients with Ischemic Heart Disease in Massachusetts," *Journal of the American Medical Association* 261 (1989): 253–257.
44. Kenneth C. Goldberg et al., "Racial and Community Factors Influencing Coronary Artery Bypass Graft Surgery Rates for All 1986 Medicare Patients," *Journal of the American Medical Association* 267 (1992): 1473–1477.
45. John D. Ayanian, "Heart Disease in Black and White," *New England Journal of Medicine* 329 (1993): 656–658; J. Whittle et al., "Racial Differences in the Use of Invasive Cardiovascular Procedures in the Department of Veterans Affairs Medical System," *New England Journal of Medicine* 329 (1993): 621–627; Eric D. Peterson et al., "Racial Variation in Cardiac Procedure Use and Survival following Acute Myocardial Infarction in the Department of Veterans Affairs," *Journal of the American Medical Association* 271 (1994): 1175–1180; Ronnie D. Horner et al., "Theories Explaining Racial Differences in the Utilization of Diagnostic and Therapeutic Procedures for Cerebrovascular Disease," *Milbank Quarterly* 73 (1995): 443–462; Richard D. Moore et al., "Racial Differences in the Use of Drug Therapy for HIV Disease in an Urban Community," *New England Journal of Medicine* 350 (1994): 763–768.
46. Council on Ethical and Judicial Affairs, "Black-White Disparities in Health Care," *Journal of the American Medical Association* 263 (1990): 2346.
47. Marlene Cimons, "CDC Says It Erred in Measles Study," *Los Angeles Times,* 17 June 1996, A11; Beth Glenn, "Bad Blood Once Again," *St. Petersburg Times,* 21 July 1996, 5D.

Article Review Form at end of book.

What are the relational dynamics of the family involved in elder abuse? What may cause elder abuse?

Elder Abuse—
The Hidden Crime

Jim Bentley

bentley@cambridgeoh.com

Mildred, 82, is tied to her bed while her brother is outside working on the farm. She cries a lot. Scars, mixed with open flesh wounds, mark her wrists. This is obviously not the first time that she has been tied to her bed. She is a victim of Alzheimer's disease and her brother ties her to her bed because she wanders away from the house.

Louise, 74, wears sunglasses to hide the bruises on her face from the driver who delivers her noon meal. The driver notices a tear coming from under the glasses, "what's the matter Louise"? Louise begins sobbing and closes the door. She financially supports her 52-year-old alcoholic son who lives with her. He regularly threatens to put her in a nursing home if she doesn't give him money. Although she feels trapped in her home, she can't make her own son move. Yesterday, in a drunken rage, he demanded money, then slapped her when she refused. She gave him the money.

Esther, 69, leans over the bed in her nursing home room and rings for the nurse. No one comes. She rings again. She is lonely and knows that she calls the nurses station a lot, but this time she really needs someone. A few moments later, a woman storms into Esther's room, "Esther, that's the fourth time today that you've rang that bell for no reason, if you ring it one more time I won't bring your mail to you!" With a broken hip, Esther tries to move away from the pool of urine in her bed.

John, 89, wakes up in an ambulance, the last thing that he remembers is getting ready to cook lunch. The paperboy had called the police when John's paper began to pile up for 5 days. John becomes disoriented and loses consciousness when he does not take his medicine. His medications cost $440 a month, and his Social Security is only $510. Sure, John has some savings, but he feels that he may need that some day.

Mildred, Louise, Esther, and John are all victims of Elder Abuse, a grossly under reported crime that affects one out of 20 older Americans each year, ac-cording to a 1990 report by the House Subcommittee on Health and Long-Term Care of the Select Committee on Aging.

Victims are usually dependent upon the abuser for daily care and isolated from society with little social support. They can be frightened, embarrassed, or mistrustful, and have a fear of outside contacts. They are ambivalent about dependency versus independence, and have internal conflict about being cared for like a child.

The Ohio Department of Human Services, through its Adult Protective Services program, which investigates abuse complaints for older persons living in the community, indicates that over 12,700 elderly Ohioans were reported as having been abused, neglected, or exploited during 1992. Since it is estimated that only one in eight cases are actually reported, the 12,700 reported cases becomes a staggering indicator of how widespread the problem really is.

Facts about Elder Abuse

Elder abuse occurs with a rate and frequency only slightly less

"Elder Abuse --The Hidden Crime" by Jim Bentley, LSW, Area Agency on Aging Region 9, Inc. Byesville, Ohio. Reprinted by permission.

than child abuse. Although any older person can become a victim, the frail and impaired, especially women, run a greater risk of becoming victims. Abuse may consist of physical, verbal, or psychological abuse, neglect, violation of rights, financial exploitation or self-neglect.

The Ohio Revised Code defines elder abuse as, "Abuse means the infliction upon an adult by himself or others of injury, unreasonable confinement, intimidation, or cruel punishment with resulting, physical harm, or mental anguish."

There is no single cause of elder abuse. Usually a combination of different factors contribute to it's development. They may include:

- stress of providing care to the older person
- mental illness, drug or alcohol abuse
- unresolved family conflict
- long-standing patterns of violence in the family
- vulnerability and dependency of the older person

Abuse may be intentional or unintentional, and usually occurs more than once. Frequently, the community is unaware that the abuse is occurring. Older people become victims of abuse because they tend to have fewer social contacts outside the home.

"In the Ohio study of elder abuse, 90% of the abusers were relatives; the highest number were daughters, followed by sons, granddaughters, husbands, and siblings," relates Georgia Anetzberger, Ph.D., Associate Director, Community Services, The Benjamin Rose Institute, and Adjunct Professor of Medicine, at the Case Western Reserve University. Anetzberger also notes that family members, or the older person, may seek to hide the abuse out of fear, guilt, or shame. "They (victims) can be frightened, embarrassed, or mistrustful, and have fear of outside contacts. They are ambivalent about dependency versus independence, and have internal conflict about being cared for like a child."

There are four main types of elder abuse:

1. **Physical Abuse,** which includes, physical injury, malnutrition, severe dehydration, lack of personal care, withholding of necessary medical care, and failure to give proper medication. What to look for (a pattern or combination of events).

Signs of Physical Abuse or Neglect

- rope burns
- bruises, especially on upper arms or clustered on trunk of body, or a combination of what appears to be old and new bruises
- illnesses which seem chronic, long-term, and untreated
- abrasions or lacerations
- burns
- fractures
- sagging skin or skin deterioration
- any injury that is not compatible with the story given
- an injury not properly cared for
- unkempt appearance (uncombed hair, unshaven face)
- poor hygiene (dirty skin, untrimmed nails)
- evidence of dehydration/malnutrition
- ravenous eating habits of elder
- evidence that elder is confined unwillingly to bed/chair/room without freedom of movement (restraints at wrist or ankles, muscle contractures)

Signs of Self-Neglect

- complaints from area merchants/neighbors who report loitering or wandering
- no food in house or lots of food in house which is spoiled
- prescription medication not taken
- evidence of alcohol or drug abuse

2. **Psychological Abuse,** which includes, threats of physical harm or nursing home placement, isolation, harassment, intimidation, withholding of affection and/or security, and refusing to allow the older person outside the home or allow visitors to see the older person.

Signs of Psychological Abuse

- expressions of fear, anger or resignation
- elder embarrassed or fearful when asked about injury
- family member afraid to leave you alone with elder
- family member acting as if elder did things on purpose
- elder refuses to walk
- elder is incontinent on purpose
- elder fails to get attention

3. **Financial Exploitation,** such as theft or misuse of the person's property or funds.

Signs of Material/Financial Neglect

- elder's rent is overdue on more than one occasion; utility and other bills have not been paid
- noticeable discrepancy between what is known about the elder's financial status and how they now appear
- discrepancy between resources available to elder, and how he or she is cared for
- condition of home
- level of personal care, nutrition, medical care, clothing, transportation, opportunities for social interaction

4. **Violation of Rights,** such as usurping decision making powers of the older person or involuntary confinement of the older person to the bed, room, or chair.

Signs of Violation of Rights

- unreasonable confinement to a bed, chair, room, or other part of the house
- possibility that elder is denied visitors or freedom to go out of the house, to visit friends or to go to church
- elder has no awareness of his/her financial affairs or what is being done with money or property

Who Is Most Vulnerable?

It appears that middle-class women, age 75 or older, who are severely disabled (mentally or physically), and/or dependent on others for daily care, are at greater risk, however, any older person can fall victim to elder abuse.

Signs of Elder Abuse, What To Look For

Individual signs by themselves are not enough, the key factor in identifying elder abuse is to look for a pattern of signs, symptoms, or events. AARP, in their brochure, *Domestic Mistreatment of the Elderly, Towards Prevention, Some Do's and Don'ts,* identified several signs and symptoms:

- Increasing depression
- Withdrawn or timid
- Physically injured
- Longing for death
- Vague health problems
- Shopping for physicians
- Anxiety
- Hostile
- Confused
- Unresponsive
- New poverty
- Anxious to please
- New self-neglect
- Conflicting stories
- Mounting resentment
- Excusing failure
- Shifting blame
- Aggressive/defensive behavior
- Substance abuse
- Unusual fatigue
- New affluence
- New health problems
- Preoccupation with depression
- Withholding food or medication

What to Do

Fortunately, there are agencies that are involved in identifying and preventing elder abuse. If you suspect that an older person, living in the community, is being abused, call Adult Protective Services, located in the local Department of Human Services.

If the abuse is occurring in an institutional setting, such as a nursing home, call the Long Term Care Ombudsman. If you feel that the older person is in immediate danger, or you're not sure who to call, call your police, or sheriff's office, or 911, if it is available in your area. If you fail to report abuse you may be fined.

You can find the phone number of the Adult Protective Services and your area Long Term Care Ombudsman from your local Area Agency on Aging. You will find them listed in the "yellow pages" of your telephone directory under the classification of "Senior Citizens' Services & Organization.

Article Review Form at end of book.

What are some ways seniors can be incorporated in the classroom?
What are the benefits of bringing the elderly into the classroom?

Helping One Another Across the Generations

Bringing older people and schoolchildren together creates a bond between the two groups and benefits both. Ms. Sellars provides guidelines for starting an intergenerational program, suggests useful resources, and describes some worthwhile activities that bring seniors and students together.

Linda Sellars

Linda Sellars, who worked in the mortgage industry for many years, is a recent graduate of the College of New Jersey and is now pursuing a career in education. She lives in Cinnaminson, N.J.

As I sat back and observed the township meeting, I witnessed two generations of citizens pitted against each other. On one side were members of the older generation, entrenched in their own world, living on fixed incomes, and lacking knowledge of anything that was happening in the district's schools that wasn't a budgetary matter. On the other side were parents, struggling economically in their own right but battling for the good of their children in a technologically backward district. I watched this struggle, realizing just how much our district's children were caught in the middle.

As a new teacher, I decided that bringing seniors and children together in the classroom would benefit the community not only politically but socially and emotionally as well. Bringing older people into the classroom would certainly involve more planning and work for already overburdened teachers, but the potential rewards seemed worth the effort.

Seniors and the young view one another with skepticism and fear. Many young people today form their image of the elderly from brief visits and from the media. Sitcoms usually portray the elderly as frail, sick, and mentally deteriorating. The elderly, for their part, form their opinions of the younger generation in the same ways. They are regularly exposed to media portrayals of young people as hoodlums given to crime and violence.

Seniors do make up a very large voting bloc, however. And school spending in many districts finds scant support among senior citizens.

Bringing the elderly into the classroom can help children develop positive attitudes toward the elderly by showing them that many older citizens remain active and are anything but frail. Moreover, seniors can provide positive role models and share the wisdom, experience, and skills they have acquired over a lifetime of learning.

The seniors benefit, too. Many older people feel frustrated and disconnected from the rest of society. Interacting with an enthusiastic and vibrant group of young people can be just what the doctor ordered to make older members of the community feel worthwhile and productive.

Starting a program to bring seniors and students together is not easy. It requires hard work, much planning, and a good deal of initiative on the teacher's part. There is no need for a teacher to be well versed in gerontology or to have years of experience with senior citizens. All that is really essential is a positive attitude and a desire to encourage mutual respect and understanding between children and the elderly.

The first step is planning what kind of program the teacher would like to institute. The roles of the teacher, the seniors, and the students need to be considered, and goals and task descriptions should be established for all parties. The demographics of the town should be examined as well. How many seniors are there? Where are they located in the town? How many students are likely to participate? Are any other teachers interested in taking part?

In order to become truly successful, an intergenerational activity should be a community endeavor. And a teacher who wishes to start such a program should encourage others in the community, including administrators and other teachers, to join in.

Each intergenerational program should have a coordinator and, if possible, an advisory board or council. Senior volunteers should fill out written applications to specify where and how they would like to help and what their special talents and interests are. The coordinator will then be responsible for making contacts with the applicants and for scheduling.

Senior volunteers can be found in a variety of places. These include senior centers, organizations whose membership includes large proportions of seniors (e.g., Kiwanis International), churches and synagogues, senior service agencies, and senior housing developments. Other seniors interested in working with today's youth might be found among the retirees of large corporations or government institutions located within a district, the American Association of Retired Persons, the Elderhostel Program, the Retired Senior Volunteer Program, or political groups that represent seniors, such as the Gray Panthers. Advertisements can be placed in the district's bulletin, posted in local establishments, and included in sections of local newspapers targeted to seniors. Once a program is established, word-of-mouth referrals will be the best source of new volunteers.

Once enough volunteers have come forward, they will need some training. The teacher and anyone else who might be involved in the program, such as office personnel or lunchroom help, may need to have some training as well. The seniors should be well informed as to what their roles will be, when they should be available, and for how long. They should also be made aware of what skills and knowledge are needed. All volunteers should be given a tour of the school building and should meet in advance the staff who will be involved in the program. The children should be taught something about aging, perhaps in conjunction with health education, before they begin to work with seniors.

Prior to instituting an intergenerational program, teachers should check that the district has liability insurance that covers volunteers. And, of course, parental permission for students to participate is a must.

Another area that commands attention is transportation. Often, lack of transportation is the greatest obstacle keeping an older person from volunteering. Public transportation and the use of school buses or community transportation for seniors are possible solutions to the transportation problem.

Once the intergenerational program is established, make sure the volunteers are acknowledged for their participation. Such recognition might include not just the seniors but also teachers, parents, administrators, and students. Thank-you letters, certificates, pins, newsletters, news releases, photos, and luncheons are all potential ways of recognizing those who make the program a success. If a senior volunteer should become ill and unable to continue, the children need to be informed and have an opportunity to express their emotions by sending cards or artwork.

After your intergenerational program has been in existence for some time, it should be evaluated. Again, such an evaluation should seek the opinions of everyone involved: community members, teachers, students, parents, administrators, other volunteers, and parents. Encourage everyone to submit written comments. After gathering as much evaluative information as possible, try to project the likely future of the program. Is it meeting its goals? Is expansion justified? Should it be scaled back or altered in some other way?

The Temple University Center for Intergenerational Learning has a number of resources available, and these can be invaluable sources of guidance.

- The *Linking Lifetimes Program Development Manual* explains how to set up an intergenerational mentoring program. It provides forms for establishing and evaluating a program.
- The *Elder Mentor Handbook* provides senior mentors with many resources for dealing with at-risk youngsters. It includes "child development

issues, tips for effective communication, suggested activities, and other useful information" in an easy-to-read format.

- Four videos are also available: *Linking Lifetimes: A National Intergenerational Mentoring Initiative; Elders as Mentors: A Training Program for Older Adults* (which includes a facilitator's guide); *A Vision Shared*; and *Creating a Spark*.

For more information, contact Temple's Center for Intergenerational Learning, 1601 North Broad St., Rm. 206, Philadelphia, PA 19122. The center can be reached by phone at 215/204-6970.

Material to supplement intergenerational activities is also available from Generations Together. Generations Together is a program of the University of Pittsburgh, and one of the projects it sponsors is the Senior Citizen School Volunteer Program (SCSVP), which, according to the project's Web site, involves "older adults as classroom resources to small and large groups of children in grades K–12. Older adults tutor, provide curriculum enrichment, assist in special academic projects, coordinate extracurricular activities, offer friendship to students, and reinforce teacher-directed activities" (http//:www. pitt.edu/~gti). Generations Together holds workshops and offers support and training to both teachers and seniors.

Many activities can be used to bring seniors and students together. I'll present here just a smattering of ideas that can be instituted within a single classroom at the elementary level. Remember, though, that the kinds of interaction between seniors and students depend to some ex-

tent on the maturity of the children. Young children need a more nurturing, grandparent-like relationship, whereas older children can engage in a more equal kind of give-and-take.

Throughout the elementary grades, teachers can invite senior citizens to discuss such topics as their careers, their hobbies, or other volunteer activities in which they participate. To show children that seniors can remain active for many years, a field trip to attend a Senior Olympics event might be arranged. Perhaps one of the participants would agree to speak to the class about keeping one's body and mind engaged throughout life.

Seniors can add a new dimension to social studies classes. Many of them will have lived through the historical events covered in textbooks. They can give firsthand accounts of how things used to look and can tell stories that cannot be found in any textbook. Children can brainstorm questions that they would like to ask, and they almost always want to know about the children of a particular period. If the senior volunteers immigrated to this country, children can ask about their trip, about difficulties encountered after arriving in the U.S., and about any assistance the volunteers or their families might have received. These interview sessions can be videotaped and kept for future classes. Perhaps a copy can be presented to the volunteers to share with their families.

Many of today's intergenerational programs make use of technology. Two recipients of the Michigan Bell/Ameritech Teacher Excellence Aware, Jan Simms and Bruce Simms, suggest bringing intermediate students and the elderly together on-line to produce biographies.

This project requires preparation prior to actually going on-line. The seniors might need to be briefed about basic computer use, and the children should read biographies, write imaginary biographies, and write their own autobiographies before they communicate with their senior partners. The students should brainstorm questions to ask the seniors. When the children make their initial overtures on-line, they should share with their senior partners some information about themselves—favorite foods, sports, and so on. This introduction should be followed by a few questions developed during the brainstorming session.

At the end of the projects the Simmses suggest that a party be given to bring students and seniors together in person. Both young and old find this experience very rewarding. "You'll never know how easy it's been for me to get up in the morning," said one senior. "This project has made me feel needed." Seniors have an equally profound effect on students; more than one has been heard to say, "I'm going to write a biography about my grandparents."[1]

Of course, if the required technology is not available, the seniors and students could just swap journals. Indeed, there is a letter-writing program, called "Write Partner," which is a pen-pal activity sponsored by the Family Literacy Center at Indiana University. Children are given the opportunity to explore a senior's life and history through an exchange of letters. This project can be instituted even in the lower grades.[2]

Another program associated with advanced technology began in Upper Arlington, Ohio. It is called Computer Ease. In this program the elderly are paired with intermediate students who lead them through programs associated with grades K–5. The seniors also learn a graphics program to use in writing to family and friends. The children experience the role of teacher and realize how critical time management and organization can be. The elderly meet teachers and see firsthand the educational facilities and classes offered in their school district. Thus they are able to see for themselves how their tax dollars are being used and to pass on this information to others.

Another possibility is a student/elder gardening program. Support for such a program can be obtained through grants and awards, perhaps from a local education foundation. If there is not enough land available on the school grounds for everyone or if there are not enough seniors to go around, then the children can take turns working in the program. Special events, such as book readings or science experiments, could take place in or near this very special garden.

Senior volunteers can also participate in the classroom as aides, helping with shows and school projects or possibly making items for the classroom (easels, bookcases, puppets, and so on). They can also tune pianos, tutor students whose native language is not English, or even translate during parent/teacher conferences.

Outside the classroom, seniors might be able to help in the school office, lunchroom, or media center. There is a senior group called Meals with Manners that models appropriate behavior for eating. The senior citizens can also chaperone school trips or dances. They can be tutors in reading, keyboarding, computer labs, language arts, math, and science, and they can read to the young and help classes celebrate holidays and special occasions. Young and old can work together toward community projects that would benefit all, such as planting trees and flowers in a community park.

A program started in 1989 in Cowley County, Kansas, is known as Phone Pal. In this program senior volunteers phone latchkey children before and after school. Often the morning call provides reminders prior to leaving home. "Be sure to wear your warm coat, hat, and gloves" tells Johnny that it's cold outside. Proper screening and training are imperative for the seniors, and experience has shown that a program coordinator is a must. The seniors and students should meet in person several times a year at the school.

An intergenerational project that was started in Cook County, Illinois, is called Senior Exchange. Many seniors on a fixed income find it hard to pay property taxes. Under this program, seniors who help out in the elementary and middle schools are compensated by having credits (at the minimum-wage pay rate) applied directly to their property tax bills. Applicants to the program are interviewed to determine where their abilities and interests lies. They work in computer labs, resource centers, the lunchroom, the school office, and in the classrooms. Through this program a free medical exam is also given to the seniors, and their backgrounds are investigated.[3]

Margaret Mead once wrote, "Somehow we have to get older people back closer to growing children if we are to restore a sense of community, knowledge of the past, and a sense of the future."[4] Intergenerational programs within America's schools are one way to help bring these two generations closer. Progress might be slow at first, and much planning is required in advance. But the results will be long-lasting, and the memories the seniors and the children create together today will help these generations form a bond rather than wage a war.

1. Jan Simms and Bruce Simms, "Life Stories," *Instructor*, November/December 1994, pp. 50–51. See also idem, "The Electronic Generation Connection," *The Computing Teacher*, April 1994, pp. 9–11.
2. Carl Smith, "Grandparent Pen Pals: Authentic Writing at Work," *Teaching K–8*, May 1995, pp. 40–41.
3. John G. Conyers, "Building Bridges Between Generations," *Educational Leadership*, April 1996, pp. 14–16.
4. Quoted on the Web site of the Temple University Center for Intergenerational Learning (http//:www.temple.edu/departments/CIL/what.html).

Article Review Form at end of book.

WiseGuide Wrap-Up

- Cooperation between society and the health care delivery system is essential to meeting the needs of the elderly.

- Approaches to health care that accommodate the changing needs of the elderly are available.

- Intergenerational programs have been successful.

R.E.A.L. Sites

This list provides a print preview of typical **coursewise** R.E.A.L. sites. There are over 100 such sites at the **courselinks**™ site. The danger in printing URLs is that web sites can change overnight. As we went to press, these sites were functional using the URLs provided. If you come across one that isn't, please let us know via email to: webmaster@coursewise.com. Use your Passport to access the most current list of R.E.A.L. sites at the **courselinks**™ site.

Site name: ElderAction: Ideas for Older Persons and Their Families
URL: http://www.aoa.dhhs.gov/elderpage.html#ea
Why is it R.E.A.L.? This site provides a variety of information for older persons and their families. It covers a wide range of topics, such as talking with your doctor, information on prescription drugs, information on key elderly housing concerns, and retirement and financial planning online resources.
Key Topics: medications, long-term care, Medicare
Activity: Identify a resource from this site that deals with aging and society.

Site name: Administration on Aging Fact Sheets
URL: http://www.aoa.dhhs.gov/factsheets/
Why is it R.E.A.L.? Clear and concise fact sheets designed for elders and their families as well as health care providers are available at this site. A variety of elder issues are discussed including elder abuse, age discrimination, protecting elders' rights, transportation and the elderly, and ombudsman programs.
Key Topics: Medicare, long-term care
Activity: List some resources for grandparents raising grandchildren.

Site name: Caregivers Support
URL: http://www.agenet.com/caregiver_support_page.html
Why is it R.E.A.L.? This is a resource developed by the AgeNet Information and Referral network to provide support and information for people with the primary responsibility of caring for a loved one. It offers a wealth of information on caregiver support, including articles and a resource directory.
Key Topic: long-term care
Activity: What is the book highlighted in the "Special Book Selection" component?

section

6

Key Points

- Technology has complicated the process of dying and death.

- The elderly are often more aware of and concerned about dying and death issues.

- Many ethical and moral dilemmas are involved with dying and death concerns.

Dying and Death

WiseGuide Intro

Developing an understanding of the life span involves not only the aging process but also the process of dying and death. As we age, we become more cognizant of our own mortality and the mortality of those around us. Section 6 opens the door for discussion and reflection on those final stages of life.

The treatment and care of people at the end of the life span has become a complicated issue. Several readings in this section look at the ethical and legal concerns of decisions at the end of life. Issues such as the right to die, living wills, assisted suicide, and euthanasia are debated in the readings, providing an opportunity to explore and review personal opinions and beliefs.

The grieving process is also examined from the perspective of the elderly as well as the medical care professional. One reading provides an excellent overview of the changes that older people experience. Medical care professionals need to be aware of these changes and reactions to effectively provide treatment. Essays from individuals about dying and death are provided in another reading, which adds a human, compassionate component to the issues in Section 6.

? ? ? Questions ? ?

Reading 30. Currently, the right-to-die laws in the United States make a clear distinction between what two categories? Do we have the legal right to refuse treatment in the United States?

Reading 31. What are the typical attitudes of the elderly toward death compared to other age groups? Can we measure attitudes about death?

Reading 32. What is meant by "palliative care" in the context

of the elderly person? What has complicated the long-term care of the aged in our country?

Reading 33. What is a common way many elderly cope with loss? How does "spirituality" help people deal with death?

Reading 34. How does the Patient Self-Determination Act (PSDA) impact dying and death. How could "ageism" affect medical treatment of the elderly?

Currently, the right-to-die laws in the United States make a clear distinction between what two categories? Do we have the legal right to refuse treatment in the United States?

Deciding Life and Death in the Courtroom

From Quinlan to Cruzan, Glucksberg, and Vacco—A brief history and analysis of constitutional protection of the 'right to die'

Lawrence O. Gostin

From the Georgetown/Johns Hopkins University Program on Law and Public Health, Washington, DC, and Baltimore, Md.

Abstract

The U.S. Supreme Court has recognized the constitutional right of terminally ill patients to die, but has found no similar right to be assisted in their death by a physician. Courts have widely upheld the right of patients to refuse treatment, or food and water, even when it causes their death. Despite public and physician

support, however, the Court believes there are legitimate state and ethical interests in banning assisted suicide. Although finding no constitutional right to assisted suicide, the Court may uphold state laws which permit it.

The Supreme Court decisions on the constitutionality of physician-assisted suicide in *Washington v Glucksberg*[1] and *Vacco v Quill*[2] stand as an important moment in the rich and storied history of judicial determinations about life-and-death choices in America. The role of medicine in the dying process—like procreation, abortion, and research on fetal tissue—poses

politically charged questions about how and why human life has meaning. Who should make intimate life-or-death decisions, under what circumstances, and with what safeguards? The judiciary—more than the political organs of government or the medical profession—has opined on these questions during its last two decades of case-by-case determinations on the "right to die."

Until the seminal decision of the New Jersey Supreme Court in *In re Quinlan*[3] in 1976, few judicial cases involving the role of medicine in the dying process had been decided. Since Quinlan, however, to Cruzan,[4]

Glucksberg,[1] and Vacco,[2] the courts have rendered more than 200 judgments about the lawfulness of medical decisions to intervene, or the failure to intervene, in the dying process.[5,6] Courts have considered the rationality of categorical distinctions that have long perplexed philosophers and physicians, such as the difference between acts and omissions. The judiciary has transformed not only the practice of medicine and the rights of patients, but has also shaped societal values. To understand contemporary moral and constitutional arguments about physician-assisted dying, one must first appreciate how the courts have dealt with the termination of life-sustaining treatment.

Withholding and Withdrawing Life-Sustaining Treatment

The legitimacy of patient claims—both moral and constitutional—for withholding or withdrawing life-sustaining treatment now appears so well settled, it is easy to forget that they were bitterly contested but a short time ago.[7] Prior to the era of judicial activism on the right to die, many regarded decisions to terminate life support as unethical and unlawful.[8] According to this view, if a physician discontinued treatment that would foreseeably result in a patient's death, the physician potentially could be held civilly or criminally liable. Consequently, some physicians refused to respect patient requests to terminate treatment, and others did so covertly. Cases came to the courts primarily because physicians feared what the Quinlan court called "the brood-ing presence of such possible liability."[3]

In Barber, for instance, two physicians were convicted of murder for terminating life support at a patient's request, only to have the conviction vacated on appeal.[9] Although physician concerns about liability have been exaggerated (no reported cases have held physicians liable for complying with the wishes of their patients),[10,11] it is well to recall the long history of uncertainty about the lawfulness and morality of terminating life support.

Derivation of the "Right to Die"

In Cruzan, the Supreme Court proclaimed, "This is the first case in which we have been squarely presented with the issue of whether the United States Constitution grants what is in common parlance referred to as a right to die."[14] The Supreme Court may now rue the day it characterized the constitutional right in quite this way, for the cases that preceded and post-dated Cruzan did not hold that patients possess a pure, autonomous right to decide the manner and timing of their death. Rather, the cases developed a narrower principle that patients possess a right to forgo medical treatment. The body of law known as "right-to-die" cases, in reality, extends ordinary treatment-refusal doctrine to end-of-life decisions.

The right of competent persons to refuse medical treatment is derived from three distinct sources of law—the common law, statutes, and the Constitution (both federal and state). Shortly before the turn of the century, the Supreme Court observed that "no right is held more sacred, or is more carefully guarded, by the common law, than the right of every individual to the possession and control of his own person, free from all restraint or interference of others, unless by clear and unquestionable authority of law."[12] This right to refuse treatment is embodied in the doctrine of informed consent under tort law and holds that physicians have a duty of care that requires the disclosure of relevant benefits, risks, and adverse effects of medical treatment.[13]

The right to refuse treatment can be found in state statutes that explicitly permit patients to discontinue life support.[14] These statutes authorize a patient to make an advance directive to "rude treatment decisions in the event that he or she becomes incompetent—either a living will or a durable power of attorney." A living will allows a patient to specify the circumstances under which he or she would choose to decline life-sustaining treatment. A durable power of attorney allows a patient to specify an agent or proxy to make health care decisions on his or her behalf. All 50 states provide statutory authority for some form of advance directive: 46 states and the District of Columbia authorize both living wills and the appointment of health care agents; Alaska recognizes only living wills; and Massachusetts, Michigan, and New York[15] recognize only health care agents.[5] In 1990, Congress enacted the Patient Self-determination Act, which requires health care institutions to disseminate written information at the time of admission about the patient's rights under state law to refuse treatment and to formulate advance directives.[16]

The right to refuse treatment, most importantly, has been grounded in the Due Process Clause of the Fourteenth Amendment to the Constitution. At least since the turn of the century,[17] the Supreme Court has recognized that a competent person has a constitutionally protected "liberty interest" in refusing unwanted medical treatment.[13] The Supreme Court in Cruzan embraced this liberty interest and extended it to the "dramatic consequences" of refusing life-sustaining treatment.[4]

The courts, having affirmed a constitutionally protected interest in refusing life-sustaining treatment, held that certain categorical distinctions that had been drawn lacked a rational basis.[19]

Competency vs Incompetency

The right to refuse treatment characteristically requires the patient to be competent to make an autonomous choice. The question arose whether this same right should logically extend to persons who are not competent. Reasoning that an incompetent person retains the same rights as a competent person "because the value of human dignity extends to both," courts have adopted a "substitute judgment" standard, whereby a proxy determines what an incompetent person would have decided.[20] To effectuate the right to decline treatment for the incompetent, courts have, to some extent, engaged in a legal fiction. For those who have never been competent, such as severely mentally retarded persons or those who have never seriously contemplated such issues, the judiciary, at least implicitly, found that avoiding life-sustaining

treatment was sometimes in the patient's "best interests."[21]

Withholding vs Withdrawing Treatment

The courts have perceived no rational distinction between withholding and withdrawing life support. To some, withdrawing treatment was regarded as morally and legally troubling because the physician was engaging in an affirmative act that was a causative factor in the patient's death. Under this view, withholding treatment was defensible because the physician was merely failing to act. However, the moral difference between an act and an omission has long been challenged on the grounds that physicians have a duty of care that may require them to act, or fail to act, depending on the medical circumstances and the patient's desires. As the Conroy court stated, "Whether necessary treatment is withheld at the outset or withdrawn later on, the consequence—the patient's death—is the same."[22] Physicians also observed that a rule that permitted withholding treatment but penalized withdrawing treatment might have the perverse effect of deterring physician decisions to initiate emergency treatment.[7]

Ordinary vs Extraordinary Treatment

The courts have rejected the distinction between "ordinary" and "extraordinary" treatment. Judicial affirmation of the right to refuse life support has extended to a wide range of treatments without regard to the scientific, technical, or economic aspects of the treatment or the consequences of treatment withdrawal.[23,24] Treatments such as hydration and

artificial nutrition have a particularly intimate association with nurturance, care, and life itself. Yet courts, with a new notable exceptions, have had little difficulty in finding a right to refuse this form of medical intervention, despite the inevitably resulting death.[20] Justice O'Connor in her concurrence in Cruzan agreed with four other members of the Court that "artificial feeding cannot readily be distinguished from other forms of medical treatment."[4] An individual's deeply personal decision to refuse consent to an invasive bodily intrusion, including the delivery of food and water, is constitutionally protected.

Physician-Assisted Suicide

When the issue of physician-assisted dying came before the courts, it was within the context of a generation of cases carefully examining the rights of patients to make decisions at the end of life. Courts had already given patients on life support the broad authority to decline medical intervention, had extended this right to persons who were incompetent to express their views, and had rejected distinctions among forms of treatment and between acts and omissions. The courts, however, had persistently affirmed one categorical distinction: that between withdrawing or withholding life-sustaining treatment on the one hand, and active euthanasia or physician-assisted dying on the other.[25] Since the founding of the republic, no court of final jurisdiction has found a constitutional right to participate, or assist, in a suicide.[36]

The states have long established criminal penalties both for directly causing another person's death (euthanasia) and for assisting in the dying process (assisted suicide). A person who directly causes the death of another by administering an injection[27] or by placing a lethal dose of medication in the patient's hand or mouth[28] risks prosecution for murder or manslaughter. In *People* v *Cleaves*, for example, Cleaves was convicted of murder when he actively participated in the death of a friend who was in the terminal stages of AIDS. Neither his friend's consent nor the absence of malice justified the crime.[29]

Suicide is not prohibited in any state. However, in most jurisdictions, it constitutes an offense to assist in a suicide (e.g., to provide advice about the most effective or painless methods or to supply the means, as in writing a prescription). The Model Penal Code establishes an independent offense for a person who purposefully aids or assists another to commit suicide.[30] Thirty-five states explicitly criminalize assisted suicide by statute, and 9 additional states and the District of Columbia criminalize assisted suicide through the common law.[5] The Assisted Suicide Funding Restriction Act of 1997 also prohibits the use of federal funds in support of physician-assisted suicide.[31] Prohibitions against physician-assisted suicide have never contained exceptions for persons near death or for those who have granted consent.

Social values surrounding life-and-death choices have progressed so dramatically since Cruzan that two federal courts of appeal were prepared to critically challenge the deeply ingrained categorical distinction between "killing" and "letting die." The Second and Ninth Circuits, for different reasons, held that physician-assisted suicide was constitutionally protected and that no rational distinction could be drawn between physician-assisted suicide and termination of life support.[32,33]

Public concern and democratic action are sharply focused on physician assistance in the dying process: opinion polls among the general public[34] and physicians[35,36] show significant support for physician assistance in dying. Many physicians, moreover, say they have engaged in, or would engage in, the practice.[37] A referendum supporting physician assistance in dying passed in Oregon,[38,39] while referenda in Washington State and California were narrowly defeated. In the Kevorkian cases, juries refused to convict even in the face of the most blatant transgressions of the "hard rule" against physician-assisted suicide.

It was within this context that the Supreme Court agreed to review the Second and Ninth Circuit Court opinions in the momentous cases of *Washington* v *Glucksberg*[1] and *Vacco* v *Quill*.[2] The intensity of contemporary interest in physician-assisted suicide is demonstrated by the 60 amicus curiae briefs that were submitted to the Court, notably by the Solicitor General of the United States,[40] bioethicists,[41,42] moral philosophers,[43] and law professors.[44]

Washington v *Glucksberg*: Is There a Fundamental Liberty Interest in Assisted Suicide?

The Fourteenth Amendment to the Constitution provides that no state shall "deprive any person of life, liberty, or property, without due process of law." The Due Process Clause guarantees more than fair procedures. It proscribes government from acting in an irrational, arbitrary, or unreasonable manner (substantive due process). The Supreme Court uses a heightened standard of review when government interferes with certain fundamental rights and liberty interests involving, for example, reproduction,[45] abortion,[46] and marriage.[47] Most importantly, the rights to bodily integrity[48] and to refusal of unwanted life-saving medical treatment[4] are constitutionally protected.

The Supreme Court's substantive due process analysis requires, first, a "careful description" of the asserted fundamental liberty interest and, second, that the interest is, objectively, deeply rooted in the nation's history and traditions. The Chief Justice, writing for the majority in Glucksberg, essentially reframed the description of the fundamental liberty interest enunciated by the courts below.[1] Rather than characterize the case as involving the right to "determine the time and manner of one's death" or, more simply, the right to die, the Court identified the liberty interest as the "right to commit suicide which itself includes the right to assistance in so doing."[1] Having framed the question in this way, the Court demonstrated an opposition to, and condemnation of, suicide assistance as an enduring theme in the nation's philosophical, legal, and cultural heritage[49]: "We are confronted with a consistent and almost universal tradition that has long rejected the asserted right, and continues explicitly to reject it today, even for terminally ill, mentally competent adults." The asserted right to assistance in committing suicide, according to the Supreme Court, is not a fundamental liberty interest protected by the Due Process Clause.

The State Interests in Physician-Assisted Dying

During oral arguments, Justice Rehnquist commented that if the Court found a fundamental liberty interest, but permitted the state to prohibit it entirely, "that would be rather a conundrum." If a person has a constitutionally protected interest in physician-assisted suicide, how could the state effectively "snuff out" that personal interest by a complete ban?

By finding no constitutionally protected liberty interest, however, the Court adopted its lowest level of constitutional scrutiny. The Court simply had to demonstrate that physician-assisted suicide was rationally related to legitimate state interest.

Preservation of Human Life

Perhaps the paramount state interest is the preservation of human life, and according to the Court, the prohibition on physician-assisted suicide reflects and advances this commitment to life. Under this reasoning, the prohibition on assisted suicide demonstrates the gravity of taking a life and the limits in human relationships.[50] Clearly, the state ought not to make subjective assessments about the quality of a person's life or afford less than full protection of the law to all persons. Nonetheless, the Supreme Court did not take into account that the state's interest in preserving life is diminished if the person it seeks to protect is terminally ill or permanently comatose and has expressed a desire to die.

When competent, terminally ill patients feel that their physical health no longer permits them to pursue liberty or happiness, and they no longer wish to live, the state's interest in forcing them to do so appears less important.[32]

The Supreme Court relied on the related state interest in suicide prevention, aptly referring to suicide as a "serious public health problem."[1] Yet, in drawing its arguments from the broad range of suicides in society, including teens and the mentally ill, it considered a class of persons much broader than the competent, terminally ill persons specified in the litigation. Certainly, terminally ill patients, like others seeking suicide, may have undiagnosed and untreated depression. It follows that the state ought to provide adequate mental health services and rigorous safeguards to assure fully considered and competent decision making. It does not follow, however, that all terminally ill persons who seek physician assistance in dying do so irrationally.

Integrity and Ethics of the Medical Profession

The Supreme Court deferred to the considered views of the American Medical Association and others that assisted suicide is fundamentally incompatible with the healing role of physicians and that the practice would undermine the physician-patient relationship.[51,52] Yet, equally thoughtful opinion in medicine and ethics holds that physicians have a duty to honor patient wishes, provide comfort, and relieve suffering. Under this view, physician assistance in the dying process, consistent with the wishes and best interests of patients, may not only be compatible with the physician's role, but

may be an obligation inherent in it.[53,54] Some patients, of course, may lose trust if their physician is permitted by law to assist in suicide. Other patients, however, may have greater confidence if they know that their physician will abide by their wishes should they decide that they can no longer endure suffering and that it is time to die.

Protecting the Vulnerable

During oral arguments before the Supreme Court, those who were protesting assisted suicide made a powerful symbolic statement. Persons with disabilities chained their wheelchairs together on the steps of the Court, poignantly asserting that assisted suicide would render them more vulnerable and would devalue their lives. The Supreme Court reasoned that assisted suicide would place vulnerable groups (e.g., the elderly, the poor, and persons with disabilities) at risk from abuse, neglect, and mistakes. Others have expressed concern that, in an era of managed care and cost containment, patients may be exposed to subtle pressures to seek a quicker, less expensive alternative to aggressive treatment or extended comfort care.[55,56] Under this view, patients may be subjected to external pressures from health care providers, insurers, and families seeking to minimize cost. But equally important, vulnerable individuals may experience internal pressures wherein they perceive themselves to be less valued and may wish to spare their loved ones the financial and emotional burdens of an arduous dying process. While careful regulation of assisted suicide could minimize the undue influence of others,[57] the state could not fully protect vulnerable individuals from their own perceptions and fears. At its core, society must decide between the paternalism inherent in banning assisted suicide and the respect for autonomy inherent in permitting competent, terminally ill individuals to make the final decision.

The Slippery Slope

The Supreme Court expressed concern that permitting physician-assisted suicide would start down an inexorable path toward voluntary and perhaps even involuntary euthanasia. From a legal perspective, the Court reasoned that if assistance in suicide were a constitutional right, everyone must enjoy it, including the incompetent, the physically disabled, and the nonterminally ill. Why, for example, shouldn't a person with a physical disability who is unable to self-administer prescribed medication have the right to euthanasia? The Court also drew support from the Netherlands where the practice of euthanasia has not been restricted to the terminally ill or to those who have explicitly requested assistance in dying.[58,59]

Slippery slopes are always possible in medicine as they are in most public forums. The central constitutional question is whether there is a principled basis for limiting a right to assisted suicide to competent terminally ill individuals and whether that line reasonably could be enforced. Adoption of rigorous safeguards would restrict, but not eliminate, inappropriate uses of assisted suicide such as a young person influenced by depression or a feeling of hopelessness. Some argue that current prohibitions on assisted suicide are not enforced; society's failure to regulate at all may create an even greater potential for abuse.[44] The evidence from the Netherlands—which is a very different country with unique legal procedures—is decidedly mixed. Finally, the legislature or the judiciary may in the future extend the right to assisted death to the noncompetent or nonterminally ill, but making assisted suicide lawful does not render these decisions inevitable.[54]

Autonomy, Community, and the Patient-Physician Relationship Under the Constitution

The decisions of the Second and Ninth Circuit Courts of Appeals, together with many of the amicus curiae briefs, strenuously argued that the central constitutional and ethical issue was not assistance in suicide but, instead, the right of self-sovereignty. Under this view, the core principle is whether the Constitution safeguards the right of autonomous adults to exercise personal control over their manner of death, to seek professional medical assistance toward that end, and to avoid unnecessary and severe physical and mental suffering. The Supreme Court acknowledged that many of the rights and liberties protected by due process sound in personal autonomy, but held that "all important, intimate, and personal decisions" are not so protected.[1]

Interestingly, the Supreme Court's decisions resonate with the importance of community and the interrelatedness of people in society. Justice Stevens, quoting John Donne's observation that "No man is an island," proclaimed the importance of "preserving and fostering the benefits that every human being may provide to the community. . . . The value to others of a person's life is far too precious to allow the individual to claim a constitutional entitlement to complete autonomy in making a decision to end that life." Justices Scalia and Stevens implied that in many, if not most, cases, the individual's right of autonomy—including the right to refuse treatment—would yield if necessary to effectuate a vital community interest.

Notably, five members of the court wrote or joined in opinions that took a decidedly more liberal view of autonomy and decisional privacy, suggesting the majority of the Court favors a more expansive methodology for substantive due process. Justice Stevens insisted that due process embraces a patient's "interest in dignity, and in determining the character of the memories that will survive long after her death." Justice Souter would ask whether the statute sets up one of those "arbitrary impositions" or "purposeless restraints" at odds with the due process clause. Justice Breyer suggested that America's legal traditions would provide greater support for a formulation of interests using words roughly like the "right to die with dignity. . . . But irrespective of the exact words used, at its core would lie personal control over the manner of death, professional medical assistance, and the avoidance of unnecessary and severe suffering." Finally, Justice O'Connor, joined by Justices Ginsburg and Breyer, saw no need to reach the question of whether "a mentally competent person who is experiencing great suffering has a constitutionally cognizable interest in controlling the circumstances of his or her imminent death."

The Supreme Court's jurisprudence provides ample reason to believe that the Constitution safeguards, in the words of *Planned Parenthood* v *Casey*,[46] "the most intimate and personal choices a person may make in a lifetime, choices central to personal dignity and autonomy." Even the amicus brief for the United States,[40] which rejected assisted suicide, argued that the term liberty in the Due Process Clause is broad enough to encompass the right of self-determination for terminally ill, competent adults. The moral philosophers' brief[43] defended the autonomy principle vigorously: "certain decisions are momentous in their impact on the character of a person's life. . . . Such deeply personal decisions pose controversial questions about how and why human life has value. In a free society, individuals must be allowed to make those decisions for themselves, out of their own faith, conscience, and convictions."

Vacco v *Quill:* Is There a Rational Distinction Between "Killing" and "Letting Die?"

The Equal Protection Clause of the Fourteenth Amendment provides that no state shall "deny to any person within its jurisdiction the equal protection of the laws." Equal protection, simply put, requires that similarly situated individuals must be treated similarly, but that unlike cases may be treated differently. If a legislative distinction neither burdens a fundamental liberty interest nor creates a suspect class, the courts are highly deferential. Since the Glucksberg court found no fundamental liberty interest in assisted suicide, and no suspect class such as race was involved, the state had to show merely that its distinction was rationally related to a legitimate governmental purpose.

As explained above, states not only permit withdrawal of life-sustaining treatment, they constitutionally protect it. At the same time, states criminally proscribe physician-assisted suicide. If no rational distinction exists between a right to withdraw treatment, which states constitutionally safeguard, and physician-assisted suicide, which states criminalize, then, according to proponents, there is a denial of equal protection. The basic constitutional questions are whether the groups indeed are similarly situated (do important moral differences exist between physician-assisted suicide and withdrawal of life support?) and, if so, whether the state has a rational basis for applying unequal treatment.

The Supreme Court in Vacco found the distinction between assisted suicide and withdrawal of life-sustaining treatment to be "important, logical, rational, and well established."[2] Yet, its reasons for differentiating between the two practices fly the face of a body of philosophic literature examining questions of causation and intention in medicine. Before I turn to the Supreme Court's reasoning, it is well to explore a logical distinction between these two practices. Although not enunciated by the Court, the distinction I offer provides a plausible reason for treating assisted suicide differently from withdrawal of life-sustaining treatment.

A person who is on life support which she requests be discontinued is receiving unwanted medical treatment. She is claiming a right to be free from a burdensome physical restraint. The patient's claim is "negative" in nature; she is merely seeking to avoid an invasion of her bodily integrity. The physician has a

duty to respect the patient's request not to be treated, for the physician's privilege to treat is wholly dependent on the patient's consent.

A person who is not on life support, but who wishes to hasten his death, is making a materially different request. This patient's claim is "positive" in nature, for he is affirmatively soliciting the assistance of another in achieving his desired ends. A patient's request for medical treatment, particularly if it lies outside of the standard of care, does not create a corollary duty on the physician to comply. The Supreme Court has long seen a "negative" Constitution that provides rights against restraint, but not necessarily affirmative obligations to assist.[60] The difference between a claim of avoidance of restraint and affirmative medical assistance provides a reasonable distinction between "killing" and "letting die." The Court's reasoning, based on causation and intention, is less certain.

Causation

The Chief Justice accepts the argument that when a patient refuses life support, he dies of an underlying disease or pathology, but if he ingests lethal prescribed medicine, he is killed by the physician. In both cases, however, the physician engages in an act from which the patient dies. Consider a patient who requests termination of nutrition and hydration. The physician affirmatively acts to remove a nasogastric tube, and the patient dies of starvation, not the underlying disease. It is possible, of course, to argue that the disease initially prevented the person from eating and drinking, but to many observers, the causation argument is weakened by the close connection between the physician's act and the inevitable result.

Intention

The Chief Justice resorted to "purpose" or "intent" in justifying the distinction between "killing" and "letting die."[2] A physician who withdraws life-sustaining treatment, it is said, may hasten death, but the purpose is to relieve pain and suffering. A physician who assists a suicide, however, "must necessarily and indubitably, intend primarily that the patient be made dead."[1]

Intent may be defined as the state of a person's mind that directs his actions toward an objective. Whether one focuses on the physician's motivation, knowledge of the result, or justification for the act, the intent behind assisted suicide and withdrawal of life support appears similar.

First, in both cases, the physician's motive is benevolent in the sense that she seeks to do good for the patient. The well-intended physician does not desire the patient's death, but recognizes that the patient is terminally ill and suffering. The wish to end that suffering motivates the physician, whether she is withdrawing life support or assisting in the death.

Second, the physician knows the likely result of her action and understands the consequences that likely will follow from that act. Training and experience in medicine will usually enable the physician to accurately predict the result of an act, whether it is withdrawal of life support or assistance in death. It is sometimes said that the resulting death is much more certain with physician-assisted suicide than with withdrawal of life support,

but this is not necessarily so. Certainly, a patient may continue to breathe if a respirator is disconnected, but there is no such ambiguity of result if nutrition and hydration are removed. On the other hand, a patient who obtains a prescription to assist in suicide may, or may not, fill the prescription or self-administer the medication.

Finally, and most importantly, in both instances, the physician acts in accord with the patient's wishes. The physician's act is justified by the patient's autonomous expression of will, and it is the patient's consent that is controlling. Absent the patient's consent, both withdrawal of life support and physician-assisted suicide would be unethical.

The Double Effect and Aggressive Palliation of Pain

Physicians who prescribe high levels of sedation for patients may not know the results. The sedation may have a so-called double effect—it will help relieve pain and provide comfort, but it may also retard respiration possibly leading to the patient's death. Prior to the physician-assisted suicide cases before the Supreme Court, there was uncertainty whether a physician could engage aggressively in palliation of pain, knowing that a possible, perhaps likely, result was the patient's death. The Supreme Court, citing the New York State Task Force on Life and the Law, argues that it is "widely recognized that the provision of pain medication is ethically and professionally acceptable even when the treatment may hasten the patient's death, if the medication is intended to alleviate pain and severe discomfort, not to cause death." It is of some

consequence that the Supreme Court concludes its opinion in Glucksberg by emphasizing the importance of palliative care. Justice O'Connor makes the point without equivocation: "A patient who is suffering from a terminal illness and who is experiencing great pain has no legal barriers to obtaining medication, from qualified physicians, even to the point of causing unconsciousness and hastening death."[1] While the issue of double effect was not squarely before the Court, the justices' perspective of extant state law appears to be that aggressive pain palliation is lawful. More importantly, the Court's decision could be read for proposition that the state could not, consistent with the Constitution, prosecute a physician for causing a patient's death, where that death was a secondary consequence of aggressive pain management.

The Future of Physician-Assisted Suicide

The Glucksberg and Vacco decisions culminate more than two decades of judicial opinion on decisions at the end of life. Despite its unanimity, the Court left open the door to further constitutional adjudication and invited the nation to pursue an earnest discussion of physician assistance in the dying process. By declining to find a constitutionally protected interest, the Court ceded to the political organs of government the future lawfulness of assisted suicide. The assisted suicide cases are fully consistent with the Court's reassertion of state authority in our federal system of government. Although the Court did not categorically state that statutes legalizing assisted suicide would be upheld as constitutional, it broadly hinted that it would tolerate state experimentation in a democratic society. State experimentation, of course, indicates that some states, like Oregon, might legalize assisted suicide, while the majority may not. This could lead to the troubling consequence of "forum shopping," where individuals might cross state lines to die. In her concurring opinion, Justice O'Connor observed[2]:

Every one of us at some point may be affected by our own or a family member's terminal illness. There is no reason to think the democratic process will not strike the proper balance between the interests of terminally ill, mentally competent individuals who would seek to end their suffering and the State's interests in protecting those who might seek to end life mistakenly or under pressure. . . . States are presently undertaking extensive and serious evaluation of physician-assisted suicide. . . . In such circumstances, "the . . . challenging task of crafting appropriate procedures for safeguarding . . . liberty interests is entrusted to the "laboratory" of the States. . . .

In the words of Justice Stevens, there is "room for further debate about the limits that the Constitution places on the power of the states to punish this practice."[2] In Glucksberg, the Court found that the state of Washington's statutory ban on assisted suicide was constitutional "on its face," meaning that it would be valid in most, but not necessarily all, cases in which it was applied. That holding, however, does not foreclose the possibility that an individual "seeking to hasten her death, or a doctor whose assistance was sought, could prevail in a more particularized challenge" (Stevens J, concurring).[1] The Chief Justice, moreover, in a footnote (note 24) did not disagree with Justice

Stevens' assessment. Thus, the Court left open the possibility that it would uphold the right to assisted suicide, say, in a case where a physician faced a severe criminal penalty for complying with the request of a patient who was unquestionably competent, terminally ill, and experiencing intractable pain and suffering.

Beyond the heated and prolonged conflict on assisted suicide dawns one area of consensus. The enhanced consciousness about the dying process underscores the importance of high-quality end-of-life care. Resources and professional training naturally should focus on the management of pain, the alleviation of depression and mental illness, and the physical and emotional needs of patients nearing the end of their lives.

References

1. 117 SCt 2258 (1997).
2. 117 SCt 2293 (1997).
3. In re Quinlan, 355 A2d 647 (NJ), cert denied, 429 US922 (1976).
4. Cruzan v Director, Missouri Dept of Health, 497 US 261 (1990).
5. Choice in Dying. *The Right to Die Law Digest*. New York NY: Choice in Dying; 1997.
6. Meisel A. *The Right to Die*. 2nd ed. New York, NY: John Wiley & Sons, 1995.
7. President's Commission for the Study of Ethical Problems in Medicine and Biomedical and Behavioral Research. *Deciding to Forego Life-Sustaining Treatment: A Report on the Ethical, Medical, and Legal Issues in Treatment Decisions*. Washington, DC: US Government Printing Office; 1983.
8. Solomon M. Decisions near the end of life: professional views on life-sustaining treatments. *Am J Public Health*. 1993;83:14–20.
9. Barber v Superior Court, 195 Cal Rptr 484 (Ct App 1983).
10. Glantz LH. Withholding and withdrawing treatment: the role of the criminal law. *Law Med Health Care*. 1987–1988;15:231–241.
11. Gostin LO. Drawing a line between killing and letting die: the law, and law reform, on medically assisted dying. *J Law Med Ethics*. 1993;21:71–78.
12. Union Pacific Railway Co v Botsford, 141 US 250, 251(1891).
13. Canterbury v Spence, 464 F2d 772 (DC Cir), cert denied, 409 US 1064 (1972).
14. Conservatorship of Drabick, 245 Cal Rptr 840 (Ct App), cert denied, 488 US 958 (1988).
15. While ease law in New York recognizes living wills, health care agents are preferred under state legislation. Eichner v Dillon, 420 NE2d 64 (NY Ct App 1981).
16. 42 USCA [subsections] 1395cc(f)(1), 1396a(a)(1997).
17. Jacobson v Massachusetts, 197 US 11, 24–30 (1905).
18. Washington v Harper, 494 US 210, 221–22 (1990).
19. Gostin LO Weir R. Life and death choices after Cruzan: case law and standards of professional conduct. *Milbank Q*. 1991;69:l43–173.
20. Superintendent of Belchertown State School v Saikewicz, 370 NE2d 417 (Mass).
21. Dubler N. Balancing life and death: proceed with caution. *Am J Public Health*. 1993;83:23–25.
22. In re Conroy, 486 A2d 1209 (NJ 1985).
23. In re Storar, 420 NE2d 64 (NY), cert denied, 454 US 858 (1981).
24. Brophy v New England Sinai Hospital, Inc, 497 NE2d 626 (Mass 1986).
25. Weir R. *Physician Assisted Suicide*. Bloomington: Indiana University Press;1997.
26. Compassion in Dying v Washington 49 F3d 586, 591 (9th Cir 1995).
27. State v Cobb, 625 P2d 1133 (Ky 1981).
28. Aven v State, 277 SW 1080 (Tex 1925).
29. People v Cleaves, 280 Cal Rptr 146 (Ct App 1991).
30. American Law Institute. Model Penal Code 210.5(2) (Official Draft and Revised Comments 1980).
31. Pub L 105–12,111 Stat 23 (codified at 42 USC [subsections] 14401 et seq).
32. Compassion in Dying v Washington, 79 F3d 790 (9th Cir 1996) (en banc).
33. Quill v Vacco, 80 F3d 716 (2d Cir 1996).

The author is grateful to Kathleen Maguire , RN, JD, James G. Hodge, Jr, JD, LLM, and Joanne Hewitson for their valuable contributions to this article.

34. Blendon RJ, Szalay US, Knox RA. Should physicians aid their patients in dying? The public perspective. *JAMA*. 1992;267:2658–2662.

35. Bachman JG, Alser KH, Doukas DJ, et al. Attitudes of Michigan physicians and the public toward legalizing physician-assisted suicide and voluntary euthanasia. *N Engl J Med* 1996;334:303–309.

36. Lee MA, Nelson HD, Tilden VP, et al. Legalizing assisted suicide: views of physicians in Oregon. *N Engl J Med*. 1996;334:310–315.

37. Back AL, Wallace JI, Starks HE, et al. Physician-assisted suicide and euthanasia in Washington State. *JAMA* 1996;275:919–925.

38. Ore Rev Stat [subsections] 127.800 et seq (1996)

39. Lee v Oregon, 891 F Supp 1429 (D Or 1985), vacated, 107 F3d 1382 (9th Cir 1997).

40. Dellinger W, Humger FW, Waxman SP, et al. Brief for the United States as Amicus Curiae Supporting Petitioners, November 1996.

41. Annas GJ, Glantz LH. Brief for Bioethics Professors Annicus Curiae Supporting Petitioners, November 12, 1996.

42. Gold MR. Brief for Bioethicists Amicus Curiae Supporting Respondents, December 9, 1996.

43. Dworkin R, Nagel T, Nozick R, et al. Assisted suicide: the philosophers' brief. *New York Review*. March 27, 1997:1.

44. Hoffman DA, Baron CH, Gostin LO. Brief Amicus Curiae of Law Professors in Support of Respondents, December 10, 1996.

45. Griswold v Connecticut 381 US 479 (1965).

46. Planned Parenthood Southeastern Pennsylvania v Casey, 505 US 833 (1992).

47. Loving v Virginia, 388 US 1(1997).

48. Rochin v California, 342 US 165 (1952).

49. Marzen TJ, O'Dowd MK, Crone D, et al. Suicide: a constitutional right? *Duquesne Law Rev.* 1985;24:1–56.

50. New York State Task Force on Life and the Law. *When Death Is Sought:A$$is$d Suicide and Euthanasia in the Medical Context.* Albany, NY:Health Education Services, 1994.

51. American Medical Association. Code of Ethics. Chicago, Ill: American Medical Association;1994:para2.211.

52. Council on Ethical and Judicial Affairs, American Medical Association. Decisions near the end of life. *JAMA* 1992;267:2229–2235.

53. Orentlicher D. The legalization of physician-assisted suicide. *N Engl J Med.* 1996;335:663–667.

54. Angell M. The Supreme Court and physician assisted suicide: the ultimate right. *N Engl J Med.* 1997;336:50–53.

55. Wolf SM. Physician assisted suicide in the context of managed care. *Duquesne Law Rev.* 1996;35:455–479.

56. Annas GJ. The promised end: constitutional aspects of physician-assisted suicide. *N Engl J Med.* 1996;335:683–687.

57. Miller FG, Quill TE, Brody H, et al. Regulating physician-assisted death. *N Engl J Med.* 1994;331:119–123.

58. Wilfert CM. Euthanasia in the Netherlands: good news or bad? *N Engl J Med.* 1996;335:1676–1680.

59. van der Mass PJ, vender Wal G, Haverkate I, et al. Euthanasia, physician assisted suicide and other medical practices involving the end of life in the Netherlands. *N Engl J Med.* 1996;335:1699–1705.

60. DeShaney v Winnebago County Dept of Social I Services, 489 US 189 (1989).

Reprints: Lawrence O. Gostin, JD, Georgetown University Law Center, 600 New Jersey Ave NW, Washington, DC 20001 (e-mail:gostin@law.georgetown.edu).

Health Law and Ethics section editors: Lawrence O. Gostin, JD, the Georgetown/Johns Hopkins University Program on Law and Public Health, Washington, DC, and Baltimore, Md: Helene M. Cole, MD, Contributing Editor, JAMA.

Article Review Form at end of book.

What are the typical attitudes of the elderly toward death compared to other age groups? Can we measure attitudes about death?

The Understanding of Death and Dying in a Life-Span Perspective

Brian de Vries, PhD

Assistant professor, School of Family and Nutritional Sciences, University of British Columbia, 2205 East Mall, Vancouver, BC, Canada V6T 1Z4.

Susan Bluck, BA

Graduate student, School of Social Ecology, University of California, Irvine.

James E. Birren, PhD

Director, Borun Center for Gerontological Research, University of California, Los Angeles.

Abstract

Fifty-four men and women from across the adult life span wrote two-page essays about death and dying. Content coding assessed the extent to which essays were concerned with death or dying (i.e., as a subject of discussion) and self, others, or more abstract conceptions (i.e., referent), as well as levels of impact, involvement, and acceptance. Structural analysis revealed that for both genders discussions of death were both more frequent and more complex than were discussions of dying, and individuals referred to others more often and in more simplistic terms than to self. The middle-aged writers placed greater emphasis on dying. All discussions were characterized by high impact and involvement and low levels of acceptance.

A sizable body of literature attests to life course variations in attitudes toward death. Erikson (1968) has proposed that the realization that time is short and death is imminent precipitates the integrity-despair crisis of the terminal period of life. Attempting to cope with death, however, does not wait for the final developmental period. Fears and expectations about death begin forming early and may be shaped by the impersonal and seemingly daily contact with death through the media and by the loss of loved ones, which may occur at any age. Our concern, then, in this article, is not only to study the aged, who are most directly confronting death, but to chart differences and development that occur across the life span. Woodruff-Pak (1988) reports on a number of studies that have replicated Hall's (1922) original finding that fear of death is greatest in adolescence and that young adults fear death whereas older

The work herein was supported, in part, by a Social Sciences and Humanities Research Council of Canada Special Post-doctoral Fellowship to the first author. The authors thank Glen Bradford, Kim Cote, Dolores Fischer, and Dennis Shannon for their data coding assistance. Portions of this work were reported at the annual meeting of the Gerontological Society of America. San Francisco, November 1991.

adults worry more about the circumstances of their death (e.g., Kalish, 1976; Kastenbaum, 1992).

In young adulthood, death may be seen as inevitable, but it remains distant, based on a normative understanding of the life course. Gesser, Wong, and Reker (1987–1988) suggest that there is a tendency to avoid or brush aside thoughts of death and that fear of death probably underlies this tendency. Alternatively, because younger individuals know fewer people who have died (e.g., Kalish & Reynolds, 1977), a case can be made that such inexperience is a causal factor in their attitudes and their relative insensitivity to some of the potential issues of death.

Neugarten (1968) has written that middle age is a time of stock-taking. Life becomes restructured in terms of time-left-to-live rather than time-since-birth with an attendant focus on time left and tasks to be completed prior to death. The middle years of life have been characterized by the increasing awareness of the agedness of parents coupled with the maturing of children into adults. These contribute strongly to the sense of aging—that it is one's own turn to grow old and die (Jaques, 1965). The individual has stopped growing up and has begun to grow old, and a new set of external circumstances has to be met (Levinson, 1977). Death is no longer a general conception or experienced as the death of another (i.e. bereavement) but becomes a personal matter (Jaques, 1965). Middle-aged individuals have been underrepresented in studies of death attitudes/beliefs, and research is equivocal in its support of the theoretical propositions elucidated above.

Studies that have compared death attitudes of the elderly with those of other age groups have shown, with fair consistency, that the elderly think and talk more about death, although death appears less frightening for them (Kalish, 1976; Wass, 1977). At the same time, there is increasing evidence of the nearness to the end from one's own body and from the health and death of one's age peers. Wass (1977) reports that significantly more elderly persons than those of younger ages consider with distaste the possibilities of their own pain in dying and the grief their death would cause loved ones (see also Birren et al., 1981).

A modest literature also exists on gender differences in death attitudes, specifically death anxiety. The majority of research shows that women report more death fear than do men (e.g., Pollack, 1979–1980). The most commonly used instrument is the Death Anxiety Scale (DAS; Templer, 1970) and the most commonly examined group of participants is college students. Some studies using the DAS with mature professional people fail to find gender differences as do studies using the Threat Index (TI; Neimeyer, Epting, & Rigdon, 1984), a cognitive measure that taps the meaning structure that individuals use in the construal of death. Dattel and Neimeyer (1990), however, found that women scored higher on the DAS than did men even when controlling for social desirability and self-disclosure, suggesting that higher scores on the DAS are not attributable to expressiveness as a factor.

Gesser, Wong, and Reker (1987–1988) have written that much research has assumed the death fear/anxiety construct to be

unidimensional and scales have been constructed accordingly. Nelson and Nelson (1975), however, reported four dimensions of death anxiety: death avoidance, death fear, death denial, and reluctance to interact with the dying. Several other studies have recognized the distinction between fear of death and fear of dying, suggesting that some individuals might not fear the event of death but fear the process of dying (or vice versa). Collett and Lester (1969) devised separate measures of death fears, attempting to distinguish the fear of death from the fear of the process of dying and to differentiate further between these fears depending on whether they are for oneself or for another. An extensive discussion of the multiple ways in which death has been treated (e.g., as a variable, event, state, analogy, and mystery) may be found in Kastenbaum's (1975) writings. The analyses described herein focus on death as an event (i.e., a loss) and dying as a process.

Although fear and anxiety are the terms that probably first surface with regard to thoughts of death/dying, attitudes toward death need not be negative. Unfortunately, positive attitudes such as death acceptance have received little attention (Gesser, Wong, & Reker, 1987–1988). Compounding the problem in the thanatological literature is the tendency to interpret the absence of fear/anxiety as avoidance or denial. Simpson (1980), in scathing critique, has suggested that death anxiety scales reveal significant anxiety because they do not allow any alternatives. "Death acceptance is not necessarily the opposite of death anxiety and the two can correlate positively and be distinguished from death denial" (p. 143).

A clear exception to the often muddy waters of the foregoing empirical literature is the work of Neimeyer and others (e.g., Dattel & Neimeyer, 1990; Neimeyer & Moore, 1989). In their use of the Threat Index and a companion measure, the Death Attitude Repertory Test (DART), they have moved away from expressive measures of anxieties and fear about death (sometimes confounded with dying) to a more cognitive assessment of the meaning underlying the construct "death." They use personal construct theory to guide their work, with its inherent assumption that "human beings literally construct the meaning of their own lives, by devising, testing, and continuously revising personal theories that help them anticipate their experience" (Neimeyer & Moore, 1989, p. 229). Neimeyer, Fontana, and Gold (1984) have also developed a coding procedure to describe the actual content of individuals' constructs pertaining to death to be used in scoring the DART or other open-ended materials. Neimeyer and Moore (1989) have reported on pilot data suggesting that older respondents tend to construe death-related situations in more coherent ways and that more educated individuals display greater flexibility and less uncertainty in their views of life and death than do their less educated peers. Data are not presented differentiating death from dying, or among varying referents.

Objectives

A primary purpose of this study was to see whether it was possible to reliably differentiate death (as an event) from dying (as a process) using essay-type materials, and if so, to also code the extent to which men and women of different ages used these constructs in reference to themselves, to others, and/or in an abstract form.

We were also interested in examining structural differences in discussions of death and dying. For this purpose, we used a measure called integrative complexity (Baker-Brown et al., 1992), an information processing variable from the same personal construct theoretical roots as the DART. Integrative complexity provides for an analysis of the structure underlying thought as represented in verbal and written materials. Integrative complexity has been assessed in a wide variety of contexts—from the public statements of international politicians and policymakers (e.g., Suedfeld & Bluck, 1988; Tetlock, 1984; Wallace & Suedfeld, 1988) and the writings of famous authors (Porter & Suedfeld, 1981) to the expositions of undergraduate students on a moral issue (de Vries & Walker, 1987) and the life stories of men and women from across the life span (de Vries, 1991).

Finally, we used several categories from the Manual for Content Analysis of Death Constructs (Neimeyer, Fontana, & Gold, 1984) to assess the levels of involvement, impact, and acceptance with which participants in the study discussed death and dying. Besides our basic aim of charting differences in individuals' writings about death across the life span, our coding of the data in these various manners allowed us to examine relationships between the content and structure of the death construct.

Method

Participants were 27 women and 27 men, drawn from three age groups (early, middle, and late adulthood). The age ranges for the three groups were 20–39, 40–59, and 60 and above, with mean ages of 30.6, 48.8, and 65.3 years, respectively. Mean ages did not differ by gender. Level of education was positively skewed: 10% of men and 13% of women had only a high school education. The remainder had at least one college or university degree. Ninety-three percent of the men and 86% of the women were Caucasian, 7% of the men and women were Asian-American, and the remaining 7% of women were Afro-American. The following results must be couched in terms of the limiting demographic characteristics of this sample.

The participants were drawn from a group of individuals who had completed Guided Autobiography workshops conducted primarily at the University of Southern California between 1976 and 1988. The Guided Autobiography (GAB) is a structured thematic approach to life review (see Birren & Deutchman, 1991; de Vries, Birren, & Deutchman, 1990). A series of nine themes is presented to individuals over the 2-week course of GAB, including such themes as family relationships, aspirations and achievements, and death. In preparation for each session, individuals write two pages dealing with the specific theme assignment. In this study, responses to the theme "The History of My Experiences with Death and/or My Ideas about Death" were used for analysis. The complete list of sensitizing questions is included in Birren and Deutchman (1991). These questions were provided to stimulate thought about the issues rather than as a list of questions requiring specific answers.

GAB data are unique in that they provide for the examination of the individual's perceptions of death, tapping constructs developed throughout the life span from experience with and reflections on this topic. The data were coded for both thematic and affective content as well as structure, with the paragraph as the basic scoring unit. Information as to respondent's age, gender, race, and educational level did not appear on the protocols.

Thematic Content

Each paragraph was assigned a score reflecting its emphasis on death or dying, and whether this related to self, other, or was discussed in the abstract. Paragraphs that did not concern death or dying or that discussed the death or dying of pets (approximately 10% of the sample) were excluded from the data set. Interrater reliability between the two scorers of thematic content was 80%.

Death was scored when the focus of a paragraph was the social or emotional reactions of self or others to a loss; the readjustment of one's life as a result of another's death, or concern for others after one's own death; funerals or other social rituals around a death; talk of an afterlife or the possibility of seeing the deceased, or missing the decreased; or the lessons we learn through loss.

Dying was scored when the focus of a paragraph was pain, suffering, or other aspects of the physical dying process, or a view of life as a battle with illness; attitudes that have developed as part of an ongoing illness; psychological or social withdrawal, or changes in relationships, in preparation for death, or preparation for others to be taken care of

financially after one's death; or ways of dying, being able to choose the way that one will die, or the quality of life in one's final days or years.

In general, then, death was conceptualized as an event, and dying as a process. Within these conceptualizations there is the opportunity to discuss these issues as they related to one's self, others, or in the abstract. Content was scored "self" when the emphasis of the paragraph was on one's own death or dying, and "other" when the emphasis was on the death or dying of a specified other or group of others. Included in this definition of others were individuals varying in emotional distance from the writer (e.g., spouse, childhood friend, public figure). Content was scored "abstract" when participants spoke of death or dying without any specific reference to themselves or others, often in philosophical or hypothetical terms.

This coding scheme allowed for analysis of the following categories:

Death-Self (DS). E.g., I can remember the closing days of the Korean war and several national emergencies when I was in high school and college causing me the fear of death. I thought "I will probably have to go to war and be killed. I will never know what it is like to be married, to have children and to experience the more mature situations of life."

Death-Other (DO). E.g., Afterwards when the ceremonies were over, when the family reassembled once more there were things that bespoke of sadness. No one touched the piano or played the victrola, not for a whole

year. Engulfing silences where there had been laughter. At seven, I felt all this but I didn't understand it. Content was fragmented, meaning, I know not what.

Death-Abstract (DA). E.g., I still can't really say what I know about death. The aloneness, the hole where someone I cared for had been. The unsolved mystery of life, and thus death is always present. But what happens when the physical part of an individual dies? The clinicians have these antiseptic definitives couched in precise language of science. I only know that I don't know.

Dying-Self (DyS). E.g., How do I view my own death? I think not about death but about dying. I fear the slow deterioration that might come to rob me of my faculties, that can make jest of the reason and sense of life. To lose the most important part of myself, to be condemned to live as a vegetable. That really shudders my soul.

Dying-Other (DyO). E.g., When my sister died I was there with her too. She'd had surgery and afterwards, the Doctor came and told us she only had six weeks to live. He felt that he wanted her to be told. But her husband said no in loud and strident tones. He believed that she would have more happiness without that knowledge. I feel that she had the right to know. She was a strong spirit. She ought to have had the right to prepare herself in whatever way she wished.

Dying-Abstract (DyA). E.g., In a way we are all dying from the moment we are born but most of the time we don't think about it. Dying is part of life but the tragedy of it is the pain it brings to the individual and their loved ones.

Affective Content

Three content categories—personal involvement (high/low), impact (high/low) and acceptance (low)—from "A Manual for Content Analysis of Death Constructs" (Neimeyer et al., 1984) were chosen as especially relevant. The presence or absence of each category was scored with reference to category definitions and an appendix of key constructs. Prospective coders read the manual and achieved interrater reliabilities of at least 80% on practice material before beginning to score the data set. Interrater reliabilities calculated on the ratings of the data set were 83%, 84%, and 88% for personal involvement, impact, and acceptance, respectively. The three categories are conceptualized by Neimeyer and colleagues as follows:

Personal Involvement. High is scored for constructs connoting personal involvement in dying or death (e.g., "close to me," "self loss," "relates to a friend," "I care about it") and low is scored for constructs depicting death or dying as remote or not pertaining to the self (e.g., "distant from me," "stranger to me," "Merely factual," "unlikely to affect me").

Impact. High is scored for constructs dealing with the impact of death or dying (e.g., "shocking," "severe," "grievous," "important") and low is scored for constructs implying that death or dying has minimal impact (e.g., "trivial," "unimportant," "no shock," "doesn't matter").

Acceptance. Low is scored for constructs depicting the death or dying as something to be rejected or resisted (e.g., "unacceptable," "loss," "disturbing," "traumatic"). No high acceptance category is included in the manual, as interrater reliability did not reach sufficient levels to consider it a reliable category.

Structure

In order to examine the thought structure of participants' ideas on death and dying, materials were also scored for integrative complexity according to the standard scoring procedure (Baker-Brown et al., 1992). The material was scored by two trained individuals who had reached interrater reliability of 81% agreement on this data set. The scoring system proceeds along a 7-point continuum based on the hierarchical constructs of differentiation and integration. A score of 1 represents the perception of only a single acceptable perspective or dimension; 3, the recognition that there are legitimate alternative ways of looking at the issue (differentiation); 5, the generation of combinatorial or interactive positions (integration); and 7, integrations involving multiple levels of schemata, Scores of 2, 4, and 6 are transition points between the major scores.

The following are examples of the four major scoring levels of integrative complexity:

Score of 1. The funeral seemed like another church service. The trip to the cemetery gave me one of my very infrequent rides in an automobile. Just our family was in our car, three vehicles back from the hearse.

Score of 3. At other deaths in our large family, we duplicated the same ritual. The prevailing philosophy was obvious: do everything you can to maintain and fulfill life, but understand that death is the time to honor not to grieve.

Score of 5. I pray frequently but never so fervently and dependently as when I have to deliver a death message in person to the next of kin. I need divine guidance and sensitivity to permit the next of kin to grieve in their own way and to comfort them effectively. By attitude and proximity, I invite the survivor to lean on me psychologically and physically to lighten their burden of sorrow. There is no harder and more rewarding task for me.

Score of 7. Preparing men and women for death in their years requires a great deal. Not to deny its coming is step number one. Putting one's affairs in reasonable order is next. Then the deeper religious preparation. The New Testament teaching is clear and theologically approved by all faiths: the understanding of Christian death permits a richer earthly life. This must be accepted affectively as well as cognitively. Both dimensions require time and demonstration to penetrate the deeper level. The presenter and facilitator must be sensitive, gentle, patient, and consistent. But when a person overcomes the fear of death, life has an inexhaustible dimension.

Standardization of the Scored Data

As mentioned above, the basic unit scored was the paragraph. Since participants wrote essays of differing lengths, it was necessary to create standardized scores for each individual. To analyze the thematic content, percentages of the essay concerning each theme (death, dying, self, other, abstract) were calculated. In order to relate affective content to thematic content the percentages of each affective content measure were calculated for each theme (e.g., each participant's paragraphs about death were broken down by percentage into those scored as high impact, high personal involvement, and low acceptance, and so on for each theme). Mean integrative complexity scores were calculated by theme. These percentages and means were used in analyses.

Results

Our initial examination of the data was in terms of the frequencies with which individuals discussed death and dying of the self, another, or in the abstract as represented in their essays. Surprisingly, gender was found not to be a significant factor and therefore was excluded from subsequent analyses. A 3 (age group) × 2 (subject: death, dying) × 3 (referent: self, other, abstract) ANOVA revealed a main effect for subject, $F(1,51) = 57.3$, $p = .001$, with death ($M = 64.92$, $SD = 22.02$) greater than dying ($M = 24.02$, $SD = 20.79$). A main effect for referent was also found, $F(2,102) = 58.03$, $p = .001$, with other ($M = 54.56$, $SD = 21.36$) greater than self ($M = 21.06$, $SD = 14.60$), both of which were greater than abstract ($M = 13.32$, $SD = 16.00$), as supported by Student-Neuman-Keuls multiple comparisons ($p = .05$). Both of these main effects were qualified by their interaction, however, $F(2,102) = 12.55$, $p = .001$. The mean frequencies (and standard

	Death	Dying
Age Group	**% (SD)**	**% (SD)**
Young	61.53 (28.23)	31.23 (25.72)
Middle-aged	72.20 (14.70)	12.52 (11.06)
Old	61.04 (20.36)	28.31 (18.70)

Table 1 Mean Percentages of Essay Paragraphs Focused on Death and Dying Themes, by Age Group

Note: Each age group included 18 respondents. Frequencies do not sum to 100 because parts of respondents' essays (11.05%) were concerned with neither death nor dying.

deviations) for the six categories on which this interaction is based are (in descending rank order): death-other ($M = 39.82$, $SD = 19.44$); dying-other ($M = 14.75$, $SD = 14.71$); death-self ($M = 12.57$, $SD = 12.51$); death-abstract ($M = 12.54$, $SD = 15.44$); dying-self ($M = 8.50$, $SD = 12.51$); and dying-abstract ($M = 0.77$, $SD = 4.05$). All comparisons were significantly different (t-tests; $p = .001$), except that death-self did not differ from either death-abstract or dying-self.

Significant differences were also found in the age-group-by-subject interaction, $F(2,51) = 3.04$, $p = .05$. Subsequent analyses of the simple main effects revealed no differences in the frequency of usage of the death theme across age groups. However, the main effect for dying was significant, $F(2,51) = 4.83$, $p = .01$, and Student-Newman-Keuls multiple comparisons ($p = .05$) indicated that the middle-aged group differed from both the younger and the older respondents in their focus on this theme, as seen in Table 1.

In order to investigate differences on the structural variable, integrative complexity, two repeated measures ANOVAs were conducted with mean complexity scores as the dependent measure. Neither subject nor referent were included as within-subject variables in a single

analysis due to insufficient cell sizes (i.e., a single analysis would have required respondents to have scores in all subject-referent combinations). Gender was again excluded from analyses on the basis of nonsignificance in preliminary findings. A 3 (age group) × 2 (subject) ANOVA with repeated measures on the subject factor yielded only one significant effect: discussions of death $M = 2.13$, $SD = .599$) were more complex than discussions of dying ($M = 1.85$, $SD = .772$), $F(1,38) = 4.14$, $p = .04$. A 3 (age group) x 3 (referent) ANOVA with repeated measures on the referent factor yielded one significant main effect: discussions of death/dying of others ($M = 1.69$, $SD = .613$) were less complex than discussions of death/dying of self or abstract (self: $M = 2.25$, $SD = .938$; abstract: $M = 2.25$, $SD = 1.102$), $F(2,42) = 3.13$, $p = .05$ (paired t-test comparisons self vs. other, $t(44) = 1.81$, $p = .08$, and abstract vs. other, $t(27) = 3.06$, $p = .01$).

Repeated measures ANOVAs were used to examine the affective content measures: personal involvement, impact, and acceptance. Dependent measures in these analyses were the mean frequencies of high personal involvement, high impact, and low acceptance; analyses based on low personal involvement and low impact would be redundant. The 3 (age group) x 2 (subject) ANOVAs were nonsignificant on all three measures. The 3 (age group) x 2 (referent) ANOVAs (abstract was not included due to small cell size) showed a significant main effect for referent only for impact, $F(1,39) = 11.82$, $p = .01$. Discussions of death/dying of other ($M = 60.59\%$, $SD = 30.63$) were more frequently coded high impact than were discussions of self ($M = 32.93\%$, $SD = 32.55$).

The absence of age and gender differences in the usage of the affective content categories is surprising and provocative. This is not to say that these categories were infrequently used. Overwhelmingly, high impact ($M = 87.88\%$, $SD = 44.592$) and high personal involvement ($M = 82.00\%$, $SD = 49.136$) characterized these discussions, with low acceptance ($M = 64.51\%$, $SD = 38.318$) occurring to a lesser degree, $F(2,80) = 4.66$, $p = .01$. Even though there are differences in the frequency with which death and dying were discussed by individuals across the life span, the affective content and the structure of these discussions were uniform.

Discussion

The results point to several interesting and provocative issues in the understanding of conceptions of death and dying across the life span. First, and perhaps most fundamental, is the reliable and meaningful distinction between the death and dying categories in both the frequency of their usage and the structure of their representation. Collett and Lester (1969), Kastenbaum (1975), and others have called for the recognition of the multidimensionality of

death as a construct for some time, specifically distinguishing between the event and the process (i.e., subject) and among referents (i.e., self or other). The participants in this research spontaneously addressed both subject and referent, unequally, suggesting that the distinction is of subjective, theoretical, and empirical significance.

That death was discussed more frequently and in more complex terms than dying may support Kastenbaum and Costa's (1977) assertion that the construct of death is more familiar to most people than is the construct of dying. Perhaps this reflects a general orientation to event over process or perhaps, more specifically, life holds more constant reminders of the loss of a loved one than the process by which that loss occurred. This interpretation presumes, of course, that individuals prefer to discuss that which is familiar to them or about which they know more. Support for this comes from previous research in complexity, which has suggested that discussions of issues within an individual's realm of experience or sphere of expertise, broadly defined (e.g., de Vries, 1988), are represented by greater complexity than are discussions of more foreign issues. The greater complexity of discussions is the outcome of more extensive thought.

Such a pattern is mitigated, however, by heightened anxiety and stress. A well-substantiated finding in the complexity literature is decreased complexity in the face of increased stress (e.g., Suedfeld, 1981; Suedfeld & Rank, 1976). Recall that other was used as a referent significantly more often than self or abstract, although these latter two were presented in more complex ways

than the former. Kastenbaum and Costa (1977) have written that "death, for many people, is neither an abstract, generalized thought, nor concern for personal demise; rather, it is the actual or threatened loss of a significant person" (p. 243). Although another's death is a more frequent experience than one's own and may be a more frequent thought, it is also the substance of bereavement, grief, and mourning. Discussions of the death/dying of another were more often coded for high impact than were the discussions of death/dying of the self. The stress and emotional turmoil associated with such an event/process may serve to constrain the complexity with which it is discussed. Alternatively, the less familiar thoughts of one's own death are, almost by definition, abstract and discussed in more complex ways and with less emotional impact. Recall Freud's (1959) observation that "our own death is indeed unimaginable, and whenever we can make the attempt to imagine it we can perceive that we really survive as spectators" (pp. 304–305).

The lack of age differences on the structural variable of complexity was surprising at first. Our expectation was that there would be changes in the complexity of thought (and specifically thoughts about the death/dying of self) over the age groups, as in the pilot work reported by Neimeyer and Moore (1989), in which older respondents construed death-relevant situations in more coherent (e.g., similar) ways. The somewhat skewed demographic characteristics of this sample, however, may have precluded the uncovering of age-related complexity differences. That is, complexity has a modest correlation with education (e.g., Coren & Suedfeld, 1990) and the vast majority of this sample had at least one college or university degree, perhaps attentuating the range on the complexity measure. Phrased differently, "controlling" for education might have removed much of the variability otherwise attributable to age. The age groups in this sample were more similar than different in the ways in which they thought about death and dying as it applies to the self, another, or in the abstract. Kastenbaum (1985) has written that general cognitive level and style are relevant because death-related thoughts are formulated within the context of an individual's overall ability to interpret the self and her or his world. It is also too simplistic to assume that death/dying has any singular meaning to any one age group or to any one individual; as Kalish (1976) has written, "death means different things to the same person at different times . . . and it means different things to the same person at the same time" (p. 483). Perhaps changes in an individual's death construct are more a reflection of life history and experience than life course position.

Interesting age differences did emerge, however, in the respective proportions of discussion devoted to issues of death and issues of dying. Overall, death was discussed more frequently than dying without significant age variations. Discussions of dying, however, were more common among younger and older participants than among those in the middle years, a pattern similar to that reported by Gesser, Wong, and Reker (1987–1988) in their analyses of death attitudes over the life span.

This is not to imply that the similarity in frequency of thought about dying between the old and young is matched in the foci of their discussions. That younger people have frequently witnessed the graphic portrayal of dying in the popular media and make attempts at, as well as reporting thoughts of, suicide with greater frequency than other age groups may play a pivotal role in the understanding of these differences. Additionally, Kalish and Reynolds (1977) have suggested that "the subterfuges of the recent past, so evident in regard to sexual and other intimate relationships, are less acceptable to younger people today" (p. 211). Dying is a subject, like so many others, open for discussion among younger adults. Shneidman's (1971) 30,000, primarily young (ages 10–24 years) respondents to the *Psychology Today* survey on death seem to support such a statement. Kastenbaum (1985) has written that those theories of psychosocial development that have found any "task" at all for the elderly person tend to emphasize preparing oneself for death. As described above, several studies report that the old are concerned with the circumstances of their death. Perhaps the relative nearness of death, on a probability basis, mandates the asking of more pragmatic questions of "how" and "when," fueled by the mounting evidence of physical decline from one's own body and from the failing health and demise of one's peers.

The relative infrequency in the middle years of thoughts of dying may come about as a consequence of the restructuring of time and experience (e.g., Neugarten, 1968) and the recogni-

tion that one is no longer growing up and has begun to grow old. This sort of existential stock-taking and counting of life in terms of time-yet-to-live raises issues of the meaning of life and the embedded question, "What is death?" The responsibilities of being a member of the omega generation may weigh heavily. A relative exaggerated concern with time left to achieve life's goals, as well as the multiple practical tasks of daily living, then, may usurp a more pronounced concern with the process of life's ending.

The work reported herein is necessarily more evocative than it is definitive. The sample has demographic peculiarities that hinder generalizability. Also, the nature of the data, although allowing for a more naturalistic and open examination of the concept of death, requires a sacrifice of precision. These are constant tensions and trade-offs in the use of open-ended, narrative documents. Several interesting patterns have been uncovered, however, and several intriguing questions have arisen.

For example, what is it about death that promotes its more frequent consideration relative to dying? We hypothesize that bereavement plays a crucial role, while suspecting that other factors are also relevant: how would relative considerations of death and dying differ in association with high and low levels of anxiety, denial, or fear? It may be useful to combine standard scalar measures (e.g., the DAS) with more open-ended approaches, such as that adopted in this study.

The absence of gender differences and the relative paucity of age differences are also curious. Is education or "general cognitive level and style" sufficient to so dramatically attenuate the range on which variables? Socioeconomic status and selected personality dimensions must play some role. We infer that dying and perhaps death may mean different things to different age groups. Are such differences cohort-bound and what role does experience play? How do prevailing societal attitudes affect the death construct? Nearness to death is not the exclusive domain of older persons; how do conceptions of death among the young terminally ill compare with those of the elderly? Perhaps, also, gender is not as relevant as relationship or caregiving status in conceptions of death as personally involving and having high impact. A unique synthesis of contextual and developmental influences may hold the greatest promise for understanding the cognitive terrain and affective dimensions of death and dying.

References

Baker-Brown, G., Ballard, E., Bluck, S., de Vries, B., Suedfeld, P., & Tetlock, P. (1992). The conceptual/integrative complexity scoring manual. In C. Smith (Ed.), *Motivation and personality: Handbook of thematic content analysis.* Cambridge: Cambridge University Press.

Birren, J., & Deutchman, D.E. (1991). *Guiding autobiography groups for older adults: Exploring the fabric of life.* Baltimore: Johns Hopkins Press.

Collett, L., & Lester, D. (1969). The fear of death and the fear of dying. *Journal of Psychology, 72,* 179–181.

Coren, S., & Suedfeld, P. (1990). A power test of conceptual complexity: Textual correlates. *Journal of Applied Social Psychology, 20,* 357–367.

Dattel, A., & Neimeyer, R. (1990). Sex differences in death anxiety: Testing the emotional expressiveness hypothesis. *Death Studies, l4,* 1–11.

de Vries, B. (1988). *The concept of self in a life-span, life event context.* Unpublished doctoral dissertation, Department of Psychology, University of British Columbia, Vancouver.

de Vries, B. (1991, August). An integrative complexity analysis of life events. In P. Suedfeld (Chair), *New directions in research on integrative complexity.* Symposium conducted at the meeting of the American Psychological Association, San Francisco.

deVries, B., Birren, J.E., & Deutchman, D.E. (1990). Adult development through Guided Autobiography: The family context, *Family Relations, 39,* 3–7.

deVries, B., & Walker, L.J. (1987). Conceptual/integrative complexity and attitudes toward capital punishment. *Personality and Social Psychology Bulletin, 13,* 448–457.

Erikson, E. (1968). *Identity: Youth and crisis.* New York: Norton.

Freud, S. (1959). Mourning and melancholia. *Collected Papers,* Vol. 4, New York: Basic.

Gresser, G., Wong, P., & Reker, G. (1987–1988). Death attitudes across the life-span: The development and validation of the Death Attitude Profile (DAP). *Omega, 18(2)* 113–128.

Hall, G.S. (1922). *Senescence, the last half of life.* New York: Appleton.

Jaques, E. (1965). Death and the mid-life crisis. *International Journal of Psychoanalysis, 46,* 502–514.

Kalish, R. (1976). Death and dying in a social context. In R. Binstock & E. Shanas (Eds.), *Handbook of aging and the social sciences* (pp. 483–507). New York: Van Nostrand Reinhold.

Kalish, R., & Reynolds, D. (1977). The role of age in death attitudes. *Death Education, 1,* 205–230.

Kastenbaum, R. (1975). Is death a life crisis? On the confrontation with death in theory and practice. In N. Datan & L. H. Ginsberg (Eds.), *Life-span developmental psychology: Normative life crisis* (pp. 19–50). New York: Academic.

Kastenbaum, R. (1985). Dying and death: A life-span approach. In J. E. Birren & K.W. Schaie (Eds.), *Handbook of the psychology of aging,* 2nd edition, (pp. 619–643). New York: Van Nostrand Reinhold.

Kastenbaum, R. (1992). *The psychology of death,* 2nd edition. New York: Springer.

Kastenbaum, R., & Costa, P. (1977). Psychological perspectives on death. *Annual Review of Psychology, 28,* 225–249.

Levinson, D. (1977). The mid-life transition: A period in adult psychosocial development. *Psychiatry, 40,* 99–112.

Neimeyer, R, Epting, F., & Rigdon, M. (1984). A procedure manual for the Threat Index. In F. Epting & R. Neimeyer (Eds.), *Personal meanings of death: Applications of personal construct theory to clinical practice* (pp. 235–241). Washington, DC: Hemisphere.

Neimeyer, R., Fontana, D., & Gold, K. (1984). A manual for content analysis of death constructs. In F. Epting & R. Neimeyer (Eds.), Personal meanings of death: Applications of personal construct theory to clinical practice (pp. 299–320). Washington, DC: Hemisphere.

Neimeyer, R., & Moore, M. (1989). Assessing personal meanings of death; Empirical refinements in the threat index. *Death Studies, 13,* 227–245.

Nelson, L., & Nelson, C. (1975). A factor analytic inquiry into the multidimensionality of death anxiety. *Omega, 6(2),* 171–178.

Neugarten, B. (1968). The awareness of middle age. In B. Neugarten (Ed.), *Middle age and aging* (pp. 93–98). Chicago: University of Chicago Press.

Pollack, J. (1979–1980). Correlates of death anxiety: A review of empirical studies. *Omega, 10(2),* 97–121.

Porter, C.A., & Suedfeld, P. (1981). Integrative complexity in the correspondence of literary figures: Effects of personal and societal stress. *Journal of Personality and Social Psychology, 40,* 321–330.

Shneidman, E. (1971, June). You and death. *Psychology Today,* pp. 43–47.

Simpson, M. (1980). Studying death: Problems of methodology. *Death Education, 4,* 139–148.

Suedfeld, P. (1981). Indices of world tension in the *Bulletin of the Atomic Scientists. Political Psychology, 2,* 114–123.

Suedfeld, P., & Bluck, S. (1988). Changes in integrative complexity prior to surprise attacks. *Journal of Conflict Resolution, 32,* 626–635.

Suedfeld, P., & Rank, A.D. (1976). Revolutionary leaders: Long-term success as a function of changes in conceptual complexity. *Journal of Personality and Social Psychology, 34*, 169–178.

Templer, D. (1970). The construction and validation of a death anxiety scale. *Journal of General Psychology, 82*, 165–177.

Tetlock, P.E. (1984). Cognitive style and political belief systems in the British House of Commons. *Journal of Personality and Social Psychology, 46*, 365–375.

Wallace, M., & Suedfeld, P. (1988). Leadership performance in crises: The longevity-complexity link. *International Studies Quarterly, 32*, 439–451.

Wass, H. (1977). Views and opinions of elderly persons concerning death. *Educational Gerontology, 2*, 15–26.

Woodruff-Pak, D. (1988). *Psychology and aging.* Englewood Cliffs, NJ: Prentice-Hall.

Article Review Form at end of book.

What is meant by "palliative care" in the context of the elderly person? What has complicated the long-term care of the aged in our country?

Decisions and Care at the End of Life

Michael Gordon

Baycrest Centre for Geriatric Care, North York, Ontario, Canada, Division of Geriatrics, Mount Sinai Hospital, Toronto, and Department of Medicine, University of Toronto

Peter A. Singer

Centre for Bioethics, and Department of Medicine, University of Toronto and Toronto Hospital

Abstract

The geographic dispersal of families has complicated long-term care of the aged. Furthermore, while government supported long-term care is expensive, community-based care often becomes the responsibility of women in families. Treatment decisions become difficult when an elderly patient's mental abilities are compromised by dementia or depression. Living wills, which may designate an alternative decision-maker or dictate decisions ahead of time, have gained a lot of attention but actually are not common. Cardiopulmonary resuscitation may not be beneficial in many cases, however it is difficult to avoid without a previous order not to resuscitate. Care which relieves symptoms and provides comfort is vital,
though complicated by the ability to use advancing technology to attempt treatment. Euthanasia and assisted suicide remain illegal in most parts of the world, however, in individual cases they seem like ethical options.

Successful public health and social policies and apparently inexorable medical advances are now compelling physicians and others who care for the elderly to confront clinical issues and ethical dilemmas that hardly existed fifty years ago. In North America and Europe more than 12% of the population are now over 65 years of age and all are facing decisions at the end of life which will affect their families and society.[1,2] Older people deserve to be cared for with respect and dignity.[3] They have more years of function and potential life fulfillment than any previous generation.[2,3] Indeed, so compelling is this positive image that some old people, when they become ill, question their bad luck or wonder what they did wrong. Despite the call for massive programmes of health promotion, many age-related conditions that cause disability (e.g., Alzheimer's and Parkinson's diseases) and many malignancies and muscu-

loskeletal syndromes have no identified pathophysiological process for which preventive measures are beneficial.[4] Although treatments for the underlying disease vary in efficacy, old people who become unwell will often benefit from interventions targeted at improving function even when no cure can be offered. Virtually all countries find that they cannot afford all that medicine has to offer and are looking at ways to decrease health care costs.[3,5] The elderly population, especially when life is drawing to a close, often become the focus of such efforts as cost control.[6,7]

Many issues arise at the end of life—where should one's last days be spent, consent to treatment, advance directives, aspects of clinical care such as resuscitation and palliation, and the controversies of euthanasia and assisted suicide—and this review cannot cover all of them in detail.

The Ties That Bind

The modern family is mobile and dispersed in many western countries, especially the USA and Canada. On retirement many

"Decisions and Care at the End of Life" by Michael Gordon and Peter A. Singer from THE LANCET, July 15, 1995, Vol. 346, No. 8968, pp. 163–167. Reprinted by permission.

people go to warmer climates while children move away from their parents and grandparents because of educational, work, and social opportunities. While family members remain well and independent this geographical separation is of limited consequence since visits and communication by telephone and letter remain possible. The impact on families of prolonged illness and disability can be profound because a son's or daughter's ties and obligations of kinship to parents may conflict with their responsibilities to their own families and their jobs.

Old people usually want to live independently for as long as they can and many struggle with their own financial and living arrangements and with how best to spend the rest of their lives. Governments are grappling with the same issues as expenditure on social services and residential care mounts. Many government-supported options seem costly and attempts are being made to transfer the expense to old people themselves and their families. Although attractive conceptually, community-based systems of care may not always be cheaper than comparable facility care, and much of the burden of so-called community care is borne by families, usually the women.[8,9]

When the level of care required or a lack of community support means that admission long-term to a nursing home or the like is unavoidable the important question for the family is how to ensure that the care provided will be of high quality. For government the challenge is to maintain sufficient places without embarrassing the agencies appointed to oversee standards. And for those who run such long-term care facilities the goal is to provide a standard of service that is both acceptable to their clients and affordable.[8]

Consent to Treatment

During the past two decades there has been a major shift in the relation between doctor and patient. "The doctor proposes, the patient disposes" is an aphorism that accurately encapsulates a large body of bioethics literature, policy guidelines, and health law. Capable (competent) people have the right to make their own health care decisions, a right based on the ethical principle of respect for autonomy and the legal doctrine of informed consent.[10]

How can physicians determine that a patient is competent? This question is becoming increasingly important as medical decisions have to be made for more and more individuals whose mental function is undermined by age-related conditions such as delirium, dementia, or depression. Capacity—the ability to understand the information needed to make a treatment decision and to appreciate the reasonably foreseeable consequences of that decision—is specific to the particular situation and may vary over time. We do not yet have any reliable clinical measure of capacity to consent to treatment.[10,11] Physicians must rely on questions that attempt to establish a patient's understanding of what he or she is being told.[12] The doctor might, for example ask "What is your medical problem?," "What treatment has been proposed?," "What will happen if you receive the treatment and what will happen if you do not?," and "What have you decided about receiving treatment and why?" Such questions can serve as a screening tool to help health-care providers to assess the capacity of the patient to make important clinical decisions. In certain cases, the physician may want to consult an expert in the assessment of capacity, such as a geriatrician, neurologist, or psychiatrist well versed in the subject.

An incapable person retains in theory the right to make treatment decisions but that right must be exercised by someone else on the patient's behalf. Who should make the decision for the incapable person, and how? The goal is to reach the decision the person would have made, if capable, and that can often be achieved through an advance directive or, if one is not available, on the basis of the patient's earlier, verbally expressed wishes, or their known values and beliefs, or, failing those pointers, on what the substitute decision maker sees as the patient's "best interests."

Advance Directives

An advance directive or "living will" is completed by a capable person to guide future health-care decisions when the person becomes incapable. It has two parts: one names the substitute (proxy) decision maker, the other states what decisions a person wants. While many people include both components, either may exist separately.

Advance directives have gained wide endorsement in Canada and the USA. All American state laws support advance directives and the federal Patient Self-Determination Act requires health care facilities to advise patients of their statutory right to complete one.[13] In Canada five provinces have passed legislation on advance directives and the momentum is growing. In the UK, the Bland case and the House of Lords Select Committee on Medical Ethics both supported advance directives. Surveys of patients and providers show strong endorsement of advance directives.[14,15] However, their use has been disappointing. One study found that only one-quarter of Americans had completed a directive.[16] The barriers include lack of information, a fatalistic attitude towards death, cultural beliefs, and non-support of loved ones. Some of these obstacles may be amenable to sensitive counseling by physicians and other caregivers. Perhaps the completion of written documents is the wrong endpoint. Discussion of and publicity about advance directives could stimulate a discussion between patient and family or friends about end-of-life care that is useful in itself.

Most advance directives are generic (i.e., not disease specific) and contain many choices that may be irrelevant to the affected person. Disease-specific documents, tailored to specific conditions, have been recommended.[17] For example, a person with Alzheimer's disease might focus on scenarios of mild, moderate, and severe dementia, and on the treatment of intercurrent illnesses such as pneumonia, pressure ulcers, and inability to eat, that arise as the dementia worsens. The best advance directive is one developed for an individual and drawn up on the basis of that person's health situation and prognosis in consultation with his or her personal physician. Communication between health provider and patient is an important element of planning for future care.

The influence of culture on advance directives has only recently received attention. Some societies favour family decision making over the individualistic approach inherent in the directives devised to date; others may regard the completion of such a document as inviting bad luck and challenging fate. In view of western societies' increasing multiculturalism, the role of culture requires clarification, especially for elderly people who may cling to old traditions.

Astonishingly, little is known about how advance directives affect the care of incapable persons.[18,19] Nowadays no drug or medical device is introduced into practice without rigorous evaluation of safety and efficacy—yet that is exactly what has occurred with advance directives. These directives are being widely recommended and used and their impact on care must be carefully examined.

Cardiopulmonary Resuscitation

The successful development of closed chest cardiopulmonary resuscitation (CPR) held out the possibility of averting death from cardiac arrest but with time the limited chance of success in certain groups of aged individuals emerged. It is difficult to avoid being subjected to CPR in a hospital setting unless a "do not resuscitate" (DNR) order is in place. The clinical and legal climate in Canada and the USA has meant that CPR will be attempted unless there is a DNR order whereas in other western countries there is a lesser emphasis on this form of therapy.[20,21] The benefits, especially to older people, became a special focus of the CPR debate in the 1980s when reports indicated

that although age in itself was not the major determinant of outcome with CPR success strongly correlated with previous functional status and disease burden.[22] For community dwelling elderly people who are not disabled the success rate is not very different from that in younger patients.[23,24]

During the past decade the focus has been on whether the frail, highly dependent old people who live in longterm care facilities benefit from CPR.[25] Evidence thus far indicates that for this population CPR is not very successful and that in some situations it may be futile.[22,25] When the dismal results are combined with the emotional consequences of an unsuccessful attempt perhaps CPR should not be provided in certain long-term care settings except under carefully defined circumstances.[22,25] For some, this position is extreme, but there is general agreement that only for those arrests that are witnessed, that have a rhythm (when obtainable) of ventricular fibrillation or tachycardia, and for which CPR can be tried promptly should resuscitation be attempted.[23,25–27]

Palliative Care

"It is not death, but dying which is terrible" wrote Henry Fielding in his, novel *Amelia* (1751). Palliative care is, ethically, a mandatory part of the care of the dying. A byproduct of the success of modern medicine is that the dying process is prolonged. With chronic, debilitating diseases and cancer, the terminal phase is often predictable once interventions directed at the underlying disease have been exhausted—and what is then required is palliative care, aimed at providing comfort, and symptom relief, and meeting psychosocial and spiritual needs.[28,29] The hospice movement and palliative care programmes have developed in many countries, yet it is still common for patients to be deprived of palliative care in advanced malignant and other end-stage diseases states when they are in hospital or at home. Contrasting with contemporary technological advances in medical care, good palliative care is often an elusive goal.[29]

Despite apparent commitment to the principles of palliative care, necessary medical attention such as continuous analgesia is often not provided or investigations and therapies may be continued beyond the point when they can do any good. The philosophical acceptance of dying combined with support for what valuable life remains have to be incorporated into clinical practice if unnecessary suffering at life's end is to be avoided.

The distinction between palliative care and euthanasia causes conflict and confusion. If a physician's actions meet the following criteria they constitute palliative care and not euthanasia: the patient is suffering, the doctor's therapeutic response is commensurate with the degree of that suffering and there is a feedback loop between the suffering and the continuing therapy; and the actions are not intended to lead directly and deliberately to death.

Euthanasia and Assisted Suicide

"Just as I shall select my ship when I am about to go on a voyage, or my house when I propose to take a residence, so I shall choose my death when I am about to depart from life," wrote the Roman philosopher Seneca (in his Epistulae ad Lucilium). Euthanasia is a deliberate action that leads directly to death (e.g., the injection of a lethal dose of potassium chloride). Assisted suicide is the provision to patients of the medical means to commit suicide (e.g., by supplying sufficient barbiturate tablets to provide a lethal dose knowing what the patient's intentions are).

Euthanasia and assisted suicide are legally prohibited in almost every jurisdiction in the world[30] but since the late 1980s they have been gaining increasing prominence in debates on public policy. In 1994, by referendum, the voters of the U.S. State of Oregon approved regulated assisted suicide, this approval being overturned by the courts subsequently. In the Netherlands euthanasia is allowed under defined circumstances. Court decisions (e.g., the Sue Rodriguez case in Canada) and the high profile actions of individual physician advocates in the United States have heightened interest.

Proponents argue that euthanasia and assisted suicide in response to a competent patient's voluntary request should be permitted, the principle here being respect for autonomy and the right of self-determination. Supporters also quote the principle of beneficence; such acts relieve the suffering of patients and are thus legitimate responsibilities of physicians. Legalising the process would avoid the surreptitious actions that already exist and that so often result in pitiful and unsuccessful suicide attempts. Opponents argue that such interventions should not be permitted because human life is sacred, the societal risk of abuse outweighs the potential for individual benefit, and vulnerable persons, especially the frail elderly, require protection. They also argue that assisted suicide and euthanasia are anathema to the traditional healing role of physicians.

Proponents and opponents have reached stalemate. One can sympathise when a terminally ill patient requests euthanasia yet be concerned about the risk of abuse were the practice to be legalised. This is the paradox: although euthanasia appears ethically defensible in individual cases, it may represent a perilous direction for social policy. While the euthanasia debate rages, physicians should provide the best care available within the framework of the law. They should not abandon patients for whom a request for euthanasia cannot legally, morally, or professionally be complied with but continue to provide sensitive care and attention.[31,32]

References

1. Davies AM. Epidemiology and challenges of aging. In: Brody JA, Maddox GL, et al. *Epidemiology and aging: an international perspective.* New York: Springer, 1988: 1–23.
2. Campion EW. The oldest old. *N Engl J Med* 1994; 330:1819–20.
3. Farrel C, Palmer AT. The economics of aging: why the growing number of elderly won't bankrupt America. *Buisness Week* 1994; (Sept 12) 60–68.
4. Cassel CK, Rudberg MA, Olshansky SJ. The price of success: health care in an aging society. *Health Affairs* 1992; 11:87–99.
5. Decter MB. *Healing Medicare: managing health system change the Canadian way.* Toronto: McGilligan, 1994.

P A S is supported by the Canadian National Health Research and Development Program through a national health research scholar award, and by the American College of Physicians through a teaching and research scholarship. The Centre for Bioethics is supported by the Ontario Ministry of Health (grant 03006).

6. Callahan D. Setting limits: a response. *Gerontologist* 1994; 34:393–98.

7. Schneider EL, Guralnik JM. The aging of America: impact on health care costs. *JAMA* 1990; 263:23, 54–55.

8. Gordon M. Community care for the elderly: is it really better? *Call Med Assoc J* 1992; 148:393–96.

9. Weinberger M, Gold DT, Divine GW, Cowper PA, Hodgson LG, Schreiner PJ, et al. Expenditures in caring for patients with dementia who live at home. *Am J Public Health* 1993; 83:338–41.

10. President's Commission for the Study of Ethical Problems in Medicine and Biomedical and Behavioural Research. *Making health care decisions: the ethical and legal implications of informed consent in the patient-practitioner relationship*, vol I. Washington, DC: US Government Printing Office, 1982.

11. Silberfeld M, Fish A. *When the mind fails*. Toronto: University of Toronto Press, 1994.

12. Appelbaum PS, Grisso T. Assessing patient's capacities to consent to treatment. *N Engl J Med* 1988; 319: 1635–38.

13. Omnibus Budget Reconciliation Act (US Public law 101-508), s4206, 4751.

14. Emanuel LL, Barry MJ, Stoeckle JD, Ettelson LM, Emanuel EJ. Advance directives for medical care: a case for greater use. *N Engl J Med* 1991; 324:889–95.

15. Davidson KW, Hackler C, Caradine DR, McCord RS. Physician's attitudes on advance directives. *JAMA* 1989; 262:2415–19.

16. Emanuel EJ, Weinberg DS. How well is the Patient Self-Determination Act Working?: an early assessment. *Am J Med* 1993; 95:619–28.

17. Singer PA. Disease-specific advance directives. *Lancet* 1994; 344:594–96.

18. Danis M, Southerland LI, Garrett JM, Smith JL, Hielema F, Pickard CG, Egner DM, Patrick DL. A prospective study of advance directives for life-sustaining care. *N Engl J Med* 1991; 324:882–88.

19. Schneiderman LJ, Kronick R, Kaplan RM, Anderson JP, Langer RD. Effects of offering advance directives on medical treatments and costs. *Ann Intern Med* 1992; 117: 599–606.

20. Solomon DH. The US and the UK: an ocean apart? *J Am Geriatr Soc* 1990; 38:259–60.

21. Smith EM, Hastie IR. Resuscitation status of the elderly. *J R Coll Phys Lond* 1992; 26:377–79.

22. Gordon M. Should we provide cardiopulmonary resuscitation to elderly patients in long-term care? *Cardiol Elderly* 1995; 3:53–57.

23. Bedell SE, Delbanco TL, Cook EF, Epstein FH. Survival after cardiopulmonary resuscitation in the hospital. *N Engl J Med* 1983; 309: 570–76.

24. Tresch D, Heudebert G, Kutty K, Ohlert J, Vanbeek K, Masi A. Cardiopulmonary resuscitation in elderly patients hospitalized in the 1990s: a favourable outcome. *J Am Geriatr Soc* 1994; 42:137–41.

25. Murphy DG. Do-not-resuscitate orders: time for reappraisal in longterm care institutions. *JAMA* 1988; 260:2098–101.

26. Tresch DD, Neahring JM, Duthie EH, Mark DH, Kartes SK, Aufderheide TP. Outcomes of cardiopulmonary resuscitation in nursing homes: can we predict who will benefit? *Am J Med* 1993; 95: 123–30.

27. Awoke S, Mouton CP, Parrott M. Outcomes of skilled cardiopulmonary resuscitation in a long-term-care facility: futile therapy? *J Am Geriatr Soc* 1992; 40: 593–95.

28. Maddocks I. Changing concepts of palliative care. *Medy J Aust* 1990; 152: 535–39.

29. Fried TR, Gillick MR. Medical decision-making in the last six months of life: choices about limitation of card. *J Am Geriatr Soc* 1994; 42:303–07.

30. Lowy FH, Sawver DM, Williams JF. Canadian physicians and euthanasia. Ottawa: Canadian Medical Association, 1993.

31. Quill TE, Cassel CK. Nonabandonment: a central obligation for physicians. *Ann Intern Med* 1995; 122:368–75.

32. Pellegrino ED. Nonabandonment: an old obligation revisited. *Ann Intern Med* 1995; 122:377–78.

Correspondence to: Dr Michael Gordon, Baycrest Centre for Geriatric Care, 3560 Bathurst St, North York, Ontario M6A 2E1, Canada.

Article Review Form at end of book.

What is a common way many elderly cope with loss? How does "spirituality" help people deal with death?

A Significant Part of Life

Readers write about the role of faith.

Malcolm Boyd

Malcolm Boyd is an Episcopal priest and the author of Go Gentle Into That Good Night *(Genesis Press). While he cannot answer letters individually, if you wish to share a problem OR a solution please write him c/o MODERN MATURITY, 601 E St NW, Washington, DC 20049.*

Spirituality is a significant part of life for many of you, according to letters you've written me. You tell me that you frequently pray or meditate, focusing on God or a spiritual power, seeking peace of mind and unselfish service to others as major goals. You underscored this in your unprecedented outpouring of letters following my November-December 1997 You and I column, which dealt with issues of death and dying. I was deeply touched by your personal experiences, candid expressions of faith, and the positive attitudes toward life you revealed.

"I've found that I can't make it alone," a reader in Michigan wrote. "Too many hard problems have touched a raw nerve in my life, including the deaths of my husband , mother, and son-in-law. But my faith supported me and led me to help other people. I volunteer in a hospice, work actively in my church, am in a prayer group, help make lunches one day a week in a center for people with AIDS, and regularly visit people in a nursing home. My life has taken on a meaning that it never had before. I'm so very grateful to God."

I can identify with your approach. Whenever I feel overwhelmed by life's problems, I discover tremendous help in looking in another direction and focusing on what I'm deeply grateful for. A reader from Texas writes that she compiles a list of worries and an accompanying list of blessings. "The blessings are more numerous," she says. "God has some purpose for us and we must try to discern it and get on with our life."

"I lost my husband two years ago," writes a reader in Florida. "It seems like yesterday. I've learned that we should treasure people around us, give them that special hug and tell them how much they mean to us. Pray every day no matter what religion you are, taking time to say a prayer for the sick—and be grateful you're alive to say it."

I agree. In fact, one way that I deal with my own pains and problems is to pray for other people. "A key to effective spirituality," writes a reader in Ohio, "is to replace a 'me, me, me' prayer or meditation with one that recognizes our needs as a common people. A prayer or meditation can concern environmental needs, problems caused by racism, or a worldwide desire for peace. This acknowledges a wider base of suffering and a broader scale of problems."

Prayer can take the form of action as well as words. A reader in Pennsylvania recounts a moment of terrible need: "My husband and I were shopping in a department store when he fell to the floor. A clerk gave him CPR, and an ambulance arrived to take us to a hospital. Suddenly, a stranger asked to go with me. She stayed with me while a doctor gave me the devastating news that my husband was dead. She was a nurse who had watched many people suffering in such a moment. She had vowed to help those she could by staying at their side. I firmly believe she was an angel sent to me in my most difficult hour."

Let's hope that our own spirituality, yours and mine, will transform our prayers into actions, too, so that in such moments of pain and need we may be enabled to act like angels helping one another.

Article Review Form at end of book.

How does the Patient Self-Determination Act (PSDA) impact dying and death? How Could "ageism" affect medical treatment of the elderly?

Caring for the Older Patient, Part III

Ethical issues in gerontology

**Steven B. Dowd
and Ann M. Steves**

*Division of Medical Imaging and Therapy
University of Alabama at Birmingham
Birmingham, Alabama*

This is the third article of a four-part series on gerontology and its applications to the care of elderly patients in nuclear medicine. This article reviews some of the ethical issues that arise in caring for the elderly.

Upon completion of this article, the reader should be able to: (a) discuss the relationship between autonomy and competence; (b) differentiate between competence and decision-making capacity; (c) identify guidelines for determining decision-making capacity; (d) define ageism and provide examples of it; (e) describe the way American society views death and the issues this view raises for health care professionals; and (f) describe the grieving process.

Key Words: aged; ageism; communication; death and dying; decision making; euthanasia; geriatric assessment; grief; informed consent; mental competency; suicide.

J Nucl Med Technol 1997;25: 171–178.

> *Cast me not off in the time of old age;
> forsake me not when my strength faileth.*
>
> Psalms 71:9

Old age is often euphemistically referred to as the golden years, indicating a time in life that one can look forward to. Is this a correct view? Peter Townsend, a British pioneer in the discipline of gerontology, used to claim that one could measure a culture, society or civilization by how well it treated the elderly. It is a sentiment recently echoed by Kosberg and Mangum.[1,2] Certain ethical issues arise in caring for the elderly. Ethical decisions can be viewed as the allocation of resources towards a goal. If resources were unlimited, each individual in a society or group would receive unlimited care, and there would be no ethical decisions required.

Ethical issues arise in health care, however, because only so many resources are available. If we invest our resources in MRI scanners, we may not have enough money for basic health care, such as childhood immunization. If we invest in a system that encourages acute care, we will have less money for preventive and wellness care and, in fact, may not value such care. In ethics, these are known as justice concerns. Although it is often assumed that health care is not rationed in the U.S., in reality, every society has a method for rationing health care. The dominant method of rationing health care in the U.S. has been the merit (price

For correspondence or reprints contact: Ann Steves, MS, CNMT, University of Alabama at Birmingham, 1714 Ninth Ave. South, Birmingham, AL 35294–1270.

or laissez-faire) method, which rations resources based on an ability to afford them, with some resources available on a charity basis.

How much health care, then, do the elderly deserve? At what point should care (or for that matter, efforts to cure) be terminated? Do the elderly deserve special treatment? Do we view the elderly with disdain and, therefore, provide them with less treatment than we would a younger person? This article will attempt to answer these questions in reference to both health care in general and nuclear medicine technology, in specific.

Ethics

The worst sin towards our fellow creatures is not to hate them, but to be indifferent to them; that's the essence of inhumanity.

George Bernard Shaw
The Devil's Disciple, Act II

In medical ethics, the consideration of autonomy is particularly important. Autonomy is one of three concepts related to respect for people: autonomy, confidentiality and privacy, and veracity (truth-telling). At its most basic level, autonomy refers to the right of the individual to make decisions. However, it is not a simple concept in its execution. For example, one can differentiate between autonomy as a negative right (freedom from interference) as opposed to autonomy as a positive right (support and enhancement of choice).

Autonomy literally means self-rule. In American society, autonomy has typically been seen as the right to make one's own decisions free from interference, as well as the right to exercise those decisions. As our society becomes more multicultural, this view of autonomy may change.

One legal means of recognizing patient autonomy is through the Patient Self-Determination Act (PSDA). This law requires hospitals and nursing homes to inform clients of their rights at the time of admission. These rights include the right to participate in health care decisions and execute advance directives, such as living wills. The implementation of the PSDA has been erratic to date, and its full effects are not yet known.

Autonomy also may conflict with the principle of beneficence (doing good) since health care professionals may reflect their values in an attempt to do good for clients. Beneficence and nonmaleficence provide the underpinnings for most codes of ethics for health care workers. Beneficence refers to "doing good," and is a primary goal of any health professional. Most individuals enter a health profession with at least one of their stated goals being to help people. Since the health professional's view of what is good may conflict with the client's view, beneficence may clash with autonomy. Nonmaleficence refers to the "first, do not harm" admonition seen in health care codes of ethics. It is often seen as the first goal in health care, with beneficence the second goal.

Autonomy also must be balanced with safety concerns. In some cases, it becomes easy to assume that an older person cannot care for himself due simply to frailty. This is an example of ageism, discussed later in this article. There also is task-specific competence, which recognizes that individuals may have the capacity to make some decisions but not others.

There are many ideas about how health professionals should view their relationship with a client. These views represent a continuum ranging from strict paternalism, or acting as a parent (a good example is the play and movie *Who's Life Is It Anyway?*), to the physician as a procedural expert whose advice may be taken or ignored. In the middle of this continuum is a contractual model in which the patient agrees, based on trust of the health professional, to a course of treatment unless some factor intervenes. This is similar to a fiduciary relationship.

Autonomy and Competency

Does one's integrity ever lie in what he is not able to do? I think that usually it does, for free will does not mean one will, but many wills conflicting in one man. Freedom cannot be conceived simply.

Flannery O'Connor
Wise Blood

Most ethical issues related to the care of the elderly center around autonomy. Autonomy refers to the right to maintain one's independence and make decisions. In America, autonomy (life, liberty and the pursuit of happiness) is a valued philosophical ideal.

Old age with its concomitant losses, however, has the potential to threaten autonomy. Aging is a universal and irreversible process; all humans who live long enough experience decline in their physical and mental abilities.[3] Fortunately for most individuals, these changes are not severe enough to bring about the need to be institutionalized. In fact, most elderly are healthy enough to carry on the activities of daily living. Simply because

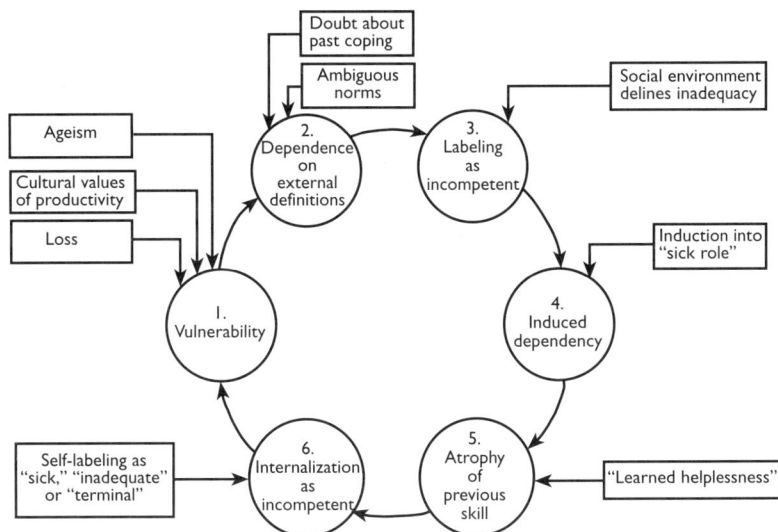

Figure 1. Social breakdown in old age: a vicious cycle of induced incompetence.[4]

one takes longer to perform tasks does not mean one is unable to do them. Similarly, normal forgetfulness that occurs in aging does not mean that one is senile.

Older individuals may become impaired or, even worse, be viewed as impaired simply because they are old. In their social breakdown model, Kuypers and Bengtson[4] show how the elderly may enter a cycle that leads them into a role of "learned helplessness" based on the way in which they are perceived by others (Fig. 1). This may happen when elders move from an environment in which they are functional to one in which their capabilities are insufficient to meet the demands of the new environment, such as an extended stay in a hospital. In the hospital, the daily routine, food, certain equipment and terminology are unfamiliar, making even the most basic activities more difficult. In addition, the emphasis is on treating the acute illness for which the patient was hospitalized rather than returning the person to the previous level of function. The patient becomes dependent on hospital personnel,

loses functional capacity and becomes less self-sufficient.

If an elder does become impaired, caregivers must perform a delicate balancing act between the rights of the individual and the risk the older person poses to self and others.[5] Even when impaired, an older person still has rights, which in some situations includes the right to make decisions. Unfortunately, thinking on this issue is often binary; once an older individual loses full competence, they must be impaired and, thus, unable to make decisions.

In the clinical setting, the patient's ability to give informed consent, a concept that develops from the ethical principle of autonomy, is closely related to competence. Informed consent contains three elements: (a) adequate information about the procedure; (b) voluntary assent without external coercion; and (c) competence.[6] Competence is a legal term that lacks a clear set of standards, hence a ruling of incompetent strongly depends on the facts of the individual case.[7] Answers to the following questions have served as criteria in a court of law for determining the

competency of individuals who refuse life-sustaining treatment: (a) Can the patient make and express a choice concerning life? (b) Is the outcome of the choice that the patient makes reasonable? (c) Is the choice based on rational reasons? (d) Does the patient understand the implications and consequences of the choice?[8]

One example from case law involves a 72-yr-old man, Robert Quackenbush, who refused bilateral amputation of his gangrenous legs.[9] The hospital wanted the court to declare the patient incompetent because he withdrew consent for surgery. Discussions between Mr. Quackenbush and the judge and a psychiatrist demonstrated that the patient understood his condition and its severity, and that he would die as a result of the gangrene. The patient "hoped for a miracle," but knew one was unlikely. Mr. Quackenbush also stated that the burdens of the surgery and living with the amputations outweighed his desire to live. While refusing the amputation may not have been the medically rational choice, it was the patient's treatment of choice, consistent with his goals and values. The definition of rational may be different for patients and health care professionals, and competency may never be questioned until a patient disagrees with the course of treatment or refuses a procedure. However, agreeing to a medical intervention does not imply competence either. It has been suggested that in assessing the patient's decision-making ability, the process of decision making, rather than the final choice, is the better indicator of competence.[7]

In contrast to the Quackenbush case is the Northern case.

Mrs. Northern also refused bilateral amputation of her legs.[10] Although her feet were "dead, black, shriveled, rotting and stinking," she believed that they were dirty from soot or dust. In this case, the court judged Mrs. Northern to be incompetent because her choice to forego surgery was not based on a rational reason. In the words of the judge, "she was incapable of recognizing facts which would be obvious to a person of normal perception"[10] If, as in the case of Quackenbush, her reason for refusing medical treatment was that she preferred death to the loss of her feet, the judge probably would have declared her competent.

In fact, most determinations of competency are not made in a court of law, but rather in the clinical setting by the consensus of the patient's caregivers who may include both family members and health care professionals.[6,8] Since competence is a legal term, the use of the term decision-making capacity is preferred to describe what is actually being assessed. Also, rather than considering competency or capacity in a broad general sense, a patient's capacity should be considered in relation to making a particular decision. A patient may not have the decision-making capacity to manage financial affairs, but may have the capacity to make decisions about medical care. Guidelines for the assessment of decision-making capacity are similar to those used in court and described in the paragraphs above. If all the criteria are met, then the decision-making capacity is not impaired, but the situation becomes more difficult when only some of the criteria are met. It has been proposed that a sliding scale associated with the risk of the patient's decision be used in assessing decision-making capacity. The more serious the risk posed by the patient's decision, the more stringently the criteria for capacity must be met.[7]

Just as patients may have decision-making capacity for certain decisions but not others, their decision-making capacity may change over the course of the day. For instance, patients may alternate between periods of confusion and windows of lucidity. Some patients exhibit greater confusion in the evening, a condition known as "sundowning." However, these patients may be able to give informed consent during their lucid periods.[11] Those who know the patient best can identify these periods of peak function. Other conditions, such as dehydration, medication or electrolyte imbalance, can cause reversible dementia that can temporarily impair decision-making capacity.[7]

Niemira[12] notes that ethicists prefer to discuss what he considers to be obscure issues such as active euthanasia, but that they choose to ignore the ethical issues that have the most relevance for professional practice, such as how to deal with the frail elderly and what it means to be incompetent. He believes this traps health care workers into being overly paternalistic.

Paternalism, like any other stance, is not bad itself. Paris et al.[13] solved one patient care problem, elder abuse, by adopting a "short-term paternalistic stance" and later allowing the patient to make decisions. The danger is that a short-term paternalism can extend into a long-term or permanent paternalism.

As dedicated health care professionals, we believe in the power of intervention. However, often interventions have no positive effects, and sometimes leave the patient worse off than before. Curtin[14] has written an interesting case study in which she notes that, "It is idealistic to think of intervention as a swift blade that slices cleanly between the patient and the problem, leaving the patient disease free and the ailment to wither and perish."

Consider further the case of the elder abuse. Often, as health care professionals, we believe that no competent person would choose to live in an abusive situation; therefore a refusal to accept intervention is proof of incompetence.[15] This is a circular logical trap. Curtin notes that we can take just as much away from a patient when we intervene, and that leaving the patient in an abusive situation may be necessary. In her case study, the abused person would have lost her caregiver and possibly have been placed in a worse situation.

Health care professionals are sometimes told that they should treat all patients as if that patient were their parent. A far more effective analogy might be to put themselves in the place of an older person, a process known as interpathy[16] and ask the following questions, continuing to use elder abuse as the example:

- Why might you *not* want the abuse to be reported? For many elders, the label of abuse indicates that something is wrong with the caregiver, who is often a family member, or that there is something wrong with the elder that makes them deserving of abuse.

- Does an older person have the right to have abuse not reported? Accepting elders as autonomous individuals gives them the right to make bad or wrong decisions as well as correct ones.

- At what point does that no longer hold true? Most would indicate that a loss of competency would negate the elder's right to make such decisions. This is correct, but the determination of competent is rarely simple.

After that analysis, the following questions may help clarify the health care professional's position:

- How can you best be an advocate for the abused older patient?
- Would there ever be cases in which you would be an advocate for the abused older person by *not* reporting abuse? Is this such a case? In some cases, only a temporary amelioration of the situation is possible. Although it is difficult for many health care professionals to accept, sometimes problems can only be solved for the short term.[17]

It is sometimes difficult for young individuals to imagine themselves as aged. In some cases, there is such a fear and avulsion to aging that it results in a prejudice known as ageism.

Ageism

Every man desires to live long, but no man would be old.

Jonathan Swift
Thoughts on Various Subjects

Holding prejudiced attitudes against the elderly is known as ageism. The concept was first developed by Butler.[18] He later noted that ageism was:

. . . a process of systematic stereotyping of and discrimination against people because they are old, just as racism and sexism accomplish

this with skin color and gender. Old people are categorized as senile, rigid in thought and manner, old-fashioned in morality and skill . . . Ageism allows the younger generations to see old people as different from themselves; thus they subtly cease to identify with their elders as human beings.[19]

Ageism allows younger generations to stereotype, avoid, act hostile toward and make inappropriate jokes about the elderly. What causes ageism is unclear. Selective exposure to the elderly, the media and expected social roles have all been attributed as the cause.[20-22] Schoenfield felt that ageism may be a myth.[23] Others believe that the former myths of aging may be gone, but have been replaced by several new myths and stereotypes (such as, most elderly are well-off and a drain on resources and are politically self-motivated).[24] Thus, some young people may see no need to continue social security benefits to the aged and feel that the aged are all well-off and would only spend money on greens fees at the golf course.

The construct of ageism is difficult to measure. It is relatively easy for a prejudiced, yet intelligent, subject to answer "false" to a statement such as "All old people are pretty much alike." Some reports indicate that health care workers tend to have stereotypical views of the elderly.[25,26] One reason often cited for this is that most health care workers have their clinical experiences in institutions that offer acute care to the elderly and are thus denied exposure to the well elderly.[27]

Ageism In Nuclear Medicine Technology

There are numerous examples of age stereotyping in the practice of nuclear medicine technology,

some subtle and some not. One of the most common, perhaps, is a technologist's assumption that, because of the patient's age, the physical ailment is accompanied by a mental deficit, or that the physical ailment has totally debilitated the patient. The first article of this series described an approach to elderly patient care that views the elderly on a continuum.[28] The two extremes of the continuum, the well elder and the frail elder, have very different needs that should be recognized by the technologist. However, it is equally important to appreciate that many elderly are neither fully well or frail, requiring a combination of approaches to their care that is tailored to each individual's needs. The JCAHO accreditation standards acknowledge the validity of this approach in the age-related competency requirements.[29]

Failing to respect differences in the elderly that are normal age-related changes or to address the special needs that these individuals may have can lead to actions that compromise patient autonomy. Hearing impairment is a good example. Communicating with a patient with a hearing deficit requires time and patience. It is sometimes difficult to convey even simple directions or collect routine information. Explaining an unfamiliar, and sometimes involved event, such as a nuclear medicine procedure, makes the communication process even more arduous. It can be frustrating and confusing to the patient, and disconcerting to the harried technologist. In an attempt to do good for the patient and promote clinical expediency, a technologist may not explain the procedure as fully as necessary for the patient to give informed consent. Likewise, the patient may acquiesce to end a frustrating and possibly embarrassing experience. Thus, the patient's autonomy may have been sacrificed.

An attitude of disrespect that devalues the elderly patient as a person illustrates how ageism can affect clinical practice. An insidious expression of this attitude occurs when the technologist questions the appropriateness of a procedure based solely on a patient's age. Such an attitude may be expressed overtly when a technologist calls elderly patients by their first names without being requested to do so, or uses unwelcome terms of endearment or speaks condescendingly to patients in a way that places adult patients in a child-like role. Similarly, carrying on discussions in front of elderly patients because the perception is that they do not hear well or that they do not understand conveys that the technologist is in control. This can frighten a patient unfamiliar with the environment whose caregiver appears to be focusing attention on unrelated matters rather than on the patient.

While these examples may seem like just bad manners, they express an uncaring attitude about the concerns and needs of a particular group based on misinformation and stereotyping. As a result, the elderly sometimes receive inappropriate or substandard care.

Case Study

Consider the following true story. A 65-yr-old man was admitted to the hospital and scheduled for a nuclear medicine procedure. When the technologist requested that the patient be sent from his unit to the nuclear medicine department, she learned that he was seven feet tall and weighed approximately 400 pounds. The nurse told the technologist that the patient would be sent to the nuclear medicine department as soon as a stretcher could be found that would accommodate him. About two hours later, the patient arrived looking very uncomfortable with his legs suspended from the end of the stretcher. The technologist explained to the patient that he had to be moved from the stretcher onto the imaging table. The patient energetically got up from the stretcher, walked to the imaging table and lay down on it, commenting that "no one believed me when I said I could walk."

What is the basis for the assumptions that have been made here? The original premise that a large man in his sixties could not possibly be mobile enough to move from his hospital bed to a wheelchair or even walk to nuclear medicine was obviously false. After informing the staff that he was capable, the patient was still made to conform to uncomfortable transport, possibly because it was considered to be more expedient. In this situation, ageism is responsible for uncaring treatment. In addition, it made hospital staff appear inept and compromised their relationship with the patient by doubting his credibility.

Death, Dying and Grief

Death be not proud, though some have called thee mighty and dreadful, for thou art not so.

John Donne
Holy Sonnets

Death is a universal event, common to all humans. There is no question that as we age, we come closer to death. Although death can come at any age, most individuals will face death in old age. Since health professionals must deal with the dying and may encounter death in their clinical practice, they especially need to confront death, just as they must confront ageism, in order to deliver effective patient care.

The American View of Death

It has been said that, in the U.S., we are a death-denying society.[30] Some critics have even said that death has become the new pornography for Americans. That is, whereas once sexual subjects were taboo, now death is the taboo subject that we lie to children about and avoid in polite company.[31] Some individuals believe that technology can free them from death, and dying at home has only recently been rediscovered as a viable option.[32] Other ways in which we deny death include attempts to rename the hospital morgue, the romanticizing of violent death in the movies and the separation of the elderly (they dying) from the rest of society.

The Health Professions and the Terminally Ill

Few health professions programs provide much education about death, including nuclear medicine technology. When death education is offered in the health professions curriculum, it tends to be integrated throughout the curriculum, offered as an elective or, more rarely, required as a course.[33] There are obvious problems with the first two, in that required material for the health professional to confront death may not be covered. In the final example, the problem, as always, is time. Most health professional curricula focus on the provision of technical skills needed to be a competent radiographer, nuclear medicine technologist, nurse, physician and so on. There is rarely time for adequately covering everything that needs to be taught and; thus, some subjects suffer, especially those easily ignored.

What this cursory coverage can do is perhaps best shown in the patient care textbooks of the radiologic sciences. All of them, based on literal interpretations of the work of Kübler-Ross[34] categorize grief into five stages: (a) denial and isolation; (b) anger; (c) bargaining; (d) depression; and (e) acceptance. They also indicate that mourners pass through these stages in sequence. Of these, Adler and Carlton are the least restrictive, indicating that this staging is generally accepted.[35–37]

Kübler-Ross never intended to indicate that all mourners pass through all of these stages, or as some have interpreted, that this is a linear process. Establishing a set of rigid stages for individuals to follow does not allow for the natural unfolding of each individual's grief process. In the care of the terminally ill patient in nuclear medicine technology, Thomas[38] made the following appropriate remarks:

Unfortunately, the stages of grief are not systematically experienced from denial to acceptance. A patient can be accepting in the morning, angry in the afternoon and depressed at the conclusion of his exam. Working with this patient can be a roller coaster ride that is emotionally damaging for you if you do not understand the emotions associated with the grief process.

It has been well-documented that physicians have a high death anxiety, and some studies have indicated that many physicians choose medicine as a career to try to control death.[39] One deficit in not providing sufficient death education, according to Noyes and Clancy,[40] is that physicians tend to confuse the dying role with the sick role. Thus, a pretense exists to confirm that both physician and patient want the patient to get better. This is perhaps one reason why physicians are often hesitant to prescribe pain-killing drugs "to prevent them from becoming addicts," even when the patients are terminally ill.

Euthanasia

There are two basic types of euthanasia or good death. Active euthanasia is when death is hastened by an act of commission and passive euthanasia is when an individual is allowed to die by the omission of an act (such as by "no-codes"). This is one of the most basic ethical issues confronting us today. Most Americans and health professionals (although not a substantial majority) tend to oppose active euthanasia while approving of passive euthanasia. It seems wrong to us to assist suicide or allow someone to kill themselves. Passive euthanasia, however, usually is associated with a lack of using extraordinary measures and allowing someone to die in peace. In reality, things are never that simple.

There certainly are times when individuals are in great pain and suffering, have no chance of recovery, but will not die for some time. Do such individuals have a right to end their lives? Euthanasia is irrevocable, even when voluntary. One cannot change one's mind later. Another, perhaps frightening, problem is the hesitancy of physicians to *not* honor no-code situations and do-not-resuscitate (DNR) orders. One

study in radiology found that this was not uncommon due to the "emotional weight that results from withholding resuscitation from a patient in whom cardiac arrest probably could be reversed" or, as they later note in cases of interventional radiology, "they believe that the DNR order is not applicable in these situations because they do not think the order was designed to prevent these types of deaths [during interventional procedures]".[41] From the patient's viewpoint such actions are extremely paternalistic and reflect a view that the physician is the decision maker or is the only individual affected by death.

A Possible Solution?

One possible solution lies in adopting the Dutch attitude toward euthanasia. As with all proposals for euthanasia, the Dutch method of euthanasia is compared to the Nazi "euthanasia" programs.[42] However, the Dutch attitude differs significantly. In Holland, euthanasia is still technically illegal but there are guidelines that make a doctor immune from prosecution. These guidelines include a persistent, voluntary and durable request by the patient, unacceptable and hopeless suffering, and require a coroner's visit to determine whether charges should be filed against the physician.

What makes the Dutch program appealing to many advocates is that it does not approve of euthanasia per se, since it is still technically illegal, but makes physicians and patients adhere to strict guidelines to avoid prosecution. The Dutch program eliminates many of the "slippery slope" issues that we encounter in euthanasia decisions. As

Veatch has noted, the lever for Nazi euthanasia was not compassion or a desire to respect the views of others, it was a view of the sick, weak, old and undesirable as unrehabilitative and not contributing to an ideal society.[43]

Suicide

It may seem strange to address suicide, especially outside the subject of euthanasia, within the context of this article. Many assume that primarily the young commit suicide and may not see this as a topic that needs to be discussed in nuclear medicine technology. However, the elderly have a documented rate of suicide twice that of the general population, and this rate is highest in white males over the age of 85.[30]

It has been estimated that 75% of all suicides see a physician within 4 months of their suicide.[44] It is a recognized prodromal indicator for suicide. It has been theorized that, although some of these individuals have real physical complaints, others use these complaints of real or imagined problems to seek help. Such patients may be present in nuclear medicine. There is no way that a technologist knows whether the patient on the table is there for real or imagined complaints. By offering legitimate caring and concern for the patient's distress, the technologist may help the patient to decide against suicide. Suicide is always an act of ambivalence and a single marker event of concern may help the patient choose to live.[45] Shneidman[45] notes the example of "intentioned suicide," in which "older hospitalized persons in the terminal stage of fatal illness . . . with remarkable and totally unexpected energy succeed in killing themselves." It is not illogical to assume that such energy can be directed positively, rather than negatively.

Grief and Bereavement

The terms grief and bereavement are used differently by different authors and, in some cases, are used interchangeably. This article will use the definitions of Rando,[46] who says that bereavement is the actual state of having suffered a loss, whereas grief is the process involved with any loss, encompassing psychological, social and somatic reactions.

Due to the problems associated with viewing grief as a linear process, most death educators and counselors prefer terms other than "stages" of grief. For example, Worden[47] prefers to use the term tasks of mourning, describing them as: (a) accepting the reality of the loss; (b) experiencing the pain of grief; (c) adjusting to the changed environment; and (d) withdrawing emotional energy and reinvesting it in another relationship or other activities. Martocchio[48] prefers to view the grieving process as nonlinear, but expressed in clusters or phases that are not in any particular order nor with any discrete boundaries between the reactions of grief.

It is important to use the correct names to refer to things. One example is categorizing grief that is not "normal" as "pathological" grief, as if there were certain types of grief that were correct and those that were incorrect. Such unusual forms of grieving may include absent, distorted, converted or chronic grief. The preferred term for such grief is complicated grief, as it indicates that grief is a normal process but may be complicated by a variety of psychosocial and other factors.[49]

It should also be noted that grief can occur due to a variety of losses in addition to death. Such losses can include those associated with the aging process or perhaps the loss of function of a limb. Many elderly individuals go through anticipatory grief in preparation for death, and it is important to allow them to talk about death.[50] Ignoring them simply because we have not come to grips with death ourselves or belittling their concerns is death-denying. It is important for the elderly, in many cases, to talk about and prepare for death.

Cross-Cultural Perspectives

"Every culture provides for its members a way of thinking about death and responding to it."[30] Whereas once ethnocentrism was the norm, today we realize that we must acknowledge the views of other cultures. This not only lets us better understand other cultures and how to respond to their needs, but often helps our understanding of our own humanity. As a society decried as death-denying, perhaps we can learn something from other societies to better help us face our own deaths. Hindus view psychological readiness for death as part of a good death: "It's like if you start getting ready for a holiday a long time before the holiday. People . . . who are all ready for it will never die, the body dies, the soul just takes over for the next form.[51]

It is not only non-Western cultures that have such diametrically opposed views of death from the U.S. The German proverb, "Tod und Leben sind über einen Leisten geschlagen," (dying is as natural as living) shows an attitude towards death that is accepting without being pessimistic.[52] As we saw in the look at Dutch euthanasia, it is possible to have a system that is regulated in such as way that assisted death is technically illegal, but still allowed when circumstances demand.

All cultures have some view of a potential life after death, and all cultures must mourn and bury or dispose of the corpse. Mourning rituals exist primarily to reintegrate individuals, such as spouses and other survivors, into society and to invest the psychic energy of mourning in a culturally appropriate way.[30]

Conclusion

It is better to know some of the questions than all of the answers.

James Thurber
The Thurber Carnival

There are no easy answers for any ethical issue. Ethical decisions are difficult almost by definition. With the elderly we find that ethical issues concern the allocation of resources and how best to foster autonomy in the midst of personal loss. If we believe, as Peter Townsend did, that the measure of our society, and perhaps the profession of nuclear medicine technology, is by how well we treat our elders, then these are issues we will have to grapple with for some time.

References

1. Townsend P. *The last refuge.* London, England: Routledge; 1962.
2. Kosbert JI, Mangum WP. Ethical dilemmas in teaching ethical issues in aging. *Eduational Gerontology* 1992; 18: 767–774.
3. Steves AM, Dowd SB, Durick D. Caring for the older patient, Part II: age-related anatomic and physiologic changes and pathologies. *J Nucl Med Technol* 1997; 25: 86–97.
4. Kuypers JA, Bengtson VL. Perspectives on the older family. In: Quinn WH, Hughston GA, eds. *Independent aging: family and social systems perspectives.* Rockville, MD: Aspen Publications; 1984:17.
5. Watkins M. Can you tread this emotional high wire? Balancing elderly people's rights and independence against risks they pose. *Professional Nurse* 1993; 8:604–606, 608.
6. Kutner JS, Ruark JE, Raffin TA. Defining patient competence for medical decision making. *Chest* 1991; 100: 1404–1409.
7. Lo B. Assessing decision-making capacity. *Law Med Health Care* 1990; 18: 193-201.
8. Haddad AM. Determining competency. *J Gerontol Nurs* 1988; 14: 19–22, 36–37.
9. *In the matter of Robert Quackenbush, an alleged incompetent.* 156 NJ Super 282, 383 A.2d 785; 1978.
10. *State Department of Human Resources v Northern.* 563 S W.2d 197; Tennessee Court of Appeals; 1978.
11. Abrams AB, Beers MH, Berthan R, eds. *Merck manual of geriatrics,* 2nd ed. White House, NJ: Merck and Company, Inc; 1995.
12. Niemira D. Life on the slippery slope. A bedside view of treating incompetent elderly patients, *Hastings Center Report* 1993; 23: 14–17.
13. Paris BE, Meier DE, Goldstein T, et al. Elder abuse and neglect: how to recognize warning signs and intervene. *Geriatrics* 1995; 50: 47–51.
14. Curtin K. Intervention in elder abuse: a swift blade or a dull-edged saw? *Can Med Assoc J* 1995; 152: 1121-1123.
15. Costa AJ. Elder abuse. *Prim Care* 1993; 20: 375–389.
16. Dowd SB. *Teaching in the health-related professions.* Dubuque, IA: Eastwind Publishing; 1995.
17. Dowd SB, Durick D. Elder abuse: the RT's role in diagnosis and prevention. *Radiology Technol* 1996; 68: 23–28.
18. Butler RN. Age-ism: another form of bigotry. *Gerontologist* 1969; 9: 243–246.
19. Butler RN. *Why survive? Being old in America* New York, NY: Harper and Row; 1975: 11–12.
20. Ansello EF. Age and ageism in children's first literature. *Educational Gerontology* 1977; 2: 255–272.
21. Bishop JM, Krause DR. Depictions of aging and old age on Saturday morning television. *Gerontologist* 1984; 24: 91-94.
22. Nardi AH. Person-perception research and the perception of life-span development. In: Baltes PB, Schaie KW, eds. *Life-span developmental psychology: Personality and socialization.* New York, NY: Academic Press; 1973: 285–301.
23. Shoenfield D. Who is stereotyping whom and why? *Gerontologist* 1982; 22: 267-272.
24. Binstock R. The Donald P. Kent memorial lecture. The aged as scapegoat. *Gerontologist* 1983; 23: 136–143.
25. Dowd SB. Radiographers' knowledge of aging, *Radiology Technol* 1983; 54: 192-196.
26. Sheffler SJ. Do clinical experiences affect nursing students' attitudes towards the elderly? *J Nurs Educ* 1995; 34: 312–316.
27. Haight BK, Heaton S, Truslow C. A staff development plan for the graying of America's hospital patients. *J Nurs Staff Development* 1994; 10: 66–70.
28. Dowd SB, Steves AM, Durick D. Caring for the older patient, Part I: the relationship of theory to practice. *J Nucl Med Technol* 1997; 25: 24–32.
29. Joint Commission on Accreditation of Healthcare Organizations. *Accreditation manual for hospitals.* Oakbrook Terrace, IL: JCAHO; 1997.
30. Backer BA, Hannon NR, Russell NA. *Death and dying: understanding and care,* 2nd ed. Albany, NY: Delmar; 1994.
31. Gorer G. *Death, grief and mourning in contemporary Britain.* New York, NY: Arno Press; 1977.
32. Fulton R, Owen G. Death and society in twentieth century America. *Omega-J of Death and Dying* 1988; 18: 379–398.
33. Degner LF, Gow CM. Evaluations of death education in nursing. A critical review. *Cancer Nursing* 1988; 11: 151–159.
34. Kübler-Ross E. *On death and dying.* New York, NY: MacMillan; 1969.
35. Ehrlich RA, McCloskey ED. *Patient care in radiography,* 4th ed. St. Louis, MO: Mosby-Year Book; 1993.
36. Torrea LS. *Basic medical techniques and patient care for radiologic technologists,* 4th ed. Philadelphia, PA: JB Lippincott; 1993.
37. Adler AM, Carlton RR. *Introduction to radiography and patient care.* Philadelphia, PA: WB Sauders; 1994.

38. Thomas KS. Effectively interacting with the terminally ill patient. *J Nucl Med Technol* 1996; 24: 92–96.

39. Benoliel JQ. Health care providers and dying patients: critical issues in terminal care. *Omega-J of Death and Dying* 1987; 18: 341–363.

40. Noyes R Jr, Clancy J. The dying role: its relevance to improved patient care. *Psychiatry* 1977; 40: 41–47.

41. Jacobson JA, Gully JE, Mann H. "Do not resuscitate" orders in the radiology department: an interpretation. *Radiology* 1996; 198: 21–24.

42. Friedlander H. *The origins of Nazi genocide: from "euthanasia" to the final solution.* Chapel Hill, NC: University of North Carolina Press; 1995.

43. Veatch RM. *Death, dying and the biological revolution: our last quest for responsibility,* rev ed. New Haven, CT: Yale University Press; 1989.

44. Colt GH. *The enigma of suicide.* New York, NY: Summit Books; 1991.

45. Shneidman ES. *Deaths of man.* New York, NY: J Aronson; 1983.

46. Rando TA. *Grief, dying and death: clinical interventions for caregivers.* Champaign, Ill: Research Press; 1984.

47. Worden JW. *Grief counseling and grief therapy: a handbook for the mental health practitioner,* 2nd ed. New York, NY: Springer Publishing Company; 1991.

48. Martocchio BC. Grief and bereavement. Healing through hurt. *Nursing Clinics in North America* 1985;20:327–341.

49. Brownson K, Dowd SB. Complicated grief. *Radiation Therapist* 1997; 6:21–26.

50. Alty A. Adjustment to bereavement and loss in older people. *Nursing Times* 1995; 21:34–36.

51. Firth S. The good death: approaches to death, dying and bereavement among British Hindus. In: Berger A, Badham P, Kutscher A, et al, eds. *Perspectives on death and dying: cross-cultural and multidisciplinary views.* Philadelphia, PA: Charles Press; 1989;69.

52. Rippley LJ. *Of German ways.* Minneapolis, MN: Dillon Press; 1970;38.

Article Review Form at end of book.

WiseGuide Wrap-Up

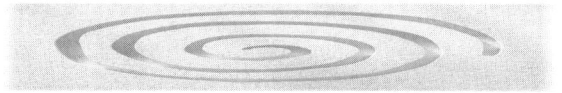

- Many legal questions about dying and death in the United States remain.

- Living wills, the right to die, and assisted suicide are all part of the "death with dignity" concept.

- The elderly have unique thoughts and insights about dying and death.

R.E.A.L. Sites

This list provides a print preview of typical **coursewise** R.E.A.L. sites. There are over 100 such sites at the **courselinks**™ site. The danger in printing URLs is that web sites can change overnight. As we went to press, these sites were functional using the URLs provided. If you come across one that isn't, please let us know via email to: webmaster@coursewise.com. Use your Passport to access the most current list of R.E.A.L. sites at the **courselinks**™ site.

Site name: Funeral Humor

URL: http://vbiweb.champlain.edu/famsa/humor.htm

Why is it R.E.A.L.? Need to take the lighter side of the road when it comes to dying and death? This site provides some relief through humor, jokes, and anecdotes.

Key topic: dying and death

Activity: Identify your favorite story at this site.

Site name: Choice in Dying

URL: http://www.choices.org/

Why is it R.E.A.L.? You order a copy of a Living Will document or download your state's advance directive packages from this site.

Key topics: death and dying, living will

Activity: Print a copy of your state's advance directive package.

Site name: Funeral Price Information

URL: http://www.nfda.org/resources/funeralprice.html

Why is it R.E.A.L.? This site has an up-to-date chart showing average funeral prices for an adult in the Unites States and an itemized list of things typically included in funeral expenses.

Key topic: death and dying

Activity: List the average cost of a funeral today.

Site name: Was the Funeral Home an Ethical One?

URL: http://vbiweb.funerals.org.edu/famsa/ethical.htm

Why is it R.E.A.L.? This site gives you ten simple questions to answer to determine if you might have been the victim of unethical practices. It also provides you with information on "How to File a Funeral Complaint."

Key topic: dying and death

Activity: When should you file a "funeral complaint?"

Site name: Center for Clinical Ethics and Humanities in Health Care

URL: http://www.wings.buffalo.edu/faculty/research/bioethics/

Why is it R.E.A.L.? This site provides resources concerning the rights of dying people, living wills, advance directives, help for caregivers, and links to other related sites that deal with medical ethics.

Key topics: dying and death, living wills

Activity: Identify some of the key topics highlighted at this site.

Index

Note: Names in boldface type indicate authors of readings.

Putting it in *Perspectives*
-Review Form-

Your name:_____   Date: _____

Reading title: _____

Summarize: Provide a one-sentence summary of this reading: _____
_____
_____
_____

Follow the Thinking: How does the author back the main premise of the reading? Are the facts/opinions appropriately supported by research or available data? Is the author's thinking logical?

_____
_____
_____
_____
_____

Develop a Context (answer one or both questions): How does this reading contrast or compliment your professor's lecture treatment of the subject matter? How does this reading compare to your textbook's coverage?

_____
_____
_____
_____
_____

Question Authority: Explain why you agree/disagree with the author's main premise.

_____
_____
_____
_____
_____
_____

COPY ME! Copy this form as needed. This form is also available at http://www.coursewise.com
Click on: *Perspectives*.